Transformations of Sensibility

MICHIGAN MONOGRAPH SERIES IN JAPANESE STUDIES
NUMBER 40
CENTER FOR JAPANESE STUDIES
THE UNIVERSITY OF MICHIGAN

Transformations of Sensibility

The Phenomenology of Meiji Literature

Kamei Hideo

Translation Edited and with an Introduction by
Michael Bourdaghs

Center for Japanese Studies
The University of Michigan
Ann Arbor   2002

Open access edition funded by the National Endowment for the Humanities/ Andrew W. Mellon Foundation Humanities Open Book Program.

© 2002 The Regents of the University of Michigan

Published by the Center for Japanese Studies, The University of Michigan, 202 S. Thayer St., Ann Arbor, MI 48104-1608

Library of Congress Cataloging in Publication Data

Kamei, Hideo, 1937–
    [Kansei no henkaku. English]
    Transformations of sensibility : the phenomenology of Meiji literature / Kamei Hideo ; translation edited and with an introduction by Michael Bourdaghs.
    p. cm. — (Michigan monograph series in Japanese studies ; no. 40)
    Includes indexes.
    ISBN 978-1-929280-12-4 (hardcover)
    1. Japanese literature—1868—History and criticism. 2. Japanese literature—Edo period, 1600-1868—History and criticism. I. Bourdaghs, Michael, 1961– II. Title. III. Series.

PL726.55 .K2613 2002
895.6'090042—dc21

2002072878

This book was set in Times New Roman.

This publication meets the ANSI/NISO Standards for Permanence of Paper for Publications and Documents in Libraries and Archives (Z39.48–1992).

Printed and bound by CPI Group (UK) Ltd, Croydon, CR0 4YY

ISBN 978-1-929280-12-4 (hardcover)
ISBN 978-0-472-03804-6 (paper)
ISBN 978-0-472-12747-4 (ebook)
ISBN 978-0-472-90142-5 (open access)

Contents

Editor's Introduction:
Buried Modernities—The Phenomenological
Criticism of Kamei Hideo

MICHAEL BOURDAGHS

The decade between the mid-1970s and the mid-1980s saw a revolution in the study of modern Japanese literature. It is, first of all, within this context that Kamei Hideo's work should be understood. A new generation of scholars arose in revolt against the largely positivistic methodologies that had dominated postwar scholarship, including author studies (*sakkaron*), studies of a single work (*sakuhinron*), and literary history (*bungakushi*). Works such as Maeda Ai's *The Establishment of the Modern Reader* (*Kindai dokusha no seiritsu*, 1973), Noguchi Takehiko's *The Japanese Language in Fiction* (*Shōsetsu no Nihongo*, 1980), and Karatani Kōjin's *Origins of Modern Japanese Literature* (*Kindai Nihon bungaku no kigen*, 1980), began the process of challenging orthodox interpretations, often introducing new methodologies in the process, including semiotics, narratology, structuralism, postmodernism, and poststructuralism.[1] Feminist criticism by such figures as Mizuta Noriko and Komashaku Kimi launched a critical reassessment of writing by women and of masculinist assumptions that had guided literary studies in Japan.[2] From a multitude of directions, established literary knowledge found itself under attack. If there was a shared aspect to this multifaceted revolt, it was a critical stance toward modernity and Enlightenment (and toward existing scholarship that worked within the paradigm of modernization theory). Modernity was no longer perceived as the solution, but as

---

1. An anthology of Maeda's essays in English translation, edited by James Fujii, is forthcoming from Duke University Press. Karatani's work is available in English translation, edited by Brett de Bary, from Duke University Press (1993).
2. For a useful summary of recent feminist criticism in Japan, see Kitada Sachie, "Contemporary Japanese Feminist Literary Criticism," *U.S.–Japan Women's Journal* English Supplement 7 (1994): 72–97.

viii   Editor's Introduction

the problem, a problem of which Japanese modern literature and established literary studies were symptoms.

During the 1980s and 1990s, the intellectual ferment continued and in many ways the new scholarship carried the day. Among the influential works published were Asada Akira's *Structure and Power* (*Kōzō to chikara*, 1983), Komori Yōichi's *Narrative as Structure* (*Kōzō toshite no katari*, 1988) and Suga Hidemi's *The 'Birth' of Japanese Modern Literature* (*Nihon kindai bungaku no 'tanjō,'* 1995). Feminist criticism continued to flourish, including such important anthologies as *On Men's Literature* (*Danryū bungakuron*, edited by Ueno Chizuko, Ogura Chikako, and Tomioka Taeko, 1992) and *Modern Literature as Read by Women* (*Onna ga yomu kindai bungaku*, edited by Egusa Mitsuko and Urushida Kazuyo, 1992). This period also saw the rise of a postcolonial New Historicism in the work of such scholars as Watanabe Naomi, Murai Osamu, and Kawamura Minato.

As he writes in his preface to this translation, Kamei Hideo's work exists in an odd relationship to this revolution. It is certainly true that he helped pioneer this new wave of scholarship; yet it is also true that the road Kamei paved, while often parallel to the new scholarship, never quite intersected with it. The attention Kamei pays to the textual processes of subject formation, his assumption that subjectivity is a historical construct, and his use of the methodologies of close reading, semiotics and narratology all seem to ally Kamei with the young turks. Yet, on the other hand, many of the philosophical sources and historical assumptions that Kamei employs, especially his stance toward modernity, distinguish him from his contemporaries. Moreover, although he is critical of it, Kamei clearly places himself within the lineage of *kokubungaku*, of academic Japanese literary studies. Whereas his contemporaries largely positioned their critique as external to its object, in many senses Kamei's work is an *immanent* critique. It is this unique position that provides both the excitement and the difficulty in reading Kamei's highly original and provocative works.

In the present book, Kamei, like many of his contemporaries, explores the terrain of early-Meiji writing, which previous scholarship had all too often neglected.[3] Rejecting the conventional view that these works represent failed experiments mainly of interest as faltering steps toward the creation of the modern novel, Kamei instead considers these works to contain a variety of possibili-

---

3. It should be noted, though, that this reexploration of early-Meiji writings was prompted by the publication of the massive *Complete Works of Meiji Literature* (*Meiji bungaku zenshū*), 99 vols. (Tokyo: Chikuma Shobō, 1965–83), which made available in reprint form a wide-ranging selection of texts from the Meiji period (though the selection and editing practices adopted for the series have not escaped criticism).

ties, possibilities that were subsequently lost with the rise to hegemony of the "realistic novel." To recover these possibilities, he performs close readings of the "expressions" used in an astonishing variety of texts. Through these readings, Kamei describes the rise of new modes of "sensibility," modes defined by particular forms of "visual intentionality" as well as by varying degrees of sensitivity to the tonal and rhythmic qualities of spoken language.

The production of these new sensibilities is largely the result of the emergence of a new kind of fictional narrator, what Kamei calls the "immanent non-person narrator." This new narrator creates the possibility for new forms of self-consciousness, because its existence relativizes the sensibilities not only of the various characters who appear in a work, but also of the author who wrote that narrator into existence (and thereby underwent a splitting or doubling of his or her own self). Because literary texts objectify modes of sensibility, they render those modes visible to the subjects (authors, narrators, and readers) who perceive through them—those subjects become able to see the previously transparent lenses through which they view the world. The knowledge about sensibility thus gained empowers them to alter those modes of sensibility. For Kamei, modern literature is at its best moments a site for realizing new forms of self-consciousness and for the evolution of a new kind of ethicality, as it becomes possible to take responsibility for one's own sensibility.

Kamei begins with the opening chapters of Futabatei Shimei's *Ukigumo* (1887–89), long proclaimed Japan's first modern novel, and through a close reading overturns much conventional wisdom. The distinct sensibility of the narrator of those early chapters comes neither from Russian literature nor from oral storytelling genres, Kamei argues, but rather from a genre of popular comic reportage written in a Japanified form of Chinese, the *kanbun fūzokushi* of late Edo and early Meiji. Moreover, like the authors of those works, Futabatei was forced to recognize a gap between the sensibility of his narrator, inherent in its mode of expression, and the object that that narrator depicts—in Futabatei's case, the internal despair of Bunzō, his fictional hero. This recognition leads Futabatei to create the form of narrator found in the second half of *Ukigumo*, one with a new sensibility that allows it to sympathize with Bunzō, to see into his interior and to harbor a sense of shared destiny with that character. A dawning awareness of sensibility achieved through the process of writing had made possible a new form of self-consciousness—for fictional characters, narrator, author, and reader alike.

But this process is not limited to Futabatei. As Kamei's analysis continues, we see the transformation of sensibility and the emergence of new forms of consciousness across a wide variety of genres. In the political novels of the 1880s and in Mori Ōgai's works from the early 1890s, we see the non-person narrator evolve into a self-reflective first-person narrator. The drama of unfolding self-awareness now became a motif in fiction. In Higuchi Ichiyō's brilliant stories from the early 1890s, Kamei traces another line of development: the evolution of a new second-person narrator, one that—by relativizing the sensibility of narrator and author against those of other characters within the text—allows the emergence of a polyphonic novel in Japan, one marked by the dialogic encounter of numerous voices, each marked by a distinct sensibility. This permits the emergence of a new ethicality, a new way for the self to be with others, and situates Ichiyō's love suicides as an important turning point in the transition from the passion-driven love suicides of Edo literature to the ethical suicides of alienated modern characters that appear in so many twentieth-century works.

In subsequent chapters, Kamei traces the tense relations between two kinds of modern realism, one focused on mimesis achieved through visual description, the other on mimesis achieved through reproducing the tone and rhythm of spoken language.[4] It is the latter form, with its inherent stress on dialogic relations between speakers, that fascinates Kamei. In the stories of Izumi Kyōka, Kōda Rohan, and Kunikida Doppo, Kamei traces the rise of a new interiority, one based on inner speech—the language through which we speak our most private thoughts to ourselves, a language that, paradoxically, we must borrow from others outside of ourselves. Ultimately, this polyphonic, orally based realism leads to the breakdown of the Edo literary technique of *katagi* (character-types), used in works that provided humorous catalogs of various stereotyped stock characters, and the rise of the modern notion of individualized "personality." A modern literature capable of critically challenging society's norms and conventions had emerged.

The last two chapters in the book trace the waning of this form of orally oriented realism and the rise to dominance of the other, more visually oriented realism. This in turn produces alienation and discrimination, paranoid hallucinations about both domestic and foreign others. Kamei traces this problematic through the different schools of nature description and of travel writing that arose in mid-to-late Meiji and argues that the critical possibilities of modern literature, its ability to relativize human sensibilities and to allow for an ethical coexistence of multiple, autonomous voices, were repressed. In Naturalism and

---

4. This is a problematic that has been taken up fruitfully in the work of Komori, who was in fact a student of Kamei's at Hokkaido University. See, for example, Komori Yōichi, "Shizenshugi no saihyōka" in *Nihon bungaku kōza 6: kindai shōsetsu*, ed. Nihon bungaku kyōkai (Tokyo: Taishūkan Shoten, 1988), 95–113. For another recent example, see Kōno Kensuke, "Onna no kaiwa, otoko no kaiwa: *Ie* ni okeru kaiwa no gihō," in *Shimazaki Tōson: bunmei hihyō to shi to shōsetsu to*, ed. Hiraoka Toshio and Kenmochi Takehiko (Tokyo: Sōbunsha, 1996), 167–81.

the I-novel, literature could only blindly reproduce existing sensibilities, and when these genres were accepted as constituting the mainstream of Japan's modern literature, the alternative possible modernity that Kamei has traced here was lost.

Kamei's argument, then, attempts to recover an abandoned wealth of possibilities within Meiji literary writings. This is a project with important implications for the present moment. When the modern "realistic novel," especially the I-novel, emerged as the sole legitimate form of prose fiction, literary expression was no longer perceived as a relative medium for creating multiple sensibilities, but rather as an absolute medium capable of transparently reflecting the interior of the speaking subject. Such a literature could not produce knowledge of sensibility; it could only reproduce existing conventional sensibilities. According to Kamei, when we accept this as constituting "modern literature," the danger lies not only in the assumption that a homogeneous sensibility is shared by all people, but also in the implied threat that such a sensibility will be accepted as natural and inevitable. Human beings will lose the ability to actively transform their own sensibilities. Kamei's rereading of Meiji literature is aimed, ultimately, at trying to recover for us a certain margin of freedom.

* * * * *

Undoubtedly, one of the most interesting sections of *Transformations of Sensibility* for English-language readers will be Kamei's scathing criticism of Karatani Kōjin's *Origins of Modern Japanese Literature*, a work that had achieved wide influence among American specialists even before its English translation was published in 1993. Since Karatani's argument has become so well known, Kamei's critique—whether we agree with it or not—provides a useful entryway into explaining the methodological and critical issues that underpin Kamei's argument as a whole. Of course, the various methodological and political positions advocated by both Karatani and Kamei have seen significant change in the years since these works were originally published. For my purposes here, though, I will ignore those subsequent developments in order to sketch an outline of the disagreements that existed between the two when *Transformations of Sensibilities* was first published in 1983.

As we have seen, Karatani's book helped launch a direct and ultimately successful assault on the problematic assumptions that governed the study of modern Japanese literature in postwar Japan. Although Karatani was trained as an academic specialist and held university teaching positions, he wrote largely from the perspective of a *hyōronka*, that is, as a journalistic critic from outside the sphere of academia. In one sense, Kamei's rebuttal in these pages can be read as the response of one *kokubungakusha*, an academic scholar of Japanese literature, to this critique. In his defense of academic scholarship (a defense that is at times nearly as critical of established scholarship as is Karatani's attack), Kamei charges that Karatani has not only seriously misinterpreted the work of Kamei's scholarly peers, but also that Karatani has provided only the most superficial readings of the literary texts with which he deals.

Beyond differences in institutional position, the first and most obvious difference marking the two arguments lies in the opposing philosophies of history that underlie them. The version of history that Karatani presents, one focused on inversions and epistemic breaks, bears an important resemblance to the form of historiography we are most familiar with from the works of Foucault (although Karatani himself has tended to stress more his debt to Paul de Man and Hannah Arendt, among others). In contrast to Karatani's emphasis on the radical discontinuity of Japan's modernity with earlier periods, Kamei emphasizes continuity, especially with the Edo period. In Kamei, we find a dialectical model of history, one in which historical development occurs not as the result of ruptures or external impact, but out of creative syntheses that resolve internally generated contradictions. Kamei finds the seeds for literary development within literary works themselves. Hence, for example, we will see Kamei locate the beginnings of modern modes for expressing interiority in the late Edo *gesaku* works of Tamenaga Shunsui, and also the stress here on the importance to modern literature of *kanbun*, the Japanified style of writing in Chinese that dominated intellectual discourse throughout the Edo period.

One of the results, both revealing and frustrating, of Kamei's incessantly dialectical approach is his insistence on restricting his focus to written texts themselves. Because he is concerned with locating the rise of new modes of expression as the synthesis of contradictions found in earlier modes, he deliberately avoids seeking external, nontextual causes for changes in historical expressions. While he will occasionally refer to the specific historical position of an author, Kamei is mainly concerned with demonstrating that the history of modes of expression can be explained through very close readings of the literary texts involved, picking slowly through the tensions and contradictions internal to each (an approach, as Kamei notes, that he developed out of the work of Yoshimoto Takaaki). In this, he is critical of what he sees as Karatani's superficial readings of many of the same works.

This is not to say that Kamei's work lacks a political or historical dimension. In fact, the arguments made here bear tremendous implications for intellectual and social history. In the second chapter, for example, Kamei critiques the form of sensibility and subjectivity created in the political novels of the 1870s and 1880s for mistakenly confusing Japanese national liberation with imperial expansion, a sensibility that leads ultimately to the travel writing depicted in the twelfth chapter, when writers describe the "natives" of Japan's future empire in brutally prejudiced language. Likewise, chapter eleven contains a brilliant exposition of the structure of consciousness of social discrimination against domestic minority groups. But Kamei's commitment to the notion that subjectivity and sensibility inhere in our linguistic expressions, and to the idea that literature is the proper domain for the study of that relationship, leads him consistently to restrict his focus to the literary texts under examination, attempting to carry out a political and ethical critique that is immanent to them.

While Kamei's approach to history is dialectical, he does not see historical development as following a necessary or predetermined path. His readings of early Meiji works revolve around the task of uncovering lost possibilities that were opened by those works, possibilities that were eventually forgotten with the rise of the particular ideology of realism that has dominated modern Japanese literature. But Kamei argues that this rise was in no way inevitable, and he remains attentive to the existence of other possible outcomes for the historical development of expressions. Moreover, as is most apparent in the closing paragraphs of chapter one, Kamei hopes that his own work will form an intervention that will alter the dominant assumptions regarding expressions and subjectivity in late twentieth-century Japan. The book as a whole consists of an extended meditation on the possibilities and stakes of resisting the often unconscious norms for behavior and feeling through which societies discipline individual subjects. In that sense, Kamei's work should be understood as one form of reaction to the perceived collapse of the New Left in 1970s Japan (a position it shares with Karatani's work). As Kamei argues in his preface to this translation, New Left activists attempted to subvert the social order by following the dictates of their own sensibilities, unaware that sensibility was precisely the point at which they had been most effectively socialized into that order.

Their divergent philosophies of history lead Karatani and Kamei to radically different conceptions of modernity. In a sense, their clash anticipates the debate over modern visuality that would be carried out in the 1980s and 1990s by Jonathan Crary and Martin Jay.[5] For Karatani, Japan's modernity is marked by ideological interpolation into a new Cartesian subjectivity of interiority, one

---

5. I am indebted to Thomas LaMarre for this insight. See his "The Deformation of the Modern Spectator: Synaesthesia, Cinema, and the Spectre of Race in Tanizaki," *Japan Forum* 11:1 (1999): 23–42. For a condensed form of this debate, see Hal Foster, ed., *Vision and Visuality* (Seattle: Bay Press, 1988). For more detailed versions of the respective arguments, see Martin Jay, *Downcast Eyes* (Berkeley: University of California Press, 1993) and Jonathan Crary, *Techniques of the Observer* (Cambridge, MA: Massachusetts Institute of Technology Press, 1990).

marked by an unbreachable gap between a gazing subject and its object. It is something to be subjected to ruthless critique, its naturalized assumptions turned on their head and exposed. For Kamei, modernity means something quite different, beginning with its characteristic subjectivity. For Kamei, modern subjectivity follows not so much a Cartesian dualistic model as it does a phenomenological model, one that involves a stronger sense of continuity and dynamic relationality between subject and object. The in-itself of the object and the for-itself of consciousness are necessarily in sympathetic communion.[6] Moreover, for Kamei intersubjective factors are always fundamentally constitutive of the subject-object relation. Hence, whereas Karatani in his brilliant critique of landscape focuses on the binary split between gazing subject and its object, for Kamei, the verbal description of landscape is always a tri-polar relationship. It involves the gazing narrator, the object of the gaze, and the reader/listener to whom the narrator speaks. To narrate is to establish a community, and so Kamei's argument about landscape is also an argument about what sort of community modern societies should establish.

Accordingly, for Kamei, modernity represents not so much something to be rejected, but an as yet unfulfilled possibility, one that the rise of "modern Japanese literature" has (perhaps only temporarily) delayed. In short, Kamei presents us with something like the "incomplete modernity" seen in the work of such figures as Maruyama Masao, except that Kamei implies that the incomplete project of modernity is not limited to Japan, but something that Japan shares with the rest of the "modern" world. If anything, in Kamei's argument, the unique particularity of Japan's modernity harbors important lessons for the West and other regions suffering through the crisis of modernity.

Already, this suggests that, like "modernity," the meaning of the word "Japan" is quite different for Karatani and Kamei. Karatani's critique of modernity includes a skeptical view of the notion of a unified Japanese cultural identity as one of the invented traditions used to legitimate the modern nation-state. As a result, Karatani tends to stress the erasure of cultural diversity that accompanied the rise of modern Japan. Accordingly, Karatani foregrounds the similar constructions of identity, both subjective and national, that mark the various

---

6. Cf. Maurice Merleau-Ponty, *The Phenomenology of Perception*, trans. Colin Smith (London: Routledge, 1962), 212–15. For example, contrast Karatani's assertion of the subject in landscape as "the 'inner man,' who appears to be indifferent to his external surroundings" (Karatani, *Origins of Modern Japanese Literature*, 25), one that has withdrawn from the outside world, to Merleau-Ponty's assertion that "As I contemplate the blue of the sky I am not *set over against it* as an acosmic subject; I do not possess it in thought, or spread out towards it some idea of blue such as might reveal the secret of it, I abandon myself to it and plunge into this mystery, it 'thinks itself within me,' I am the sky itself as it is drawn together and unified, and as it begins to exist for itself; my consciousness is saturated with this limitless blue" (214).

Meiji writers he discusses: "it becomes clear beyond any doubt that what *all* of the writers of the 1890s encountered was 'landscape'" (Karatani, *Origins of Modern Japanese Literature*, 31; emphasis added). Kamei, on the other hand, criticizes Karatani sharply for ignoring the substantial differences that distinguish various genres, authors, and modes of expression. Kamei undertakes the task of delineating the heterogeneity of Meiji literature (though he is also concerned with arranging that heterogeneity into a sort of dialectical narrative, and though he links all of these various genres on a single ground, the presumed identity of the Japanese language). Nonetheless, in Kamei's sense of crisis regarding the state of modern literature, expressed eloquently in the opening pages of the book, we see many similarities with Karatani's belief that modernity has brought about an erasure of heterogeneity within Japan. As Kamei notes in the closing pages of the book, despite his disagreements with Karatani, they do share a number of similar concerns. What distinguishes them, of course, is the very different methodologies they adopt to approach those concerns, above all Kamei's insistence that any effective critique of Japan's modernity must be an immanent critique, one that arises from within the specificity of the actual experiences of that modernity.

* * * * *

A number of keywords are central to Kamei's argument. Kamei discusses several of them in his preface to this edition. Here, I will take up a few others to explain the translations of them that appear here and to situate them at least provisionally within the philosophical traditions of phenomenology. The discussion of each will inevitably circle back to connect with the others, and in those connections I hope to clarify the system, or more precisely, the complex process that Kamei describes in this work.

Visual intentionality (*shikōsei*): This is a neologism coined by taking the existing Japanese philosophical term for intentionality (*shikō*) and replacing its first character (*shi* or *hodokosu*: to will) with a homophonous character meaning "to see." (When Kamei uses the conventional term, we have translated it as "intention" or "intentionality"). Intentionality is, of course, one of the keywords of phenomenology, arising from Husserl's insistence that our consciousness is always consciousness of something, that it always involves a dynamic, *intentional* relationship with its object. But what is visual intentionality?

As Kamei notes in an earlier book, he was not the coiner of this word.[7] When he encountered the word, it seemed a useful tool for resolving a certain dissatisfaction he felt with the theories of J.P. Sartre and Yoshimoto Takaaki.

---

7. See Kamei Hideo, *Shintai: hyōgen no hajimari* (Tokyo: Renga Shobō Shinsha, 1982), 244–48.

Sartre, in theorizing imagination, had presumed that when, for example, we perceive four lines jotted on a piece of paper as a human face, a two-stage process had occurred: four lines were perceived by the senses, and then an image of a face was produced through imagination. Kamei's dissatisfaction lay in his belief that, in fact, our visual sense perception always imposes an order on the objects it perceives; the realization that what exists on the paper are only four lines, not a face, can only be achieved afterward, through reflection. That is to say, we are able to achieve through reflection an awareness of the actual elements constituting our perception, as they existed before they were organized into an object of our perception. This reflection can in turn lead to an abstract awareness of the structure of our own perception. Sartre was, according to Kamei, uninterested in this process, a process that is very much the subject of the present book. Likewise, Kamei felt dissatisfied with Yoshimoto's theory of self expression (*jiko hyōshutsu*), the for-itself aspect of language for the speaking subject that Yoshimoto argued was the primary fount of poetic activity. This theory too neglected the process of reflective consciousness necessary for an awareness of this aspect to become possible.

What was needed to address this problem was a word that would express the active role of the eye itself in organizing perception, prior to any intentional conscious processing of the visual image. While seeking such a word, Kamei happened to read Takeuchi Yoshimoto's afterword to his 1971 Japanese translation of Trän Dúc Tháo's *Phenomenology and Dialectical Materialism*. There, Takeuchi expressed his dissatisfaction with the standard Japanese translations for a number of terms from the vocabulary of Western phenomenology. For example, the French *viser* ("to sight," as in aiming a weapon) from Sartre and Merleau-Ponty was generally translated as *nerau* ("to aim at"). Noting that *viser* was frequently used as a French translation for Husserl's *hinblicken* ("to look at" or "to look toward"), Takeuchi argues that *nerau* lacks the proper nuance of turning one's eyes toward something and proposes using the neologism *shikō* instead, which had previously been coined by translators of Husserl (in fact, though, Kamei notes, Takeuchi did not use this phrase in his translation).

Accordingly, "visual intentionality" (a phrase more awkward in English than it is in Japanese) here refers to the ways in which our visual perception organizes its objects, even before they become objects of intentional consciousness. It expresses the way in which vision is always "already inhabited by a meaning (*sens*) which gives it a function in the spectacle of the world and in our existence."[8] As we will see below, this makes it a fundamental aspect of what Kamei calls "sensibility."

8. Maurice Merleau-Ponty, *Phenomenology of Perception*, 52.

Mode of expression or *expression* (*hyōgen*): The word *hyōgen* has long been used in Japanese literary criticism to indicate the style of language characteristic of a specific work or author. The word signifies both a particular style of expression (hence, "mode of expression") and the actual language itself (as in the English, "a particularly apt expression"), either a passage from a given work or the entire work itself. It is similar to the French *écriture* as used in recent literary criticism.

In Kamei's work, *hyōgen* is distinguished from another word that is usually translated "expression," *hyōshutsu*, used, as we have seen, by Yoshimoto Takaaki. (Here, we have translated both as "expression," but we provide a parenthetical gloss in passages that specifically discuss *hyōshutsu*.) As Kamei notes in his introduction, he is influenced by Yoshimoto's work on the history of *hyōshutsu* but wants to distance himself from the notion inherent in *hyōshutsu* of an interior self that pre-exists its manifestation, its outward expression, in speech and writing. Hence, Kamei's *hyōgen* is closer to the "expression" as used, for example, by Merleau-Ponty in his philosophy of language. Merleau-Ponty argues that we should seek not a thinking subject but rather a speaking subject:

> . . . *consciousness is inseparable from its expression* (consequently, it is inseparable from the cultural whole of its milieu). There is *no radical difference between consciousness of self and consciousness of other people*. [. . .] There is no consciousness *behind* the manifestations. These manifestations are inherent in consciousness: they *are* consciousness.[9]

For both Kamei and Merleau-Ponty, because we come to self-consciousness only through the language that we share with others, the subject produced through language is inherently intersubjective, a subject with others. Moreover, since the subject is produced through expressions, a change in mode of expression necessarily means a change in our self-consciousness—and in our way of relating to others. Repeatedly in the present work, Kamei argues that the appearance of a single word, or of a particular phrase, in the inner or outer speech of a certain character produces, by a kind of introjection and internalization, a shift in that character's self-consciousness. The character is forced to recognize him or herself as the sort of subject who would utter that word or phrase, a shift that then ripples out to alter the perceptions and expressions of other characters, the narrator, and even the author. Accordingly, when Kamei traces through a vari-

---

9. Maurice Merleau-Ponty, *Consciousness and the Acquisition of Language*, trans. Hugh J. Silverman (Evanston: Northwestern University Press, 1973), 46–47. Merleau-Ponty is here summarizing the thought of Max Scheler, with whom he is largely in sympathy.

ety of modes of expressions, he is tracing through a history of different possible modes for self-consciousness and for intersubjective existence that are realized in the various works he analyzes here.

One of the most interesting critiques of Kamei's book implicitly takes up the problem of "expression." Mitani Kuniaki, a brilliant scholar of classical literature, agrees that subjectivity is produced through linguistic expressions but argues that Kamei's analysis of the expressions of modern fiction overlooks the central problem of temporality.[10] It is the use of the "past tense" verb ending -*ta* that is the key to expression and subjectivity in modern fiction, Mitani argues. In conversational Japanese, one can use -*ta* forms in relation to one's own past internal experiences (e.g., *Sō omotta*: I thought it so), but one needs to add a conjectural suffix when reporting past experiences of others (*Kare wa sō omotta darō*: He thought it so, I suppose). In modern realistic fiction, however, the narrator can make this sort of impossible, omniscient statement (*Kare wa sō omotta*: He thought it so). Hence, in the expression of modern fiction, -*ta* signals readers that they are entering the domain of fiction, where ordinary rules of conversational usage no longer apply.[11] Mitani argues that -*ta* also enacts the unification of the text around a single, monological voice, that it constructs the fiction of an "author" as the subject who unifies the text, thereby eliding the free play of multiple voices that characterized earlier fiction. The real significance of Futabatei's *Ukigumo*, Mitani argues, is its gradual shift from a predominantly present-tense narration, one reminiscent of late-Edo *gesaku*, to a past-tense narration marked by this -*ta* form, a shift that coincides with an increasing capacity for omniscient representation of characters' inner thoughts. Moreover, the significance of later works by such authors as Mori Ōgai, Kōda Rohan, and Higuchi Ichiyō lies not, à la Kamei, in their contribution to the unfolding of this modern mode of expression but rather in their resistance to it: by composing works in the *bungotai* literary language, rather than the new *genbun itchi* style with its characteristic -*ta* forms, they sought to preserve the play of polyphony in their works against the rising hegemony of works unified around the "author."

Mitani's criticism provides an attractive alternative reading of early Meiji works, while pointing out certain omissions in Kamei's work—though in

---

10. Mitani Kuniaki, "Kindai shōsetsu no gensetsu: joshō," in *Kindai bungaku no seiritsu*, ed. Komori Yōichi (Tokyo: Yūseidō, 1986), 118–28. Kamei's rebuttal to Mitani, "Wajutsu no yukue," can also be found in the same volume, 129–41. Mitani's essay was first published in *Nihon bungaku* 33:7 (July 1984); Kamei's essay was first published in *Bungaku* 53:11 (November 1985).

11. For a useful explanation of this and other problems of the rhetoric for modern fictional narratives in Japan, see Edward Fowler, *The Rhetoric of Confession* (Berkeley: University of California Press, 1988).

fact, while Kamei may not stress the temporal aspects of expressions, temporality is implicitly inherent to the notion of expression.[12] But what we see perhaps most clearly in the debate between the two figures are different stances toward modernity and modern subjectivity. While many readers will likely share Mitani's desire for a more critical stance toward modernity on Kamei's part, it also seems to me that Mitani fails to consider the ways in which such "traditional," non-*genbun itchi* writers actively participated in the rise of modernity in Japan. There is nothing so central to modernity, after all, as invented traditions, especially those characterized by nostalgia for an imagined past of undisciplined, utopic playfulness. Moreover, in his critique of the supposedly monologic qualities of the -*ta* writing style, Mitani must ignore the materiality of language, its inherent polysemy, in order to stress its functioning at the conscious level of meaning.

This is a significant omission, because in Kamei's argument, the impact of a certain mode of expression is in many ways preconscious and occurs at the level of materiality. According to Merleau-Ponty, expressions characteristic of a given social group organize the perceptions of the members of that group. This is not so much a matter of the level of meaning, but at the nonsemantic level of phonetics. An infant who learns to repeat certain rhythms and accentuations, modulations of speech, without yet understanding the semantic content of that speech, is already acquiring certain flexible patterns for making differentiations, for organizing raw experience into perception, and for adopting certain affective and judgmental attitudes toward the objects of perception. The very organs of the child's body are being rewritten to produce only certain kinds of perceptions. This is just as true of adults: encountering an expression provokes a reorganization of one's own body, as one reorients oneself to follow the gestural intent immanent in the words of the expression.[13]

12. Expressions are objectifications of "sensibility" (defined at length below), the institutionalized form that molds our perceptions, and perception as defined in the phenomenological tradition is something that always takes place within a doubled temporal horizon of recollection and anticipation of "retention" and "protention." See Merleau-Ponty, *Phenomenology of Perception*, 69. See, for example, Kamei's explication of Masaoka Shiki's theory of "time haiku" in chapter eleven of the present work.
13. "There is, then, a taking up of others' thought through speech, a reflection in others, an ability to think *according to others* which enriches our own thoughts. Here the meaning of words must be finally induced by the words themselves, or more exactly, their conceptual meaning must be formed by a kind of deduction from a *gestural meaning*, which is immanent in speech. And as, in a foreign country, I begin to understand the meaning of words through their place in a context of action, and by taking part in a communal life—in the same way an as yet imperfectly understood piece of philosophical writing discloses to me at least a certain 'style'— either a Spinozist, critical or phenomenological one—which is the first draft of its meaning. I begin to understand a philosophy by feeling my way into its existential manner, by reproducing the tone and accent of the philosopher" (Merleau-Ponty, *Phenomenology of Perception*, 179).

Perception, then, is not a natural but a cultural or intersubjective process, spread contagiously through the culture of expressions.

> The angry Japanese smiles, the westerner goes red and stamps his foot or else goes pale and hisses his words. It is not enough for two conscious subjects to have the same organs and nervous system for the same emotions to produce in both the same signs. What is important is how they use their bodies, the simultaneous patterning of body and world in emotion. [. . .] It is no more natural, and no less conventional, to shout in anger or to kiss in love than to call a table 'table.' Feelings and passional conduct are invented like words. Even those which, like paternity, seem to be part and parcel of the human make-up are in reality institutions. It is impossible to superimpose on man a lower layer of behaviour which one chooses to call 'natural,' followed by a manufactured cultural or spiritual world. (Merleau-Ponty, *Phenomenology of Perception*, 189)

On similar grounds, Kamei critiques the notion of preserving supposedly untouched "nature," be it inner nature or external nature, as the regnant motif in modern Japanese literature.[14]

To put it simply, for Mitani the problem with modern expressions is the hegemony of cogito, the severing of mind from body in the symbolic order, a break established with the -*ta* suffix. But for Kamei, the problem is to achieve an accurate description of the fluid relationship between mind and body in experience, of the continuing connection between the realms of the imaginary and the symbolic in expressions. Our bodies, like our minds, are social products, molded through our expressions into a "sensibility" that itself is something like a language. This brings us to the next keyword in the book.

Sensibility (*kansei*): "Sensibility," one of the central themes in this book, is, as James Fujii notes, "an elusive term that overlaps such notions as sensitivity, sensual awareness, sensibility, and consciousness."[15] The term has a long usage in the Western philosophical tradition, especially in aesthetics, the branch of philosophy concerned with linking body and mind, subject and object, perception and reason, self and other. As Alexander Baumgarten, one of the founders of this "science of the concrete" vowed, "Science is not to be dragged down to

---

14. Merleau-Ponty similarly argues elsewhere that "it is impossible to establish a cleavage between what will be 'natural' in the individual and what will be acquired from his social upbringing. In reality the two orders are not distinct; they are part and parcel of a single global phenomenon." Maurice Merleau-Ponty, "The Child's Relations with Others," trans. William Cobb, in *The Primacy of Perception* (Evanston: Northwestern University Press, 1964), 96–155. This passage appears on 108.

15. James Fujii, *Complicit Fictions: The Subject in the Modern Japanese Prose Narrative* (Berkeley: University of California Press, 1993), 58.

the region of sensibility, but the sensible is to be lifted to the dignity of knowledge."[16] For aestheticians, the notion of sensibility has implied a harmonious agreement between sense perceptions, aesthetic judgments, and rational intellect.

Sensibility has also been a key term in philosophies of subjectivity. For Kant, sensibility was the faculty that produced mental representations of external objects (unknowable in themselves); it was contrasted to the faculties of the intellect and understanding, which analyzed and judged those representations. Sensibility produced the sensual appearance or mental representation of an external object, its phenomenon, as distinguished from the noumenon, the unknowable thing-in-itself.[17] In a sense, Kamei's project has a Kantian bent to it: it aims at demonstrating how a knowledge not of the object-in-itself, but rather of the sensibility through which we perceive objects, can become an object for reflective consciousness. Like Kant, Kamei is interested in defining the limits of the proper domain of sensibility.

But there is also a pronounced Hegelian dimension to Kamei's usage of the term. Whereas for Kant, sensibility was a universal feature of the working of the human mind, for Hegel (and for Marx, as well as for the later phenomenologists), sensibility was perceived more properly as a historical product, taking particular forms in specific communities at specific historical moments. The values and affects we share with those around us shape our perceptions of the outside world and structure the everyday practices that make up our culture.[18] Sensibility was in many ways the invisible bond that linked communities together; it was the internalized, organic mechanism of culture. Hence, Kamei's project, as is clear from the title of this book, is a history of changing sensibility in the literature of the Meiji period, and he shares with Merleau-Ponty and others a sense that only a return to the level of pre-analytical perception will allow us to understand subjectivities in their concrete historical situations.

Among the more immediate Japanese predecessors of Kamei who also use the term "sensibility" are Yoshimoto Takaaki, whose work Kamei discusses at length in his preface, and Nakamura Yūjirō. In *The Awakening of Sensibility* (*Kansei no kakusei*, 1975), Nakamura argues that the crisis of modern society can be overcome only by restoring the passions and sensibility to their rightful place in philosophy as well as in daily life. An excessive emphasis on rationalism, without regard for its connection to affect and sensibility, a privileging of

---

16. Quoted in Terry Eagleton, *The Ideology of the Aesthetic* (Cambridge: Blackwell, 1990), 17.
17. Cf. the discussion of the noumenon as "a merely *limiting concept*, the function of which is to curb the pretensions of sensibility" in Immanuel Kant, *Critique of Pure Reason*, trans. Norman Kemp Smith (New York: Modern Library, 1958), 155. I am indebted to Joseph Murphy for calling my attention to this passage and its relevance to Kamei's argument.
18. See Eagleton, *The Ideology of the Aesthetic,* esp. 120–52.

mind over body, has resulted not only in the environmental disaster of a devastated nature, but also an impoverishment of human nature. Reason and sensibility are not to be opposed, Nakamura argues, but rather reconnected, by way of a reconsideration of the role of language. Likewise, nature and culture—our learned customs or "second nature"—are to be reunited, and through such an exploration, we are to learn how our embodied sensibility is not only a social product but also one that is, à la Lacan, structured like a language. Nakamura concludes his book with a call for revitalizing our sensibilities, one that echoes throughout Kamei's work:

> But when our sensibility is systematized and structured like a language, then even when we feel things or harbor mental images, we are unable to escape the domination of a habitualized, rigidified linguistic system. But at the same time, out of this we are able to detect the systematic, rigid character of our way of feeling and of our mental images, we can grasp with our own eyes our ways of feeling and of imagining, we can remake and renew them, we can reassemble their hitherto existing forms of combination, and thereby live out more fully those ways of feeling and images we have accumulated in the past, while at the same time opening up a new path to a rich creativity. In this, the grasping of our own language and our way of feeling things, together with our detecting the systematicity of the "natural," do we not find the most effective strategy to employ against domination at the hands of an otherwise invisible sensibility?[19]

Sensibility, then, is a site whereby knowledge is linked to affect, and mind to body, where the sense perceptions presented to our conscious mind arrive already embedded within a network of social meanings. In that sense, Kamei follows that "broad movement in the history of philosophy [. . .] which has interrogated the primacy of consciousness or experience in conceptions of subjectivity and displaced the privilege of these terms by focusing on the body as a sociocultural artifact rather than as a manifestation or externalization of what is private, psychological, and 'deep' in the individual."[20] As one of the pioneers of what came to be known as the "theory of embodiedness" (*shintairon*) in Japan, Kamei in this book is very much writing a critical history of the senses, and attempting to trace out (while remaining immanent to them) their connections to consciousness, rational knowledge, and ethicality.

19. Nakamura Yūjirō, *The Awakening of Sensibility* (*Kansei no kakusei*) [1975], reprinted in *Jōnen ron*, vol. 1 of *Nakamura Yūjirō chosakushū*, 10 vols. (Tokyo: Iwanami Shoten, 1993), 77–353. This quotation appears on 352.
20. Elizabeth Grosz, *Volatile Bodies: Toward a Corporeal Feminism* (Bloomington: Indiana University Press, 1994), 115.

Immanent, non-person narrator (*naizaiteki muninshō katarite*): Kamei's entire argument revolves around the production of the narrator characteristic of modern fiction. In fact, he argues that the unification of a literary work around a single, consistent focal center is perhaps *the* defining feature that distinguishes modern literature in Japan from its predecessors.[21] As is well known, the *genbun itchi* movement of the Meiji period called for a reform in literary language, including the replacement of *bungotai*, the classical literary writing style, with a more colloquial style. Numerous late Edo works had already reproduced colloquial language in passages of spoken dialogue; what was new in Meiji was experimentation with colloquial language in what is called *ji no bun* in Japanese, the passages attributed not to one of the characters in the work but rather to the narrator—the passages of narratorial "background" against which the "figure" of spoken dialogue emerges. This in turn, according to Kamei, led to the rise of a new writing style for depicting spoken dialogue, one which respected the individuality of diverse speaking voices yet refracted them through the unifying consciousness of a single narrator.

The rise of a new kind of subjectivity in Meiji literature was, then, the production of a new kind of narrator. Moreover, as Kamei notes, the narrator of a literary work is involved not merely as a subject gazing at its object, but also as a speaking subject who narrates to other subjects—it is inherently an intersubjective being whose words effect a certain kind of communal bond with others. Accordingly, Kamei in this work frequently investigates the relationship established in various works between the narrator (*katarite*) and that narrator's implicit or explicit auditor (*kikite*).[22]

In essence, in Kamei's argument, phylogeny recapitulates ontogeny: he uses the processes leading to subject formation in the child as theorized by such figures as Piaget, Merleau-Ponty, and Vygotsky as a framework to explore the

---

21. Tomiko Yoda pointed out to me the similarities between Kamei's non-person narrator and the "fourth-person narrator" that Yokomitsu Riichi discusses in his essay, "On Pure Fiction" ("Junsui shōsetsu ron," 1935), which Kamei cites in chapter one of this work. Yokomitsu posits the fourth-person narrator as the necessary voice for the modern novel, in which the author must create a means for pulling together the multiple levels of consciousness and self-consciousness that characterize self-reflexive modern existence.

22. In fact, the above-mentioned debate between Kamei and Mitani revolves largely around their different conceptions of the mode of reception of the literary text. Mitani focuses on the ability of an external reader to identify with the sensibility objectified within the world of the text via the narrator's words, while Kamei focuses on the point of contact between that narrator's words and the auditor, the implied listener that those words project as an active participant within the scene of narration (an imaginary process that in turn can reshape the sensibilities of actual readers). See Komori Yōichi, "Kaisetsu," in *Kindai bungaku no seiritsu*, ed. Komori Yōichi (Tokyo: Yuseidō, 1986), 249–63, esp. 258–59.

formation of modern writing styles in Meiji Japan. Kamei uses these to explain the characteristics of what he calls the "non-person narrator" found in many early Meiji works, including the opening chapters of Futabatei's *Ukigumo*. This narrator differs from that found in earlier *gesaku* works of prose fiction and yet is not assimilable to the categories of narrator type (first- or third-person) that would be established with the rise of realism. It adopts the lively, sarcastic tone characteristic of Edo *gesaku* narrators, yet is spatially positioned within the scene described, unlike the typical third-person narrator or the earlier *gesaku* narrators, who were situated in a transcendent exterior space. While it is spatially immanent to the scene, this narrator remains invisible to the other characters in the text—unlike the typical first-person narrator. Moreover, this narrator is not omniscient; it is unable to fathom the thoughts or emotions of the characters it depicts. And this narrator's sensibility often renders it unsympathetic to the novel's protagonist, even as they occupy the same spatial setting.

This narrator, who had disappeared from Japanese fiction by early in the twentieth century, is fundamental to Kamei's argument because it represents a rough equivalent to the mirror stage in theories of subjectivity. As Kamei notes in his introduction, he encountered the notion of the mirror stage not in the works of Lacan, but in the phenomenology of Miura Tsutomu and Merleau-Ponty. According to those theories, the infant child begins to emerge into the position of an ego, a subject, by locating outside of itself an ideal image of its own coherence, in the specular image of its own body that it sees projected in the mirror. This fantasy image then carries forward the process of constructing the fragmented body into what Lacan calls an "orthopaedic" whole.[23] By identifying itself with this image, the child also begins the leap into self-awareness, because it can now demarcate its own body from other bodies and from the external world (even as this image comes into the self from outside).

> I gradually become aware of my body, of what radically distinguishes it from the other's body, at the same time that I begin to live my intentions in the facial expressions of the other and likewise begin to live the other's volitions in my own gestures. The progress of the child's experience results in his seeing that his body is, after all, closed in on itself. In particular, the visual image he acquires of his own body (especially from the mirror) reveals to him a hitherto unsuspected isolation of two subjects who are facing each other. The objectification of his own body discloses to the child his difference, his 'insularity,' and, correlatively, that of others. (Merleau-Ponty, "Child's Relations," 119)

23. Jacques Lacan, *Écrits: A Selection* (New York: W.W. Norton, 1977), 4.

The child comes to recognize itself not only in the image, but also as the "real" self who gazes at the image: the beginning of its "split subjectivity." The child also here begins the process of moving from a specular self toward a fully socialized self, because it realizes that the mirror image represents its self as viewed from the position of others.[24] That is to say, it comes to recognize the existence of others as other, beings with their own sensibilities and consciousnesses.

The child reaches the final stage of subjectivity through the acquisition of socialized language, which again requires the child to project itself into the position of the other who gazes back at the self. In using language, I must place myself into the slot opened up for a speaking subject in language, an external place that can be occupied by anyone. I must simultaneously occupy the position of the I and of the other who gazes at me, of the I who enunciates and of the I about whom the enunciation is made. What emerges is a socialized split subject, and the mirror stage is the key step in its emergence.

Kamei argues here that the non-person narrator of early Meiji resembles the mirror stage of psychoanalysis and phenomenology. Early authors such as Futabatei and the authors of the political novels discussed in chapters two and three discovered in their narrators a kind of ego ideal. A new kind of self-awareness was now possible, one that was intimately connected with notions of democracy and national solidarity promoted by activists in the People's Rights Movement of the 1870s and 1880s. But these authors and their readers quickly became dissatisfied with this narrator, because it failed to establish the sort of intersubjective relationship with others that was needed. As Kamei argues, the sensibility of the narrator in the early chapters of *Ukigumo*, for example, renders it unsympathetic to the novel's protagonist. Even as Futabatei identified with it, he was forced to step back from this ego ideal, to recognize it as such and to acquire conscious knowledge of the sensibility that shaped its perceptions. This split self-consciousness in turn allowed him (and other authors) to reshape the narrator, to relativize its position against the objects it cognized and against the words of others. This very process, the splitting off of one's own ideal image from one's consciousness of that image, a process that necessarily involved a growing awareness of one's own sensibility (and that of others), became the proper theme of modern literature. New ethical and creative possibilities were born—and almost as quickly lost, when after the emergence of Natu-

---

24. Note that for Kamei, as for Merleau-Ponty and Vygotsky, the child is from the beginning socialized, since the very perceptions through which it sees the mirror image are mediated by sensibility, and also because the child before the mirror stage is not an individualized subject but "an anonymous collectivity, an undifferentiated group life" (Merleau-Ponty, "Child's Relations," 119). But it is only after emerging into language and the ethicality of a self-consciousness that knows itself to be with others, that it can be called a socialized *subject*.

ralism and the I-novel in the early 1900s, the subject that emerged from this historical unfolding became naturalized, internalized, and accepted as a universally given entity with an unchanging sensibility.

It is the immanent non-person narrator that provides the key to Kamei's readings of early Meiji texts. It is also the key to the critiques he makes of numerous linguistic and literary theorists of subjectivity. Kamei argues that they ignore the mediating role of the narrator in the subject/object relations that are established in literary texts: in their rush to explore the terrain of the symbolic order of language, they are too eager to skip over the imaginary aspects of subject formation that arise during the mirror stage and continue to color linguistic expressions. Conversely, theories of visual subjectivity (including Karatani's "landscape") ignore the mediating ear and voice of the narrator's words. The non-person narrator, with its distinct sensibility, links voice and gaze in its expressions and functions to mediate authorial subjectivity.

The centrality of the narrator to Kamei's argument has been one source of criticism of the present book. Should we assume that the narrative passages in a given work are produced through a single coherent subject position, even one as nuanced, historicized, and socialized as is Kamei's non-person narrator? As James Fujii notes, "Kamei runs the risk of essentializing a different subject that is defined not so much in terms of flesh and bone as the locus of perception and sensibilities" (Fujii, *Complicit Fictions,* 61). Such concerns led subsequent scholarship in Japan, especially in the work of Komori Yōichi, to focus not so much on the narrator (*katarite*) as on the narration (*katari*). Moreover, we might also ask whether the narrator in a literary text can actually function as the ego ideal for its author, the author's split subject, or whether that ego ideal must lie at yet another level, beyond the explicitly designated narrator. Nonetheless, Kamei's creative deployment of the idea of non-person narrator, a brilliant theoretical innovation in literary analysis, allows him a new language by which to connect the unique specificity of early Meiji literature to broader theoretical questions and thereby to reveal how those texts challenge unspoken assumptions that underlie much structuralist and formalist criticism. It is a strategic move that makes the present work literary criticism in the best sense of that term.

* * * * *

Our goal in translating the work was to provide the most useful and readable English-language version possible, one that whenever possible clarified the more elusive passages in the Japanese original and that included supplemental information that the original assumes its reader already possesses. Nonetheless, we have repeatedly had to bend the English language in an attempt to echo the reverberations that are set off in Japanese by Kamei's unique language, as well as by the various Meiji-period texts he quotes. But all translations are of course betrayals, and with a work as dense and as dependent on the resources of the Japanese language as is this one, this is all the more true. We highly recommend that anyone deeply interested in the complexities of Kamei's argument should return to the Japanese-language text and create his or her own translation.

All footnotes in the translation have been added by the translators and editor, except where noted. The brief summaries that precede each chapter are by the editor. We have also added citations for works quoted, which the original, following standard publishing practices in Japan, did not include. When the work quoted has appeared in English translation, we have cited that translation, although we have often modified the translations. Such modifications are not meant as criticisms or corrections of the published translations, but rather were necessary in order to highlight in English more clearly the specific points that Kamei discusses in his readings. For works not previously translated, we have cited modern reprint editions where they exist, particularly the *Meiji bungaku zenshū* (abbreviated as *MBZ* in citations), the most complete and widely available collection of Meiji-period writing. For works not included in that edition, we have cited other modern editions when available. Also, in quotations, to avoid confusion with ellipses as used in Meiji fiction, we have used brackets to distinguish ellipses that mark omissions from the quoted source.

I would like to thank a few of the many persons who have contributed to this project. First of all, on behalf of all the translators, I would like to thank Prof. Kamei, not only for writing such a brilliant and challenging book, but also for answering literally hundreds of questions about the text over the four years the project required. His prompt and lucid responses to our many queries, and his careful attention to the translated texts, have contributed enormously to whatever value this translation may have. Secondly, I would like to thank the many translators who contributed their labor and intellect (and sensibilities) to this project for their fine work and patience throughout the lengthy editing process. I learned a great deal from each of you. Satoko Ogura has, as always, contributed to my work here in countless ways, large and small. I also thank my colleagues and graduate students at UCLA, who have read over and provided helpful comments on various sections of this manuscript, in particular Seiji Lippit, Shu-mei Shih, Shoichi Iwasaki, Michael Marra, and David Schaberg. Two graduate student research assistants at UCLA, Wengxia Peng and Leslie Winston, performed herculean tasks in tracking down citations, locating texts and preexisting translations, and in untying the many knots that were encountered in the editing process. I also thank Wengxia Peng for her invaluable help in translating the *kanbun* passages from chapters one and twelve. Numerous conversations with Naoki Sakai, Thomas LaMarre, K. Mark Anderson, Murai Osamu, and Takahashi Akinori have also helped me understand this work and guided my editing, even if they were not direct participants in the project. Work on this project was also supported by generous grants from the UCLA Academic Senate and the UCLA Center for Japanese Studies. Finally, I would like to thank Bruce E. Willoughby and Leslie Pincus of the University of Michigan Center for Japanese Studies, as well as the anonymous outside reviewer for the press, for their enthusiastic support of this project, which has made it possible for us to bring Kamei's remarkable work to an English-speaking audience.

Author's Preface to the English Translation

TRANSLATED BY MICHAEL BOURDAGHS

From 1978 to 1982, I published a series of twelve articles in the journal *Gunzō* under the titles "Transformations of Sensibility" ("Kansei no henkaku") and "Transformations of Sensibility Revisited" ("Kansei no henkaku sairon"). In 1983, these were published in book form by Kōdansha under the title *Transformations of Sensibility* (*Kansei no henkaku*).

I believe that this work played a certain role in changing the conception of modern literature in Japan and in setting the tendency for the way literature was viewed in the 1980s. At roughly the same time as I was writing this book, new schools of thought were introduced into Japanese literary studies, including the textual theories of structuralism and so-called poststructuralism, and these became major topics of discussion among scholars and critics. As a result, at the time of its publication this book ended up being lumped together with that trend. When I began writing these essays, though, I myself was conscious of no such connection. In fact, I originally conceived of my project as one grounded in theories that had been produced independently in Japan, but because I criticized modern views of literature and advocated a new method for reading, my work was viewed as sharing a common intention with those new methodologies.

In fact, this book at present is out of print and very hard to obtain in Japan, but now Michael Bourdaghs and other young American scholars have undertaken to translate it into English. Hoping this is of interest to American scholars, I would like to take this opportunity to describe the development of what we might call Japan's homegrown theories and methodologies, those that do not consist of the application of imported structuralist or poststructuralist methodologies to Japanese literature.

When I wrote the essays contained here, I had no idea that they would someday be translated into English. I wrote under the presumption that many of the keywords I used were familiar to my readers, and so I used them without providing any particular explanation. In addition, in the case of keywords to which I attached a particular meaning, I had previously explained them in my book *The Theory of Contemporary Expressions* (*Gendai no hyōgen shisō*, 1974) and in the revised edition of that work, published under the title *The Body: The Beginning of Expression* (*Shintai: hyōgen no hajimari*, 1982), and so I omitted explanations of those here as well. As a result, when I reread this book now, I find passages that today must be difficult to understand even for young Japanese scholars. They must be all the more difficult for scholars of Japanese literature in other countries. With this in mind, I would like to take this opportunity to explain why I undertook this sort of project by situating it in the trends of literary theory that were then current in Japan. I hope that this will also lead to a better understanding of the cultural structure of Japan at that time and my reasons for using the expression "Japan's homegrown theories."

-1-

To begin with, I must first introduce the theories of expression in Japanese of Tokieda Motoki, Miura Tsutomu, and Yoshimoto Takaaki. The research into Japanese expressions carried out by these three is responsible for the concepts of "language"[1] and "subject" that exist in Japan.

What these three share in common is the viewpoint that linguistic research should always be conducted at the level of the utterance: of language actually spoken by somebody, to somebody, and about something. To this language grasped at the level of the utterance they gave the name "language-as-expression," and set it in opposition to the view of language current in Europe. The European view of language they had in mind was Saussure's definition of *langue*, or more precisely, the definition of *langue* found in Kobayashi Hideo's translation of Saussure's *Cours de Linguistique Générale*, (*Gengogaku genron*, 1928).[2] They criticized this *langue* as being nothing more than an abstract concept that stripped away the three fundamental conditions of "language-as-ex-

---

1. Tokieda, Miura, and Yoshimoto all use the word "language" in the sense of "language as expression." It should not be confused with Saussure's concept of *langue*, or "language as system." (Kamei)
2. Kobayashi Hideo (1903–78), not to be confused with the famous literary critic whose name is homophonous but written with different characters, was an important scholar of linguistics. His 1928 Japanese-language version was the first translation of Saussure's French original to appear in any language.

pression," namely that it be spoken by somebody, to somebody, and about something. It was Tokieda Motoki who first established this point of view.

As a young man, Tokieda traveled to Germany, where he studied Husserlian phenomenology. After returning to Japan, he launched a reevaluation of the studies of the Japanese language carried out in the Edo period by nativist (*kokugaku*) scholars, developing what he called the language process theory. This theory is systematically expounded in Tokieda's *Principles of Kokugogaku* (*Kokugogaku genron*, 1941).[3] There, he takes up (Kobayashi's translation of) Saussure's definition of *langue*, namely that it exists "where an auditory image becomes associated with a concept" (Saussure, *Course in General Linguistics,* 14), so that the linguistic sign is "a two-sided psychological entity" (Saussure, 66), and that signs are therefore "realities that have their seat in the brain" (Saussure, 15).[4] Tokieda criticizes Saussure for having transformed language into a substance, a "psychological entity." He then argues:

> [If, as Saussure says] the one [the auditory image] is in concert with the other [the concept], or again, if the one summons up the other, then these two do not form a union but rather must be considered successive psychological phenomena. [. . .] As for the *langue* he sought in the speaking-circuit of *parole*, not only does it not constitute a single unit, it cannot even be considered a two-sided entity; it is always a psychological-physiological compound unit. More precisely, it is nothing other than a phenomenon consisting of successive psychological-physiological processes, combined in the form auditory image → concept, concept → auditory image (Tokieda, *Principles*, 65).

In this way, Tokieda asserted the need to grasp language within the topos of the concrete speech act, and he gave the name "language process" to the successive processes of "auditory image [physiological process] → concept [psychological process]" that occur in the relationship between speaking and listening.

Tokieda's concept of the subject [*shutai*] is closely related to this language process theory. He identifies the subject as one of the three conditions of the speech act, namely the somebody that speaks. But he is careful to distinguish this from the first-person grammatical subject [*shugo*] of a sentence.

3. Tokieda Motoki, *Kokugogaku genron* (Tokyo: Iwanami Shoten, 1941). *Kokugogaku* is the name of the academic discipline concerned with the study (*gaku*) of the national language (*kokugo*), i.e., Japanese. It is historically and structurally distinct from the discipline of linguistics per se (*gengogaku*), a distinction that will be discussed below.
4. Quotations from Saussure here are taken from Ferdinand de Saussure, *Course in General Linguistics,* trans. Wade Baskin (New York: McGraw-Hill, 1959). Page numbers are cited parenthetically.

Moreover, he divides the fundamental research methodologies of linguistics broadly into two camps: the observational standpoint and the subjective standpoint. The observational standpoint uses a grammatical research method, grasping the text of an utterance in its formal aspect and isolating its grammatical subject as one component element of its syntax. From Tokieda's perspective, Saussure's methodology falls under the observational standpoint. In contrast, Tokieda asserted that his own method took the subjective standpoint, in that it sought to understand language as it was actually uttered by someone, tracing through the successive processes described above. In the sense that Tokieda uses the word, we can say that the subject—the somebody who speaks— is in a spiral relationship with its interlocutor, the somebody who listens. This is because the subjective standpoint, that which understands the speaker's language through the successive processes, is in fact a listener's standpoint. Or, as Tokieda put it, "language consists of a form for understanding expressions."[5] Language is one of the forms by which a listener understands semiotic activity. But according to Tokieda, the capacity of the subject to understand language through processing can only be developed through the act of producing its own utterances. He called this relationship by which the listener and speaker mutually guarantee each other's existence the speech circuit of "parole," and what Tokieda called the subject referred to the subject that was realized in this relationship.

On this point, it is worth noting that Tokieda sometimes used the phrase "somebody (original situation [*bamen*])" in place of "somebody (listener)." What he called "original situation" of course included the listener, but it did not simply refer to the place where the conversation took place. Rather, according to Tokieda, what formed the base of this "original situation" was the Japanese language's constant rhythmicity of pronunciation. This referred to the form of vocalization characteristic of Japanese, in which each syllable (or, more precisely, each mora) is pronounced for an equal length of time, like a person clapping hands at constant intervals. For example, the word "McDonald" is pronounced in Japanese as MA-KU-DO-NA-RU-DO, so that when Japanese hear this, they perceive it as being Japanified English. According to Tokieda, when someone intends this constant rhythmicity of pronunciation characteristic of Japanese as they try verbally to communicate something to an interlocutor, the intentionality of that consciousness forms the "original situation" of the utterance.

---

5. Tokieda Motoki, "My View of the System of Kokugogaku" ("Kokugogaku no taikei ni tsuite no hiken") originally printed in *Kotoba* (December 1933) and reprinted in Tokieda Motoki, *The True Nature of Language* (*Gengo honshitsu ron*) (Tokyo: Iwanami Shoten, 1973), 201–4. This passage appears on 204.

* * * * *

If this is so, how is the subject [*shutai*] different from the first-person grammatical subject [*shugo*]? And what was the significance of this difference for Tokieda's research on the Japanese language? In order to answer these questions, I must first briefly turn to the history of lexical category theories in Japanese language studies prior to Tokieda.

Tokieda Motoki was named Professor of Japanese Language Studies [*Kokugogaku*] at Tokyo Imperial University in 1943. His predecessor in that post, Hashimoto Shinkichi (1882–1945), had begun the process of classifying the parts of speech in Japanese by dividing the language into two broad categories: free morphemes [*jiritsugo*] and dependent morphemes [*fuzokugo*]. Free morphemes are words in which a certain articulate sound possesses its own set meaning, such as is the case with nouns, verbs, or adjectives. In contrast to these, in Japanese there also exists a group of words that function to indicate whether a noun in a sentence takes the nominative, objective, or possessive case. In lexical category theory, these are called postpositional particles [*joshi*]. In addition, there is another group of words, auxiliary verbs [*jodōshi*], that indicate the temporal or spatial relationship between speaker and topic. These auxiliary verbs indicate, for example, whether the topic being discussed refers to something that is temporally or spatially distant, or whether it consists of a hope directed toward the future, or again of a recollection from the past. These postpositional particles and auxiliary verbs in themselves possess no set meaning, and it is only when they are attached to a noun or used to conjugate a verb or adjective that they express mode or tense. It was words in these categories that Hashimoto called dependent morphemes. This is because they possess no meaning in themselves, and only begin to function when they are appended to free morphemes.

According to Tokieda, however, Hashimoto's method did not provide a sufficient basis for classifying words. For example, the word *hinoki* (cypress tree), now a single word written with a single Chinese character, was originally created out of three words: *hi* (fire) *no* (particle indicating possession) *ki* (tree): *hi-no-ki*, or fire's tree. *Hi*, the character for fire, was originally pronounced *ho*, making it a homonym for *ho* (to excel or soar) and *ho* (a flame or an ear of grain), so that it signified something with a pointed end that emitted energy or life-force. At some time in the past, Japanese people praised a certain tree by comparing it to fire, calling it *hinoki*. But we in the present are not aware of this three-word origin and are conscious of it only as a single noun that refers to a kind of tree. Or again, there are regions where a donkey is called not a *roba*, as in standard Japanese, but rather *usagiuma*. If we classify this according to

Hashimoto's method, based only on the formal aspects of words, we would have to classify this as a compound of two words: *usagi* (rabbit) and *uma* (horse), and yet when the people of that region use this word, they are likely not conscious of *usagi* nor of *uma*, but rather are conscious of it as a single word that refers to the animal known in English as a donkey. In short, a decision as to whether a given phrase consists of one word or two can only be made by taking a subjective standpoint, one that starts from the consciousness of the person who uttered the phrase. This was the basis of Tokieda's critique of Hashimoto. According to Tokieda, Hashimoto's work was flawed because he had approached matters from an observational standpoint.

It may be difficult for people accustomed to writing systems that place spaces between individual words, as for example in English or French, to understand the importance that Tokieda placed on this sort of difference. For such people, the custom of spacing between words is already unconsciously woven into their utterances. But for people accustomed to writing systems that place no spaces between words, such as in written Japanese, the question of how to parse words is an important and unavoidable problem. As I understand it, in written Japanese it is *kanji*, Chinese characters, that fill a function similar to that of spacing in written English. In fact, it can be said that the reason that the Meiji-period movements that advocated writing Japanese solely in *kana* syllabary or in the Roman alphabet ended in failure was because they overlooked this function of *kanji*. And Tokieda argued that the subjective standpoint, which stood on the side of the writing consciousness and grasped words in adherence with its linguistic consciousness, was the superior method for solving this problem.

If one views language in this way, from the standpoint of the uttering or writing consciousness, one will notice that there are two kinds of words, words that are the result of a process of ideation or conceptualization with regard to some thing or subject matter, and words that are not the product of such an ideation. At least, this is what Tokieda thought. According to Tokieda, this approach was suggested to him by the studies of Japanese language carried out by Edo-period nativists.

Tokieda gave high praise to the work *Thesis on the Four Types of Language* (*Gengyo shishu ron*, 1825) by Suzuki Akira (1764–1837), a representative nativist scholar of the Edo period.

In this work, Suzuki divides words into four types: "body words," "words of deeds," "words of form" and "*te-ni-wo-wa*."[6] "Body words" here are similar to what are called nouns in contemporary lexical category theory, just as

---

6. These translations are adapted from the discussion of Suzuki in H.D. Harootunian, *Things Seen and Unseen* (Chicago: University of Chicago Press, 1988), 66.

"words of deeds" are similar to verbs and "words of form" to adjectives, while "*te-ni-wo-wa*" are equivalent to particles and auxiliary verbs.

Suzuki argued that the *te-ni-wo-wa* words were clearly of a different character from the other three types of words, and he explained the difference in the following terms: whereas the former three types of words all had some specific referent which they indicated, the *te-ni-wo-wa* words had no such referent. To say that a word has a referent that it indicates is to say that the referent is actualized as a phenomenon by virtue of the word's referring to it, and at the same time that the word comes to have "reality as a word."[7] Tokieda interpreted "indicates" [*sashishimesu*] as meaning to objectify or ideate some nonlinguistic matter.

On the other hand, the *te-ni-wo-wa* words, according to Suzuki's explanation, are not words that "indicate" and hence actualize some referent, but rather they are "the voice of the mind" of the speaker that attach to the other three types of words. This seems to mean the speaker's thoughts or emotions at the time he or she actualizes some matter by means of the other three types of words. According to Tokieda's interpretation, these are words that have not undergone ideation or conceptualization of an object and that are direct expressions [*hyōshutsu*] of the subject's attitude or viewpoint toward its object.

Suzuki goes on to use the metaphor of a jewel necklace to explain the difference between the *te-ni-wo-wa* words and the other three types: while the three types are the jewels, the *te-ni-wo-wa* words are the thread that runs through the holes in the jewels, without which the jewels would scatter at random. He argues that one cannot form a sentence using only words of the three types, that the *te-ni-wo-wa* words unite the other three types of words into coherent sentences. This metaphor was not original but rather was one used first by his teacher, the nativist scholar Motoori Norinaga (1730–1801), a fact which, from Tokieda's perspective, made this metaphor a keyword of the Edo-period studies of the Japanese language by nativist scholars. According to Tokieda, Suzuki's three types of words, the words classified as free morphemes in modern lexical category theory, are words selected through the processes of indicating and conceptualizing some nonlinguistic referent. In contrast, the *te-ni-wo-wa* words

---

7. To use Suzuki's own language, the three types of words "have something they point to" (*sasu tokoro ari*), whereas *te-ni-wo-wa* "do not have something they point to." The three types are "words that point to something and thereby manifest it," whereas *te-ni-wo-wa* are "the voice of the mind as attached to those [other three types of] words." Suzuki's expression, "have something they point to," is at present generally interpreted to mean "to indicate something." But more precisely, it should be understood in the following manner: a certain articulate sound is uttered, thereby manifesting something, and by virtue of this the articulate sound becomes a word that points to something. (Kamei)

determine the relationship between free morphemes and unify them into sentences, and by virtue of the manner in which they do so, they express the subject's viewpoint.

What becomes clear when we look at things in this manner is that while Tokieda out of explanatory necessity takes as his premise the existence of a subject who produces the utterance, that subject is manifested only as the *te-ni-wo-wa* words that unify the utterance. In short, we can only identify the subject in the form of the *te-ni-wo-wa* words. Tokieda called the words belonging to Suzuki's three categories *shi* [stem words, nominals, symbols] and those belonging to the *te-ni-wo-wa* category *ji* [conjugational suffixes, nonnominals, indices]. These terms are now used widely, and I will follow this usage here.[8]

If one adopts Tokieda's view, then of course the first-person pronoun that appears in a sentence, the grammatical subject [*shugo*], cannot be the subject [*shutai*]. This is because the grammatical subject is a word [*shi*] by which the subject objectifies and conceptualizes itself as "self." Tokieda explained this point using the example of an artist painting a self-portrait: "The image of the depicted self is not the subject who depicts, but rather it is the achievement of objectivity toward the subject, the subject's transformation into subject matter, whereas the subject itself here is the artist who paints the self-portrait" (Tokieda, *Principles*, 42–43). This metaphor and view of the subject would subsequently have a major impact on Miura Tsutomu and Yoshimoto Takaaki.

But at the time *Principles of Kokugogaku* was published, what attracted the attention of scholars of Japanese language was Tokieda's new method for classifying words. For example, the word *kudasaru* is a polite-form verb that describes the act of giving or bestowing something by a higher-ranking person to a lower-ranking person. If we say "*okane wo kudasai*," it conveys the meaning ("Please give me money [*okane*]") in a form that expresses respect for the addressee. According to Hashimoto Shinkichi's theory, *kudasaru* would of course be classified as a free morpheme (verb). But in Japanese, there are also expressions such as "*mite kudasai*" (lit. "please look"), in which case *kudasaru* (here conjugated as *kudasai*) no longer has the meaning of "bestowing" or "giving," and what remains is only the function of expressing respect for the interlocutor's act of looking. In Hashimoto's theory, this form of *kudasai* too is classified as a free morpheme, but Tokieda classified it as a dependent morpheme (auxiliary

---

8. Both *shi* and *ji* have the meaning of "word," but while *shi* has the nuance of communicating or transmission, *ji* has the nuance of imploring or making an appeal. It seems likely that Tokieda deliberately invoked this nuance when he used *ji* to describe the subject's expressive functions. This is because Hashimoto's category of "dependent morphemes" utterly ignored the subjective expressive [*hyōshutsuteki*] and sentence-unifying functions of the *te-ni-wo-wa* words. (Kamei)

verb). This was because *kudasai* in the phrase "*mite kudasai*" does not include the meaning of "to bestow," but rather expresses only the viewpoint of respect that the uttering subject bears toward its interlocutor, the standpoint of respect toward the interlocutor's act of looking.

The Japanese language contains many such instances where a single word is used in two distinct manners, one in which it is used together with its conceptual content, and another in which its conceptual content is stripped away and it is used only to convey the uttering subject's sense of respect. Tokieda argued for the superiority of his language process theory on the grounds that if one did not take the standpoint of the uttering subject, adhering to the concrete utterance, one would be unable to distinguish this difference.

-2-

Tokieda Motoki's theories had a strong impact on scholars of Japanese grammar, but his work was not well received by linguists.

Since the Meiji period, Japanese linguists had adopted the method of referring to European linguistic theory as general linguistics, of applying it to the Japanese language, and of regarding those aspects that did not conform to the rules of European languages as constituting the particularity of the Japanese language. On the basis of the distinguishing features of the Japanese language that they apprehended through this method, Meiji scholars of the Japanese language "discovered" the unique spirit of the Japanese people, going on to develop a theory of the Japanese spirit. Ueda Kazutoshi (1867–1937), the leading figure in Japanese language studies of this period, declared that "the Japanese national language is the spiritual blood of the nation. It is by virtue of this spiritual blood that the national polity is sustained."[9] In order to protect and purify this spirit, Ueda and his disciples asserted the necessity of establishing and propagating a standard form of the language that would serve as a norm for the nation and participated in the creation of state language policies. They were the ones who created the term and concept of *kokugo* (the Japanese national language). Later, another group emerged from this circle, one that studied mainly the grammar of Japanese. As a result, a certain division of labor developed: specialists in Japanese grammar primarily engaged in research into the vocabulary and grammar of the classical canon, while specialists in linguistics [*gengogaku*] were active in the state's national language policies.

9. Ueda Kazutoshi, *On National Language* (*Kokugo no tame*, 1895), abridged version reprinted in *MBZ* 44:108–90. This passage appears on 110.

In the curriculum of Japanese universities, literary research into the classical canon came to be called *kokubungaku* (national literature studies) while grammatical studies of the canon came to be called *kokugogaku* (national language studies), and as a result the historical role of general linguists in developing the concept of *kokugo* was obscured. Moreover, with the approach of the Second World War, exaltation of the national spirit became the central task for both *kokubungaku* and *kokugogaku*, rendering the history of their development even more obscure.

Tokieda was a scholar of the *kokugogaku* that arose from this path of historical development. On the eve of the outbreak of war between Japan and America, he criticized the tendency of Japanese linguists to theorize the particularity of Japanese against the model of general linguistics. Moreover, he asserted that insofar as Japanese was one language, the rules uncovered for Japanese could not constitute its particularity, but rather must constitute a universality that was applicable to any language. It was on the basis of this thought that he pursued his reevaluation of the research on the Japanese language conducted by nativists prior to the Meiji period. While this stance may seem in concert with the advocacy of national spiritual purity that dominated the 1930s and 1940s, in fact this is not the case. Tokieda pointed out that it was actually scholars of linguistics in Japan who gave birth to the theory of the particularity of the Japanese language and who prepared the way for the theory of a national spirit. Taking up Saussure's notions that *langue* "is the social side of speech, outside the individual" (Saussure, *Course in General Linguistics*, 14) and that

> among all the individuals that are linked together by speech, some sort of average will be set up: all will reproduce—not exactly, of course, but approximately—the same signs united with the same concepts (Saussure, 13)

Tokieda criticizes Saussure for mistakenly reifying *langue* into a social reality (Tokieda, *Principles*, 72–77). This is because Tokieda believed that Saussure's theories were no different from those that reified the Japanese language as a social substance, and the Japanese spirit as the psychological essence of the Japanese people.

Tokieda's insistence on approaching the problem of language at the level of utterances produced by individuals was his way of resisting this tendency. Above, I introduced his idea of the "original situation." According to his theory, each individual producer of utterances intended the original situation of the constant rhythmicity of pronunciation characteristic of Japanese, and it was at this moment that the Japanese language was actualized; it was impossible for the Japanese language to exist in any substantial form outside of this original situation. For this reason, following his theory, what exists in this world are those people who actualize the Japanese language by intending the original situation characteristic of Japanese—a group of people that cannot be limited to such categories as the Japanese race or nation.

But in an irony of history, after the war Tokieda was immediately reinvented by linguists who had converted to American-style democracy or to Soviet-style Marxism. He was turned into a *kokugogaku* scholar who was responsible for the wartime ideology of national purity. Prior to his joining the faculty at Tokyo Imperial University, Tokieda had served as a professor at Seoul Imperial University in Korea, then a Japanese colony. Because of this personal history, he was pasted with the label of having been an advocate of compulsory Japanese language policies forced on the Korean nation. Japanese linguists, who had created the concept of *kokugo*, who had collaborated with the government in its systematization and who had prepared the policies for forced introduction of the Japanese language into Japan's colonies, now tried to shift the blame onto Tokieda in order to escape their own responsibility.

When Tokieda took up his post in Korea, he was faced with the following problem.[10] If he applied Ueda's ideas without modification, he would need to teach the Korean nation to respect the Korean language as the "lifeblood of the nation" (Tokieda, "Korea," 59). But what was expected of him was to educate the Korean nation in the Japanese language. Tokieda's solution to this dilemma was his theory of intentionality toward the "original situation" characteristic of the Japanese language, introduced above. In this sense, his theory of intentionality was designed to bring about an internalization of the Japanese language in the colony, a method much more sophisticated than those policies that attempted to compel the use of Japanese by governmental fiat. A genuine critique of Tokieda would take up this issue, but the postwar linguists who attacked Tokieda went no further than to criticize his taking a position in a colonial university.

One incident is particularly symbolic of the way they treated Tokieda.

In 1950, *Pravda*, the newspaper of the Soviet Communist Party, published "On Marxism in Linguistics," a kind of doctrinal catechism that appeared under Stalin's name. It was subsequently translated into Japanese. In it, Stalin declares that language should not be considered part of the superstructure, giving the following reasons:

> . . . language differs radically from superstructure. Language is generated not by one base or another, by the old base or the new within a

---

10. Tokieda Motoki, "*Kokugo* Policy in Korea" ("Chōsen ni okeru kokugo seisaku '), *Nihongo* 2:8 (July 1942): 54–63.

given society, but by the entire historic development of society and the history of the bases over the centuries. It is created not by any one class but by the whole society, by all classes of society, by the efforts of hundreds of generations. It is created not to meet the needs of any one class but of the whole society, of all classes in society. This is precisely why it is created as the language of the whole people, as a society's single language, common to all members of the society. [. . .]

It cannot be otherwise. Language exists, it is created, to serve society as a whole in the capacity of a means of communication for people, to be common to the members of a society and one and the same for the society, serving the members of the society equally, regardless of their class position. Language has only to depart from this position with respect to the entire people, language has only to show preference for and render support to a particular social group, to the detriment of other social groups of the society, for it to lose its quality, for it to cease to be a means of communication of people in a society, for it to become the jargon of a particular social group, for it to degenerate and doom itself to extinction.

In this respect language, while differing fundamentally from the superstructure, is not, however, different from the tools of production, machinery, say, which can serve both capitalism and socialism equally.[11]

This was published prior to the so-called critique of Stalin, and Marxist linguists in Japan accepted its views uncritically. Kobayashi Hideo, taking a Saussurean position, approved of it, calling its theory of language as nonsuperstructural "completely correct." Moreover, interpreting Stalin's views to mean that "language is directly tied to productive activity and reflects changes in production," he gave his approval with some reservations about Stalin's views, at least in terms of issues related to vocabulary.[12] It was in this atmosphere that Tokieda Motoki published his criticism of Stalin.[13]

The central point of Tokieda's critique may already be apparent, but I will briefly summarize it here. When Stalin explains why language is not part of the superstructure, it is premised on the concept of "society as a whole" (in Japanese, *zenkokumin*, "the entire nation") as if that existed as an actual substance. Next, in order to reinforce that concept, he contrives the concept of a

---

11. English translation from "Stalin Enters the Linguistics Debate," *Current Digest of the Soviet Press* 2:21 (July 8, 1950): 3–9. This passage appears on 3.
12. Kobayashi Hideo, "Stalin's Views on Language" ("Sutaarin no gengokan"), *Bungaku* 19:2 (February 1951): 22–29. The quoted passages appear on 24.
13. Tokieda Motoki, "On Stalin's 'On Marxism in Linguistics'" ("Sutaarin 'Gengogaku ni okeru Marukusushugi' ni kanshite"), *Chūō Kōron* 65:10 (October 1950): 97–104.

single, unified national language. After expressing his skepticism regarding these, Tokieda goes on to argue that:

> As for language, even if Stalin argues that it is single and unified, as a matter of historical fact it is undeniable that it is a site of differences and conflict. If we say that these are class-based, then the class-based nature of language is a necessity, and to deny this and assert that it is single and unified is to engage in a form of idealism that confuses desire and reality. [. . .] To separate language from the individuals who compose society and to declare that it exists as a tool held in common by society is something that can only be affirmed in the most metaphorical of terms or under special conditions. In fact, language is something that can be established only in the form of individual subjective acts by the members of society. (Tokieda, "Stalin," 102–3)

Stalin had argued that language, like a tractor, was a means of production and that it was non-superstructural because it was equally useful to the members of any class. While Tokieda was skeptical of this analogy, I will borrow it here in order to highlight the nature of Tokieda's criticism. Even if it is the case that people of any class are able to use a tractor, their class position will necessarily be reflected in their "subjective" acts of production. Class relations must also be reflected in the circulation of their product as a commodity. This was the basis of Tokieda's objection.

But Japanese Marxists of that time swallowed whole the Soviet Communist Party's official explanation that in a postrevolutionary socialist state classes no longer existed. Japan's penitent linguists, who followed this line, uncritically accepted Stalin's theories on language and means of production, which were deduced from this official explanation. Accordingly, they treated Tokieda's objection with derision, claiming it was a misguided view that demonstrated an ignorance of history.

Looking back now, it seems likely that Stalin had begun to develop an understanding of the structure of language, but because his theoretical approach was not sufficiently rigorous, he fell into the error of a too hastily drawn analogy between the structure of language and the structure of class society. As a result, he modified the concepts of the structure of class society and of revolution to make them fit the structure of language.

Stalin, having noticed the "fact" that the Russian language had undergone almost no change since the Revolution, argued that the transformation in language from an old type to a new type did not occur suddenly, but rather through the gradual accumulation of various elements of the new type and through, accordingly, the gradual extinction of various elements of the old type.

He then asserted that this view alone constituted the "Marxist" view of language. At the same time, he set forth the following new theory of social reform:

> In general, it should be drawn to the attention of the comrades who have been attracted by the notions of explosions, that the law of the transition from an old quality to a new through an explosion is inapplicable not only to the history of a language's development, it is not always applicable to other social phenomena of a basic or superstructure nature as well. It is obligatory for a society divided into hostile classes. But it is not at all obligatory for a society which does not have hostile classes. (Stalin, "On Marxism in Linguistics," 8)

This explanation perplexed Japanese Marxists because they had interpreted revolution, the transformation from an old-type capitalist order to a new socialist order, via the law of the dialectic: they saw it as an explosive changeover, not a quantitative but a qualitative change. How could they accommodate this understanding to Stalin's thesis? In answer to this question, one Marxist theorist[14] declared that "Among changes, there are 'quantitative changes' characterized by graduality and 'qualitative changes' characterized by abruptness" (Terazawa, "Hiyaku to bakuhatsu," 31). Moreover, within the category of qualitative change, there were "two forms, explosive qualitative change and gradual qualitative change" (31). The shift from capitalism to socialism took the form of explosive qualitative change. But under the system of "direction from above by the existing state authority and conscious support from the masses" (31) such as characterized a socialist state, gradual qualitative change became not only possible, but desirable. It was in this form that he supported the Soviet system under Stalin's leadership.

In this sense, the problem of language was also a problem of the theory of contradiction as well as a problem of the theory of the state. Among contradictions there were two types: antagonistic and nonantagonistic. This had been a widely accepted premise of Marxism, but Stalin took the further step of apportioning antagonistic contradictions to societies "divided into hostile classes" and nonantagonistic contradictions to societies that do "not have hostile classes." This sort of mechanical differentiation can also be seen in Mao's theory of contradiction, but in Stalin's version, antagonistic contradictions, which have their basis in class conflict, are no longer possible in a postrevolutionary socialist state. The contradiction between the Party and the people consisted of a non-

---

14. Terazawa Tsunenobu, "Leaps and Explosions" ("Hiyaku to bakuhatsu"), in *The Language Question and the National Question*, ed. Minshushugi kagakusha kyōkai gengogaku-bu (*Gengo mondai to minzoku mondai*) (Tokyo: Rironsha, 1952), 24–35.

antagonistic contradiction, "a revolution from above [. . .] accomplished on the initiative of the existing regime with the support of the [. . .] masses" (Stalin, "On Marxism in Linguistics," 8). It served as the motive force behind the gradual development of the socialist state. Moreover, according to this view, the social contradictions that were internal to the capitalist order, as well as the conflict between socialist states and capitalist states, were by necessity antagonistic contradictions. This was, of course, the logic of the purge, under which criticism of the party leadership was considered an antagonistic contradiction in the same way as were the external enemies of the socialist state and required expulsion.

Another Marxist linguist[15] replied to Tokieda's criticism of Stalin in the following terms:

> In the case of honorific usage, too, Edo-period samurai used *gozaru* while townspeople used the more polite *gozarimasu*, but how does this "reflect class-based thoughts or feelings"? Doesn't the very same samurai use *gozarimasu* when he speaks in turn to his lord? (Mizuno, "Nihon gengogaku," 92)

Tokieda argued that if you abstracted words into *langue*, then certainly language appeared as something non-superstructural, unrelated to class, but if you approached language in adherence to the speech act of the utterer, then it would necessarily reflect the speaking subject's class-based thoughts or feelings. His Marxist critics tried to trip him up on this issue by pointing out that both the samurai of the ruling class and the townspeople of the ruled class used the same words, *gozaru* and *gozarimasu*.

But this is a hollow counterargument. *Gozaru* and *gozarimasu* in the Japanese system of honorifics are classified as humble expressions with the meanings of "to be" or "is." Humble expressions are words that indicate the subject's consciousness of the inferiority of its own status compared to that of its interlocutor, so that a townsperson uses it in speaking to a samurai, while a samurai too uses it in speaking to his lord. This phenomenon thus appears to be unrelated to class, and yet the lord here would never use *gozaru* or *gozarimasu* when speaking to his vassal samurai. To use a word that would indicate that the ruling lord is of lower status than his ruled vassals would be a violation of the rules of language usage. Tokieda's critics deliberately ignored this point in their attacks on him.

---

15. Mizuno Kiyoshi, "Japanese Linguistics" ("Nihon gengogaku"), in *The Language Question and the National Question*, ed. Minshushugi kagakusha kyōkai gengogaku-bu (*Gengo mondai to minzoku mondai*) (Tokyo: Rironsha, 1952), 90–106.

* * * * *

In this way, Marxist linguists of that period toed the Stalin line and behaved in an authoritarian manner toward Tokieda, a fact that they attempted to conceal after the so-called critique of Stalin. In 1977, I serialized a series of articles on postwar literary debates in the quarterly journal *Kyōiku kokugo*, but when I touched on the controversy surrounding Stalin's theory of language in my article on the *kokumin bungaku ronsō* debate over a national literature, my article was rejected for publication.[16] This was because the editorial advisory board for *Kyōiku kokugo* included some of the linguists I have discussed here, and they intervened to prevent publication of my article.

-3-

These circumstances formed the background for the positive evaluation of Tokieda's theories by the civilian Marxist, Miura Tsutomu. The phrase "civilian Marxist" might strike some people as odd. By "civilian," I mean not affiliated with the government or any branch of "official" Marxism. As is well known, after its founding in the 1920s, the Japanese Communist Part (JCP) became the target of governmental oppression and was driven into illegal underground activities because it advocated the overthrow of the Emperor system and the abolition of private property. In that sense, it may appear unnecessary to single out Miura as a "civilian," since all Japanese Marxists were driven out of public life and forced into an illegal existence within the realm of civil society. For example, the respected Marxist economist Kawakami Hajime (1879–1946) was forced to surrender his position as professor at a national university by the prewar government.

But with Japan's defeat in the war in 1945, the fascist and militarist powers were overthrown, and the JCP was recognized as a legitimate political party. Many Japanese intellectuals, reflecting on their own war responsibility for failing to check the rise of fascism and militarism, joined the party, and even those who did not officially join tended to support it. At that time, these persons referred to themselves as "progressive intellectuals," and they came to dominate the postwar university, and not just in departments of economics. From their intellectual activity came the mainstream schools of knowledge across campus, be it in the sciences, the humanities, or the schools of education: Marxist historiography, Marxist philosophy, Marxist linguistics, Marxist theories of science, Marxist pedagogical theory. The mass media also frequently employed

16. The manuscript was returned to me and is now in my possession. (Kamei)

intellectuals who held these same points of view, while in the literary world the dominant organization, the New Japan Literature Association (*Shin Nihon bungakkai*), was led by writers who were party members. The theoretical ground of the Marxism espoused by this generation of writers and intellectuals was the Leninist-Stalinist version of Marxism expounded by the JCP. Moreover, their theoretical efforts were evaluated on the basis of how faithfully they adhered to the party's official line and how much they contributed to its propagation. In short, with the legalization of the JCP and the lifting of the ban on Marxism, there appeared the phenomenon we might call the "official" Marxism as espoused by the JCP.

But the "civilian" Marxist Miura Tsutomu bucked this trend. In 1950, when Cominform, the international organization of world communist parties, criticized the JCP, the party's ranks split, not so much over whether it should accept the criticism as over what form its acceptance should take. This split extended to organizations of academics and writers as well, giving rise to many tragicomedies of expulsion and excommunication from party rolls. The roots of conflict and mutual suspicion that began at this time went very deep. While this was not the sole cause for the splits that arose in subsequent movements opposing the conservative government of the Liberal Democratic Party, when conflicts did break out among the ranks of antigovernment movements, almost without fail the aftershocks of this earlier schism came into play to intensify the new conflicts. Miura Tsutomu, however, was not drawn into these disputes and consistently played the role of a theoretical mentor to a variety of citizens' movements.

This may have been the result of his unique academic career path. He withdrew before graduation from an old-style (pre–1945) vocational school and while working at a factory in a small village, he studied on his own the works of Marx and Engels. As I have already noted, Japanese Marxism might more precisely be called Leninism, Stalinism, or Maoism, but Miura with his knowledge of the original texts of Marx and Engels was able to evaluate and criticize those tendencies.

* * * * *

Miura's theoretical investigations ranged over a wide area. The central issues in his research on Japanese expressions, as developed in his *What Sort of Language Is Japanese?* (*Nihongo wa dō iu gengo ka*, 1956), are the concepts of the ideational split self and of norms.[17]

---

17. The translations of Miura's terms are borrowed from Naoki Sakai, *Voices From the Past: The Status of Language in Eighteenth-Century Japanese Discourse* (Ithaca: Cornell University Press, 1991), esp. 190–94, except that for stylistic purposes, the Japanese word *kannenteki* is translated alternately as "ideational" and "conceptual."

Using the examples of mirrors, photographs, and pictures, he explains the "ideational split self" in the following manner. In, for example, the phenomenon of seeing my own reflection in a mirror, I am certainly seeing myself, but I am also conscious of the meeting I am about to attend or the people I am about to meet, and as I imagine how I will be seen by those people, I fix my hair and select the clothing I will wear. That is to say, together with seeing my reflected image with my own eyes, I also take the position of the people I am about to meet and gaze at myself as if I were looking from their eyes. In this way, at the level of concepts or ideas, we double our gazing perspective, which is what Miura called the "ideational split self."

Or again, when I take a photograph of the landscape before my eyes, my own figure is not depicted within the photograph, and yet the viewing position from which the photograph was taken is reflected in the composition of the photograph. Grasping this phenomenon, whereby the viewing position is objectified within the photograph, Miura believed that the visually depicted or expressed object possessed the character of a mirror. When I draw a bird's-eye-view map in order to show somebody where my house is, the real I who writes the map is standing on the ground, but I draw the map to my house conceptually as if I were looking down from a position of great height. According to Miura's theory, this map is a kind of mirror reflecting the perspective of another "I," one that is ideationally split off from the I that draws the map.

From this brief introduction, the reasons for Miura's positive appraisal of Tokieda's theories may already be apparent. Tokieda grasped the first-person pronoun not as the subject itself, but rather as the subject's objectification and conceptualization of itself. Following Miura's theory, this is the result of the self's ideational split. The Japanese language includes several words that function as first-person pronouns, including *watashi, ore, boku,* etc. Moreover, when a father speaks to his children, he often refers to himself as "father" (*otōsan*). According to Miura, we distinguish between such words as *watashi, ore, boku* depending on our conversational interlocutor because the speaker causes the original situation and his relationship to the listener to be reflected in his speech. Or again, when a father refers to himself as "father" when speaking with his child, it is because conceptually he has taken the position of the child, calling himself "father" because that is how the child refers to its father. Tokieda had broadly divided the Japanese language between words that resulted from a process of conceptualization and words that directly expressed [*hyōshutsu*] the disposition of the speaking subject. Miura called cases where ideation occurred "objective expressions," and those in which the subject's perspective or standpoint was verbally manifested through *ji* (as opposed to *shi*) he called "subjective expressions," and he argued that in Japanese sentences *ji* functioned like mirrors reflecting the subject.

The major difference between these two was that while Tokieda considered the subject, be it the speaker or writer, as a unified entity, Miura's subject was the ideational split subject, one pluralized to include the so-called fictional narrator or perspectival character.

* * * * *

The other central concept in Miura's theory was that of the "norm." The most coherent explanations of his theory of the norm come in his books *Theories of Cognition and Language* (*Ninshiki to gengo no riron*, 1967) and *What Kind of Science is the Dialectic?* (*Benshōhō wa dō iu kagaku ka*, 1968). As will be clear from the following explanation, his theory of the norm is based on Hegel's *Philosophy of Right*. At the risk of boring the reader, I would like to trace through his concept of the norm as argued in *Theories of Cognition and Language*, in so far as it is necessary to explain Miura's thinking on linguistic norms.

Miura considered norms to be the objectification of will. For example, let us assume that I have been given the following advice by my doctor: "You'd better quit drinking and smoking." Whether or not I follow this advice is up to me, but if for the sake of my health I decide to follow it and assign myself a new rule of abstinence from tobacco and alcohol, I then check my desire to consume alcohol and tobacco by means of this rule. This rule is one I have chosen of my own will, and yet it functions just as if it were an order constraining me from outside. In this sense, this rule includes a degree of fictionality and must be distinguished from pure will. Miura called this sort of rule an "individual norm."

But if, for example, I should violate this rule, it would at least for the moment cause no one any trouble. In contrast, I cannot unilaterally violate a promise or contract I have made with some other person. This is because promises and contracts consist of "shared will" created in order to realize "shared benefits." From the moment we agree to a promise or contract, it becomes a constraint on our mutual wills, and if one party violates it without the consent of the other, he will necessarily be censured by the other. Miura called this sort of "shared will" a "particular norm."

According to Miura, this sort of particular norm bore a shared will in the form of a "conceptual person." Let us say, for example, that I have contracted to lend money to somebody. If I (the lender) urge the borrower to repay the loan, or again if I release him from the obligation to repay it, phenomenally it seems as if my will is directly controlling the will of the borrower. But in fact, this takes place through the mediation of the "conceptual person" of the loan agreement, so that if I were to transfer that loan agreement to some third party, that third party in representing the will of the "conceptual person" would demand repayment from the borrower. Or, if I (the lender) were to refuse to accept the payment brought to me by the borrower, saying "you don't need to repay me" and thereby releasing him from the obligation to repay, this in fact would be a contract violation that went against the will of the "conceptual person." If the borrower consents to my will as manifested in my saying "you don't need to repay me," then we have established a new shared will, and the loan agreement is discarded, the contract cancelled.

Miura thought that most social domination took place through this sort of "conceptual person." In the relationship of an employment contract, the capitalist who controls the means of production is in the overwhelmingly advantageous position over the laborer, who has only his own labor to sell and who is therefore forced into making numerous concessions in the conditions of the contract. While this at first glance appears to be a contract entered into under the free will of both parties, in fact in many cases the will of the employee hardly enters into it. Yet the ability of a particular capitalist to control a particular laborer is at all times mediated by the "conceptual person" of the employment contract. A privately acting capitalist cannot dominate or force labor on a privately acting laborer in the absence of an employment relation. To put this another way, while a privately acting laborer may be forced into many concessions in the employment contract, once that contract is made, if the employer capitalist does not fulfill his obligations under its terms, the laborer can demand that those contractual terms be faithfully observed. In cases where that may be difficult as an individual, the laborer can demand that the law, or the state power which is the executor of the law, represent the "conceptual person" established in the contract.

When we summarize his position in these terms, it becomes clear that Miura operated within the conceptual framework of modern civil society. He grasped "law" (or, in Hegel's vocabulary, "right") as being a "universal norm" established for the purpose of sustaining an imaginary communal interest. Why did he call it a "universal norm"? The reason was that, whereas "individual norms" and "particular norms" acted to constrain only those parties who had created them, the law as "universal norm" was created as a general will that should apply to all members of a community, or again as the will of the totality that transcended the individual wills of the various members, so that it was granted compulsory power. Why did he grasp this as an expression of "imaginary" communal interest? The reason was that, while the "communal" interest in class society is nothing more than the "particular interest" of the ruling class, it is camouflaged and rationalized by the ruling class so that it appears to be the "communal" interest.

Miura unfolded his theory of "universal norms" based on Marx and Engels's *German Ideology*, but he stressed the difference between "universal norms" and the will of the ruling class. A law that has been established as a "universal norm" can conflict with and constrain the will of individual capitalists or enterprises. As in the example above, it functions to guarantee the contractual rights of the individual employee. In other words, this imaginary communal interest in its capacity as a "conceptual person" is relatively independent from and hence can function to regulate the will of the ruling class. This is because the imaginary communal interest is created in the form of the ruling class's conceptual self-alienation. But because vulgar Marxists fail to understand the structure of this "imaginary," they are only able to grasp the imaginary communal interest as being a direct reflection of the ruling class's interest, making a short-circuited mistaken equation between "universal norms" and the will of the ruling class. Miura's stress on the difference between "universal norms" and the will of the ruling class arose from his desire to critique the simplistic reflection theory and short-circuited cognition of the vulgar Marxism that dominated the antiestablishment political movements of his day.

* * * * *

This is a rough outline of Miura's theory of norms, but he also argued that the above three types of norms were all created purposively and consciously, whereas linguistic norms were developed through a process of natural growth over the long course of human history. Linguistic norms consisted of social conventions regarding the linkage between concepts and articulate sounds, as well as social conventions regarding what sound/concept pairings would be applied to what objects. We use these conventions in order to verbalize our cognition regarding some thing or event. Yet we are not normally conscious of this process when we speak. In fact, what we really encounter on a daily basis are individual, concrete utterances, and linguistic norms can be located only as a result of abstraction from these. In short, the norms developed through natural growth are located through a process of abstraction from the form of concrete phenomena, so that we must rigorously distinguish between phenomenal form and norms. This theoretical stance led Miura to declare that it was the actual, concrete utterances exchanged in everyday life that constitute language. From this standpoint, Saussure's *langue* refers only to linguistic norms.

Tokieda Motoki criticized Saussure's *langue* for being an overly conceptual abstraction. For the reasons described above, however, Miura was not entirely critical of Saussure's concept of *langue*. He was, however, critical of Saussure's lack of a rigorous theoretical understanding of the concept of norms and for his inability to grasp the link between acoustic image and concept through the theory of contradiction.

Miura considered the phonetic side of linguistic norms to form their sensible [*kanseiteki*], material side, whereas their conceptual side formed their extrasensible or nonmaterial side. This mode of being of linguistic norms, containing both a sensible and an extrasensible side, according to Miura, took the form of a nonantagonistic contradiction born out of the practice of mental communication between people. The cognition that people have in and of itself cannot be sensed by the eye or ear. In order to convey this extrasensible cognition to others, people convert this into a sensible, material form, such as articulate sounds or written letters. The recipients of these then trace through those sensible forms and thereby understand the cognition of the utterer. Miura grasped this process as a dialectical act, the negation of a negation.

To avoid misunderstanding, let me point out that Miura's "cognition" did not consist of a simple reflection of reality. It rather should be seen as an ordering of reality. When faced with a certain situation or event, we might say, "there is a box on the table," but we could also say, "there is a table under the box." Or again, we could say "the table is holding up a box" or that "the box is being held up by a table." In this case, we impose a certain relationship on two things as we conceptualize them, and using linguistic norms we call one of these "table" and the other "box." Miura grasped this sort of act as being the expression of cognition as mediated by linguistic norms. But this was not all that was implied by Miura's notion of the expression of cognition. Things exist on their own, outside their relationships to other things. From among them, we select two and impose a relationship on them: "is above," "is below," "is holding up," or "is being held up." In this sense, the expression of relationship is clearly related to our way of cognizing. To put this another way, our way of speaking manifests not only the relationship between the two things, it also reflects our own relationship to them. Moreover, our cognition and expression of this relationship is ordinarily not undertaken from the perspective or position that we hold in reality. In most cases, it takes place by way of the position or perspective of our ideationally split self.

-4-

It was Yoshimoto Takaaki who introduced Miura Tsutomu's ideas about the Japanese language into literary theory. Yoshimoto gave the clearest systematic expression of his literary theory in two books: *What Is Beauty for Language?* (*Gengo ni totte, bi to wa nani ka*, 1965) and *Preface to a Theory of Mental Phenomena* (*Shinteki genshōron josetsu*, 1971). Both had wide influence, especially among young readers, from the time they were first serialized in *Shikō*, a journal that Yoshimoto edited and published. Here I will briefly summarize his theories, with an eye toward explaining why they achieved such great influence.

In *What Is Beauty for Language?* Yoshimoto attempts to depict "theoretically" the circumstances through which humankind came to possess language, tracing out what he considers to be the necessary conditions for the appearance of language. First, he supposes a stage at which people become able to pair up articulate sounds with things. According to Yoshimoto's theory, at this stage these articulate sounds cannot yet be considered to constitute language. Next, he supposes a stage at which people start to utter consciously the articulate sound that is coupled with an object even when that object is not present and only its image has been called to mind. According to Yoshimoto, when we have reached this stage the articulate sounds have fulfilled the conditions that make them into language. To use his terminology, articulate sounds first become language when they no longer possess a directly indicative relationship to their object. This mental causality, whereby the image of a thing is capable of being intended even outside of a direct relationship to that thing, constitutes the quality that Yoshimoto calls "self expression" [*jiko hyōshutsu*].

In a sense, we can say that his notion of self expression has two sides. The first consists of a mental intention, which takes the image of something as an object for consciousness, and the second is an intention toward pronunciation, whereby one voluntarily pronounces a certain articulate sound, thereby making it an object for consciousness. He gave the name "indicative expression" [*shiji hyōshutsu*] to this latter act whereby one indicates the (image of the) thing by means of a certain articulate sound. Why did he choose to add the word "expression" here instead of simply calling this "indication"? The reason for this was that the act of indication could not take place in the absence of mental intentionality.

To look at this another way, we can say that the term indicative expression relates to the aspects of the utterance that are directed at others, whereas self expression relates to those aspects directed toward the self. When I turn toward some other and say something, unless I follow what Miura called linguistic norms, the meaning of my utterance will not be conveyed. According to Yoshimoto, it is by examining these other-oriented aspects that we discover Miura's linguistic norms. But when we turn our attention toward the self-oriented aspects, we feel a sense of estrangement from linguistic norms and become aware of a mental impulse toward disobeying them. Moreover, as for the motivation behind our desire to speak, it is more common for the self-oriented motive to be stronger than the other-oriented motive. At least, this is what Yoshimoto believed. The following passage from *Preface to a Theory of Mental Phenomena* (Tokyo: Hokuyōsha, 1971) clearly manifests this belief:

> A single ashtray is placed before the eye. This is a container made to
> answer to a certain purpose: holding ashes flicked from cigarettes

and discarded cigarette butts. In terms of function, any nonflammable container could answer to this purpose. But we give the name ashtray to those containers especially made in order to answer to this purpose. Why do we call this container "ashtray"? Why don't we call it "bowl" instead of "ashtray"? The reason for this has no other basis except that normatively we are accustomed to calling it "ashtray." Accordingly, if we arbitrarily began to call it some other name, there exist no grounds for calling this wrong. Saying that it would be inconvenient because others might not understand, or that it risks causing confusion with some other container are nothing more than unfounded pretenses. (Yoshimoto, *Preface*, 188)

We can think of language as possessing two structural factors. The first is language as expression, the second language as norm. In the study of literature normally language as expression is foregrounded, whereas in the study of linguistics language as norm is considered primary. Simple, uncomplicated "language" as such does not exist. (Yoshimoto, *Preface*, 168)

Language as expression, if viewed as a mental phenomenon, exists in the tendency to attempt self expression as we approach the near side of some "concept." The externalization of this in the form of speech or writing is only secondary. It has the tendency of reaching fruition when, in the midst of what from the perspective of another appears to be silence, a certain "concept" is formed. When we sense momentarily the presence of words that are not yet words, this is simply because mentally the words are approaching a concept as they strive to attain their true nature. (Yoshimoto, *Preface*, 170)

Here, Yoshimoto adopts a methodology similar to that of Husserl. When we produce an utterance directed toward somebody, we are at the same time hearing our own voice with our own ears. If, taking this as the point of departure in the process, we gradually distill this down to the relation between voice and self (one's own voice that one can hear, then one's own voice as directed to oneself, one's own voice as it internally arises from oneself, etc.), in the end we are able to abstract out an ideal voice, the voice that appears most directly before the self. Through this procedure, Yoshimoto tried to extract "language as a mental phenomenon."

This could also possibly be characterized as an attempt to prove psychologistically what Saussure called the arbitrariness of language. Suppose there is a person here who remains completely silent. In the eyes of another person, he appears to have completely forgotten all language. Yoshimoto posited the existence of such a person. Imagining that this person maintained his silence out of a feeling of the futility of whatever he might say to other people,

Yoshimoto tried to describe the "words that are not yet words" that he thought existed in this person. This was part of his attempt to grasp the true nature of words as they appear before the self. Seen in the light of such a true nature, linguistic norms would have to be "unfounded pretenses," arbitrary conventions. As for the grounds that justify calling a certain real object "ashtray," just because such a convention exists in reality does not necessarily mean that it has theoretical necessity.

But the arbitrariness of language as defined in Saussure's theory and the arbitrariness of linguistic norms that Yoshimoto described are not the same thing. According to Saussure, it is precisely because language is arbitrary that social conventions are necessary for its functioning. It is the arbitrariness of language that gives birth to norms, so that in this sense the ground for these norms is the arbitrariness itself. On this point, Saussure reaches the same conclusion as Miura. But whereas Miura's theory is premised from the start on the existence of linguistic norms, in Saussure's theory the arbitrariness of language is posited as the premise for the existence of norms. The theoretical implications that arise from this difference are enormous.

If we look at this in the light of actual consciousness, it is of course true that we call an ashtray "ashtray" because we are normatively accustomed to doing so. This is because "if we arbitrarily began to call it some other name" then in fact "it would be inconvenient because others might not understand." This alone surely provides sufficient grounds for calling it an "ashtray." But Yoshimoto, anticipating this sort of objection based on actual consciousness, persists in his insistence on a mental basis for language as he develops his argument in a dialogic fashion.

Note that in the passage from Yoshimoto quoted above, there is not a single phrase that ignores or deviates from linguistic norms. This, of course, is because he had to write in a way that would convey his meaning to others, so that he had no alternative but to use language that obeyed the norms of "indicative expression" in order to depict his doubts and criticisms of those norms, doubts that arose from the perspective of "self expression." But at the time *What Is Beauty for Language?* and *Preface to a Theory of Mental Phenomena* were published, few readers noticed that Yoshimoto's writing itself obeyed linguistic norms; what readers reacted to instead was the content of his argument. The younger generation, especially students involved in the various protest movements that peaked around the year 1970, was deeply influenced by his ideas and tried to carry them beyond the realm of linguistic expression, experimenting with political movements that were characterized by "self expression" in a variety of acts, movements that questioned the grounds for various social norms, including the academic and scholarly norms of the university. Not only this, they also attacked the various Marxist norms of the JCP, which by then had become part of the establishment system. This generation largely believed that Yoshimoto's theory of "self expression" provided an accurate explanation of its own mental motives and impulses.

University students proceeded to occupy campus buildings, erect barricades, and to use new words to signify the meaning of those actions. To describe their praxis in terms of Yoshimoto's example, they drank soup out of an ashtray so as to be able to call it "bowl" and flicked ashes and discarded cigarette butts into a bowl so as to be able to call it "ashtray." As praxis it was clumsy and childish, but in the students' eyes, the barricades created a space of "self authority" that resisted the actual state authority.

In the universities of that time, there were still a large number of scholars affiliated with the JCP. They viewed themselves as antiestablishment progressives who opposed the conservative government, but the new generation rejected this as a trick. These faculty members and the young student activists denounced and despised each other, each group criticizing the other for being secretly in bed with the conservative, reactionary state authorities. It was the young student activists who took the upper hand in this contest of mutual recrimination. This is because, consistent with their commitment to the principles of linguistic "self expression," they were only too happy to fall into discommunication with their professors. The professors burned their fingers on this discommunication and in the end felt they had no alternative but to rely on the power of the police, part of the reactionary government they supposedly opposed, to tear down the barricades.

* * * * *

In this manner, Yoshimoto created a theory for circumventing the unique function of norms, the significance of which had first been recognized by Miura. Yoshimoto's approach of grasping Japanese texts from two aspects was also something he learned from Miura. We can say that Miura's objective expression roughly corresponds to Yoshimoto's "indicative expression," his subjective expression to Yoshimoto's "self expression." Yoshimoto then went on to say that in tracing through the "indicative expression" of Japanese texts we uncover "meaning," whereas when we trace through their "self expression" we uncover "value." This double-structure approach is clearly a reappropriation and transformation of Miura's theory. On the basis of it, Yoshimoto argued that historical changes and innovations in Japanese literary expressions were caused by metamorphoses of "self expression" consciousness.

I wrote *Transformations in Sensibility* with the intention of critiquing and revising Yoshimoto's view of literary history, what he called the "history of expression," but I carried it out with a deep appreciation for the precision of his analysis of Japanese expressions.

For example, let us examine the following tanka by the twentieth-century poet, Otsuka Kinnosuke:

Kokkyō owareshi Kaaru Marukusu wa tsuma ni okurete shininikeru kana
Driven abroad / Karl Marx / after his wife / he died

Read for its content, what Yoshimoto would call its "indicative expression," this poem seems nothing more than the recounting of a historical episode: Karl Marx, driven into exile, meets with the death of his spouse, after which he too dies. But Yoshimoto analyzes this poem from the viewpoint of "expression consciousness" (*hyōshutsu ishiki*) in the following manner.[18] First, in the expression "driven abroad," the author is relating how a certain figure was forced to endure the cruel fate of foreign exile. From the reader's perspective, having read up to this point, the identity of that figure is still unknown. It might be the author, or some other figure. In short, the author's "position of expression" (*hyōshutsu ichi*) regarding the event of foreign exile is still unclear. With the subsequent "Karl Marx," the author's expression consciousness splits between Marx as its object and the position of expression that narrates Marx's fate. But in the next phrase, "after his wife," the position of expression shifts and now identifies with Marx himself, because the word used for "wife" here (*tsuma*) in Japanese can only be used by that woman's husband. If the author's position of expression had remained separate from Marx's, he would have used a different word, the more formal *fujin*, to describe her. By choosing the word *tsuma* here, the author stands in the position of the husband Marx and shares in his loneliness as a husband whose wife has died. After this, with "he died," the author's position of expression again separates from Marx, returning to a position that narrates the Marx who died a lonely man. The poem narrates Marx's life in the brief form of a tanka, as if it were a fast-forwarded film. According to Yoshimoto, the ability of this brief expression to make a strong impression on the reader is due to the agile shifts in the author's position of expression.

Yoshimoto's notion of expression consciousness is not exhaustively delineated by these sorts of shifts in position of expression. In discussing Tokieda's theories, I mentioned the constant rhythmicity of pronunciation that is characteristic of Japanese. The Japanese tanka is based on the number of moras (syllables) produced through this constant rhythmicity, a single tanka being composed of five clauses consisting of 5, 7, 5, 7 and 7 moras, respectively. But in

18. Yoshimoto Takaaki, *What is Beauty for Language?* (*Gengo ni totte, bi to wa nani ka?*), vol. 1 (Tokyo: Iwanami Shoten, 1965), 108–11.

the original Japanese version of the above tanka, the opening set of 5–7–5 is recomposed into two clauses of 8 and 7 moras: " driven abroad" and "Karl Marx." Moreover, the traditional tanka genre did not usually employ words such as "driven abroad," with its clear political connotations, or "Karl Marx," a foreign proper noun. In that sense, this poem represents an attempt at innovation and genre critique carried out within the traditional literary genre of tanka. The author's method here of engaging the conventions of genre also falls under Yoshimoto's category of expression consciousness.

It was Yoshimoto who used this perspective to conduct a word-by-word analysis of Japanese expressions, thereby pioneering the method that grasped historical changes in expression consciousness.

-5-

At the opening of this preface, when I used the phrase "Japan's homegrown theory," I had in mind mainly the theories of these three figures.

Of course, it is not the case that Tokieda, Miura, and Yoshimoto were utterly isolated from foreign theories. They were all well versed in non-Japanese theory. But unlike the majority of Japanese theorists, who do nothing more than apply theories developed mainly in Western Europe to Japanese texts, these three attempted to create theories that adhered to the actual expressions of the Japanese language. Those who import and apply foreign theories, as represented by the Ueda Kazutoshi school, have tended to "discover" something in Japanese texts that does not fit the imported theories, whereupon they make a 180 degree change of direction and trumpet the particularity of the Japanese language, which leads to assertions of uniqueness of the "spirit" or "culture" of the Japanese nation. In this sense, in relation to national spirit and culture, these scholars advocated a kind of linguistic determinism. But Tokieda, Miura, and Yoshimoto never became advocates of nationalism or linguistic determinism. Perhaps the actual uniqueness of the structure of Japanese culture lies in this paradox.

But my use of the phrase "Japan's homegrown theory" was not meant to refer solely to the theories of these three. The phrase is also relevant in the area of literary theory, as well. Here, I would like to provide a brief introduction to this topic.

* * * * *

As is well known, the first systematic work of literary theory written in Japan was *The Essence of the Novel* (*Shōsetsu shinzui*, 1885) by Tsubouchi Shōyō

(1859–1935), who called for a reform of Japan's traditional narrative genres (*monogatari*) based on the model of English literature. Since then, the primary role played by literary theorists in Japan has been to introduce Western European and Russian literature and literary theory and to promote (what they believed to be) "new" literary movements. Accordingly, the indispensable precondition for becoming a literary theorist in Japan was to specialize in foreign literature at the university. Following World War II, the category of "foreign literature" was expanded to include American literature, but it still remained virtually impossible to become a literary theorist without a good knowledge of foreign literature, and theoretically oriented scholars who specialized in Japanese literature continued to be exceedingly rare.

This was the general trend for literary theory in Japan, but in addition to this, there also appeared a separate genre called "literary reviews" (*bungei jihyō*), and from this there developed something we could call "Japan's homegrown theory." In Japan, it is customary for writers to contribute to newspapers or literary journals on a monthly basis a critical survey of the literary works published during that month. We call this form of criticism "literary reviews," and it is written not just by literary theorists, but also by practicing novelists. In fact, the latter are more numerous. When written by novelists, these tend to consist of impressionistic criticism, based on the author's own experience as a novelist and on knowledge of the personal relationships that structure the literary world. Among the representative anthologies collecting these sorts of literary reviews are Hirotsu Kazuo's *Impressions of Authors* (*Sakusha no kansō*, 1920), Satō Haruo's *Textbook of Boredom* (*Taikutsu dokuhon*, 1926), and Masamune Hakuchō's *Literary Reviews* (*Bungei hyōron*, 1927). These writers called their impressionistic criticism "personal criticism," or more literally translated, "I-criticism" (*watakushi hihyō*).

Today, the term "I-criticism" is no longer commonly used, but it referred to a style of criticism that formed a pair with the I-novel, the genre that has dominated modern fiction in Japan. For a detailed discussion of this genre, I refer the reader to recent works by Irmela Hijiya-Kirschnereit and Tomi Suzuki.[19] Briefly put, the I-novel is a narrative genre in which the author relates his or her own experiences and in which the ideal is to attempt a study of humanity through a frank revelation of the author's private life. Hirotsu, Satō, and Masamune were all writers of I-novels, and among them Masamune was the

---

19. Irmela Hijiya-Kirschnereit, *Rituals of Self-Revelation: Shishōsetsu as Literary Genre and Socio-Cultural Phenomenon* (Cambridge, MA: Council on East Asian Studies, Harvard University Press, 1996) and Tomi Suzuki, *Narrating the Self: Fictions of Japanese Modernity* (Stanford: Stanford University Press, 1996).

first to use the term I-criticism. In his *Literary Reviews*, Masamune repeatedly relates accounts of his own youthful interest in literature, of the rise and fall of various literary schools and factions he witnessed after becoming a reader of such journals as *Kokumin no tomo* (published 1887–98) and the original *Bungakkai* (1893–98), and of his experiences as an active writer since becoming a member of the literary world. This narrative structure itself seems to manifest clearly the character of I-criticism. Through this kind of narrative, he confirmed that the history of modern fiction in Japan almost perfectly overlapped with his own literary experiences, and he claimed that this reality-based criticism, grounded in his own experience as an author, was able to convey properly the true character of modern Japanese fiction and hence was superior to criticism that was based on imported foreign theories. When we read the anthologies of Hirotsu's and Satō's criticism, too, we sense the same self-confidence in the validity of their own experiences as authors and the pride they had in what they believe to be their own reality-based criticism. With this self-confidence and pride, they carried out their evaluations of the I-novels written during their era, and in so doing their interest naturally focused on how truthfully the events of private life were being narrated by the writer, a fellow practitioner of the I-novel genre. This is the style of criticism that was referred to as I-criticism.

From the late 1920s to the early 1930s, Marxist literary theorists appeared, carrying the banner of scientific criticism. They dismissed this I-criticism as being simply subjective and impressionistic, just as they attacked the I-novel itself for being nothing more than a solipsistic confession of bourgeois emotions. But in the late 1930s, authors who had dropped out of the now illegal JCP-sponsored movement began to publish fiction that confessed their own betrayal of class struggle and reproached their own weakness of character.[20] As a result, once again the I-novel genre flourished. It was in these circumstances that Itō Sei and Hirano Ken began their study of the history of the I-novel genre and of the historical significance of I-criticism.

The results of their respective studies are systematically expounded in two postwar works, Itō's *Methods of the Novel* (*Shōsetsu no hōhō*, 1948) and Hirano's *Art and Real Life* (*Geijutsu to jisseikatsu*, 1958). Hijiya-Kirschnereit and Suzuki both discuss the approaches of these two critics to the history of the I-novel. For our purposes here, it is important to note that neither Itō nor Hirano

---

20. This fiction is usually called "*tenkō* literature," or "literature of apostasy." *Tenkō* referred to the act by a member of the JCP to renounce the party's revolutionary theses of "destroy the emperor system" and "abolish private property" and to renounce party membership. A number of writers who committed *tenkō* went beyond a mere renunciation of these theses and moved in the direction of actively supporting the emperor system and legitimating the military invasion of China. (Kamei)

leapt to the defense of the I-novel; both foresaw that the genre would soon reach a dead end. But unlike most critics of their generation, who were content to point out the "shortcomings" of the I-novel based on the standards current in the modern European novel,[21] these two reached their conclusions based on an internal analysis of the character and structure of the I-novel. In fact, they praised the high quality of the observation of humanity that the I-novel authors had achieved through their depictions of private life. In addition, these two attempted to adapt into their own criticism the methodology of "reading" that had been deployed in I-criticism, noting the role that I-criticism had played in improving the quality of observation through its critical focus on the expressions used to depict private life.[22]

In Japan, when one illuminates a literary text by applying a certain literary theory or by comparing it to certain foreign literary works, this approach is called "external criticism" (*gaizaiteki hihyō*). In contrast, an attempt to analyze a literary text's structure to uncover its intentions or ideals and then to evaluate the text's degree of accomplishment in light of those intentions or ideals is called "immanent criticism" (*naizaiteki hihyō*). Immanent criticism had its beginning with Hirotsu and Masamune's I-criticism, but it was Itō and Hirano who brought it to completion as a methodology. Accordingly, my category of "Japanese homegrown theory" includes the literary theories of these two figures, as well.

The theories and literary histories produced by these two had a great influence on scholars of modern Japanese literature. In 1955, I traveled north to Sapporo to enroll in the national university there, where I majored in Japanese literature. Without the accomplishments of Itō and Hirano, it is inconceivable that a person of my background could have become a literary critic.

* * * * *

In today's Japanese university, perhaps more than 70 percent of the students who major in Japanese literature specialize in modern literature. That is how popular modern literature studies are today, but when I entered the university in 1955, such a state was beyond our wildest dreams.

At that time, university scholarship on Japanese literature was centered on so-called classical literature, that is, on research into texts from before 1868. Since the 1930s, there had been a handful of scholars of Japanese literature who

---

21. Nakamura Mitsuo's *Essays on the Novel of Manners* (*Fūzoku shōsetsu ron*, 1950) is representative of this group. (Kamei)
22. The theory of realism in Japan developed in relation to this question of the quality of observation of humanity. (Kamei)

touched on modern literature in their research, and in the postwar era a few private universities began to hire modern literature specialists as faculty members. But in the more prestigious national universities, hiring a specialist in modern literature was almost unheard of.

But in the decade between 1959, when I graduated from the university, and 1968, when I was hired as a professor at a national university, the situation gradually changed. The number of specialists in modern literature increased, the Association for Modern Japanese Literature (*Nihon kindai bungakkai*) was established, and modern literature studies at last won recognition. Naturally, during this period, the efforts of scholars of modern literature focused on establishing theories and methodologies appropriate to modern literature. In order to win recognition as a legitimate discipline, it was necessary for modern literature studies to possess its own theories and methodologies, distinct from those used in classical literature studies.

As a result, modern literature studies split into three broad tendencies. The first of these took as its task the positivistic ordering and transcribing of the history of modern literature. The scholars who took this approach first worked to record the rise and fall of the various literary schools, as well as to identify the distinguishing characteristics of each school; they called this methodology "literary history." Later, they worked to connect this history of literary schools to political and economic history, a methodology they called the "social science method."

Second, there were scholars whose research surveyed the forms of publication of literary texts, including the variations that existed between different editions of a single work. These scholars called their approach the "bibliographical method." Third, there were researchers who interpreted the contents or special characteristics of a literary text in relation to the private life of its author; they called their approach "author studies." It was because the actual research in the field took these forms that Itō's and Hirano's theories were able to have such a large influence on modern literature scholars.

In fact, all of these research methodologies had already been employed in classical literature studies. But due to the limitations caused by lack of materials, classical literature studies had never been able fully to carry out the first two methodologies. Modern literature specialists claimed that only modern literature studies provided the ideal circumstances for carrying out these two. As for the third methodology, even specialists in classical literature had been influenced by the form of reading that developed in I-criticism, uncritically importing it into their own research, so they were in no position to criticize modern literature specialists on this account. Following this pathway, modern literature studies in Japan won recognition as a discipline in a very short time. But we must also note that in fact what actually made its emergence possible was the rapid economic growth of the 1960s and the appearance of a large number of young readers of literature.

-6-

As I wrote literary criticism over the course of a number of years, I came to feel more and more strongly the need for a fundamental reevaluation of our idea of what modern literature was. This was because the interpretations of literary texts that were being produced were increasingly impoverished, due to the assumption that was widely shared among theorists and scholars that literature consisted of authorial self-expression, that literary works reflected the author's interior. According to the view of humanity characteristic of modern literature, as promulgated by these scholars, the human "interior," especially the "interior" of youths or writers, was delicate, pure, and easily wounded. I found myself increasingly suspicious of this notion. Weren't such notions as the "self" or the "interior" in fact created by literary texts? But they had inverted this, taking what was the product of literary texts to be their cause, transforming the "self" and "interior" into substances, into the *a priori*. As I felt increasingly skeptical about this approach, I decided to begin a reexploration of literature at the level of textual materiality, going all the way back to the dawn of modern literature in Japan.

I am roughly seven or eight years older than the generation that participated in the student movements around 1970, but among my generation too there were many admirers of Yoshimoto Takaaki. When the university called in the riot police to tear down the students' barricades and resume classes, these admirers repeatedly used the word "collapse" (*zasetsu*) to describe what had happened, by which they meant that they had been defeated and injured by the use of force on the part of the authorities. Yoshimoto himself bore no responsibility for the spread of this mood of collapse: he never used the word "collapse." But it seemed to me that the concept of self in Yoshimoto's "self expression" amounted to an evolved form, perhaps a radicalization, of the "self" or "interior" that prevailed in modern literary studies. Because of this, the student activists and their sympathizers, who based their struggle on Yoshimoto's theories, ended up playing the role of wounded youths and retreated into literary acts of expression designed mainly to demonstrate their own purity. Why was it that modern Japanese literature was only able to create such a feeble "self" and "interior"? This question defined my problem consciousness.

This critique and my attempt to construct my own theoretical perspective can be found in my books, *Theory of Contemporary Expressions* (*Gendai no hyōgen shisō*, 1974) and *The Collectivity of the Individual* (*Koga no shūgōsei*, 1977).[23] Here, I will focus mainly on how these works relate to *Transformations of Sensibility*, in particular to the set of keywords I employ in it.

* * * * *

If it were just a matter of criticizing those approaches that take a literary work to be a reflection of the author's private life or emotions, this would be a simple matter. If we use Miura Tsutomu's theory of the "ideational split self," then no matter how much a narrative may seem to relate truthfully the actual everyday life of the author, it is nonetheless necessarily narrated from a perspective or standpoint that is conceptually split off from the actual, concrete author. In so far as this conceptually split off perspective or standpoint in and of itself is a kind of fiction, the content of the narrative too must be in some respect fictional. Taking up this point, I gave the name "narrator" (*katarite*) to this conceptually split off perspective or standpoint. It is not always the case that this "narrator" occupies a single, fixed position consistently through the whole of a narrative. In fact, it is more common to see it take up multiple standpoints and positions. It is true, however, that in modern Japanese fiction there has been a strong tendency toward maintaining as much consistency as possible in this perspective, standpoint, or tone. More precisely, we are accustomed to calling those narratives in which we find this sort of narratological consistency "modern fiction." This mode of narration prepared the way for realism in Japanese fiction, just as it became the basis for the I-novel genre.

But the criticism I developed through this theory of the narrator was not solely aimed at those theories of literature that sought a reflection of authorial private life. It was also meant to be a criticism of Yoshimoto Takaaki's theories. This was because his theories always tended to return the question of literary linguistic expression back to the "self expression" of the author. It seemed to me that the flaw in Yoshimoto's theory appeared in its most egregious form in his inability to analyze the utterances produced by characters within a narrative. He was only able to see the author's self expression in passages of so-called "narrative description" (*ji no bun*). If we grasp the utterances of a character in a work as the self expression of that character, then what relation did that self expression have to the author's self expression? In order to avoid simply identifying the utterances of various characters with the overall narrative description, in order to grant them some degree of autonomy as spoken dialogue, as utter-

---

23. Kamei Hideo, *Gendai no hyōgen shisō* (Tokyo: Kōdansha, 1974). This work quickly went out of print, and in 1982 I published a revised edition under the title, *The Body: The Beginning of Expression (Shintai: hyōgen no hajimari)*. Kamei Hideo, *Koga no shūgōsei* (Tokyo: Kōdansha, 1977). (Kamei)

ances endowed with the individual qualities specific to a particular character in the work, it is necessary to acknowledge the Other as Other, to grant autonomy to the utterances of both this Other and the self based on the relational consciousness that pertains between them. Moreover, the author in fact does not have a direct relationship to the utterances of this Other (characters in the work); such a relationship is possible only for other characters or for the narrator. In this sense, the utterances of characters in a work constitute a mark of the otherness of the Other, yet Yoshimoto lacked a theory of alterity that would allow him to grasp this.

On the other hand, I found very useful Yoshimoto's concept of the structure of "indicative expression," which was excluded from his theory of value in linguistic expression. What he was trying to describe with this phrase "indicative expression" was a certain kind of relation, the ideational relation the author establishes with the worldview or image of reality that we hold in common as shared concepts, alienated from the self. At least, this is how I interpreted the notion. As I understand it, the narrator constitutes the mediating agent that determines how the author will relate to these shared concepts. It is through the position or perspective of this narrator that a spatio-temporal perspective on the shared conceptual image of reality is opened up and that the things and events within this perspective are ordered and assigned value.

Modern Japanese fiction was born as a form that grants corporeal sensation and a seemingly natural, physical voice to this narrator function. Since the early 1980s in Japan, methodologies that analyze literary texts through the concept of narrator have become quite common, but in 1978 when I published the first chapters of *Transformations of Sensibility*, such methodologies were completely unheard of, at least in the pages of literary journals. It was through my analysis of early Meiji literary texts that I became aware of this narrator, and not through a reading of Roman Jakobson's *Essais de linguistique Générale* (1963; translated into Japanese by Tamura Suzuko et al. in 1973). But subsequently translations of a number of similar works were published, including Roland Barthes' "Introduction à L'analyse structurale des récits "(1966; translated into Japanese by Hanawa Hikaru in 1979)[24], Roger Fowler's *Linguistics and the Novel* (1977, translated into Japanese by Toyoda Masanori in 1979), and Umberto Eco's *A Theory of Semiotics* (1976, translated into Japanese by Ikegami Yoshihiko in 1980). As a result, Jakobson's work was widely reread by those interested in literary theory. These events produced a new direction in theory, one that seemed to swallow up my own work.

---

24. Available in English translation as "Introduction to the Structural Analysis of the Narrative," *Stencilled Occasional Paper: Theories & Methods Series* No. 6 (Birmingham: Centre for Contemporary Culture Studies, University of Birmingham, 1966?).

* * * * *

In my theory of the narrator, I was also pursuing a critique of the theories of Miura Tsutomu. In his criticism of the advocates of egoism, he stressed that human beings are not born with self-consciousness in the form of "I = I." Nonetheless, his analysis of Japanese sentences is always premised on the existence of a person who is already in possession of self-consciousness. He lacked any interest in the question of how people acquire a consciousness of "I" through the act of uttering. In the case of Yoshimoto, too, his theories assume that at the moment primitive humans first produced articulate sounds, they already were in possession of self-consciousness.

In constructing my own theoretical approach, my primary data came from such sources as J.M.G. Itard's *De l'Education d'un homme sauvage ou des premiers développements physiques et moraux de jeune sauvage de l'Aveyron* (1802; translated into Japanese by Kotake Yashō in 1972)[25] and data related to the development of speech in Japanese children, and in theorizing this data I referred primarily to such sources as Maurice Merleau-Ponty's *Les relations avec autrui chez l'enfant* (1950, translated into Japanese by Takiura Shizuo and Kida Gen in 1966)[26] and Trän Dúc Tháo's *Phénoménologie et matérialisme dialectique* (1951, translated into Japanese by Takeuchi Yoshimoto in 1971).[27]

My choice of these materials was based on my desire to address the following questions:

1. According to Yoshimoto, the stage where humans became able to produce an articulate sound that corresponded to the intended image of some absent thing was the stage at which the fundamental condition for language was met. I am in agreement with him on this point. But in the process of reaching this stage, humans must first pass through a stage at which they become able to identify certain fixed articulate sounds in themselves as such. At this stage, for example, the articulate sound "dog" must be identifiable and recognized as such, whether it is spoken by a man or woman, in a high-pitched or low-pitched voice. Together with this, humans must also have acquired the ability to identify the category of "dog," including in it not only the specific animal that was first

---

25. Available in English translation as *The Wild Boy of Aveyron*, trans. George and Muriel Humphrey (Englewood Cliffs, NJ: Prentice-Hall, 1962).
26. Available in English translation as "The Child's Relations with Others," trans. William Cobb, in Maurice Merleau-Ponty, *The Primacy of Perception* (Evanston, Illinois: Northwestern University Press, 1964), 96–155.
27. Available in English translation as *Phenomenology and Dialectical Materialism*, trans. Daniel J. Herman and Donald V. Morano, vol. 49 in *Boston Studies in the Philosophy of Science* (Dordrecht, Holland: D. Reidel, 1986).

cognized in connection with the sound "dog" but also countless other animals that resemble that first instance. How do humans acquire these two abilities?

2. An infant sees only the people around it and does not see or know its own appearance. Speaking solely from the experience of perception, for the infant its own appearance must remain a blank. Nonetheless, the infant becomes able to recognize its own image reflected in a mirror as being "myself," and it becomes able to use in its utterances the first-person pronoun "I." What is the nature of the relationship between these two abilities?

3. When an infant shows an interest in mirrors, this interest is initially provoked not because the mirror reflects various things, but rather is directed at the mirror itself as a thing. If that is so, how does an infant come to know the difference between the mirror itself and the images reflected in it? Together with the awareness of this difference, it seems that the child's interest is shifted from the mirror itself to the images reflected in it. What is the relationship between this and another shift that occurs when the child, hearing articulate sounds spoken by some other person, begins to pay less attention to the articulate sounds themselves and more to the concepts associated with those sounds?

In my effort to answer these questions after my own fashion, I traced through the processes whereby the infant internalizes the image of itself reflected in a mirror as being "I" and whereby the infant, who previously made no distinction between itself and the people around it, comes to split itself off from and locate its own position in relation to those others. I eventually reached the conclusion that "The so-called ego is something that first appears outside of ourselves in the 'external world' and then is subsequently brought inside the self as an image, taking up residence there as an image that is accompanied by an alienation from one's relations to other people" (Kamei, *Contemporary Expressions*, 114).

In 1974, when I first presented this view, Jacques Lacan's *Écrits* (1966, translated into Japanese by Miyamoto Tadao in 1972) had already been introduced in Japan, though I had not read it. In fact, I still have not read it all the way through; I simply cannot bear the language of the translation. But I suspect that even if I had read it at the time, it would have had little impact on my interests. Lacan's theory of the mirror stage is premised on the existence of the mirror. My interest, on the other hand, as should be clear from the three questions given above, was on the process whereby the perception of the reflected image was split off from the perception of the mirror itself, so that inevitably my interest was in the manner of recognition of "self image" in a person who has no mirror.

* * * * *

As I proceeded with my investigations, I found especially fruitful Trän Dúc Tháo's concept of the "sketch" and Miura's concept of the "production and reproduction of people themselves."

For example, in the moment just before a snake strikes at its prey, it momentarily halts its movement and with great concentration takes aim. For organisms more primitive than a snake, as soon as they locate food they reflexively begin to move toward it, but a snake momentarily restrains itself and delays the act of capture. It seems that the subsequent act of swallowing the prey is already sketched in ahead of time in the snake's perception of the prey that occurs in this moment of postponement. When a cat captures a mouse, it doesn't immediately eat it but often toys with it for a few moments. For a cat to play with its prey in its front legs is an act of pinning it down at a certain distance from the mouth, but at the same time it is also a sketching out of the subsequent act of picking it up into the mouth, so that the act of playing with the mouse conforms to this sketched in act. Tháo's sketch refers to the embodied intentionality born out of this sort of momentary halting of a reflexive movement toward an object, and also to the mode of depiction whereby that intentionality sketches out the forthcoming act (Tháo, *Phenomenology*, esp. 156–72).

I tried to grasp human behavior from this perspective. People do not perform this sketching solely in relation to actually perceived objects. For example, it is because they sketch out a result that transcends the time and space of actual perception that people wait for green fruit to ripen, or plant seeds in spring and wait for the autumn harvest. In this way, human beings make their direct perception of some object conform to a sketched in result. Once they have reached this stage, people grasp the object in actual and concrete terms through this mode of seeing, embracing a mindset that we might call the outlook of ownership. Or again, we could say the following. Human beings, as they make the direct object of perception conform to some sketched in result, become able to maintain their interest in that object even after it disappears from the realm of perception. We might compare this maintenance of interest with the natural time in which the planted seed sprouts and grows fruit, but in fact what we are dealing with now is a mental (consciousness of) time that belongs to a different dimension from natural time.

But a human infant is not equipped with this sort of ability to sketch. We can detect this ability to sketch in snakes or cats, and in comparison, the degree of innate ability in humans is exceedingly low. If this is so, how is it that humans go about acquiring a level of ability that far outstrips that of snakes or cats? As I considered this question, I found valuable suggestions in Miura's concept of the "production and reproduction of people themselves."

* * * * *

In his book *Doubt from Lenin* (*Reinin kara utagae*, 1964), Miura defines our act of forming a family and raising the next generation as the production of daily life (*seikatsu*) and the reproduction of biological life (*seimei*), and he argues that it should be grasped as the objectification of labor power. This was because the view of labor held not just by Japanese Marxists of that time but by the majority of Japanese tended to limit that category to the act of producing material goods. Miura was critical of this tendency and argued for the need to grasp social structure and historical development through the production of daily life and the reproduction of biological life. As I had done with Tháo's idea of sketching, I developed this perspective after my own fashion.

What Miura called the production of daily life and the reproduction of biological life was not limited to the activities of producing the material needs of daily life, such as producing foodstuffs or sheltering the body with clothing. For example, suppose that I read to my daughter a Japanese translation of Saint Exupery's *The Little Prince*. Saint Exupery's act of writing *The Little Prince* is an objectification of mental labor, while the process of turning that into a book involves the labor of the papermaker, the typesetter, and the printer. The process of distribution that brought it to Japan also involved the objectification of labor: there was the mental labor of translating it into Japanese, just as I had to sell my own labor power to obtain the money to buy the book and then had to undertake the labor of communication as I read the book to my daughter. If by virtue of having listened to *The Little Prince* my daughter's emotional life were to be enriched, that emotional life would have been cultivated through the mediation of the objectified labor produced along this chain. In this way, Miura argued that even our emotions and sensations are cultivated through objectifications of the labor of countless persons. When I taste food, my sense of taste is cultivated. Here too, according to Miura, by virtue of my consuming the labor that is objectified in the foodstuffs and in the prepared dishes, I am both reproducing biological life and producing/reproducing my sense of taste.

In eighteenth-century rural France, a "savage boy" was discovered and taken under the care of a young doctor named Itard, where he learned to discriminate between hot and cold, to react to the taste of food, to distinguish by ear between different combinations of articulate sounds, and to pronounce voluntarily a number of articulate sounds himself. This was the result of Itard's efforts, rubbing the boy's skin with a dry cloth to awaken his sense of touch, and patiently teaching him to discriminate between sounds by using the boy's five fingers to correspond to the five vowel sounds. Eventually, the "savage boy" when faced with food began to restrain momentarily the act of eating, no longer immediately bringing the food to his mouth but rather pausing to enjoy the color and shape of the food; he also began to show a preference for certain flavors and to express through bodily gestures his request for certain favorites that were not present before him. He left behind the realm of animal desires and entered into the dimension of culture. I gave the name sensibility (*kansei*) to the intentionality (including the ability for sketching) of our bodily senses that is produced through this sort of multilayered objectification of labor.[28]

As should be clear even from the brief introduction above, in *Theory of Contemporary Expressions* I approached the human being as an interpersonal texture. In my 1977 book *The Collectivity of the Individual* I analyzed the intertextuality of Ōoka Shōhei's *The Battle for Leyte* (*Reite senki*, 1967–70) and concluded that "With this work, such methodologies as the organic analysis of a single work [*sakuhinron*] or author studies are once and for all demolished" (Kamei, *Collectivity*, 8).

The Battle for Leyte is a text that assembles a wide variety of documentary records and eyewitness accounts, so that it may seem only too obvious that it should be approached from the perspective of intertextuality. But in fact, at that time there was still no textual analysis from that perspective being performed in Japan, and the articles on *The Battle for Leyte* that did appear all treated it as the reflection of the author's emotions or as a statement of his personal philosophy. It was not until the latter half of the 1980s that the method of intertextual interpretation became common in Japan. In my book, I did not use the word "intertextuality," using instead such expressions as "the compound structure of expressions that include the experience of simultaneity with others" (e.g., Kamei, *Collectivity*, 26). I approached *The Battle for Leyte* through the views of humanity and language that I had developed in *Theory of Contemporary Expressions*, stressing not only that *The Battle for Leyte* was a texture of quotations, but also that even the individual records and eyewitness accounts themselves—including the accounts of experiences of individuals who were in completely isolated situations—were intertextual narratives, all grasping an interpersonal experience.

At the same time, I also began a critical investigation of the view of nature held by Japanese people. In Japanese, the word for nature, *shizen*, signifies not so much the so-called natural world as it does the state of being unaltered by human hands, of being unorganized and unprocessed. In short, it is not so much a word that indicates a specific object as it is a word that summons up a particular state or manifests a certain attitude. At first glance, this seems to be

---

28. Subsequently, with the publication of such works as Ichikawa Hiroshi's *The Body as Spirit* (*Seishin toshite no shintai*, 1975) and Takiura Shizuo's *Language and the Body* (*Gengo to shintai*, 1978), the theory of the body became a topic of debate in philosophy and literature. (Kamei)

not unlike the "nature" found in the Western binary opposition culture/nature. And yet in Japan, leaving something unaltered or unorganized is itself a cultural and cultured act, so that acts of altering or organizing are apt to be seen as uncultured. This discourse of the binary opposition altered/natural is also used to describe human existence. One can easily imagine what sort of discourse forms when this discourse of nature links up with the above-mentioned concept held by young people and writers, that the "interior" was something pure, spotless, and fragile.

The key issue lies with how Japanese people, having equated a cultured attitude with respect for nature, apply this understanding to what they find before their eyes. When this attitude is adopted, one's understanding of the processes that produced what one sees lapses into ahistorical abstraction. Japan's scenic beauty in mountains, forests, and meadows were brought into being through the labor of countless generations of people, through their intentionality toward daily life, but this process is abstracted away, and the natural scene that appears before the eyes is taken as existing in a pristine "natural" state. Human sensibility should be regarded as a cultural texture that results from the multilayered objectification of labor, but this is abstracted away and sensibility comes to be regarded as an individual's unique endowment. Only the individualistic phases of sensibility are acknowledged. The phrase "respect for individuality" used by Japanese speakers means to uncover in this way the essential, original endowment of an individual and to adopt the cultured attitude toward it of respecting the natural. To put this another way, the very act of adopting this cultural attitude of respecting the natural renders the object into something "natural." Mushanokōji Saneatsu, the Shirakaba school novelist, emphasized the "natural" flow of emotions in his works. The protagonists in Shiga Naoya's fiction regard the sensibility that manifests itself in their personal feelings of like and dislike as being the most natural part of their selves. As a result of their excessive efforts to respect this absolutely, they behave as emotional tyrants toward others. It was the authors of I-novels who took this attitude as their model. Japanese critics praised these novels as representing not only the highest perfection of Japanese Naturalism, but also as having achieved the establishment of individualism in Japan. The view of nature I have discussed here lay behind this praise.

This view of nature held by the Japanese led to disastrous and horrible results on the battlefields of Asia. Clarifying this was the theme I pursued in *The Collectivity of the Individual.*

* * * * *

It was after these projects that I began work on *Transformations of Sensibility*.

-7-

It seems to me that among English-speaking Japanologists, the name of Miura Tsutomu is hardly known. The situation is not much better for Tokieda Motoki, although there is a discussion of his work in Naoki Sakai's *Voices of the Past*, and Tokieda's name appears in all the works written in Japan about the history of Japanese language studies. But Miura's name does not appear in histories of modern Japanese literature or of Japanese language studies, nor in works of intellectual history or the history of philosophy. He is even omitted from histories of Japanese Marxist theory. The standard reference dictionaries for Japanese modern literature, Japanese linguistics, and intellectual history do not contain entries on him. He is not cited in scholarly articles in the fields of Japanese linguistics or intellectual history or philosophy, and in the field of Japanese literature he is cited by only a handful of scholars, including myself. While his own books and articles still exist, Miura's name is practically absent from those written by others.

The main reason for this odd phenomenon is that Miura lacked the credentials that in Japan would qualify him as a scholar of some discipline. Another reason is that from the 1970s, research based on Saussure's theories began to flourish in Japan, and as certain weaknesses in Tokieda's understanding of Saussure became apparent, the scholarship on Japanese language that had rejected Saussurean methodologies found itself discarded and labeled the "old linguistics."

In the realm of Japanese literature studies, I and a few others continue today the process of a critical reconstruction of the theories of Tokieda and Miura, but the mainstream is occupied by textual theories that have arisen in the wake of Saussurean linguistics and structuralism. This phenomenon might best be understood not so much as a confrontation between different academic schools but rather as a guild-like "segregation" rooted ultimately in the cultural structure of Japan. As I have already noted, Japanese literary theorists, who largely concern themselves with the business of introducing and importing foreign literature and theory, publish their essays primarily in literary journals or in magazines that focus on theory. In contrast, scholars of modern literature, a discipline that won recognition in the postwar, publish their articles in the organs of learned societies or in specialized academic journals. It is extremely rare for the former to publish in academic journals, just as it is unusual for the latter to write for literary journals. Since the mid-1980s, a new generation of modern literature scholars has actively begun to negotiate with the work of nonacademic literary theorists, but the "segregation" itself continues to exist today.

I myself studied Japanese literature at the university and subsequently am in the position of a modern literature scholar, yet for roughly fifteen years beginning around 1970, I also wrote essays that tackled the sorts of problems addressed by nonacademic literary theorists, making me something of an exception. In the mid-1970s, when I began to grasp the ego as the internalization of the self-image that appeared in the "external world" and became critical of theories that saw literature as the expression of individuality and advocated in their place methods that stressed intertextuality, I seemed to attract more reactions of offended criticism than of sympathy. From the mid-1980s, as the theories of Lacan, Derrida, and Foucault were digested, the sorts of views that I held became a broadly shared common sense, at least in the realms of literary theory and research, but my works met a fate like that of Miura's: they remained absent from the texts written by others. I think I can say, however, that *Theory of Contemporary Expressions* and *The Collectivity of the Individual* did play a certain role in encouraging the current tendency among younger scholars to actively negotiate with the work of literary theorists. I take the interest shown by Michael Bourdaghs and other American scholars of Japanese literature as evidence that efforts to break down the boundaries of "segregation" using this book continue today.

In the future, I intend to continue my research into Tokieda's and Miura's theories. One project I hope to pursue is a re-tracing of the history of the discourse on language, beginning in the Edo period. Another is to pursue the issue of the alienation that accompanies what Miura called the "production and reproduction of people themselves." The act whereby a parent raises a child is certainly the production and reproduction of biological life by means of the objectification of labor, but in this case the product is different from other products: the parent cannot possess this product, consume it, or exchange it as a commodity for other commodities. To borrow Hegel's language from *The Phenomenology of Spirit*, "[the dutiful reverence] of parents towards their children is emotionally affected by the fact that the objective reality of the relationship does not exist in them, but in the children, and by their witnessing the development in the children of an independent existence which they are unable to take back again . . . ."[29] It is clear that Hegel took as his model the family of modern

---

29. G.W.F. Hegel, *Phenomenology of Spirit*, trans. A.V. Miller (Oxford: Oxford University Press, 1977), 273.

civil society in writing this passage, and we can sense the feel of reality in his subsequent words: "the independent existence of the children remains an alien reality, a reality all its own" (Hegel, *Phenomenology of Spirit,* 273). We can of course say that in taking as his model the stable family of civil society, Hegel reveals his limitations, but if he had possessed Miura's understanding of the parent's conflict with the child as the parent's self alienation, he would have been able to provide greater depth to many of his philosophical concepts, including those of the subject, the transmission of linguistic norms from parent to child, and the norm as it takes the form of a "conceptual person."

The theorists in Japan who concern themselves with importing foreign theory are now engaged in a critical rereading from a postmodern perspective of Freud's theories, carrying on a debate over the questions of subject formation and the infant's psychological development, but they always grasp the roles of the father and mother as fixed entities. From my perspective, their work is marked by a leitmotif of always wanting to diagnose the child as victim, avoiding an encounter with the reality whereby parents witness "the development in the children of an independent existence which they are unable to take back again," because they want to play the role of one who understands children. The fatal flaw in their understanding of power derives from the same reason. In *The Collectivity of the Individual* I touched on this Hegelian problem to a certain extent, but was unable to think through all of its implications. It is my hope to challenge this problem again, taking up the task presented to us by Miura.

Chapter One
The Disappearance of the Non-Person Narrator: Changing Sensibilities in Futabatei Shimei

TRANSLATED BY BRETT DE BARY

Here, Kamei begins by identifying a certain crisis in contemporary consciousness, an inability to distinguish representation from reality, in which even literature has abandoned its role of questioning the sensibility through which we perceive the world. As a possible solution, he proposes returning to the fiction of early Meiji, when writers were forced through the process of writing into a conscious awareness of their own sensibilities. Kamei explores this first in the opening passages of Futabatei Shimei's Ukigumo, where he detects the emergence of an unusual narrator, one he christens the non-person narrator. Kamei traces a genealogy for this narrator in the genre of kanbun fūzokushi by such writers as Narushima Ryūhoku and Hattori Bushō. In attempting to write through the sensibility of formal kanbun prose about the informal affairs of everyday life, and in recognizing the gap between the two, these writers were forced into a heightened awareness of their own sensibilities and their own relatedness to the object world they depicted. This foreshadows the development in the later chapters of Futabatei's novel, where an increasing awareness of his own sensibility leads the author to alter his approach and to fashion a new narrator, one more in line with his desire to portray sympathetically the interiority of his fictional characters. While this development produced a new libratory mode of expression, the diminished role of the narrator in it also harbored a tendency to abandon the questioning of conventional sensibilities, and hence foreshadowed the contemporary crisis of literature.

Perhaps it was because I already had a dawning awareness of the problem myself. At any rate, my interest in embarking on this study was aroused by Nakajima Azusa's essay, "Transforming Modes of Expression," and her discussion of the characteristic mode of expression found in Tsuka Kōhei and other contemporary writers. "When we try to determine the distinctive characteristics of that assemblage of intentionalities we call the writer Tsuka Kōhei," Nakajima observed, "we must bear in mind that we are dealing with a reality that is from start to finish a matter of representation, of verbal expressions."[1] It was my encounter with this idea that prompted me to reexamine the modes of expression in the Japanese literature of the 1880s and 1890s, the second and third decades following the Meiji Restoration.

At the time I read Nakajima's article I had for a few years been experimenting with the practice of reading newspapers and weekly magazines, or watching television, without assuming they could enable me to glimpse reality. I had, as it were, subjected the reality we learn of through such media to a phenomenological reduction and sought to concentrate instead on the enunciative apparatus of the media themselves. If I were to regard, for example, a television drama, a commercial, and a news report as being of absolutely equal value as expressions, what then might I discover about the kinds of logic or visual techniques employed by each? I experimented with the hypothesis that "reality," the greater situation that we cannot see or hear directly, is not discernible through the media, but rather through the resistance we feel as we try to carry out the tasks of our everyday life. It was because I had already chosen to undertake such an experiment myself—indeed, only insofar as I had some experience with the problems she was writing about, even though I come from a slightly older generation—that the contemporary world she described held such intense interest for me. That world, she wrote, "is already for all of us, if I can dare to speak of an 'us,' simply an assemblage of patterns." That "world" was the object of inquiry I was already half immersed in, the world created by a new generation for whom "experience can be defined as nothing more than a choosing among styles" (Nakajima, "Transformations in Expression," 221–22).

But in deciding to base my study on such a problematic would I not be assenting whole-heartedly, I wondered, to what critics such as Karel Kosík have scathingly defined as "the world of the pseudoconcrete"?[2]

What Kosík calls the "pseudoconcrete" is, of course, a negative way of referring to our everyday, phenomenological world, the individual's fragmented

1. Nakajima Azusa, "Transformations in Expression" ("Hyōgen no henyō"), in *Gunzō* 32:9 (September 1977): 214–31. This quotation appears on p. 221. Tsuka Kōhei (b. 1948) is a playwright and novelist who first gained popularity in the early 1970s.
2. Karel Kosík, *Dialectics of the Concrete*, trans. Karel Kovand and James Schmidt (Dordrecht, Holland: D. Reidel Publishing Co., 1976), 1. Kosík's work was translated into Japanese as *Gutaisei no benshōhō* by Hanazaki Kōhei in 1969.

life environment in a society atomized through the division of labor and pervaded by what Kosík calls "the spiritual atmosphere in which the superficial shape of reality comes to be fixed as the world of fictitious intimacy, familiarity and confidence within which man moves about 'naturally' and with which he has his daily dealings" (Kosík, *Dialectics of the Concrete*, 2). But however much we might label this world "pseudoconcrete," is it not the familiar world of our daily lives, the only one thoroughly tangible for our sensibilities and clear beyond a doubt? Certainly there is no world apart from this one, nothing more essential that exists elsewhere. For individual human beings, this is the sole existing actuality that they can directly access, and yet the instant what appears "natural" to us becomes completely familiar to our sensibilities, the instant we start to affirm those sensibilities (forged in our negotiation of everyday actuality) as "natural," the "thing itself" disappears. For these reasons Kosík proposes that

> . . . if man can at all search for the structure of the thing and if he wants to investigate this 'thing itself' [. . .] then prior to any investigation man already has to have a certain cognizance that there exists something such as the structure of the thing, the essence of the thing, the 'thing itself,' that there exists a hidden truth of things which is different from phenomena that reveal themselves immediately. (Kosík, 3–4)

As we can see here, Kosík wants to reject the sensibility naturalized in daily life and assert the necessity of "a certain cognizance" that would enable us to transcend it. He assumes, in other words, the existence, prior to praxis (which here must mean a kind of "practice" of sensibilities) or any investigation, of a kind of a priori knowledge. For Kosík this a priori knowledge is science and philosophy. As he puts it, "the concealed basis of things has to be *exposed in a specific activity*. This is precisely why science and philosophy exist" (Kosík, 4, italics in the original).

But isn't the activity of human sensibility something that has always already commenced, before we can even begin seeking "a certain cognizance"? Isn't it necessary for us first to elucidate how, from within that activity itself, a distinct awareness of "pseudoconcreteness" unfolds? Neither science nor philosophy can undertake this project. It seems to me that literature, as the site where the sensibility-laden expression of an object produces in turn an objectification of our sensibilities, is the most appropriate starting point for such a task.

In Tsuka Kōhei's *The Atami Murders: The Novel* (*Shōsetsu Atami satsujin jiken*, 1975) we find a work that carries to an extreme the theory of art set forth by Itō Sei in "The Art of Prose."[3] Itō defines prose fiction as "the art which uses as its *means* the elements of reality that have been manifested in language. [. . .] In other words, [once they are transformed into words] politics, ethics, morality, and all the practical values that are efficacious in actual life serve merely as means for the art of prose" (Itō, 96). Tsuka's work carries this theory of art through to such an extreme that it becomes a parody of itself. Tsuka reveals how the medium of television, in pursuing its own protocols of expression (including the commercial) creates a system within which all actual "incidents" are used simply as "means" to intensify the effect of its visual expressions. Tsuka's *Introductory Lectures on Revolution: The Soaring Dragon Transmission* (*Shokyū kakumei kōza hiryūden*, 1977), for example, caricatures how even the revolutionary energy of student revolt can become mere spectacle the moment a television camera is introduced. And in *The Atami Murders* we find the explosive hilarity of a tale about a group of detectives whose vision and sensibilities are the product solely of the modes of expression found in and desires incited by television detective shows, and who try, in all seriousness, to project their stylistic preferences in those media onto an actual case. By showing how sensibility now functions only as a matter of preferences for certain preexisting styles, and restricting its focus to this subject matter, Tsuka's story vividly asserts the comicality of our times, when human sensibilities can produce nothing more than a world of "pseudoconcreteness." In Tsuka's work sensibility, as it were, exposes its own true nature.

The world of this self-exposing sensibility is undoubtedly humorous. And yet at the same time, how quickly we lose interest and become bored with it. Tsuka is not alone in having had to confront this problem. Indeed, the modern literary tradition that his caricature debunks has met the same fate: in taking truthfulness in the expression of sensibility as a guarantee of the "reality" conveyed by the literary work, that tradition succeeded in producing nothing more than a sham "world of authentic concreteness." We could even say that it was precisely because of Tsuka Kōhei's unwavering faithfulness to the literary tradition that seeks to capture the sensibility of its times that, paradoxically, his work ends up as an exposé of that tradition. There is something sterile and predictable about the intricately sensuous worlds created by concentrating on the expressions of sensibility of an age, thereby implicitly affirming that age's con-

---

3. Itō Sei, "The Art of Prose" ("Sanbun geijutsu no seikaku"), originally published in the August 1948 issue of the journal *Gunzō* and subsequently included as chapter nine in Itō's *The Method of the Novel* (*Shōsetsu no hōhō*, 1948), reprinted in *Itō Sei zenshū*, 14 vols. (Tokyo: Kawade Shobō, 1956), 13:5–150.

ventional sensibility. Tsuka himself has not managed to escape this trap, his legacy from the past.

In his study *The Awakening of Sensibility* (*Kansei no kakusei*, 1975), Nakamura Yūjirō observes that the discourse of *philosophia* has historically placed greater emphasis on wisdom (*sophia*) than on love (*philos*), and thus subordinated sensibility to reason.[4] While the problematic I am taking up in this book owes much to Nakamura's superb argument, which seeks to restore a sense of the human being's totality, I must insist that as far as modern literature is concerned both the historical situation and the necessary problematic are the reverse of what Nakamura proposes. In the history of modern Japanese literature, it is reason that has been subordinated to sensibility.

How has linguistic expression of sensibility been understood in modern Japanese literature? It has been seen as language's apprehension of sensibility, and a kind of "knowledge" about sensibility is seen as inevitably emerging out of the accumulation of acts of expression. Under the influence of such "knowledge," whatever expressions were deemed unnatural or unnecessary to the individual were denounced as false, and in this way the so-called "modern" literary style, which abhorred rhetorical exaggeration and ornamentation, came into being. Moreover, since there was a strong belief that human nature was repressed by the political (or by political ideology) and by social formations and the norms associated with them, a view emerged of sensibility as that which should be protected and, first and foremost, affirmed. Thus the activity of a kind of immanent "knowledge" was accepted only insofar as it limited itself to supporting, in a way that was not seen to be "unnatural," sensibility in its existing state. Nor was the activity of criticism easily tolerated if it exceeded these limits. With the workings of immanent knowledge thus constrained, modern writers proudly poured forth their highly individuated expressions of sensibility within the categories that were, of course, valorized as "natural." Insofar as critical reflection on the self-evidence of "what is" had been anaesthetized in this mode of expression, however, it eventually began to inflict an inescapable sense of tedium and stagnation on its readers. Modern Japanese literature had not fostered within itself a visual intentionality[5] toward totalization.

---

4. Nakamura Yūjirō, *The Awakening of Sensibility* (*Kansei no kakusei*) [1975], reprinted in *Jōnen ron*, vol. 1 of *Nakamura Yūjirō chosakushū*, 10 vols. (Tokyo: Iwanami Shoten, 1993), 77–353.
5. "Visual intention" (*shikō*) is a neologism coined by replacing the first character in the standard philosophical term "intention" (*shikō*) with another homophonous character that carries the specific meaning of "vision." It refers to the active role in organizing visual images played by the (socially mediated) eye itself, prior to conscious reflection on that image. See the discussion of this term in the editor's introduction.

The time has come when we can no longer believe in the existence of individuality. But, perhaps for that very reason, the expression of sensibility continues to flourish. Our sensibilities are now seen as natural and inevitable to the contemporary world precisely insofar as they are understood to be something forced on us by our situation. Literature no longer seeks to point to the "thing itself," but simply attempts, in a paradoxical way, to reveal the "world of the pseudoconcrete" into which our age has degenerated. This is why at some point midway through a text by Tsuka Kōhei we suddenly become bored. One might suggest the parallel, for example, with a group of today's middle school or high school students who adopt an aggressive attitude toward their teacher. Their stance is imitated directly from behavior they see on television shows of the "campus drama" genre, and they themselves know there is something hackneyed about it. Then, when another student derides them for this, he too borrows a certain pattern from television shows where, for example, a comedian imitates with exaggeration the gestures of a guest and thus reduces the guest to a laughing stock. This is the kind of vicious circle in which Tsuka Kōhei is trapped, one from which any escape seems difficult. Nakajima Azusa's essay, too, seems able to interpret this aspect of contemporary expression solely in terms of a reflection-of-the-times paradigm. The best she can do is talk about the transformation of modes of expression that is on the verge of taking place.

Nevertheless, I found Nakajima's remark about a "reality that is from start to finish a matter of representation, of verbal expressions" provocative. This is related to her observation that what is undergoing transformation today is "the very dichotomous structure of consciousness that opposes expression to actuality, fiction to nonfiction" (Nakajima, "Transformations in Expression," 218).

A certain "knowledge" about sensibility emerged out of the almost licentious riot of forms that characterized the situation of expression on the eve of modernization and incited the establishment of what was called the "modern" literary style. But this "knowledge" itself became impoverished under the influence of realist notions such as "sketching" (*shajitsushugi*) and "description" (*byōsha*). As a result, we lost the ability to draw out fresh possibilities from those richly variegated modes of premodern expression we had sloughed off. Not only that, although it is possible to speak of a kind of negative energy generated in the initial phases when this "knowledge" first arose, giving rise to expressions that included a visual intentionality toward the totalization of sensibility, that too has now been lost to us. It is my hope in this book to affirm the possibility of a revolution in sensibility by studying the history of that process.

*****

One very rare example of a writer in whose life we can find a real overlap between the evolution of individual expression and the evolution of an era's expression is Futabatei Shimei.[6] Here we can see how, under the sway of an immanent "knowledge," a writer developed a style that was both library for him
personally and at the same time a "natural" and "necessary" mode of expressing
sensibility. But I will postpone examining the process of formation of this new
mode in order first to explore the possibilities that existed in those styles of
expression that were eventually abandoned. In this light, let us examine the
opening passage of Futabatei's first novel, *Ukigumo*.

> It is three o'clock in the afternoon of a late October day. A swirl-
> ing mass of men stream out of the Kanda gate, marching first in ant-
> like formation, then scuttling busily off in every direction. Each and
> every one of these fine gentlemen is clearly interested in the appear-
> ance of his face. Look carefully and you will see what an enormous
> variety of individual types are represented in the huge crowd. Start
> by examining the hair bristling on their chins and under their noses:
> mustaches, side whiskers, Vandykes, and even extravagant imperial
> beards, Bismarck beards reminiscent of a Pekinese, bantam beards,
> badger's beards, meager beards that are barely visible, thick and thin
> they sprout in every conceivable way.
>   Now see how differently they are dressed. Here is a dandy in a
> fashionable black suit purchased at Shirokiya [lit.: White-Tree Store]
> set off by shoes of French calfskin. And now confident men oblivi-
> ous of the ill-fit of their tweeds worn with stiff leather shoes—trou-
> sers that trail in the mud like the tail of a tortoise; suits bearing the
> indelible stamp of the ready-made clothes rack. "I have a beard, fine
> clothing, what more do I need?" they seem to say. Glowing like em-
> bers on the fire, these creatures swagger home, heads erect. Enviable
> beings, indeed.[7]

This is clearly not an example of what later Meiji writers called the
"sketching" (*shajitsushugi*) style. Surely what dominated Futabatei's interest
was not so much producing a realistic description of government bureaucrats
going home from work as conveying to his readers a strong sense of the exist-

6. Futabatei Shimei (1864–1909) is often credited with being Japan's first modern novelist and is
   conventionally designated as one of the founders of "realist" fiction in Japan.
7. All quotations from *Ukigumo* are adapted from the translation in Marleigh Grayer Ryan, *Japan's
   First Modern Novel:* Ukigumo *of Futabatei Shimei* (New York: Columbia University Press,
   1967). This passage (slightly modified) appears on pp. 197–98. The narrator here is employing a traditional comic device, the *monozukushi*, a cataloging of things belonging to a certain
   category. Beards and mustaches were a new fashion among Meiji elite. The passage is also
   marked by skillful and humorous jumps in level of politeness of speech, embedded puns, and
   other rhetorical devices.

ence of a narrator who relates the event. His narrator never manifests himself (more precisely, itself) distinctly within the novel by referring to himself with first-person pronouns such as *yo* or *watakushi*. Nor does this narrator participate in the action of the plot. At the same time, it would be impossible to say that this narrator is merely constituted as an observer's gaze, as a third person disconnected from any specific perspective on the depicted scenes or as a kind of omniscient presence that moves fluidly throughout. Rather, this is a narrator who trails one specific office worker, the young man Utsumi Bunzō, and who, when he sees Bunzō enter "the third house from the corner, a two-story building with a lattice door," asks the reader, "Shall we go in, too?" (*Ukigumo,* 199). This is a narrator, it appears, who has a strong sense of his own existence, and who by revealing this causes the reader, on the other hand, to depart from the position of a merely passive auditor[8] and to enter into a kind of complicity with him. Consider the description of Honda Noboru's first meeting with Bunzō. The narrator comments that, "His face will be familiar to the reader; it belongs to the man we saw passing through the Kanda gate with Bunzō the day he was dismissed" (*Ukigumo,* 245). Here we see the narrator appealing to the reader's memory. When Honda goes up to Bunzō's second-floor room, the narrator stays on the first floor with Omasa and her daughter, Osei. He listens to someone descending the stairs, winking and signaling to the reader. This is a narrator with a very strong awareness of where he is situated.

This self-awareness is readily observable in the opening passage I quoted above. It is quite clear from which position the narrator is viewing the scene. His tone even has a hint of self-exhibitionism in it. We can't overlook the half-joking, sarcastic import of the use of honorific verb forms (e.g., *tamau*) in the sentence, "Each and every one of these fine gentlemen is clearly interested in the appearance of his face," which conveys a sense of very lukewarm politeness. This remark, with its malicious innuendoes, is followed by the ironic exclamation "Enviable beings, indeed!" (ending with the familiar, nonhonorific form of the copula, *da*) thrown out as a parting shot (*Ukigumo,* 198).

Even if we were to consider Futabatei here to be experimenting with the *genbun itchi* style, as has often been maintained, there are simply too many deviations for this thesis to be plausible.[9] As Terada Tōru observed in 1958,

---

8. The "auditor" (*kikite,* lit. "listener") and its relationship to the narrator (*katarite*) are concepts that Kamei will explore at greater length below, especially in chapter ten. Its use highlights the intersubjective nature of speech, which is central to Kamei's argument.

9. G*enbun itchi* (lit., "union of spoken and written languages") is the new standardized and supposedly "colloquial" writing style that was developed out of Meiji language reform movements. After much experimentation, it achieved a roughly stable form around 1900 and thereafter came to dominate modern "realist" literature in Japan. Futabatei's *Ukigumo* is frequently cited as the first novel written in *genbun itchi,* a convention that Kamei is contesting here.

"Even granted that we are now at a distance of 76 years from the colloquial speech of Futabatei's day, the rhythms and ornamental language he uses could in no way have been the *gen*, or spoken language, we associate with the *genbun itchi* style. They may have been words used in the storytelling halls or on the *kyōgen* stage, but they are not words that were used in the streets or in the common people's homes. Or, if in some way Futabatei heard them in those settings, he was listening to people known for their virtuosity as speakers, trying to impress others."[10]

Terada's interpretation makes sense to me, although I would not concur that Futabatei's writing is "just one step away from being a transcription of *rakugo* or *kōdan* storytelling, or even the linked verse of the eighteenth century" (Terada, "Modern Literature," 9). But before we take up this issue, we must give some consideration to the extent to which this type of expression represents Futabatei's own originality. We must recall that when *Ukigumo* was first published, the covers of volumes one and two listed "Tsubouchi Yūzō" as the author, while the main body of the novel was attributed to the joint authorship of Harunoya Shujin and Futabatei Shimei.[11] The opening passage of *Ukigumo* bears a strong resemblance to the opening of Shōyō's *Children of the Capital* (*Kyō waranbe*, 1886). This makes it easy to conjecture that the *engo* and *kakekotoba* in *Ukigumo* were either added to the manuscript by Shōyō or inspired by him.[12] But all the similarities with Shōyō notwithstanding, there is one thing we would never find in Shōyō's writing that we find in *Ukigumo*—its narrator, and his somewhat discomfiting moments of self-exhibition.

In the latter half of the second volume of *Ukigumo*, however, this self-exhibitionist narrator gradually fades from view, posing a difficult question for us. I will argue that these overt indications of the narrator's existence interfered with Futabatei's own scheme for the novel, so that the disappearance of the narrator represents a conscious decision on Futabatei's part. In that case, our question becomes, just what kind of entity might this narrator have been?

Let me repeat again that the narrator of *Ukigumo* is not a character who mingles with the other characters appearing in the work, as would a typical first-person narrator. But this does not mean that this narrator then somehow overlaps with the author and has free access to the physical and psychological space of the tale (including the protagonist's interior), as would the typical third-

---

10. Terada Tōru, "Modern Literature and the Japanese Language" ("Kindai bungaku to Nihongo"), *Iwanami kōza Nihon bungaku shi* 13:7 (Tokyo: Iwanami Shoten, 1958–59), 1–27. This passage appears on p. 9.
11. Tsubouchi Yūzō is the real name of the author better known by his pen name, Tsubouchi Shōyō (1859–1935). He also sometimes used the pen name Harunoya Shujin (and other variations).
12. *Engo* (conventional verbal associations) and *kakekotoba* (puns that function as pivot words) were rhetorical devices widely used in classical Japanese literature.

person narrator. Rather, we might see him as a non-person narrator, one set apart and yet aware in his own way of the distinct position he occupies in a given scene. On the one hand, after proposing all sorts of amusing similes to suggest the garb and hairstyles of the returning office-workers, this narrator mockingly expresses false envy for them. On the other hand, he seems equally disparaging of the "pitiful" sight of those workers he describes in the next paragraph whose "duties are so negligible they can easily work in old-fashioned Japanese clothes" (*Ukigumo*, 198). What kind of relationship to the object of perception is this? Can we say this mode of expression arose as a necessary and natural product of the sensibilities of Futabatei himself? Without implying that this mode was simply something he borrowed from elsewhere, we must still admit that, on the basis of what we see in the latter half of *Ukigumo* or in Futabatei's other works, he seemed neither particularly enamored of, nor particularly skilled at, using this sort of expression. The non-person narrator of the opening passages of *Ukigumo*, then, must, for a start, be distinguished from the author.

At this point, let me introduce the concept of the emergence of an "I-ness" (*watakushi-sei*) within expressions to designate the kind of unified style that we assume to result from an author's firm grasp of his or her own sensibility and that author's deployment of language which is both necessary and natural to that sensibility. Our logic in modern Japanese literature has assumed that, without the attainment of this kind of "I-ness," it is impossible to write an I-novel. But of course this is a style of expression that is not unique to the I-novel, but rather characteristic of all writing we designate "modern literature." In *Ukigumo*, the passages where Futabatei Shimei's "I-ness" seems best developed are those expressions that adhere to the psychology and perceptions of the protagonist Bunzō. These are the passages that have often struck readers as involving the author's projection of feeling onto that character, the creation of an alter ego in him. What we call the "modern sense of self" is a reification that arises when we take the unfolding of personal sensibility, of the I-sensibility, of a specific character to be an expression (*hyōshutsu*) of the author's own "interiority."

It is difficult to know exactly why the narrator in *Ukigumo* gradually fades from view. Probably what Futabatei initially intended was to have this non-person narrator, who was relatively independent from the characters in his tale, report his observations as a way of presenting a detached, objective perspective on events. But the frivolity of tone and vulgar fascinations that mark the narrator's grasp of events early on in *Ukigumo* seem to represent a crass sensibility, something Futabatei may have mimicked from the narrators he found in other works, but which was at odds with Futabatei's own sensibility of "I-ness." Alternatively, it may have been the case that in the process of manipulating the narrator of *Ukigumo* Futabatei came to have a clearer grasp of his own

"I-ness," or personal sensibility, eventually becoming seduced by the freedom this gave him to create the psychology and perceptions of the character Utsumi Bunzō. But it is perhaps most likely that Futabatei was propelled along by his own discovery that it was the latter method of composition which made him feel writing *Ukigumo* truly was necessary for him. Whatever the real situation, it seems to have been inevitable that this non-person narrator would disappear. Yet I cannot shake my fascination with him. Did his existence necessarily represent an impediment to the emergence of the modern novel?

Let me repeat again that the narrator of *Ukigumo* frequently departs from the sensibility Futabatei must have grasped as his own "I-ness." He seems to take on a life of his own that has little to do with the kind of self-consciousness that accurately and faithfully passes along news of things seen and heard. Futabatei's narrator is, in fact, single-mindedly oriented toward the reader. His role is nothing more, nor less, than to bring to life interests—and, indeed, a sensibility—that are shared in common by narrator and reader. In sum, this narrator bears a sensibility it shares with the reader; he lives within the space of the work yet is invisible to the other characters and chooses his own position within that space, a position which then functions to constrain him.

On the one hand, we have the world of the protagonist's sensibility, supposedly produced out of the author's inner necessity. A world inlaid, as it were, with passions and sentiments and constructed on the presupposition that whatever form the author's truths take shape in will also be "true" for the reader. A world that often, from the reader's point of view, seems to lapse into a kind of self-righteous coercion. But in addition, this world needs a narrator, immanent within it, who can act as a bridge between it and the reader. If we say that the former, the protagonist's world, is the product of the writer's motivation to create, then the narrator functions to objectify the desire for narrative, to endow textual space with a three-dimensional quality, to establish distinctions among things—in short, to guarantee the objectivity of the textual world. Once this function was lost, the literary work became a composition based purely on authorial motif, one that could convey only the unfolding of the I-sensibility, and its inner structure was rendered monotonous, impoverished. Such writing could only strengthen the tendency toward what ultimately became the I-novel, regardless of the inclinations of individual writers. Readers, too, had no choice but to understand the work as such an entity.

* * * * *

It seems that an awareness of sharing a common situation, of having to live it in common, was needed. In *Ukigumo*, the non-person narrator is clearly incapable of discerning and bearing witness to the tragedy of Utsumi Bunzō. His observations are too earthy and irresponsible, his sensibility too coarse. This seems to represent Futabatei's estimation of the interests and sensibility of the readers of his day. In other words, the contemporary prose narratives (*monogatari*) that Futabatei consulted had not attained a level beyond this.

If, on the other hand, Futabatei's narrator had been endowed with the awareness of sharing the situation lived by the characters in the novel, we can be sure that as his understanding of their common situation deepened, he would have embarked on a process of self-reflection that would enhance and broaden his interests and sensibility, no matter how crude some aspects of that sensibility may have been at the start. Through such a process, the sensibility of readers, insofar as it was presented in the novel as a matter of lived commonality, would also be transformed.

In the 1870s and 1880s, it was not only *Ukigumo* but a number of works that through their point-of-view, conception, and style sought to develop the sense of a lived commonality with the reader. These texts, however, were all seen as vulgar, popular writing, and were soon suppressed. Their presence attests, however, that through a kind of spontaneous blossoming an awareness of living a shared situation began to emerge during these decades. That it has become most difficult for us to discern this today is because most of this writing can be found in the largely forgotten genre of *füzokushi* ("descriptions of everyday life"), written in the now-archaic *kanbun* style.[13]

Let us consider the following passage from *Random Notes from Shinbashi* (*Tōkyō Shinkyō zakki*, 1878), published under the name Matsumoto Bannen:

> On the bridge with iron railings, people's shoulders jostle each other and carriages bump into each other. The carriages are like flowing water, the horses like wandering dragons. If the carriage driver raises his whip and shouts as he passes by, then his passenger is either a high-ranking official returning, slightly the fatter, after a day's work, or a nobleman on his way to the bank. But if it is an old carriage with its paint peeling, pulled by emaciated horses carrying three or four— even five or six—passengers, and the driver calls out the names of

13. *Kanbun* (lit., "Chinese writing") refers to a style of writing texts in Chinese characters and following Chinese syntax. These texts were often accompanied by superscript annotations enabling readers to reconstruct Chinese sentences according to Japanese phonetical and grammatical patterns. It thus differed markedly from more vernacular writing styles that followed more closely the usages of spoken Japanese (a distinction whose breakdown Kamei will trace here). *Kanbun* was a formal style used for official or public communications of the Tokugawa shogunate and samurai-bureaucrat class, as well as in diaries, particularly those written by men. It continued to enjoy wide usage in the Meiji period, but gradually lost favor, especially after the turn of the century.

places like "Eyeglasses Bridge" or Asakusa, then it is one of the low-cost carriages run by the Senriken Company. The different carriages weave in tangled threads, while among a thousand passengers, not a single one resembles another. Men with concubines on their arms are the scholars who boast of equality between men and women; those holding foreign books before their eyes are students making a show of their intellectual accomplishments. Men who have fallen asleep with their hats pulled over their eyes are playboys returning from Shinagawa, older women with children in their arms and their possessions bundled in sacks on their backs are geisha leaving the city for Yokohama. There are the passengers whose hair is already half gone and those in Western dress, and there are the carriage drivers who gather at the northern and southern ends of the bridge, noisily accosting customers. One can imagine the chaos of the scene, with its never-ending throng of people and carriages rumbling like thunder.[14]

This passage occurs near the opening of Matsumoto's text. The method here is clear: first a place is chosen, a specific point of view is determined, and then the scene is described. The phrase depicting officials returning from work is obscure for the contemporary reader, but that is because Matsumoto uses a form of word play that employs *engo* (conventional verbal associations). Punning on the similarities between the words *choku* (or "imperial decree" used in the phrase *chokunin kanshi* with which the text designates imperial functionaries) and *shoku* ("to eat," the character Matsumoto substitutes for the character *shoku*, or "employment," usually used in the word *taishoku*, to "return from work"), Matsumoto's text produces the phrase *chokunin kanshi no taishoku* ("high-ranking official returning, slightly the fatter, after a day's work"), which derides the bribe-devouring, avaricious attitude of these high officials. If the passengers in speeding carriages do not belong to this class of officials, they must be aristocrats on the way to the bank.

I know nothing about this author. But one can imagine that he started writing after being inspired by the success of other *fūzokushi* works, including Narushima Ryūhoku's *The Latest from Yanagibashi* (*Ryūkyō shinshi*, 1874) and Hattori Bushō's *New Prosperity in Tokyo* (*Tōkyō shinhanjōki*, 1874–81). This author's use of the literary devices *engo* and *kakekotoba* in a work written in *kanbun* style, however, makes his mode of expression closer to that of the writers of *gesaku* than to the writings of Ryūhoku or Bushō.[15]

14. Matsumoto Bannen, *Random Notes from Shinbashi* (*Tōkyō Shinkyō zakki*; Tokyo: Inada Madakichi, 1878), vol. 1, no page numbers. There is no modern reprint of this work.
15. *Gesaku* (lit., "playful works") refers to various genres of popular prose fiction written in late Edo and early Meiji. These works, frequently comic in nature, often used such classical literary techniques as *engo* and *kakekotoba*, and included passages of highly colloquial Japanese, especially in direct depictions of spoken dialogue.

The narrator of the Matsumoto text is certainly observing the scene on Shinbashi Bridge. But one does not have the feeling that the author is trying to capture *exactly as they were* the scenes that made the deepest impression on him personally. Rather, he has abstracted and selected materials anyone would readily associate with Shinbashi, depicting the most striking activity on the bridge— that of the horses and carriages of the government officials and wealthy aristocrats—from the cynical perspective of the common people. Compare this passage to the opening of Shōyō's *The Temper of Students in Our Times* (*Tōsei shosei katagi*, 1885–86).

> Ah, our ever shifting, changing world! One in which the very name of our capital Edo—formerly frequented only by the warrior class— has been changed to Tokyo! Each new year opens greater and greater change! Today there is no distinction between high and low, noble or commoner; anyone with skill will be used. Anyone can acquire fame and status in the twinkling of an eye. The sons of poor peddlers now grow majestic beards and take on aristocratic-sounding names as they ride in lacquered carriages down the great avenues. Once mighty men are reduced to pulling the rickshaw of the aristocrats. (*MBZ* 16:59)[16]

As we can see from this citation, the opening of *Random Notes from Shinbashi* can be considered a forerunner of Shōyō's description.

After describing the carriage riders, Matsumoto Bannen moves on to the rickshaw, and then to the appearance of the pedestrians on the bridge. The order in which the narrator's gaze moves is from people of higher to those of lower status, just as would be the case in *Ukigumo*. Let me stress that I am not attempting to trace a direct influence of *Random Notes* on the writing of Futabatei and Shōyō. I simply want to point out that, in the process through which *gesaku*-like conceptions became an increasingly pronounced feature of *kanbun fūzokushi*, a method of writing emerged that would later be used for scenes (and the gaze that surveyed them) such as the opening passages of *Ukigumo* and *The Temper of Students in Our Times*.

The attempt to capture everyday life in *kanbun* writing can be seen, conversely, as a process of *kanbun* being captured by everyday life. For example, Matsumoto used the three characters *ō* (large), *fuku* (cloth), and *boku* (hood) to write the word "large sacks," but then indicates that this should be

---

16. *MBZ* is used in citations as an abbreviation for *Meiji bungaku zenshū*, 99 vols. (Tokyo: Chikuma Shobō, 1965–83). This passage too is filled with *engo* and *kakekotoba*. The "peddlers" sell paste (*nori*) while their sons ride (*nori*) in carriages; the "aristocratic-sounding names" they take on end with Chinese characters that mean "small road," providing comic contrast to the "great avenues" down which they parade, etc.

pronounced as *ōburoshiki*, the colloquial name for this kind of sack. This kind of device, a standard practice in *kanbun fūzokushi*, could already be seen in Narushima Ryūhoku's *Latest from Yanagibashi* and, even earlier, in the writings of Terakado Seiken.[17] Matsumoto's phrase, "older women with children in their arms, and their possessions bundled in sacks on their backs, are geisha leaving the city for Yokohama," almost conveys the colloquial tone of a gawking passenger who whispers, "Look over there, that's a geisha down on her luck, if I ever saw one, moving out to Yokohama. . . ." We could say that such phrases, in which *gesaku*-like conceptions are woven into the very fabric of the narrator's *kanbun* prose, represent a process of colloquializing *kanbun* and are different from the device of directly recording conversations in the text, which Ryūhoku also used.

Perhaps my point is already clear, but let us reconsider the mode of expression Futabatei uses in *Ukigumo* to describe "extravagant imperial beards, Bismarck beards reminiscent of a Pekinese, bantam beards, badger's beards," or the "trousers that trail in the mud like the tail of a tortoise." Here too we find *kanbun*-like compounds of Chinese characters assigned colloquial Japanese readings. If we read these passages aloud using the *kun* or Japanese-language reading of the Chinese characters, we have a rhythmical narrative voice very much in accord with Terada Tōru's observation that *Ukigumo* includes elements that seem like transcriptions of *kōdan*, *rakugo*, or linked verse. But if we consider this as in every sense a *written* text, a text that sought, in fact, to use Chinese characters and *kanbun*-like expressions to artistic effect, then we discover a prose that has as its forerunner the *kanbun fūzokushi*. Moreover, patterns very reminiscent of Matsumoto Bannen's *Random Notes from Shinbashi* also appear in the first chapter of part two of *Ukigumo* ("Chrysanthemum Viewing at Dango-zaka"), where we again find the technique of listing up the very diverse phenomena that the narrator encounters in the chosen site. We, of course, also glimpse here the preferences and obsessions characteristic of Futabatei's writing about outdoor scenes, but the methods that he uses can be best explained as deriving from the examples we have just noted.

* * * * *

We might conjecture that an awareness that one necessarily exists in a situation that is shared with others arose in the course of writing about such scenes, and

---

17. Terakado Seiken (1796–1868) was a late-Edo period writer of *kanbun fūzokushi*, most notably *Prosperity in Edo* (*Edo hanjōki*, 1832–35).

that this was followed by the emergence of a method of expression according to which the writer selected the scene itself on the basis of just such an awareness. Consider the following passage from Hattori Bushō's *New Prosperity in Tokyo*. These are sentences found in a chapter entitled "The Bookstore," in volume three, published in 1875.

> Nowadays the number of bookstores is multiplying rapidly. There are some five hundred we could call "old stores," but when we begin to talk about their branch stores, the number is beyond counting. Some of these sell foreign books; some sell miscellaneous books; some publish new editions; some sell ancient books; some are open-air stalls and then there are the lending libraries. Both the main thoroughfares and the back streets are filled with such stores. This is because there are many readers, and they are the ones who have created a booming business. Scholarship by its nature advances knowledge. As knowledge leads to enlightenment, there will be many inventions. As inventions appear, books will need to be constantly updated. Ten years from now, all the books of today may be worthless scrap paper. A friend of mine said to me, "A book like your *New Prosperity in Tokyo* is worthless, it will certainly become scrap paper. If it doesn't continue to sell, how can you make a living?" I said, "Why worry? What is there to fear? If my book does not sell out, when the current boom fades, my book will be recycled into paper to record a future era of prosperity." (*MBZ* 4:186)

Hattori's depiction of a scene bustling with souls eager to gain a windfall from the booming book market is quite amusing. Note how the writer who depicts this scene is in no way portrayed as being superior to it. Since the Edo period this self-parodying style, which brought out a commonality between the observing self and its object, had been unavoidable—indeed, had been absolutely indispensable—for any writer of *gesaku*. It was a method of self-rationalization, one that Hattori Bushō had clearly adopted.

Hattori's writing, nevertheless, displays one particularly significant departure from the *gesaku* of late Edo. This lies in the fact that, when he depicts his activity of writing itself as one of the fascinating social phenomena he wants to capture, he can only depict it as one phenomenon among many. He recognized that this relativized perspective on his own activity provided a greater degree of humor. By the time Hattori Bushō began writing, it appears, the writer was no longer permitted the luxury of being a mere onlooker who parodied others. Reflection on the scene at hand makes the writer aware that his own books are merely one part of the larger situation he describes; his writing itself is merely a product of it. He has no choice but to share in common the fate of the world he describes.

This kind of self-awareness never emerged in Narushima Ryūhoku, a writer to whom Hattori Bushō is frequently compared and who has come to be esteemed more highly than Hattori. The flip side of Ryūhoku's sense that, as a *gesaku* writer, he was a superfluous being, "useless to society," was his proud awareness that his education was in no way inferior to that of high government officials, a pride so strong that it prevented him from developing a perspective like Hattori's. Ryūhoku, like a spider spinning its web in Yanagibashi, waits for the proper moment to expose the ugly nature of those temporarily inflated with success. In the pleasure quarters he has no trouble finding material of a scandalous nature. It is a site where anyone with eyes and ears can find the makings of a devastating critique, no matter who does the writing. But it is definitely not a scene into which Ryūhoku imaginatively projects himself, anxious that the fate of those he observes could also be his own. In Maeda Ai's excellent critical biography *Narushima Ryūhoku* (1976), we find the convincing suggestion that volume two of *The Latest from Yanagibashi* exemplifies Narushima's rather perverse manner of self-expression. But if we look carefully at the structure of Ryūhoku's mode of expression, we can see that Ryūhoku lacks the visual intentionality of one who lives within the depicted scene, such as we found in Hattori. Ryūhoku himself appears as a participant only in the scene where he reminisces about the close friendship between the characters Ase and Ei Hōzan (*MBZ* 4:26), a scene that parodies *Random Notes from a Wooden Bridge* (*Banqiao zaji*, published 1697) by the Ming literati Yu Huai (1616–96). Ryūhoku's textual alter ego, it seems, can only come to life in the mode of reminiscence.

The device Ryūhoku uses in place of a participatory, immanent narrator is that of the geisha character. I do not mean that in real life, he actually planted geisha to expose the scandalous activities of high government officials, but rather that he used the geisha character as a technique of expression. For Ryūhoku, the geisha was a kind of puppet who could be manipulated to produce a desired scene. Let me provide just one example.

> There was a certain geisha who loved to talk but was not very intelligent. People called her "Chatterbox" or "Dumbbell." One day she was waiting on a certain high-ranking minister at a banquet, along with some other geisha. At the height of the party, she asked him matter-of-factly, "I hear all the nobles in the Kyoto court are making ends meet by selling *hana-awase* cards these days. Do you make them, too?" The lord was speechless with shock. But after a while he responded. "Well, I suppose in the old days people had more leisure time and, I wonder . . . perhaps they made them to amuse themselves. But this must have been people of lower rank, if it is true at all. These days we have all been so busy attending to the affairs of state that people no longer have time for that sort of thing." The geisha slapped

her hand on her knees and said, "Ah, so that's it! There haven't been as many *hana-awase* cards on the market these days and the price has gone up. My father has been complaining about it and I myself had no idea what was going on. Now, thanks to you, I understand!" (*MBZ* 4:22)

This is a well-known scene, and it must have afforded readers of the time with an outlet for their feelings of contempt toward the new government's high officials.

However, in this scene, the responsibility for touching on a sore point and injuring the pride of an official (who we may surmise was something of an *arriviste*) lies with a talkative geisha who has no idea of the faux pas she has just committed. Moreover, by making the geisha herself an object of ridicule, Ryūhoku places himself outside of this totalized scene. The reader, too, can share in this detached position and hence enjoy being titillated by the scene. The historical Ryūhoku, of course, bore responsibility for writing this text and, as we know, even met disaster at the hands of the Meiji government, which in 1876 banned the book as injurious to public morals under the provisions of the newly promulgated publication regulations. Both this book and Hattori's *New Prosperity in Tokyo* were banned, and it was only through the appeals of the publisher Yamashiroya Masakichi that they were able to continue selling them until the end of the year. Nevertheless, in his textual production, Ryūhoku is never more than a bystander in every respect and is never a character who assumes agency within the depicted scene. To have an urbane sophisticate overhear the conversation between a geisha and a pretentious boor from behind the sliding door of an adjoining room, and thus expose its ludicrousness, was a technique much favored by the writers of late Edo *sharebon*.[18] If we assume that the events in this all-too-perfect teahouse scene were completely fabricated by Ryūhoku, then the mechanisms at work in its structure of expression are revealed even more clearly.

Thus we can see that the geisha used in various scenes in Narushima's *The Latest from Yanagibashi* do not constitute an "I" who is made to participate in the scene as an objectified alter-ego (or product of the author's ideationally split self), nor do they constitute a narrator immanent to the scene who has been set up as a bridge to effect a sensibility shared with readers. The kind of self-awareness according to which one makes oneself a butt of humor in order to draw out comic aspects of others is not bestowed onto these geisha characters; they are merely puppets Ryūhoku uses to poke fun as he stands outside the totalized situation. Ryūhoku did not possess the visual intentionality of one who inevitably must share the same situation as the character he depicts.

---

18. *Sharebon* constituted a genre of *gesaku* that depicted events occurring within the pleasure quarters.

Lacking such a sensibility, he did, nevertheless, try to push to its limits the technique of making his characters vehicles for a withering humor. What happens in such a case? The only means open to Ryūhoku to achieve this goal was to move in the direction of social satire, such as we find in *Ryūhoku's Tales of the Strange* (*Ryūhoku kibun*, 1878). Matsumoto Bannen, on the other hand, facing a similar dilemma, loses sight of the kind of device Ryūhoku uses in *Yanagibashi*, and in the latter half of *Random Notes from Shinbashi*, suffers from the delusion that humor in and of itself is the sole link between authorial and reader sensibility. It becomes necessary for him to push his humor in an ever more vulgar direction, as for example in a passage where characters joke about venereal diseases shared by publishing world executives who frequent the pleasure quarters. As Matsumoto himself admits at the end of the book, his writing here is on the same level as the jocular, pun-filled gossip that was featured in such tabloid newspapers as the *Kanayomi shinbun* and *Byōbyō kibun*. Even in Hattori Bushō's *New Prosperity in Tokyo*, we find passages of Ryūhoku-like narration everywhere. In this sense, it seems almost accidental that a scene like the one Hattori sets among the bookstalls, with its self-parodying perspective, emerged in this text.

Accident or no, certainly what precipitated the emergence of this new perspective was the fact that Bushō, unlike the Ryūhoku who cast his web over the pleasure quarters but kept himself hidden from view, was a writer of reportorial *fūzokushi* who actually trod the ground of the places he depicted. As the son of a Confucian official in the minor feudal domain of Nihonmatsu (whose castle had fallen after it opposed pro-Restoration troops in the Boshin War of 1868), Bushō could not afford to adopt the pose of viewing things from the aloof position of a person "useless to society," the pose that Ryūhoku adopted. For Bushō, to be a "useless person" was rather a pressing fact of real life in the fate that had befallen him. In order to write his articles, Bushō had to go out into the bustling areas of the city. These were places where people gathered, exchanging gossip in the hope of gleaning bits of information they might turn to profitable ends. However much Bushō's standpoint may have been that of an observer or a reporter, he was, in fact, just another member of this throng that gathered in search of something to put to profitable use. Bushō became able to see himself among the throng. It was an "I" that never would have become visible had he not transported himself to these sites. The writer Nakajima Sōin (1779?–1855) once shrewdly observed that since the city was overflowing with beggars even though it required a gift of three or four *kan*[19] of copper coins to gain membership in the guild of beggars at the time, this might be considered an

---

19. One *kan* equaled eight and three-quarter pounds.

index of the prosperity of the merchants who were doling out alms. Bushō sought to achieve a similar shrewdness of insight, but he was forced to the realization that he, too, had to chase after profits, alongside the characters he satirized.

As *New Prosperity in Tokyo* proceeds, Bushō's more *gesaku*-like conception that sought to create a comic effect through puns and word play and through satirizing the events he sees and hears gradually fades. It leaves in its wake a prose style that aims to inform readers of the true nature of social affairs. In order to expose the mechanisms at work in a social scene, word play had to yield to narrative. In the last chapter in volume six (published 1877), Bushō traces the way in which lawyers, the system of business incorporation, and government regulations for filing lawsuits form an unholy trinity that fleeces an elderly farmer of all his worldly possessions.

The following scene describes a farmer who has been bilked of a thousand yen by a man urging him to invest in a new business. The farmer has asked a lawyer to help him reclaim his money, but the lawyer first asks for half of his payment up front (fifty yen), and then charges the farmer several fees for transcribing his deposition. The farmer wins his verdict, but:

> The old farmer was very happy and bowed several times. He was very grateful, saying: "I really appreciate your help. Without it, how could I be so happy today? I am deeply indebted to you. Please help me get the compensation money quickly so I can go back to my hometown and reassure my wife and my children." The employee of the law firm spoke slowly and used a regretful voice. "The property of the man you sued is worth only a few yen. He also has many debts. They divided up his property equally to pay off the debtors. What we got from them is only two yen and some change. They will let the defendant pay the remainder if and when he recovers; that is how it is when official stock shares are concerned. Although I understand your difficult situation very well, the judge made his decision based on the law. There is nothing that can be done. Please drop the issue." In his shock and fear, the old farmer did not know what to say. Finally, in a trembling voice, he asked, "Is this a dream or reality?" (*MBZ* 4:241)

Of course there was no impropriety in these legal proceedings. But knowing full well that this could be the only result of the suit, the employee of the legal firm, "secretly laughing" (*MBZ* 4:240), contracted to take on the case at a high fee. Bushō presents us with a blunt narrative of the events that the situation he describes can trigger, and thus produces a penetrating insight. Regardless of whether or not he could empathize in every respect with the situation of this poor farmer, his sensibility has evolved beyond the point where he could turn this into a comical scene or indulge in word play. It is, after all, a social reality that envelops both self and other.

* * * * *

While it would not be valid to describe *fūzokushi* as a genre that always sought to reproduce reality faithfully, it was a genre that could never have emerged without the writer visually intending his own encounter with the scenes depicted. We might even define *fūzokushi* as a mode of expression characterized by the attempt to encounter the actual situation, the "thing itself." Kosík proclaims the need for "a certain cognizance that there exists [. . .] a hidden truth of things" (a knowledge that is "prior to any investigation"), but it was not on the basis of such an a priori knowledge that Hattori Bushō and other early Meiji writers developed their practice of expression. During Hattori's day there were many *fūzokushi* guides to Tokyo that were written either in classical Japanese or in colloquial styles. But these writings did not succeed in producing a mode of expression we find compelling today. It was only in *kanbun fūzokushi* texts that such a perspective could emerge, precisely because of the disparity between their *kanbun* language and the Japanese everyday life (and the sensibility that grasped it) that they tried to convey with that language. Out of the stratagems writers concocted to overcome this distance from their object there emerged a reflexivity about their own situatedness. For the first time, writers became self-conscious about how they positioned themselves. It was out of these efforts that the so-called "techniques of description" of the modern novel emerged. As we have just observed, it was from the act of determining how to position oneself in relation to the scene before one's eyes that the practice of self-consciously choosing a particular point-of-view towards one's object evolved, along with a method of grasping oneself as someone who ineluctably shared a given situation with others. Over and above these two developments we find the gradual splitting off from the writer's own consciousness of the non-person narrator, immanent to the diegetic world and sharing interests and sensibilities in common with readers.

If these techniques had continued their spontaneous evolution, what would the outcome have been? As "knowledge" about the "thing itself" deepened, so too would a self-critical "knowledge" about our own sensibilities—the understanding that, if what we refer to as "sensibility" is itself a social product, "sensibility," as well as reality, can be transformed. Or, if we were to restrict the scope of our answer to literature alone, we might envision that the techniques of writing Yokomitsu Riichi (1898–1947) made a desperate plea for in his "On Pure Fiction" ("Junsui shōsetsuron," 1935) would already have become clear to us.

However, in the portrayal of events by the media of today we see no trace of the perspective developed by early Meiji writers. Contemporary media impose their own styles of expression on events, yet simulate the transmission of an authentic reality. The effort to forge modes of expression that are themselves a way of encountering reality has been abandoned. The writer Takahashi Kazumi (1931–71) articulated his sense of crisis about this situation in his novel, *White Grave* (*Shiroku nuritaru haka*, 1971), but few have pondered his words. On the contrary, as this mechanism of information-as-expression, expression-as-information comes to dominate our everyday reality, our sensibilities have become more and more homogeneous, to the extent that the very I-sensibility, the individualistic, egoistical consciousness celebrated in the modern Japanese novel, has itself disappeared. With it has gone any hope that a metamorphosis of our I-sensibility can be achieved, except by developing it through a kind of "automatic writing" in which the differentiation between self and other is utterly erased. This is the cause of the contemporary situation of expression described by Nakajima Azusa.

It is against this background that I want to open up the question of why the convention of a narrator who was immanent to the diegetic world of a text— a technique that blossomed in *kanbun fūzokushi* and in *Ukigumo*—was abandoned by modern Japanese writers. It is a question that forces us to reconsider the very foundations of modern literature.

Chapter Two
The Transformability of Self-Consciousness: Fantasies of Self in the Political Novel

TRANSLATED BY JOHN MERTZ

Kamei turns his attention in this chapter to the political novel, a genre that enjoyed wide popularity in early Meiji. Kamei argues that it provided a key transition toward the modern novel in that it not only centered on the problem of the "self," but in particular on the self as a split subject, suspended between the self as an ideal projected figure (the fictional protagonist or narrator) and the self as the source of that projection (the author). Moreover, continuing his stress on the importance of kanbun *for modern literature, Kamei traces through the variety of styles developed out of* kanbun *in the attempt to create a modern writing style that would transcend the hierarchy-bound sensibility of the now-discredited feudal era. Only such a style could permit a new kind of narrative of solidarity, of romance between men and women as equals, a necessary precondition for the appearance of the ideal fantasy figure of the male hero, whose very existence is mediated by the gaze of women, in Tōkai Sanshi's* Chance Encounters with Beautiful Women. *Furthermore, Yano Ryūkei's* An Illustrious Tale of Statesmanship *overthrew the hierarchical structure that had hitherto characterized Japanese fiction, whereby the author's sensibility dominated over all of the characters in a work. Each individual character now saw the world through his or her own sensibility, thereby relativizing the sensibility of the author—and that of his readers. The newly emerged split subject was now a subject with others, and a means for achieving conscious recognition of one's own sensibility through literature had been attained.*

The placement of the writer's own image in the role of the protagonist, the characteristic choice of modern literature in Japan, was motivated by the imaginary projection of an ideal self. It did not arise from a desire to confess as truthfully as possible the actual self, just as it was. This fact is still often misunderstood.

Kobayashi Hideo in "Discourse on Fiction of the Self" ("Shishōsetsu ron," 1935) writes that:

> We can begin by saying that an "I-Novel" is a sincere self-confession written in fictional prose. At first glance it would also seem that in the novel's formative years, all writers had recourse to this method of writing. But history is strange, and until a sense of the individual had grown to become of profound human significance, a fiction of the self did not appear in European literary history.[1]

In the context of Japanese literature, the question that Kobayashi fails to consider is when and in what form this so-called self became a problematic of expression for writers themselves. For that, one must backtrack all the way to the time of the political novel, the genre that achieved wide popularity in Japan during the 1870s and 1880s. For the authors of this genre, as they projected the image of an ideal self, their mode of expression forced them to recognize that the self was inevitably twofold, split between a projected and a projecting entity. Any consideration of the birth of modern literature must take this process into account. When the doubled nature of the self became visible, movement toward a "real" self-recognition could commence. Modern literary expression was born only when the psychological process whereby this bifurcated self was rendered visible became a central motif.

That said, we may now ask in what forms this doubled self was experienced by Japanese writers. When the answer to this becomes clear, we can then examine the question of whether or not the "real" self-recognition attained by Japanese writers in fact constituted the only legitimate form of selfhood.

* * * * *

I will begin my consideration of these problems from the perspective of writing style.[2] Publications of the late 1870s were frequently written in *kanbun*. These writings often employed notations such as *kaeriten* (word-order markings to aid

---

1. Kobayashi Hideo, *Literature of the Lost Home: Kobayashi Hideo—Literary Criticism 1924–1939*, trans. Paul Anderer (Stanford: Stanford University Press, 1995), 67–68. Kobayashi Hideo (1902–83) is perhaps the most influential literary critic in modern Japan. He first achieved recognition in the late 1920s and remained active in the postwar era.
2. Much of the following discussion of writing style is more a summary of Kamei's argument than a direct translation. Kamei's argument relies on close readings of examples of several styles used to render *kanbun* texts into vernacular Japanese styles, examples whose differences would necessarily vanish in English translation. Those interested in the topic should refer to the original Japanese version of this section, which appears on pp. 32–35.

readers in rearranging the words back into vernacular Japanese syntax) and *okurigana* (Japanese suffixes such as verb endings appended to Chinese characters in superscript annotations). We can view this style of expression as a close antecedent to *yomikudashi* (i.e., *kanbun* that has been rewritten to appear on the page in Japanese syntactical order and with Japanese suffixes). Then, after the appearance of the *kanbun fuzokushi* discussed in the previous chapter, fictional narratives began to appear that were presented in the already-rearranged order of the *yomikudashi* style. Representative works include Yano Ryūkei's *An Illustrious Tale of Statesmanship* (*Keikoku bidan*, 1883–84) and Tōkai Sanshi's *Chance Encounters with Beautiful Women* (*Kajin no kigū*, 1885–97).[3]

I must note that there were two tendencies to the *yomikudashi* style. What drew my attention to this was Fukuchi Ōchi's "Prose Styles in Present-Day Meiji" ("Meiji konnichi no bunshō," 1893).[4] Fukuchi cites examples where a pure *kanbun* sentence containing only unannotated Chinese characters is rewritten to follow Japanese syntax and to include various honorific expressions, in order to make it fit as closely as possible the parameters of classical Japanese writing. Fukuchi calls this *yakudoku* style (lit., "translated-reading style"; i.e., *yomikudashi* with extra honorifics, aspect markings, etc., that would not otherwise appear in the original *kanbun*).

A reverse example of this can be found in a passage from Rai Sanyō's *Unofficial History of Japan* (*Nihon gaishi*, 1837), written in *kanbun*. The chapter concerning the Kusunoki clan is based on the *Taiheiki* (*Record of the Great Peace*, 1372), which was written in the vernacular Japanese literary style (albeit including some modified *kanbun* expressions). Rai's readers may well have appreciated the language of Rai's adaptation for its twofold nature.[5] Japanese honorific expressions such as *gorōzerarubekarazu* and *oboshimeraresōrō* that are used in the *Taiheiki* version are of course impossible to express in true *kanbun*

---

3. Yano Ryūkei (1850–1931) and Tōkai Sanshi (real name Shiba Shirō, 1852–1922) were both political activists and writers. Their two works cited here are perhaps the most famous examples of the political novel genre. An abridged translation of *An Illustrious Tale of Statesmanship* can be found in John Mertz, *Meiji Political Novels and the Origins of Literary Modernity*, Ph.D. dissertation, Cornell University, 1993.

4. Fukuchi Ōchi [Genichirō] (1841–1906) was a prominent journalist, playwright, and novelist who first achieved widespread recognition in the mid 1870s. The essay cited here was serialized in the journal *Kokumin no tomo*, nos. 204–6 and 208 (October 3–November 15, 1893). It is reprinted in Yamamoto Masahide, ed., *Kindai buntai keisei shiryō shūsei: hassei hen* (Tokyo: Ōfūsha, 1978), 701–16.

5. The specific passage Kamei is discussing is translated as "Since the way of warfare is as it is, let not the sovereign look at the outcome of a single battle. While he hears that Masashige alone still lives, let him believe that he will prevail at last." *The Taiheiki*, trans. Helen C. McCullough (New York: Columbia University Press, 1959), 69.

and are accordingly omitted from Rai's text. But if readers of this account were familiar with the original *Taiheiki*, then surely part of the pleasure of reading must have come from recalling the passage on which it was based, including its honorifics. During the Tokugawa period, a style that mixed Japanese honorifics into *kanbun* prose was quite ordinary for notices issued by the government, for petitions submitted to the government, and for written communications among peasants and townsmen. As the period progressed and the *yakudoku* (elaborated *yomikudashi*) style noted by Fukuchi Ōchi matured among the educated elite, it was doubtless fully expected that even documents composed in pure *kanbun*, with no annotation, would nonetheless be read with all the honorifics and circumlocutions that were characteristic of *yakudoku*. For peasants and townsmen, who wrote on a daily basis in a style that mixed Japanese honorifics into *kanbun* prose, it would not have been difficult to read pure unannotated *kanbun*, even if they could not understand the full corpus of Chinese classical literature.

Because *kanbun* was used in this way at all levels of society, it easily could have become the national literary standard for Japan, had it been adequately promoted. This was the view that Fukuchi held, and there is a certain logic to it. As we shall see below, a similar view was held by Yano Ryūkei, who criticized the very foundations of the *genbun itchi* movement in *A New Thesis on Japanese Style and Orthography* (*Nihon buntai moji shinron*, 1886). Moreover, the desire to formulate a new national writing style is clearly evident in the style of his political novel *An Illustrious Tale of Statesmanship*.

What destroyed the possibility for the adoption of this style, according to Fukuchi, was the predominance of another style among the young generation of Meiji intelligentsia, the so-called *bōdoku* (plain gloss) style. As we have seen, any *kanbun* passage could be rewritten into *yomikudashi*, by rearranging the words into Japanese order and adding appropriate suffixes. However, whereas the *yakudoku* style of *yomikudashi* sought to adjust the honorific language of the text to accord with Japanese practice, the *bōdoku* style eschewed such adjustments and used only a bare minimum of suffixes. It also demonstrated a strong preference for the Chinese (*on*) readings of characters, as opposed to the Japanese (*kun*) readings that were stressed in *yakudoku*. The *bōdoku* style originated in techniques used by Japanese Confucian scholars to recite their Chinese texts aloud. Toward the end of the Tokugawa period it became especially popular among the politically inclined samurai of the various domains, who used it to present petitions to the government; hence, it was also sometimes referred to as the *kenpaku* (memorial) style. In the Meiji period it was used in public documents issued by the new government, and so the style was endowed with the aura of official recognition. That, at least, is how Fukuchi explains it, though he errs slightly by using as his example the gazette published by the new Meiji government, which actually employed only a slightly simplified version of *yakudoku* style.

In any case, the first group to decisively employ the rarified *bōdoku* style seems to have been the Westernist intellectuals of the Meirokusha group.[6] Though the *bōdoku* style proliferated in the media, it seems fair to say that educated commoners who were accustomed to *yakudoku* probably found it quite difficult to adjust to the terseness of this new mode of expression. This style was chosen in answer to the pressing problem of how to incorporate into Japanese the ideas and expressions of European humanities and sciences, and as a result the gap in terms of both ideas and writing style between high and low grew even wider than it had been during the late Edo period. It was the intellectual class that was responsible for the enormity of that gap, and Fukuchi wryly observed the irony that those very intellectuals were now using the especially difficult *bōdoku* style to lament the low level of literacy among commoners and to call for language reform.

The style chosen by Tōkai Sanshi for his political novel was a form of *kanbun yomikudashi* produced in accordance with the *bōdoku* style.

* * * * *

However, I would not claim that these styles of *yomikudashi* are the reason why Yano's and Tōkai's political novels did not succeed as modern literature. It must be understood that, in the same way that the *kanbun* of Rai's *Unofficial History of Japan* could not be realized except by excising the honorific expressions in the *Taiheiki*, the stylistics of the political novelists negated and thus overcame the status-bound hierarchical (honorific-based) sensibility that characterized the mode of expression in traditional Japanese literature. Furthermore, the epoch-making literary fantasy of international solidarity cherished by the politician-novelists of the People's Rights Movement could not have arisen in the absence of such a style.

It is never fully possible for an author to avoid expressing the status-bound sensibility whereby one character relates to other characters in a work. Often enough, moreover, the status-bound sensibility of the author himself is overlain onto these intratextual relations. Such a sensibility in fact had long pervaded the Japanese literary tradition, to the extent that authors could find no

6. The Meirokusha group was one of driving forces in the Civilization and Enlightenment movement, which sought to modernize and Westernize Japan in early Meiji. Its members included such prominent social critics and philosophers as Fukuzawa Yukichi (1834–1901), Nishi Amane (1829–97), and Katō Hiroyuki (1836–1916).

other means of involving themselves or their readers into their works except through expressions that embraced such a sensibility as if it were utterly natural. In this sense, this sensibility had formed practically a motif within Japanese literature. Yet the authors who employed the *bōdoku* style, whether they were aware of it or not, produced a decisive rift in that tradition. If, as Fukuchi Ōchi noted, the modern writing style had been modeled on the *yakudoku* style, it would have been nearly impossible for writers (as speaking subjects) to overcome this inherently hierarchical sensibility.

For example, in the case of Tōkai Sanshi's *Chance Encounters with Beautiful Women*, this type of sensibility is practically nonexistent, whether in the relations between the protagonist and the other personae or in those between the author and the totality of the intratextual relations. With this new conception, reft of social-hierarchy markings, the author constructs a protagonist marked by the self-awareness that he lives the same political situation as the other characters in the work. But what was the end result? This is what interests me about this work.

Here is the opening passage of the first volume of *Chance Encounters with Beautiful Women*:

> Tōkai Sanshi one day climbed Independence Hall [. . .] in the city of Philadelphia. Looking up to see the broken Liberty Bell, looking down to read the Declaration of Independence of the time when the Americans had raised the flag of righteousness and expelled the tyrannical government of the King of England, he contemplated the virtues of a people independent and self-governing, and he was overcome with emotion. Tearfully he approached the window and gazed out. At that moment, two damsels came circling up the stairway. Their faces covered in celadon veils, in fragrant shadow and white-feathered bonnets of spring, wearing fine chemises and trailing long and civilized skirts, their stylish elegance was truly surprising. Pointing to Carpenters' Hall they spoke to one another: That is where, in the year seventeen hundred and seventy-four, great men from the thirteen states first met and took the first steps to plan the establishment of their nation [. . . .] And pointing to a distant river they said: That hill is called Valley Forge, and that river is named the Delaware. Ahh, Bunker Hill. (*MBZ* 6:4)

Many critics have noted a similarity between this work and later I-novels, in that the author seems to make himself into the protagonist. Yet the question remains as to what sort of self-consciousness it is that the author objectifies here in the third-person as "Tōkai Sanshi."

In his autobiographical preface to the work, the author remarks that as a foreign student in the United States he had on many occasions "feared for his country and sighed for the age" and that he had amassed more than a dozen volumes of "notes on things seen and felt" (*MBZ* 6:3). These notes, which formed a kind of rough draft for the novel, were written in an assortment of *kanbun*, classical literary Japanese, and occasionally even English. In the author's words, they did "not yet constitute a unified style" (*MBZ* 6:3). After returning to Japan in 1885, the author took leave for two months to "compile and edit them in accordance with present-day Japanese literary style, under the title *Chance Encounters with Beautiful Women*" (*MBZ* 6:3).

It is of course to be expected that the work includes many autobiographical elements. If one were simply to extrapolate from these statements, then the opening scene too was likely compiled and edited "in accordance with present-day Japanese literary style" from one of his "notes of things seen and felt" while in the United States. But the truth is hardly this simple.

In the work, after the opening passage cited above, there is a description of Bunker Hill, followed by recollections of the author's visit to that area in the late spring of 1881. This in turn leads to a citation of *kanshi* (poetry written in Chinese) that the author exchanged at that time with a friend Tekkenshi—it seems clear that the idea for these poems arose during the visit to Bunker Hill. The protagonist's poem includes the phrases:

> The East cannot compete with the winds of freedom.
> The valiant man in vain embraces a thousand sorrows
> [. . .]
> And suffers an age of calamity in another's homeland.
> The grief of his journey multiplies like the scattering blossoms.
> (*MBZ* 6:5)

This may seem an overly fine point, but the poem as it appears in *Chance Encounters with Beautiful Women* does not function to describe the situation of the author's visit to Bunker Hill. Instead, it is situated at the scene of Independence Hall one year later, in the spring of 1882. The first half of the poem is as follows:

> The lone traveler ascends and looks down from Bunker Hill.
> A grassy monument marks many seasons elapsed.
> Here was raised the flag to expel a tyrannical government,
> With a vow to slay the despots and take vengeance upon the country's
>   enemies.
> Soldiers and horses were loosed upon the sunlit mount
> In a chorus of triumph for the thirteen states' union.
> The government values public debate, popular customs are pure.
> Policies protect the country without bias. (*MBZ* 6:5)

When we compare this expression to that of the opening scene, it is clear that the opening scene consists of a prose rendering of the motif of the Chinese poem, transferred to Independence Hall. Tōkai likely judged that the sincerity of the bitter sentiments expressed in the phrase "the East cannot compete with the winds of freedom" would only be amplified by the context of his situation and mental state while climbing Independence Hall, when he "contemplated the virtues of a people independent and self-governing, and was overcome with emotion." He used the patriotic Chinese poetry of "things seen and felt" from his notebooks as a bridge linking him to contemporary readers. In order to achieve this, he borrowed a "present-day Japanese literary style" (*bōdoku*) and chose— or rather, invented—a scene that would strengthen the sense of necessity of the poem's motif and topic.

In creating this scene, the author also interposes a visual intentionality that belongs to an imaginary projection of the author's own self. When the two women happen to climb the staircase and discuss the War of Independence while pointing physically to Carpenters' Hall, soon enough the protagonist too begins to acquire a similar interest. Expressions such as "long and civilized skirts" reveal also how the two women are reflected in Tōkai Sanshi's eyes: in even a single hem touching the ground, he sees the beauty of this country's civilization. Moreover, his adoration of the "virtues" of America, whose people had historically achieved "independence and self-governance," is suffused with a sense of oppression, as I will touch on again below. These sensibility-laden expressions provide his readers with a bridge to the direct experiences, "things seen and felt," of the protagonist.

When, next, the women point toward the Delaware River, the author calls to mind the figure of himself far off in the distance, one year previously, when he visited Bunker Hill and confirmed his life's purpose. The finger-pointing of the women is nothing other than an externalized expression of his own internal visual intentionality, as he recalls his prior experience. The floating phrase "Ahh, Bunker Hill" which concludes the opening scene is ostensibly a quotation of the women's speech, but when it is viewed in the context of the recollections that follow, it can be none other than a sigh on the part of the protagonist himself. Furthermore, following the citation of Chinese poetry, the narration suddenly returns to the women's conversation, ". . . and thus the Declaration of Independence was inscribed at this hall" (*MBZ* 6:5). One might wish to call this a clever transition, but it would rather seem that the author is unable to differentiate clearly between the ideas and visual intentionalities of the protagonist and those of the two women: they blur together in this work.

This also suggests that the author had not yet developed a clear consciousness of the difference between himself as author and himself as narrated protagonist. But having created two female characters to embody externally the visual intentionality of the protagonist, it was necessary then to project for the protagonist an imaginary self that was adequate and appropriate to those women. The intensity of this imaginary projection is heightened by their location in a scene that emphasizes his common destiny with the two women.

The fact that the protagonist shares the same interests as the women forms the preamble to subsequent scenes. When he meets them again the next day, he learns of the political conditions of Spain (from the character Yolanda), of Ireland (from Colleen), and then of the Chinese mainland (from Fan Qing). Hearing these, he trembles with fear at the fate of peoples who have been decimated and invaded by the Western powers, because his own country Japan is potentially threatened with the same destiny.

The fundamental point of difference, though, is that Japan is fortunate enough not to be under the control of foreign powers, and Tōkai Sanshi is accordingly not in political exile like the others. He has come to America in order to study economics, and his friend Tekkenshi demonstrates full confidence in his future in the *kanshi* he composes:

> Perhaps these are affairs best left to the elder statesmen,
> Yet there are many who grow feeble by the day,
> Their wealth dwindling as the masses cry out in cold and starvation
> [. . .]
> You alone can expound the techniques of economics
> And utilize grand strategies to save them from drowning. (*MBZ* 6:5)

While he might not be able to expect the government to greet him with open arms, at least he is in a position where he can work in concert with government policies to stimulate national wealth and self-reliance. In this sense, he has relatively few worries—he does not live under the cruel situation of Yolanda and the other expatriates, who are prevented from returning to their homelands so long as their present governments hold power.

Yet in *Chance Encounters with Beautiful Women*, though he can hardly avoid a consciousness of this fundamental difference, he rejects his actual position and, out of the blue, leaps to the claim that "Sanshi, too, is the surviving vassal of a ruined nation," and that "I, too, am a child of the true Japan" (*MBZ* 6:16). The expression "child of the true Japan" refers to his status as a former samurai vassal of the now defunct Aizu domain.

Of course, he was not entirely fabricating his experiences. In a passage concerning the battle of Aizu, he relates how the forces of the new Meiji government ignored the real motives of the domain leader and scattered the defeated Aizu army across the land. The chagrin of the Aizu soldiers at being forced to live through unspeakably miserable circumstances is described vividly, and it is no exaggeration to call this the most moving passage of the text for Tōkai Sanshi's readers. Paradoxical though it may seem, it is precisely because he narrates these past misfortunes in order to reposition himself more closely to the present circumstances of Yolanda and the other expatriates that his self is transformed into an imaginary projection.

Altogether, the enunciations of the characters in this work are little more than long-winded speeches that are inappropriate to a novel, seemingly driven by a consciousness of grand performance in front of the reader (audience), yet this results in a certain unified effect. This appeal to the reader is further strengthened by the motif of the protagonist attempting to ally himself with the expatriates. Yet in order to achieve this, he commits almost unconsciously a substitution of Japan for the feudal domain of Aizu. In fact, the battle that was fought by his father and elder brother was never a war of liberation by and for the people of Aizu. He himself lacks any real understanding of the problem of national (or domainal) liberation. Nevertheless, he purports to belong to the alliance of Yolanda and the others. The conclusion he draws is that, "the urgent task which faces us is not to extend freedom by ten steps internally, but rather to extend our national authority by one step to the outside" (*MBZ* 6:19). This is nothing but an expression of a Japanese desire for self-expansion at the expense of others. In the end, he can only consider allying himself with the expatriate group on the basis of policies that undermine the most basic principles of national liberation and independence.

* * * * *

Perhaps we should see in this imaginary projection a desire on the part of the author to transcend his own actual self. The memories of the war that inflicted on him the loss of his father and brother and an adolescence spent drifting from house to house were too oppressive for him to escape, and yet too cruel for him to face directly. It was impossible for him to achieve a recognition of the true nature of that war, during which the Meiji army acted unjustly, but during which the Aizu army too lacked any legitimate goal shared in solidarity with the common people of their domain. Moreover, as long as the Meiji coalition government continued to exist, he would bear the burden of being identified with the old Aizu domain, and he would be forced to live in compromise with the political system of the present government. Under such circumstances, there was little for him to do but absorb the ideals of the American War of Independence and convert its sentiment into an ideological force, one that could critically strike out at contemporary political conditions in Japan. He travels to the United States to become an expert on finance, yet once there, he is appalled to witness the Western powers ravaging weaker nations. The sense of urgency that he feels for Japan's position in this struggle causes his visual intentionality to bifurcate. On the one hand, he would return to Japan and use his skills as a finance specialist to aid his country in its quest for wealth and independence. On the other hand, he would pursue the world-historical ideals of national liberation and overthrowing the domination of weak peoples by the Western powers.

He rationalizes his pursuit of the first and more concrete of these paths—returning to Japan—by interpreting it as a "realistic" political choice, a necessary step in his pursuit of the ideals of the second. That is to say, the self that was moved by the ideals of the second path could only be realized, for the moment, within the space of a fictional narrative. Thus he introduces his protagonist, Tōkai Sanshi, atop Independence Hall bearing these two visual intentionalities, one of which is then reallocated and externalized onto the gesture of pointing made by the two women. Additionally, he endows the women with the destiny of the Spanish and Irish nations, using their personal adventures as the springboard for setting out on his own pursuit of ideals. After the women leave for Spain, the protagonist (who remains behind in America) exists as a reflection of the author himself, who pursues the other, more realistic path. Still, despite this separation from the women, the author attempts to demonstrate the necessity of the protagonist's alliance with them by introducing the romance between Yolanda and him, that is, the consciousness of a relationality to difference (in this case, the opposite sex).

The author's positioning his self at the site of some historical incident is very likely patterned after Rai Sanyō's *Unofficial History of Japan*, where chapters open with the following sort of statement: "The Unofficial Historian tells us: Many times in my travel through Harima Province I have visited the station known as Sakurai. . . ."[7] However, in creating an imaginary self who lives in relation to the women who have been split off from his own visual intentionality, the author of *Chance Encounters with Beautiful Women* has no alternative but to bestow on this self the objectivity of the third-person: "Tōkai Sanshi one day climbed Independence Hall, in the city of Philadelphia."

The writing style of *Chance Encounters with Beautiful Women* as well, while similar to the quasi-*bōdoku* style of *Unofficial History of Japan*, may have simply been chosen "to imitate present-day Japanese literary style," yet the result was an elimination of the existing status-bound hierarchical sensibility. It now became possible to portray a relation between the sexes as an alli-

7. *Rai Sanyō Nihon gaishi,* ed. Andō Hideo (Tokyo: Kondo, 1982), 102.

ance of equals, and thus to realize a transformation in the sensibility of love that had typified the *ninjōbon*, the late-Edo genre of *gesaku* that focused on love affairs. Furthermore, it was owing to this new conception of love that the author was able to introduce into the novel an international perspective on politics, one capable of ranging from Europe to Asia. For these reasons, we must acknowledge *Chance Encounters with Beautiful Women* as a watershed work.

A heroic and benevolent self, appropriate to the adoration and respect showered on it by an idealized partner of the opposite sex: the tension between this idealized self and the author's own self was most likely a displacement of the tensions he felt after returning to Japan and entering into politics. Even if he had truly visited Independence Hall and met with foreign women while studying in America, this real self would after all be different from the fantasy self that appears in his fiction. In a process that can be rightly termed self-transcendence, an idealization of the self is carried out in this fantasy self through the mediation of a member of the opposite sex, one who has been allotted a portion of the self's own visual intentionality. The urgent appeal of this motif attracted a wide readership to the novel, though it also gave rise to the weaknesses in its political consciousness that I discussed above.

The subsequent loss of that motif also meant becoming aware of the true nature of the self as something that was obsessed, even possessed, by this imaginary self. It was precisely at this point that Japan's so-called "pure literature" arose. In terms of literary history, this juncture has been equated with the birth of modern literature. A process of reflection begins within the fantasy self, one that leads to an awareness that the fantasy self is an illusory contrivance and ultimately to the disintegration of this imaginary projection. This process of disintegration itself is the privileged object of expression specific to the modern Japanese novel. We find it in Saganoya Omuro's *Tasteless* (*Ajikinashi*, 1888) or Mori Ōgai's "Maihime" ("Dancing Girl," 1890), yet both of these are predated by Futabatei Shimei's *Ukigumo* (*Drifting Cloud*, 1887), where we find it in a transitional form: the breakdown is displaced onto the idealized image of a member of the opposite sex (the female character Osei). A similar movement can be found in the mode of expression of *Chance Encounters with Beautiful Women*, as well.

When Yolanda and the others leave for Spain, the protagonist meets with a Miss Parnell, leader of the Irish Independence Party, and they affirm that they share the same political goals.[8] Soon after, he is shocked to learn of her death from a newspaper:

---

8. The character's name is of course borrowed from that of Charles Parnell (1846–91), the Irish nationalist politician.

As the twilight grew deeper the dark fog dispersed, leaving not a single cloud in the long, brilliant sky. Looking up, one could see the pine trees glistening, as if blossomed with ice. Sanshi opened the window and leaned out, searching the four directions and thinking back to his homeland far away, remembering old friends. Some he had lost track of, others had left this world. As he thought back over many things, a hundred memories overcame him until he could endure it no longer. He remembered Miss Parnell. Her body, yet to be interred, lay at a Philadelphia cemetery. Sanshi desired to fulfill his friendship and mourn her in person. He set out on foot to the cemetery. [. . .] **Seeing what appeared to be the shadows of a group of people, he knelt down and gazed at them.** *Thin clouds veiled the moon and blurred his vision.* **They lay in white gowns with hair astray, the moonlight drifting over their legs like smoke, like mist.** *A piercing wind arose of a sudden, thrashing leaves and rattling branches. In an instant the shadows vanished and their spirits gave chase.* **When Sanshi had been a child still ignorant of the world, he had heard of ghosts and demons, and though he would not believe in such things now,** *at the back of his mind there was something from his childhood that could still be felt.* **His heart pounded, his flesh crept, his body quivered.** (*MBZ* 6:35; italics and boldface in original)

Thus he describes, in the present time of the narrative, his situation in being alone. Such descriptions are infrequent in the text, yet we have already witnessed in the opening scene his tendency to lapse into a mental state in which, gazing at his surroundings in the present, he finds himself overwhelmed by memories from the past. If it is possible to generalize from this particular passage, we may note the difference between phrases marked in italics (superscript open circles in the original), which describe particularly memorable scenes surrounding the protagonist yet written from the point of view of the author, and phrases marked in bold (superscript solid teardrops in the original), which consist of expressions adhering more closely to the sensibility of the protagonist himself. The aesthetic descriptions we find in these expressions depicting his environment of course represent an ideal nature, an aesthetic idealization that is only fitting to the heroic and benevolent fantasy self. Yet the I-sensibility that emerges from within this imagery defines a protagonist for whom the past is inseparably bound to the object that appears before his eyes in the present, one who is easily overcome with fear by the illusion that something from the other world is calling to him. It is indeed startling how passively receptive his sensibility is to such sentiments.

The problem is that human beings can possess only a passive relationship to the past. Poignant memories and passions incurred by historical instances of domination can generate an aggressive energy against the existing order, but in the case of Tōkai Sanshi it is rather the fear of his own inability to withstand the overwhelming sense of oppression he feels from his past that forces him into an aggressive posture, as he seeks self-transcendence and a liberation from that past. The fierce passion that marks his narration of the fate of the Aizu retainers is rooted in this kind of sensibility.

The mode of expression found in *Chance Encounters with Beautiful Women* had thus advanced to the point of directing the reader's gaze toward the author's own particular I-sensibility. If the author had continued to pursue this reflexivity, perhaps his literary task would not have stalled at the level of a self-consciousness represented by the assertion that "I, too, am a child of the true Japan" and its consequent drive for expansion of the fantasy self. Instead, he might have produced a critical analysis of that form of self-consciousness, one that pursued the questions of political freedom, both internal and external. What Tōkai Sanshi needed was to formulate a visual intentionality that would "extend freedom by ten steps." Yet in the end, owing to his inability to go beyond his own fixed consciousness of self, his inability to go beyond the unquestioning affirmation of the self's passions, he could move only in the direction of an other-oriented form of self-exhibition.

Once again, I want to stress that, as paradoxical as it may seem, what is important here is the appearance of the imaginary projection of an idealized self. In terms of literary expression, the form of self-consciousness attained by satirists like Narushima Ryūhoku and Hattori Bushō in their *kanbun fūzokushi* may have given birth to a *methodology of the scene*, but it could not have produced a *methodology of the plot*. One cannot construct a truly dramatic narrative space out of their sort of awakened self-consciousness. The use of aesthetically idealized depictions of physical surroundings as a means to create a bridge linking readers to an imaginary projection of self, such as "Tōkai Sanshi," ends up inciting the readers' own desire for such an imaginary projection and causing them to visually intend the tempering of their own sensibilities. Readers are then forced into an awareness of the tension between their own selves and this projected self. Once this tension has formed, the distance between the projected and the projecting self—between the aesthetic idealization of physical surroundings and the I-sensibility—becomes evident. At that moment, a new literary movement arises that seeks to grasp as its object this very process of achieving self-awareness. Such a movement began with Shōyō's *The Temper of Students in Our Times*, but the writers who participated in this movement also erred in their grasp of the process of attaining self-knowledge, although their error differed from that of Tōkai Sanshi. While these writers were able to move beyond Tōkai Sanshi's fantasy self, hardly any of them realized that their own protagonists were blind to the questions of freedom and politics.

* * * * *

Incidentally, Yano Ryūkei employed the colloquial tone of the late-Edo *yomihon* genre in parts of *An Illustrious Tale of Statesmanship*, but otherwise wrote it in *bōdoku* style, albeit with a preference for Japanese (*kun*) pronunciations for Chinese characters. The reasons for this are described in his "Remarks on Usage"[9] of the first volume and in the "Preface" of the second volume of that novel. But it should also be noted that he opposed the *genbun itchi* style. According to his *New Thesis on Japanese Style and Orthography*, he rejected *genbun itchi* because, "in the colloquial language of our country [. . .] the class relations of rich and poor, high and low, are attached to every phrase."[10] In other words, there were too many expressions having to do with social status in ordinary conversational speech and in the *genbun itchi* style that was modeled after it. Ryūkei writes, "Literary language works to the contrary, lacking the markings of class distinction." He defines literary language (*bungo*) in this case to mean "not *kanbun*, but the native literary language of Japan." Yet this should also be differentiated from the so-called pure Japanese (*wabun*) style. Ryūkei was referring, in essence, to a form of *bōdoku* style that favored Japanese (*kun*) readings even as it employed Chinese character compounds that were characteristic of *kanbun*. Ryūkei's claim that this "native literary language" lacked expressions of hierarchical social status is of course a perception that did not exactly accord with reality, but we must remember that this was before the standardization of -*de aru* sentence endings (which avoid mention of status distinctions and became the standard for later *genbun itchi* novels). Insofar as one lived in a world dominated by -*desu/-masu* sentence endings (which indicate an unequal relation between speaker and addressee), as did Ryūkei, it was difficult to overcome completely a status-based hierarchical sensibility. At any rate, Ryūkei's true intention was to devise a writing style that was free of class sensibilities in order to narrate the restoration of political democracy in ancient Thebes.

Moreover, Ryūkei culled and translated a variety of Western sources for this work, which he then presented as a "true historical record." Given the times, his was a highly logical style, rich with empirical evidence. Without the

---

9. Ryūkei's "Remarks on Usage" (*Hanrei*, reprinted in *MBZ* 15:4–5) introduces the punctuation and stylistic practices he will follow in the novel; it was necessary given the lack of standardization in these matters that existed in early Meiji.

10. One chapter from *New Thesis on Japanese Style and Orthography* is reprinted in Yamamoto Masahide, ed., *Kindai buntai keisei shiryō shūsei: hassei hen* (Tokyo: Ōfūsha, 1978), 290–308.

value judgment implicit in the notion of a "true historical record," a work written in a superficially colloquial style that was actually a compromise between
the *bōdoku* and *yomihon* styles could only end in failure, as was the case with
Suehiro Tetchō's *A Record of Twenty-three Years into the Future* (*Nijūsannen
miraiki*, 1886). Ryūkei had such a criterion, but once his mode of expression
had been initiated, the very process of writing with it gave birth to something
new, something that could not simply be explained under the category of "true
historical record."

Here is a particularly obvious example of this:

> Until this time, Pelopidas and Leona had hardly spoken to each other
> for several months. They were rarely left alone together, and their
> words had hardly exceeded a few rote politenesses, yet when Pelopidas
> now called out Leona's name so familiarly it was like beautiful mu-
> sic to her ears. Leona advanced toward the iron railing [that sepa-
> rated them in the courtyard]. Stopping still several feet behind the
> rail, she could only occasionally glance at Pelopidas, and did not dare
> to look him straight in the face, so she continued looking down. Pres-
> ently, Pelopidas thanked her for her favor of the previous night, and
> asked how she had come to know his true name. He would stop at
> nothing to repay his debt to her. Whatever thing, whatever deed she
> desired, he would devote his heart and soul to obtain, and while pro-
> claiming this he watched her, enraptured by the beauty of her face
> and figure, a beauty apart from this world, a beauty that would put to
> shame even the spring flowers and the autumn moon. He had never
> thought about it until now, he wondered, so why should she stop his
> heart on this of all days? Filled with sentiments of her goodness, a
> love was born in his heart, thus here he started to feel a love for her
> for the first time. (*MBZ* 15:37)

In this scene Pelopidas, who has escaped to Athens, is in hiding at the estate of
Lycius, an official. His social status and real name are known only to Lycius,
yet Lycius' daughter Leona is able to deduce them. When she learns of a secret
plan by the Evil Party of Thebes to assassinate Pelopidas, she sends urgent word
to him. Having only barely escaped the danger, Pelopidas expresses his gratitude to her in this scene.

As is clear in this excerpt, we must differentiate between a certain objective reality and the ways in which individual characters perceive that reality
as an object for their sensibilities. This was the standpoint from which Ryūkei
wrote. Under the *idée fixe* that held sway in fictional narratives before this,
once the author had described the beauty of a female character, then it was assumed that her beauty was equally visible to all of the other characters from
start to finish. This is because the act of describing her aesthetic value was at

the same time an act of establishing the moral value of that character. *Yomihon* and *ninjōbon* writers such as Takizawa Bakin (1767–1848) and Tamenaga Shunsui (1790–1843) composed their narratives with this expectation, and this tradition was carried over into the Meiji period. The author's sensibility was rendered into something absolute and compulsory. Under this convention, the beauty of the heroine would always at a single glance incite in the protagonist a feeling of good will toward her, just as the same beauty would always fill the villain with lust. No deviations were permitted: the villain would always be filled with a lust that would spur him into action. The prevalence in earlier fiction of scenes in which beautiful women repeatedly come within a hair's breadth of danger was entirely due to the compulsory force of the author's sensibility.

The role that Yano Ryūkei fulfilled in changing this was perhaps only minor. When Pelopidas has moved to the mansion of Lycius, Ryūkei introduces Leona as "a beauty apart from this world, nineteen years old at the time, with perfect figure and clever personality" (*MBZ* 15:30). The manners and customs of ancient Greece are described as "different from the customs of present-day Europe. Unless it was a time of a great rite, such as a funeral, women and men would not mix with each other; wives would remain in the house and would almost never speak to any man except if he were extremely close to the family" (*MBZ* 15:30). Ryūkei claims that the source for this was George W. Cox's *A General History of Greece* (1876). According to research by Maeda Ai, Lycius was an entirely fictional character, one that Ryūkei created by borrowing the name of a philosophy teacher known to have instructed Epaminondas (a friend of Pelopidas), so that the "true historical record" that Ryūkei took from Cox concerned only the depiction of Greek manners and customs. Thus we are left with the question of how and why Ryūkei fabricated this *ninjōbon*-style encounter between a handsome youth and a beautiful girl. From the perspective of readers who were accustomed to the *ninjōbon*, it might well seem that an "emotional bond ought to come to life in the chance encounter between such a beauteous couple" (*MBZ* 15:31). Yet until this point in the story, Pelopidas has been in no position to attend to such emotions: "Pelopidas was entirely concerned with the restoration of his country, and had no time to consider other things" (*MBZ* 15:31). One must wait until the moment that he thanks Leona for saving him before her beauty can become visible to his eyes, or rather, for him to develop an awareness of having seen it.

For something to become visible implies also that one becomes conscious of its visibility, just as the experience of a sensation elicits a self-reflective consciousness that seeks the reasons for having sensed it. Ryūkei's language is filled with hackneyed phrases and is far more simplistic and monotonous than that of Tōkai Sanshi, yet precisely because of this he was forced to consider in detail how to make each cliché into a necessary expression of some specific sensibility. The character of Leona, little more than a pretty doll at first, comes to life for the reader only at the moment she is internally apprehended through the sensibility of Pelopidas and becomes the object of his affection. Yet in the eyes of Mellon, whose simpleton nature does not allow him to probe the details of human emotion, Leona is never more than a pretty doll, nor does he suspect that she might attract the romantic attentions of his friend Pelopidas. Whereas in *Chance Encounters with Beautiful Women*, a character such as Yolanda is perceived in the same way by all of the other characters, abstracting away, as it were, the individuality of sensibility, in *An Illustrious Tale of Statesmanship* we have a work in which for the first time the various characters are brought to life by having their beauty and flaws be perceived and internally apprehended through the distinct sensibilities of the other characters.

Of course, the process of sensibility described above for Pelopidas regarding Leona was entirely fabricated by the author, Yano Ryūkei. Even if actual historical figures had experienced a similar process of sensibility—a likely occurrence—it is uncommon to find that process written down as a "true historical record." In fact, this depicted process of sensibility is the result of a new mode of expression that objectifies the sensibility of the author Ryūkei, a sensibility that left him no recourse but to imagine such a scene in his "true historical record." Ryūkei seems to have been fully aware of this point.

Until this time, the Japanese literary tradition had been bound by a hierarchical sensibility that had come to seem natural and by the absolute authority of the author, whose evaluative descriptions (the aesthetic and moral judgments contained in expressions that described an environment in adherence to the author's sensibility) functioned as a kind of a priori determination for the characters in the work. Both of these constraints, which had become thoroughly manneristic, were thrown off in this work. Yano Ryūkei consciously apprehended his own sensibility as it was manifested in his visual intentionality toward the various scenes in the novel, and he then created a mode of expression that objectified that sensibility as a bridge linking him to his readers.

To state it simply, it was a matter of living a shared interest with his readers. In *A New Thesis on Japanese Style and Orthography*, Ryūkei himself posited that the decisive factor in determining the quality of expression was discernment of "what the audience wishes in its heart." This was not at all the same as pandering to his readers' likes and dislikes. What he meant was that it was possible to transform his readers' hierarchical sensibility through a mode of expression that would increasingly clarify their self-apprehension of the sensibility through which they visually intended a given scene.

In its portrayal of the unfolding of a sensibility-driven visual intentionality that is immanent to each scene, Ryūkei's work is reminiscent of the non-person narrator in Futabatei's *Ukigumo*, but it aims higher and is qualitatively superior, because the narrator of *Ukigumo* has a tendency to be dragged along after the most vulgar proclivities of his readers.

There is another similarity between the two works. In *An Illustrious Tale of Statesmanship*, we find a narrative development that stretches from the time that Pelopidas first encounters Leona until he takes notice of his own love for her. Likewise, in Futabatei's *Ukigumo*, we have the depiction of the process through which Bunzō finally realizes the true nature of Osei, who the narrator has early on declared to the audience is "a shallow faddist by nature,"[11] a process that unfolds both externally through Osei's behavior and internally through the depiction of Bunzō's thoughts and emotions. The language of *Ukigumo* is vastly more dense and detailed than that of *An Illustrious Tale of Statesmanship*, yet in both cases we find the temporal unfolding of a process, from the moment an object is first seen by some character until the achievement by that character of a self-awareness of the implications of that object for him. When a narrative relates such an unfolding, both to the characters in the work and to its readers the events that occur all seem to arise out of a certain necessity, whereas in narratives that lack this, every event seems coincidental and random. In this sense, *An Illustrious Tale of Statesmanship* and *Ukigumo* belong to the same moment of literary development. Yet this begs the question of why later literature (following the tendency set by *Ukigumo*) would abandon the practice of placing its protagonists in specifically political situations and instead focus its gaze inward, on the internal workings of the mind and heart. What we are faced with here is the problem of the birth of "pure literature."

* * * * *

My interest in works such as *An Illustrious Tale of Statesmanship* and *Chance Encounters with Beautiful Women* is not simply a matter of seeing in them a necessary transitional stage on the way to the birth of pure literature. To adhere excessively to an I-sensibility and thus lose a sense of tension vis-à-vis one's own self is to lose sight of an important aspect of self-consciousness. It is to forget the possibility for transformation, be it of self-consciousness or of sensibility.

To quote once again from *Chance Encounters with Beautiful Women*, "As the twilight grew deeper [. . .] looking up, one could see the pine trees glistening, as if blossomed with ice." In this expression, the one who looks up is not the protagonist, Tōkai Sanshi. Though the protagonist does appear in this

---

11. Adapted from the translation in Marleigh Grayer Ryan, *Japan's First Modern Novel:* Ukigumo *of Futabatei Shimei* (New York and London: Columbia University Press, 1967), 209.

scene, it is the "self" of the author (i.e., the narrator split off from the author) that is objectified here, and the description of the setting here adheres to this perspective. This "self" is already an imaginary projection. It was mediated by the self-awareness of the position of the observing "self" that was first achieved in *kanbun fūzokushi*. The non-person narrator of *Ukigumo*, who embodied the gaze and speech of the common public, further clarified the fictional, projected nature of that self. At the time, no writer yet possessed a methodology for unfolding an expression directly out of his own position. Futabatei Shimei and Tsubouchi Shōyō gave much thought to this problem, eventually moving in the direction of an I-sensibility to rectify the projected fictionality of this "self." Yano Ryūkei meanwhile moved in the opposite direction of actively utilizing that projected fictionality, molding it, for example, into the narrator Inoue Seitarō in the wholly fabricated world of *Tale of the Floating Castle* (*Ukishiro monogatari*, 1890).

The *bōdoku*-style political novels of writers like Tōkai Sanshi and Yano Ryūkei aimed at transforming sensibilities and at achieving an imaginary projection of the "self." Accordingly, they possess an unshakable value as literature: among the various genres of Meiji literature, they alone sought to introduce the political situation and the idea of solidarity into the space of fictional narratives.

Chapter Three
The Captured "I":
Tsubouchi Shōyō and the Doctrine of Success

TRANSLATED BY LESLIE WINSTON

Kamei here turns his attention to journalistic criticism directed at political novels in the 1880s. Tokutomi Sohō and others railed against these works and the readers who devoured them for harboring a deluded understanding of politics and the world: individual worldly success, both in material and romantic terms, was mistakenly seen as constituting an appropriate political ambition. This criticism of both an infatuation with success and an excessively idealistic romanticism is also found in the writings of Tsubouchi Shōyō. Shōyō anticipated the critics' insistence on a "realistic" grasp of the world, and in his various works of criticism, translation, and fiction, he experimented with a method for achieving such a realism. In particular, Shōyō was concerned with how to conceal the author, avoiding intrusive editorial comments, by means of rendering his sensibility immanent to depicted scenes via the narrator, the imaginary "self" split off from the author. In his novel The Temper of Students in Our Times *depictions are unified through a single sensibility, that of the narrator (at the risk of overwhelming the sensibilities of the individual characters), so that descriptions of external objects and of interior states merge into a coherent whole. In this and other Meiji works that portray romances between students and young women they meet while away from home in the city, the rejection of idealism and the embrace of realism becomes an ethical issue: the selfish desire for success and love in the city is revealed as a refusal to grasp the reality of one's own hometown. The ethics of this literary realism are further developed in the later chapters of Futabatei Shimei's* Ukigumo, *where for the first time we find an ethical realism of the individual— that is, a mode of expression in which the gap between a character's own sensibility and his real situation drives him into a new, more self-reflexive form of consciousness.*

43

The writers and critics associated with the journal *Kokumin no tomo*, which began publication in 1887, launched an accurate—and therefore scathing—criticism aimed at the youth of their day.[1] It is possible to view this trend as anticipating the subsequent appearance of Futabatei Shimei's *Ukigumo*.

Imagine a frivolous but talented youth, clever at maneuvering about and skillful at ingratiating himself with senior officials and superiors. He is intoxicated by a fantasy self: if only he can capture the affections of the daughter of a powerful and wealthy family, he will be blessed with instant political success (*seikō*). We can also, of course, imagine this the other way around: that in his fantasy self, he believes himself to possess all the qualities of a great political leader, burning with the passion of solid-gold ideals inferior to none. Rationalizing his real-world conduct through this inner confidence, he blindly pursues vulgar material success.

No, his reality was perhaps even more miserable than that. An 1887 editorial in *Kokumin no tomo*, "Comments on the Boom in Political Novels," describes the then-popular political novel in the following terms:

> In most, we find nothing other than the plot from Rosei's dream in Kantan. Specifically: 'Here we have a poor student, who happens to come across a certain young lady from a wealthy family at such-and-such a hot spring, and they become enamored of one another. They endure a variety of difficulties, but finally overcome them and marry felicitously. With his wife's dowry the poor student becomes a man of means, and together the couple become active in politics. Soon he becomes the brilliant, famous leader of a People's Rights Party.' Of course, it isn't just Rosei; all the poor students cooped up in their second-floor boardinghouse rooms in Kanda wallow in this pleasant dream. That is why we should call these works "The Dream Tales of Poor Students."[2]

1. *Kokumin no tomo* (Friend of the Nation; its title was adapted from the American journal *The Nation*), published from 1887–98, was one of the most influential intellectual and literary journals of the Meiji period. Edited by Tokutomi Sohō (1863–1957) and published by Minyūsha, it tended (particularly in the later years of its existence) to adopt a more nationalist stance in reaction to the Westernizing trends that had dominated the first decades of Meiji. Many important literary works were first published in its pages.
2. Tokutomi Sohō, "Comments on the Boom in Political Novels" ("Kinrai ryūkō no seiji shōsetsu o hyōsu"), *Kokumin no tomo*, no. 6 (July 1887): 7–15. This passage appears on 11. Rosei is a character from Chinese and Japanese classical literature, a poor student who dreams of glory while sleeping on a magical pillow, only to awaken again to his impoverished reality. Kanda is a neighborhood in Tokyo that is home to several universities.

Tokutomi Sohō authored this editorial, probably with a work like Suehiro Tetchō's *Plum Blossoms in the Snow* (*Setchūbai*, 1886)[3] in mind, but he was not the only one to write this kind of scathing criticism. We can detect the same critical consciousness in other *Kokumin no tomo* articles, including the unsigned reviews of Suehiro Tetchō's *Song Thrushes Among the Flowers* (*Kakanō*, 1887)[4] and of Oda Junichirō's *Gentlemen of Osaka* (*Ōsaka shinshi*, 1887).[5] Evidence that this criticism was not entirely off the mark can be seen in such subsequent works as Sudō Nansui's *Golden Oriole Chicks* (*Hina kōri*, 1889) and Okamoto Jun's *Dreams in the Wake of the Peace Preservation Law* (*Hoanjōrei gojitsu no yume*, 1889), narratives that demonstrated no scruples about continuing to wallow in the "pleasant dream" of success (including the dream of sexual gratification), as if they were deliberately thumbing their nose at Sohō's criticism.

It was a situation in which political aspirations were linked up to the dream of being loved by a beautiful woman and thereby transformed into what Sohō called a "delusion" (*mōsō*) that could only satisfy selfish individual desires of a worldly and vulgar nature. A mood of stagnant corruption had settled over the popular political parties, as symbolized by the following imaginary dialogue from a *Kokumin no tomo* editorial: "Give it up! Give it up! What's the point in debating the national Diet? It's old hat. [The inauguration of the Diet] has been set for 1890. Whether we stand up and wait for it, or lie down and wait for it, makes no difference: it will come in 1890, all the same."[6] For the political novel, written and read as compensation for this apathetic stagnation, only the dream of being loved by a renowned, wealthy man's daughter could provide a workable plot. I believe that one of the keys to unlocking the true essence of Japan's modern literature lies hidden in these circumstances. Seeking it is one of my objectives in this chapter, but, of course, Sohō in his criticism of the current situation didn't have the latitude to mull leisurely over a literary-theory koan. He was driven forward by his indignation at the state into which the People's Rights movement activists had fallen: "Every time we analyze the minds of self-styled politicians, we cannot but be surprised at how little thought they

---

3. Together with Yano Ryūkei and Tōkai Sanshi, discussed in chapter two, Suehiro Tetchō (1849–96) was one of the most popular authors of political novels. *Plum Blossoms in the Snow* is his most famous work.
4. Unsigned book review, "Kakanō," *Kokumin no tomo*, no. 4 (May 1887): 42–43.
5. Unsigned book review, "Ōsaka shinshi," *Kokumin no tomo*, no. 5 (June 1887): 41.
6. Unsigned editorial, "What We Hope from Opposition Politicians" ("Zaiya no shinshi no nozomu tokoro ari"), *Kokumin no tomo*, no. 3 (April 1887): 1–7. This passage of imaginary dialogue appears on 2.

have of the people."[7] Sohō attacked their political aspirations, calling them a "delusion" that had decayed into a simple lust for power, with no thought of the people. It became a motif in his writing, as he couldn't but bitterly censure the present state of Meiji youth, intoxicated by dreams of political "success."

This "delusion" had to be destroyed. If they were stripped of these deluded, self-idealizing political aspirations, then the majority of protagonists in political novels would be revealed as belonging to the scheming, Honda Noboru-type of character later found in *Ukigumo*. Sohō anticipated the type in a *Kokumin no tomo* editorial: "He has a little cleverness and pluck, is good in his studies and has practical ability, is liked by the ladies, and knows how to curry favor with others" ("Boom," 14). I am not arguing here that Sohō directly influenced Futabatei. Rather, my point is that the Honda Noboru-type had already been sketched in by Sohō.[8] Moreover, Sohō also provides a foreshadowing of the protagonist of *Ukigumo*, Utsumi Bunzō, a youth who is deprived of even the possibility of Honda-like worldly success, who is "cooped up" in his "second-floor" room and compelled to wage a bitter struggle with his own "delusion."

Around the time the first volume of *Ukigumo* was published, Nakae Chōmin wrote in *Kokumin no tomo* to urge young men to abandon politics.[9] There was a strong tendency, particularly among the sons of ex-samurai families, to believe that achieving something in the world of politics was the most valuable goal one could achieve in life. Therefore, many youths participated in political movements or plunged themselves into officialdom. Sohō saw this, too, writing that they "see the government as a panacea and think that if only the government were as they liked, then everything else in the world would be as they liked [. . .] That is why they fail so terribly. Nothing in the world is more frightening than such a delusion" ("New Japanese Youth," 10). Chōmin likewise could not help feeling concerned at this state of affairs. As long as the youth of Japan were caught up in this sort of "deluded notion," they were in danger of wasting their lives and losing sight of their individual true natures. Not only that, if they looked at the actual conditions of Japan in the international environment, they would realize that "at present, the degree of our civilization is such that our military force is weak, and we cannot protect ourselves

---

7. Unsigned editorial, "New Japanese Youth and New Japanese Politics (4)" ("Shin Nihon no seinen oyobi shin Nihon no seiji [4]"), *Kokumin no tomo*, no. 9 (October 1887): 9–16. This passage appears on 10.

8. See Kamei's explanation of the term sketching, borrowed from the dialectical phenomenology of Trän Dúc Tháo, in his introduction to this translation.

9. "Deluded Notions in the Minds of Youth" ("Seinenhai nōzui chū no mōnen"), *Kokumin no tomo*, no. 12 (November 18, 1887): 26–27. Nakae Chōmin (1847–1901) was an important writer and political activist in the People's Rights movement.

from foreign invasion. But in order to strengthen our military force, we must first create economic wealth" ("Deluded Notions," 26–27). They must engage in more practical business and trade, not politics, in order to make this possible. Therefore, Chōmin concluded, "I cannot help but want you to wake up one morning and reject these deluded notions and to use your brains to observe the real state of things" ("Deluded Notions," 26).

Seen in the context of its day, Chōmin's statement includes an implicit critique of Tōkai Sanshi's *Chance Encounters with Beautiful Women*. As we saw in the previous chapter, Tōkai Sanshi, who had pursued studies in the practical area of finance in America—and perhaps precisely because of that background—developed a self-consciousness that was closely linked to the political world, the impetus coming from his sentiments as a former retainer of the Aizu domain (as "a child of the true Japan"). Chōmin dissected this sort of political ambition (and its concomitant fantasy self) and advocated in its place the need for a practical mode of being, in which each person's life goals were established on the basis of a firm grasp of the nation's real circumstances.

But when the political system became the primary intentional object in the minds of Meiji youths, it made them lose sight of reality, both their own and that of the people, and gave rise instead to counterproductive "deluded notions" and "self-delusions" about political success. Sohō, Chōmin, and others tried to reinvert this inversion. As if in concert with their efforts, Futabatei Shimei dared to open up a course that stuck steadfastly to the real private situation, the I-situation faced by contemporary youths. In that sense, the appearance of *Ukigumo* came neither too early nor too late: it was a work written precisely in sync with the needs of its time.

* * * * *

When we try to extract from the various mid-Meiji genres, including both social commentary and literature, the type of visual intentionality they share in common, what becomes apparent is an ideal that defines this period (*jidai rinen*): the insistence on adhering to reality. This ideal seems at times to have mustered an irresistible, compelling force on writers of this generation.

For instance, let us examine an editorial serialized in *Jogaku zasshi*, "On the Novel" (*Shōsetsu ron*, 1887), probably written by Iwamoto Yoshiharu.[10]

---

10. *Jogaku zasshi* (Magazine of Women's Education), published 1885–1904, was one of the most important intellectual journals in Meiji Japan. Founded and edited by Iwamoto Yoshiharu (1863–1942), the magazine was aimed primarily at female students in Christian mission schools, though its readership extended widely across mid-Meiji intellectual circles. In literary history, the magazine is closely associated with the Romantic school of writers of the 1890s, including Kitamura Tōkoku and Shimazaki Tōson. The editorial "On the Novel" is reprinted in *MBZ* 32:3–7.

Judging from the editorialist's tone in describing "the idle gossip at a failing butcher shop or hot spring resort that form the backbone of *The Temper of Students in Our Times*, or the frivolous, impudent male and female protagonists in *Ukigumo*" (*MBZ* 32:4), we can surmise that he personally could never approve of a novel of worldly passions, one devoted to the portrayal of personal emotions even when they were vulgar and insincere. Still, when he considers the matter from the perspective of the development of modern fiction, he argues that "Generally speaking, when we reflect upon the history of scholarship, we see that at first delusional philosophy was practiced, only after which empirical science arose" (*MBZ* 32:4); likewise, "among novelists, those who steadily cultivate their talent will with effort leave their delusions behind, and single-mindedly devote themselves to recording just as it is the reality that exists everywhere in the world" (*MBZ* 32:5). In this respect, he grudgingly acknowledges that "among the fiction published in recent years, works such as *The Temper of Students in Our Times*, [Shōyō's] *The Newly Polished Mirror of Marriage* [*Imotose kagami*, 1886] and *Ukigumo* belong to the category of the so-called pure novel and are notable works that approach the first rank" (*MBZ* 32:6). By "delusion" (*mōsō*) here, he means a fictional world that "the writer contrives as his stage, all within the narrow confines of his mind" (*MBZ* 32:5), a world peopled by the work's characters, over whom the writer adopts a stance of absolute power. His view of the novel, which rejects this stance, is clearly a simplified version, or in a certain sense, a misunderstanding of the view Shōyō expounded in *The Essence of the Novel* (*Shōsetsu shinzui*, 1885–86). It is easy to sympathize with the plight of this editorialist, who had to suppress his feelings of "loathing [. . .] to the extent of disgust" (*MBZ* 32:6) in order to acknowledge the importance of these works; he too apparently had no alternative but to conform to the period's reigning ideal of adhering to "reality just as it is" (*jissai no ari no mama*). The nature of his misunderstanding of *Essence of the Novel* hints that his praise for these works was offered only grudgingly.

If only he had stuck more tenaciously to his feelings of "loathing" and "disgust"! By tenaciously, I do not mean that he should have rendered these feelings into an absolute. Rather, if he had stuck tenaciously to his feeling of "loathing," which is mainly directed at Shōyō's *The Temper of Students in Our Times* (*Tōsei shosei no katagi*, 1885–86), and if he had carried out a thorough analysis of the mode of expression in that work, he would have reached a moment of self-reflection, in which he would have had to reflect on the legitimacy of his own sensibility. But to evaluate the works of this period, his own period, without employing this sort of procedure was to risk producing, both in relation to the works and to other readers, only insincere conclusions.

If he had persevered with this kind of tenacity, he perhaps would have encountered a new realization. We have already examined a technique found in *Chance Encounters with Beautiful Women*: while reconstructing a real event that one has experienced, one projects an ideal self-image, the image of what one wanted to be at that time and of what one still wants to be in the present. Whether they were conscious of it or not, the authors of the so-called futuristic novel inherited this mode of writing, including Suehiro Tetchō in *Plum Blossoms in the Snow* and Sudō Nansui in *The Local Self-Government* (*Ryokusadan*, 1886). The futuristic novel was a genre that imaginatively depicted the imminent victory of the People's Rights movement, symbolized by the impending inauguration of a national Diet. In order to depict this outcome as necessary and inevitable, these authors observed the actual state of Japan with a realistic eye and then produced a dramatic depiction of the future events that could be expected to arise inevitably from that state. They projected their ideal self-image onto the protagonist, who emerges as the final victor. Unfortunately, in order to render the protagonist's political success into a certainty, they had to arrange astonishingly propitious conditions around that protagonist: he had to be a handsome man of eloquent speech and unshakable political convictions, accompanied by a beauty who loved him and lent him her father's fame and fortune, and so on. Here we see the intellectual limitation of these authors. The unashamed stereotyping of character types in these works and the vulgar passions and ideas shared by their readers and authors were unsparingly exposed by Sohō in his criticism. Moving in tandem with this critique, Tsubouchi Shōyō also made his own efforts to slough off and bury this projected fantasy self that had become standard practice in the political novel. We see an example of this in *The Temper of Students in Our Times*, when Shōyō has the character Komachida criticize Shōyō's own translation-adaptation of Bulwer-Lytton's *Rienzi* (*Gaisei shiden*, 1884). Viewed in terms of the history of modes of expression, this was an inevitable development. However, the "reality" that Shōyō claimed to uncover was itself distorted; it too was at least partially imaginary, a projection of "reality" that from start to finish included nothing more than the vulgar passions that arise from ordinary everyday human relationships.

The "loathing" and "disgust" felt by the *Jogaku zasshi* editorialist were likely a manifestation of the discord registered by his sensibility in the face of this distortion. Moreover, when we read the following passage from the *Jogaku zasshi* editorial, keeping in mind the technique of the non-person narrator found both in Shōyō's *Newly Polished Mirror of Marriage* and Futabatei's *Ukigumo*, we find that the editorialist has in fact stumbled onto the true nature of the mode of expression in these works.

They describe what passes through the mind over the course of pro-
saic journeys and unexceptional events, discerning in great detail the
core of human feelings. They reveal the unshed tears and unexpressed
resentment, as if the character's heart were clearly reflected in a mirror. [. . .] I feel as though I have entered into the small world of the
novel to stand next to the other characters, quietly observing their
movements. (*MBZ* 32:5)

The method by which the "I" of this reader perceived the fictional world of
these novels was to assume the point of view of the author, which had been
rendered immanent to that world. I have already discussed how in *Ukigumo* the
author's doubled "self" (*jiko*) is split off and situated within the world of the
novel in the form of a non-person narrator. As Miura Tsutomu notes, when we
express something verbally, we undergo a doubling, as we are split between the
"I" who is actually speaking and the "self" who appears before us in the imaginary world that our expression depicts.[11] What I call the "self" of the author
refers to the latter case, which I frequently also call the "non-person narrator."
As we have already seen in the example of *Ukigumo*, he exists as a latent "self"
within the fictional scene, invisible to the other characters, yet we also see in
his expressions a strong degree of self-exhibitionism in such aspects as his tone
of voice and in his self-awareness of his own positionality. The reader's experience of feeling "as though I have entered into the small world of the novel"
amounts to perceiving the fictional world of the novel through (and hence con-
senting to) the sensibility of the author's "self" as it is objectified in that world.
This was the central problem of expression in this period.

Let us examine the following passage from Shōyō's translation of Edward Bulwer-Lytton's *Rienzi: The Last of the Roman Tribunes*.

In this way, Princess Nina turned the pages of Petrarch's odes, her
eyes turned downward. Reciting them silently, she rested her eyes
not on the page. Whenever the boughs on the trees stirred in the
evening breeze, she glanced at one corner of the garden. Across from
her lay an ancient pond. When the moon appeared from between
clouds, starlight sparkled in reflection on its surface, like the scatter-
ing of a myriad fireflies. From the half-neglected garden, one could
draw a look of satisfaction. There was, after all, something charming
in the image of the grapevines draping down, dancing in the moonlight. The night deepened. The scene was still and the wind died down;
beauty reigned as far as the eye could see; a most beautiful nightscape,
but Princess Nina thought not of gazing at its beauty. She single-

11. See the discussion of Miura Tsutomu in Kamei's "Introduction" to this translation.

mindedly turned her gaze only toward the other side of the garden, as
if expecting someone, toward the wall where trees stood densely
massed together. The boughs on those trees stirred gently, and now
from the copse emerged, slowly and cautiously, a solitary figure. It
stealthily approached the window where Princess Nina was reading,
and in a low voice breathed "Is it going well, Nina?"[12]

Shōyō appears to have been deeply struck by this scene. In the lengthy preface
to his translation of the novel (which in many ways foreshadows his later, more
famous *Essence of the Novel*), he criticizes the mode of expression used to depict human passions by such Edo-period authors as Takizawa Bakin and
Tamenaga Shunsui, and then concludes: "When we read the scene in which Nina
sees Rienzi in chapter seven, we see the biggest difference between Eastern and
Western authors of novels. It seems mysterious that such a superior, intrepid
man would have such an effeminate heart, but that is truly human nature. When
reading this, the reader should sense an inexpressible delicacy" (*TSS* 14:457–
58). Here, Rienzi steals into Princess Nina's chamber at night, reversing the
situation from a famous episode in Bakin's *The Story of Eight Virtuous Heroes*
(*Nansō satomi hakkenden*, 1814–41), where the beautiful Hamaji calls upon the
hero Shino in his bedchamber.[13] Subsequently, Rienzi laments the difficulty of
his efforts to overthrow aristocratic oppression, but is encouraged by Nina and
regains his valor. Somehow, from this unremarkable scene, Shōyō received a
deep and lasting impression, as the comment above shows. His goal in translat-

---

12. Tsubouchi Shōyō, *Shōyō senshū* (hereafter abbreviated *TSS*) (Tokyo: Daiichi Shobō, 1977–
78), 14:573–74. Bulwer-Lytton's original English version of this passage: "But it was not
those ingenious and elaborate conceits in which Petrarch, great Poet though he be, has so
often mistaken pedantry for passion, that absorbed at that moment the attention of the beautiful Nina. Her eyes rested not on the page, but on the garden that stretched below the case-
ment. Over the old fruit-trees and hanging vines fell the moonshine; and in the centre of the
green but half-neglected sward, the waters of a small and circular fountain, whose perfect
proportions spoke of days long past, played and sparkled in the starlight. The scene was still
and beautiful; but neither of its stillness nor its beauty thought Nina: towards one, the gloomiest
and most rugged spot in the whole garden, turned her gaze; there, the trees stood densely
massed together, and shut from view the low but heavy wall which encircled the mansion of
Raselli. The boughs on those trees stirred gently, but Nina saw them wave; and now from the
copse emerged, slowly and cautiously, a solitary figure, whose shadow threw itself, long and
dark, over the sward. It approached the window, and a low voice breathed Nina's name."
Edward Bulwer Lytton, *Rienzi: The Last of the Roman Tribunes* (London: George Routledge
and Sons, 1903), 95–96.
13. While no complete English translation of *Hakkenden* exists, an abbreviated translation of the
Hamaji-Shino episode can be found in Donald Keene, ed., *Anthology of Japanese Literature,
from the Earliest Era to the Mid–Nineteenth Century* (New York: Grove Press, 1955), 423–
28.

ing this work likely was to promote popular rights, a purpose he shared with political novels such as Yano Ryūkei's *Inspiring Instances of Statesmanship*. But Shōyō's work also harbored a critique of the tendency to produce stereo-typically heroic protagonists that characterized the contemporary political novel.

That he was so deeply impressed by Bulwer-Lytton's mode of expression and felt that it touched on the reality of human emotion shows how immature the mode of expression in early Meiji fiction was. Yet at the same time, it also demonstrates the shallowness of Shōyō's understanding of Japan's own traditional fictional narratives. However, insofar as this scene had moved him, he was driven to deepen his understanding of its mode of expression by analyzing it in detail. In *Essence of the Novel*, Shōyō once again takes up this scene from *Rienzi*. He argues that there are two methods for describing a character's nature, positive and negative. "The positive method [. . .], favored by Western novelists, acquaints the reader from the beginning with a character's disposition by describing it openly in passages of narrative description [*ji no bun*],"[14] he explains. Of course, passages of narrative description must do more than simply describe the dispositions of the various characters. "To describe only the attitudes of characters, to the exclusion of inanimate objects, is like drawing an ascending dragon without clouds" (*Essence*, 101). Accordingly, a character and his or her environment must be expressed in a form that is unified through a single sensibility. Moreover,

> Unlike other ordinary forms of writing, the novel requires more than a frank description of the author's own thoughts and feelings. *Its duty is to hide those as well as it can so that they do not show*, to portray vividly and with animation human nature as it exists in other people in its infinite variety. (*Essence*, 99; emphasis added)

To adopt an objective attitude meant to conceal oneself within one's expressions. Shōyō here clearly identified the essential problem.

Precisely speaking, the description of scenery in the passage from Shōyō's translation introduced above, the passage that extends from "Across from her lay an ancient pond" through "a most beautiful nightscape," are not necessarily expressions that adhere to the sensibility of Princess Nina. It begins by adopting the perspective of Nina as "she glanced at one corner of the garden," but the description of the garden's charm and elegance belongs to the

---

14. Translation adapted from Tsubouchi Shōyō, *The Essence of the Novel*, trans. Nanette Twine, *Occasional Papers: Department of Japanese, University of Queensland*, no. 11 (Brisbane, Australia: Department of Japanese, University of Queensland, 1981), 101.

"self" of the author objectified within this scene, that is, to the gaze of the narrator who is immanent to the scene. Then, the expression "Princess Nina thought not of gazing at its beauty" causes the reader to imagine the figure of Princess Nina, whereupon we once again return to gazing from her position: "She single-mindedly turned her gaze only toward the other side of the garden. . . ." The narrator depicts the appearance of the garden, even though it does not interest the novel's character, who is engrossed in other matters. However, the narrator's perspective is carefully manipulated so as not to create any sense of discrepancy that might seem to contradict the character's viewpoint. Here the authorial duty to "hide" oneself, which Shōyō insisted upon, is realized almost perfectly, insofar as was possible at this stage.

In this way, the concealment of the author was accomplished, and the sensibility of the characters in the work and the narrative description of their environment were unified in a seemingly unforced manner. The reader now could live the fictional world of the novel in adherence to the sensibilities of the characters in the work. At this time, to borrow the words of the *Jogaku zasshi* editorialist, it became possible for readers to savor the experience of seeming to touch "reality just as it is."

But what mode of authorial concealment did Shōyō employ in his own novels? The following is a scene from his *Temper of Students in Our Times*:

> The crescent moon, like the eyebrow of a beautiful woman, has risen in the western sky. It has already become dark, so the autumn wind feels bitterly cold. This is part of the city, but it is not a flourishing quarter, and few people come walking by at night. One can only hear the clatter of the rickshaw rolling by from time to time. Who is living in this house with the tasteful lattice door? There are dark wooden fences around here, and over there, the figure of pine tree branches draped over the fence is very fine. The one stone lantern standing far over there with the twining ivy is lovely. The chirping of the insects from within the grass sounds wistful. The small tatami room beyond the garden must be the master's room. It must be about six tatami mats wide. The light is unfortunately faint and soft, but the silhouette on the shōji screen seems to be that of a young man and woman. If Sei Shōnagon had seen it, she would have added it to her list of "Unpleasant Things." The woman seems uncomfortable. She puts her slender hand to her forehead, and her loosened hair falls hanging in her face, so even the silhouette tells of her emaciated condition. (*MBZ* 16:122)

The mode of expression in this scene of a clandestine meeting between a young man and woman does not of course adhere to the standpoint of any of the characters in the novel. This does not mean, however, that we find here a diffused, arbitrary description registered through an omniscient gaze, the work of an author who has not yet clearly grasped the relative independence of his projected "self." Rather, we are given here a description of the surroundings that could only have been attained through the senses of a person standing in a specific position within the scene. In that sense, the immanent narrator in this scene is saddled with self-limitations quite similar to those of the non-person narrator in *Ukigumo*. Immanent within the scene yet invisible, this perspectival character takes up a specific position within the garden and views the home with the lattice door. But he continually throws in superfluous comments: the home is "tasteful," Sei Shōnagon would have found the silhouettes "unpleasant," etc. This is a sensibility that bears no relation of necessity to the characters about to appear in the scene, Komachida and the geisha Tanoji. Rather, the mode of expression here is driven by an apparent need to stir up the reader's curiosity toward the scene and thereby to create a shared interest between narrator and reader.

The author Shōyō "hides" here by projecting himself in the form of this immanent yet invisible narrator, taking up the position of a reader who gazes at this scene with an interest that arises at least partly from prurient envy. It is a mode of expression quite different from that in his translation of *Rienzi*, but it was one that he was bound to arrive at, whether via the *kanbun fūzokushi* style of Narushima Ryūhoku and Hattori Bushō or the comic *gesaku* style of Shikitei Samba's *Up-to-date Bathhouse* (*Ukiyoburo*, 1809–13) and Ryūtei Rijō's *Eight Laughing People* (*Hanagoyomi hasshōjin*, written 1820, published 1848). In that sense, Shōyō after his own fashion devised a writing style capable of touching on the reality of everyday customs and human passions, a clear advance over the techniques of his predecessors. However, when he portrays other characters through the eyes and ears of this narrator, there is always the danger that those characters' individual sensibilities will be overlaid and permeated by that of the narrator, thereby reducing whatever lofty spiritual qualities they might possess to the base level of his prurient, vulgar interests. Here lay the chief weakness of this method. It is for this reason that we can say that the *Jogaku zasshi* editorialist was surprisingly accurate in his criticism; his feeling of "loathing" was not without justification.

In another passage from *Temper of Students in Our Times*, we find Shōyō once again returning to analyze *Rienzi*, this time through the mouthpiece of one of his characters:

> You suspect without reason and imagine that I'm thinking only about 'that,' but my mind is in an entirely different place. Though I am nothing special, I have aspired in my heart for years to one aim in life and promised myself *to be something*, so I am not about to mistake the direction of my entire life just for a woman. However, sad to say,

because I am so idealistic, I sometimes give rise to strange delusions, *fallaciously* applying Western ideas to Japanese society. Therefore, I make blunders. But I'm not the only one, the whole of Japan does likewise—including you. Just now you cited the case of Rienzi, but why should that become our *example* for conduct in life? Having the ambition of restoring his enfeebled country, it is only when he is emboldened by a beautiful woman that he finally accomplishes his purpose. Isn't he the weakest of them all? Lytton was talented enough to see through the mysteries of human passions, but that doesn't make Rienzi's example any more praiseworthy. (*MBZ* 16:118–19; italicized words are given in English in the original, followed by parenthetical translations in Japanese)

This is a part of Komachida's answer to his friend, Kurase, who has drawn on an example from Shōyō's translation of *Rienzi* in his effort to convince Komachida not to abandon his love for Tanoji. As previously, Shōyō maintains here that Bulwer-Lytton has touched on the reality of human passions. But we also see here an indication of an important change in Shōyō's thinking: now, he rejects as a "delusion" the idea that the love depicted in Bulwer-Lytton's story can be directly applied to Japanese reality.

Just before this passage, Komachida engages in a moment of critical self-reflection over his own yearning after an "idealistic love," his "unreasonable conduct, pursuing out of envy the hackneyed dream of a chance encounter between a talented youth and a beautiful woman" (*MBZ* 16:115). When he subsequently encounters Kurase, their conversation turns to their fellow students who have entirely lost their "strong will," and they discuss the affected heroic pose of their friends who have joined various political parties (*MBZ* 16:117). The author goes out of his way to include a commentary explaining the "idealism" that Komachida speaks about: "It is the habit of trying to put into practice in reality that which is unlikely ever to take place in the world; the Frenchman Victor Hugo's views on political affairs are very much idealism" (*MBZ* 16:119). Given this context, it goes without saying that the "delusion" Komachida attacks here includes the fantasy self that characterized the contemporary political novel. What we encounter here is the distress of a student who awakens from this delusion and begins to confront the reality of Meiji Japan. In its having grasped this, this scene helps pave the way for Tokutomi Sohō's subsequent critique of the political novel. Hence, the work in fact contains a form of social criticism, but this seems to have eluded the grasp of the *Jogaku zasshi* editorialist.

* * * * *

Here I would like to call attention to one more issue. For the youth of that time, it seems, romantic love required a particular supplementary condition. The geisha Tanoji was raised as Komachida's adopted sister.[15] Osei from *Ukigumo* is Bunzō's cousin, almost his sister, since they were raised together by his Aunt Omasa. It is precisely because of the unspoken assumption that they will marry in the future that Bunzō assumes she should be his sweetheart.

In short, what we find in these cases is a lover who is like a sister. The influence of Niwa (Oda) Junichirō's *Springtime Tale of Blossoms and Willows* (*Karyū shunwa*, 1878), a translation of Bulwer-Lytton's *Ernest Maltravers*, is probably responsible for the prevalence of this pattern. Shōyō's *Newly Polished Mirror of Marriage* was clearly conceived as an antithesis to this work, and it includes social criticism reminiscent of Komachida's complaint about those who engage in "*fallaciously* applying Western ideas to Japanese society." Shōyō's writing a novel at least partly in order to criticize it demonstrates the power of the influence exerted by *Springtime Tale of Blossoms and Willows*.

Yet, viewed from a different angle, perhaps *Newly Polished Mirror of Marriage*'s tragic conclusion was meant as a warning against falling in love with a woman whom one first met only after migrating to the city.[16] Perhaps the supplementary condition we noted in *Temper of Students in Our Times* and *Ukigumo* was also born from a consciousness that wanted to distance itself from that sort of love. In fact, in the above scene of the clandestine meeting from *Temper of Students in Our Times*, Tanoji herself refers to "the story of Wakashika Yoshie that was splashed all over the tabloid newspapers" (*MBZ* 16:124) when she avows the sincerity of her feelings to Komachida. According to the various versions of this story[17] that were published around 1882–83, the geisha Wakashika (Asao Yoshie) was from Miyazaki in the Hyūga region. She fell in love with

---

15. Tanoji was born into a respectable family yet was lost as an infant when her mother is killed in the battle of Ueno at the dawn of the Meiji Restoration. Her real identity unknown, she is subsequently adopted by Komachida's father, yet becomes a geisha when her adopted family's fortunes decline. Her adopted brother Komachida falls in love with her, an affair that brings him into disrepute, but all ends happily when Tanoji's true identity is revealed at the end of the novel. No English translation of the novel has been published, but a detailed summary can be found in Marleigh Grayer Ryan, *The Development of Realism in the Fiction of Tsubouchi Shōyō* (Seattle: University of Washington Press, 1975), 30–55.

16. The novel tells the tale of the unhappy marriage between Tatsuzō, an educated bureaucrat of high social standing, and Otsuji, the illiterate daughter of a poor merchant family. Tatsuzō, after reading *Ernest Maltravers*, resolves that he too, like the hero of that novel, can educate and cultivate his socially inferior lover into a proper wife. But the marriage turns sour, as Tatsuzō comes to despise his wife. He divorces her, and at the novel's conclusion we learn that she has drowned herself. No English translation has been published, but a detailed summary can be found in Ryan, *Development of Realism*, 56–86.

17. These include *The Career of Asao Yoshie* (*Asao Yoshie no rireki*), ed. Fukugawa Kairai (attributed) (1882), reprinted in *MBZ* 2:282–353; and *The True Contrast between Asao and Iwakiri* (*Asao Iwakiri makoto kurabe*), ed. Matsutei Kakusen (1883).

Iwakiri, a young local official, and they exchanged vows of eternal love. But before long, Iwakiri left to pursue his studies in Tokyo, leaving behind Wakashika, who faced increasing hardships. After many wretched experiences, she achieved a happy ending: she was brought into Iwakiri's household as his concubine. The published versions are obviously embellished, but they seem to be based on a true story. We can discern part of the character of this age in the way these works seriously promote as up-to-date the practice of having a man's legal wife and his concubine live under the same roof, rather than setting up a separate household for the concubine. This is precisely what Kurase encourages Komachida to do, to bring Tanoji into his household as a concubine. To hope to become Komachida's lawful wife may have been beyond Tanoji's station in life, yet her unrestrained idealism causes her to pursue this dream. But Komachida, who rejects the unrealistic idealism touched off in Japan by Western thought, cannot accept this. Rather, he seeks in her a sister. *Ukigumo*'s Bunzō, too, after his ordeal of jealousy toward Honda, finally adopts the attitude of a brother toward Osei.

As a literary theme, the love affairs of students away from home pursuing their studies have produced (and continue to produce) a great many works: think of *Chance Encounters with Beautiful Women*, Mori Ōgai's "Maihime" (1890), and Natsume Sōseki's *Sanshirō* (1908). Setting aside the political novels that Sohō attacked for their unrealistic linking of romantic love with political success, what we find in many of these works are cautionary or even punitive climaxes that seem to advise against this sort of love affair. This tendency is particularly pronounced in works from the late 1880s. Why was the combination of romantic love and success so difficult to countenance? When we look at the problem in this way, Kikutei Kōsui's (1855–1942) *Diary of Life's Journey* (*Sero nikki*, 1884) comes to mind as a work that straddles these two series. What we find at work here is a taboo against forgetting the reality of one's hometown.

The protagonist of *Diary of Life's Journey* is Hisamatsu Kikuo, a schoolteacher "not yet twenty-years-old" (*MBZ* 2:355) who falls in love with his student Matsue Take. Yasui Sakuta, the son of a local influential family, makes illicit advances toward Take and schemes to have Kikuo transferred to a remote school. Moreover, because of her stepmother's calculations, Take must marry a wealthy relative who is a hard man "already more than thirty years old, with a dark face and flat nose [. . .] as well as a naturally stubborn personality" (*MBZ* 2:368). Kikuo learns of this and, encouraged by Samuel Smiles' *Self-Help* (translated by Nakamura Keiu in 1870 as *Saikoku risshi hen*), rouses himself to action. He leaves for Osaka, where he launches into a new course of study. At this point, the narrative divides into two. Take, now the wife of her vulgar and arrogant relative, is unjustly suspected by her husband due to another trick of

Sakuta's, and because she can no longer endure this ill treatment, she rushes back to her parents' home. There too, though, she endures cruel treatment from her stepmother. She finally reaches her wits' end and tries to drown herself, only to be rescued by a passerby. Kikuo in Osaka, of course, does not know of Take's plight. Or rather, because it would be immoral to continue to love a woman who has married another, he has abandoned all thought of Take since leaving his hometown. He works very hard at his studies and wins the affections of the daughter of Akita Yutaka, a wealthy businessman. Akita favors Kikuo with his friendship as well, and Kikuo is brought into their household as a tutor. In short, Kikuo seems bound to win both the beautiful woman and "success."

But the author does not grant Kikuo such good fortune. When Akita's daughter sneaks into his bedroom, Kikuo scolds her for it and resists the temptation. Then, when word arrives that his own father is on his deathbed, Kikuo leaves the Akita family and returns to his hometown. Following the funeral, when he is visiting the house of a friend from his student days, he unexpectedly meets Take there. In addition, Take's stepmother explains to the already startled Kikuo an even more startling state of affairs: she had deliberately split the two and forced Take to marry a relative because the two were still too young and because she wanted to shield Take from Sakuta's threats; therefore, Take's marriage was a marriage in name only. All along, Take's stepmother says, "I thought that the best way was to have Take wait for the day you, Kikuo, made a success of yourself and returned to your hometown" (*MZB* 2:394).

Clearly Kikutei Kōsui borrowed the foundation for his novel from the translated *Ernest Maltravers*. But he seems not to have recognized that the romantic career narrated in *Ernest Maltravers* signified a sentimental education, a Bildungsroman. Maltravers, who had to part reluctantly from Alice, goes on to experience a long series of romantic attachments, all the while holding fast to his love for Alice—he is able to pursue an eventful romantic career with no consciousness of having betrayed her. Alice too never forgets Maltravers, even after she marries a wealthy man old enough to be her father. Apparently, Kikutei found this depiction of human psychology unconvincing. For that reason, he had no choice but to concoct the farfetched, coincidence-driven plot described above. But to dismiss this plot on the basis of the author's lack of skill or his immature grasp of modern human nature is to miss the point. If he had tried to depict with no alteration the events from *Ernest Maltravers* as if they had occurred in Japan, he would have risked regressing back into the sort of fictional world found in Edo-period *ninjōbon gesaku*, such as Tamenaga Shunsui's *Colors of Spring: The Plum Calendar* (*Shunshoku umegoyomi*, 1832–33). Hisamatsu Kikuo, in choosing not to pursue Take because she has married another man, adheres to an ethical precept. Take, on the other hand, is left behind in their hometown to face an unimaginably cruel and miserable fate, one that is hard to resolve with the stepmother's subsequent explanation of her secret plan to protect them. Neither can know anything about the other's situation. Nonetheless, Kikuo, in accordance with the ethicality that the author bestows on him, has to return to their hometown in order to save Take from her unhappy fate. For Kikuo, a student who moves away to pursue his studies, Take symbolizes his hometown, to which he must return in order to rescue it from its backward plight, while Akita's daughter becomes a symbol of the opportunity for individual success that exists only in the city.

In that sense, this was a work that attempted to clarify the ethics of a new generation of intellectual, the student. The existence of a student is an unstable one; the only meaning his present existence has lies in his potential, the possibility that he will accomplish something in the future. This new type of youth places himself in the alien and alienating environment of the city, where he lives under a sense of crisis, always threatened by such dangers as disease and sexual temptation. In his expanding fantasy self, he is pressed by the ethical problem of having to choose between Take or Akita's daughter. Take signifies the expectations of his hometown; Akita's daughter the urban dreams of individual glory and success. Therefore, when the lure of the hometown (the pull of those who "wait for the day you, Kikuo, made a success of yourself and returned to your hometown") functions strongly, choosing a girl from the alien city can only be seen as an egotistical pursuit, a betrayal of the hometown. In the case of *Chance Encounters with Beautiful Women*, the protagonist student's good fortune in winning the affections of Yolanda and Colleen is offset by the cruel political situation into which the women are cast, and mediated by his awakened sense of responsibility for his homeland (Japan, or perhaps Aizu), it is sublimated into a relationship of political solidarity—a remarkable denouement. We also find many works in which the hometown is symbolized by the mother or by the hometown girl chosen by the mother to be her son's wife. Out of resentment at this, *Ukigumo*'s Bunzō and *Sanshirō*'s protagonist choose to pursue the egocentric dream (the girl) in the city, and for that very reason they are punished. Their punishment takes the form of betrayal at the hands of the city girl. Ōta Toyotarō in "Maihime" falls into his relationship with Elis in Berlin only after he hears of the death of his mother back in his hometown. The ethical debt incurred through his egocentrism is alleviated somewhat by the obvious necessity to rescue Elis from her pitiful existence, but from the moment this youth, who had once betrayed the hopes of his hometown, chooses to return home, he must carry forever a guilty conscience.

In the case of *Plum Blossoms in the Snow* and the other futuristic political novels, the life of the protagonist, including his winning of the beautiful woman, is legitimated on the grounds that it contributes to the "success" of the People's Rights movement, that it is ultimately for the sake of the people. However, once this "for the sake of the people" decays into a mere pretext, the protagonists' egotism must be denounced. This was part of Sohō's critique; his insistence in his *Kokumin no tomo* editorials that youths return to private life in their hometowns and develop practical abilities was both a realistic and an ethical reproach. Donald Keene argues that Tetchō simply wrote his political novel "in the guise of a love story,"[18] but the connection between politics and love in the political novel was hardly a matter of arbitrary stylistic choice. And when the role of the beautiful woman in these works degraded into a cheap pretext by which to provide needed backing for the protagonist, the feebleness of these quasi-*ninjōbon* political novels became all too apparent.

We have already seen how the critique of idealism offered by Komachida in *Temper of Students in Our Times* strikes at both the unreality of the sort of love depicted between Nina and Rienzi and the falsity of the typical political novel plot. But, when viewed in the context of literary history, we see that it goes even further: it rejects unrealistic, coincidence-driven narratives of romantic success, such as the tale of Iwakiri and Asao that Tanoji cites. This critique goes so far as to expose the falsity of Maltraver's sentimental education and his dream of saving Alice, and of Hisamatsu Kikuo's image of Matsue Take. It was for this reason that Shōyō inevitably followed *Temper of Students in Our Times* with a work like *Newly Polished Mirror of Marriage*, a work apparently intended as a critique of *Ernest Maltravers*.

To achieve this criticism of idealism in *Temper of Students in Our Times*, to expose the reality of the Meiji student, Shōyō needed to contrive a new, original method for writing. The method he developed was to position the author's critical viewpoint concretely within the scene, to narrate in the manner of the passage we examined above: "The crescent moon, like the eyebrow of a beautiful woman, has risen in the western sky." If we consider this mode of expression solely in terms of how faithfully it describes an object, it clearly is far from satisfactory, as for example in his choice of a hackneyed trope to describe the "crescent moon." But the clear placement of the locus of expression within the depicted scene is quite effective in lending the reader a sense of presence. Previous works of fiction had been narrated from the aloof, transcendent perspective of an omnipresent gaze, one that was content to pile up at random aestheticized phrases borrowed from the stockpile of customary idioms. In contrast, Shōyō's expressions are unified, all adhering to the sensibility of a single

---

18. Donald Keene, *Dawn to the West: Fiction* (New York: Henry Holt, 1984), 90.

person standing in a specific position within the scene: "the crescent moon [. . .] has risen in the western sky [. . .] One can only hear the clatter of the rickshaw rolling by from time to time [. . .] There are dark wooden fences around here." It was a brilliant method, one that Shōyō used in full self-awareness.

The author also attempts to bestow on this narrator, immanent to the depicted scene, a sensibility that will elicit the reader's sympathy and interest. Hence the use of seemingly superfluous expressions: "the silhouette on the shōji screen seems to be that of a young man and woman. If Sei Shōnagon had seen it, she would have added it to her list of 'Unpleasant Things.'" These mark a desire to enjoy this scene together with the reader. We find this in even purer form in the opening of the second chapter in *Temper of Students in Our Times*, a passage that seems to have influenced the opening of *Ukigumo*:

> Fancy rickshaws crashing through, children toddle uncertainly, the clamoring horns of hansom cabs. An old man might lose his cane. In the dust of the clear, windy day, his newly purchased hat whitened, a bureaucrat, a Yan Ying, wrinkles up his nose. With great pompadours just coiled about, irritated by the swirling dust, women affecting Xi Shi's knitted brow. This is the summer scene at the crossroads. "Surely for protection from this dust one needs the help of eyeglasses," mumbles an awkward country bumpkin; his idle words contain some sense. The season is the end of May. It is already dusk. Rushing down the side-alley by the martial arts training hall, he looks about nineteen or twenty years old, a student with a pleasant look.[19]

While the passage does harbor a visual intentionality toward clearly depicting the object, its words drift off into exaggerated tropes and jokes. The mode of expression is hardly that of a realistic sketch; we find instead continual digressions from the object. And yet, these puns and tropes achieve a critique of certain aspects of the object, thereby revealing its humorous true nature. Herein lies the practice of realism of this period, which aimed above all at creating interest that could be shared with the reader. With this method, Shōyō's literature advanced to the extent that he was able to reveal the reality of the Meiji student's world, even to narrate a self-reflexive criticism of idealism though the mouthpiece of one of his student characters.

* * * * *

19. Translation adapted from Marleigh Grayer Ryan, *Japan's First Novel: "Ukigumo" of Futabatei Shimei* (New York: Columbia University Press, 1965), 82–83. Yan Ying, an official, and Xi Shi, a famous beauty, are both figures from classical Chinese literature. The passage contains *engo* and other rhetorical devices. "Eyeglasses," for example, puns on the popular nickname of a bridge in Tokyo.

When compared to the opening of *Ukigumo*, we see that this opening paragraph from chapter two in *Temper of Students in Our Times* employs a mode of writing that introduces the characters who appear before the reader in order of the strength of impression that they make. In contrast, as we saw in chapter one, when *Ukigumo* describes a similar spectacle, it arranges its characters (the civil servants' whiskers, attire, and so on) in order of their status and social ranking. Its mode of expression manifests the sure density of the controlling consciousness that Futabatei achieved, the strength of the subjective self-awareness that bestows a unity onto the depicted phenomenon, an ordering onto the interests it arouses. Even when it satirizes its object, it rejects hackneyed tropes and contrives as much as possible to produce original observations and rhetorical figures, ones that adhere to its own individual sensibility. Because of this, it achieved a higher clarity in its observation of the object. Its incessant drive for individuality in its tropes gave birth to excesses, such as the excessive use of "riddle-style adjectives" (*MBZ* 23:264) that Ishibashi Ningetsu (1865–1926) attacked in his 1887 review of the novel in *Jogaku zasshi*,[20] but these were an inevitable byproduct of the new subjective self-awareness it had achieved.

Be that as it may, this consciousness with its strong tendency toward controlling and ordering its object enabled Futabatei to depict even simple human relationships in a manner that carried out a critique of contemporary society, including its most pressing intellectual problems. Although Shōyō had already expelled from literature the idealism of romantic love that had dominated the political novel, it was still possible to use a method whereby private circumstances, the I-situation, became a metaphor for politics. In a word, romantic love could still be presented as an ethical problem. We see this clearly in the way that Bunzō seeks not sexual love in Osei, but rather the possibility of mutual human trust. In the novel, however, this expectation is gradually revealed to be nothing more than Bunzō's egotistical presumption, in short, his "delusion." Bunzō, wallowing in this self-centered dream, is made to realize by Honda and Osei the "self-evident truth" (*Ukigumo*, 302; the words are in English in the original) that it is nothing more than an egotistical love, a truth evident only to himself. Osei's betrayal—at least, from Bunzō's perspective it is a betrayal— manifests the inevitable self-punishment that was implied all along by his egotism. Futabatei's depiction of romantic love transforms it into a symbol of the problematic idealism rampant among mid-Meiji youth.

---

20. Ishibashi Ningetsu, "Evaluating *Ukigumo*" ("*Ukigumo* no hōhen"), serialized in *Jogaku zasshi*, nos. 74–80 (September 3–October 15, 1887) and reprinted in *MBZ* 23:259–65.

But the writing style used in the opening of *Ukigumo* was not well suited for depicting Bunzō's mental suffering. As long as the novel's writing style conformed to the mocking sensibility of the non-person narrator, who pokes fun at the absurdity of external appearances in order to reveal the true nature of his object, the narrator's gaze could never draw near to the internal crisis of Bunzō's mental situation. But eventually, a more suitable perspective did become possible, as can be seen in the following scene.

> Suddenly there was light in the west. Bunzō turned, his reveries interrupted. His neighbors had forgotten to close their second-floor shutters and the shōji were exposed to view. A human shadow was reflected through the paper. The form bulged grotesquely and turned into a monster. All at once the shadow disappeared and everything was dark again.
>
> Bunzō sighed and looked down into the garden of his own house. The densely crowded flowers and trees were filled with the lonely drone of insects. The trees emerged from the darkness. They reflected the dim light that came through the glass doors below and looked like so many figures lurking there, spying on the house. The night wind rustled through the foliage and blew against Bunzō's face. He shivered. He stood up, went into the house, and, groping about, lit the lamp. With his hands clasped on his knee, he sat staring off into space. Then he poured hot water from the kettle at his side into a teacup and drank it down in one gulp. He stretched out, resting his head on his arm, and stared at the flicker of light from the lamp reflected in a circle on the ceiling. He smiled, chuckling to himself; but then his open mouth became twisted and distorted and an expression of grief appeared on his face.
>
> "Oh, what on earth shall I do? I certainly have to say something. I must make up my mind to tell them when they come home tonight and get it over with. My aunt will make a very nasty face, I'm sure."
> (*Ukigumo*, 224–25)

This is reminiscent of a passage I quoted in chapter two from *Chance Encounters with Beautiful Women*, the scene depicting the ghostly nightscape seen by Tōkai Sanshi after he learns of the death of Miss Parnell. But of course the mode of expression here is more analytical and visually detailed. And whether Bunzō was forced into this situation of solitude or whether he chose it himself, note how deeply he is made conscious of it. This difference in degree of awareness produces a difference in the way that the two descriptions are psychologized. In *Ukigumo*, the description of surroundings bears a necessary relation to the psychology of the desperate Bunzō; they are psychologized so that each of his external actions is rendered meaningful in terms of his internal situation.

Shōyō was unable to go this far. It is true that Shōyō had experimented with an internal monologue mode of expression in *Newly Polished Mirror of Marriage*, a method that Hirotsu Ryūrō (1861–1928) would assimilate even more skillfully in his political novel, *Women's Participation in Politics Is Just a Dream* (*Joshi sansei shinchūrō*, 1887). But Shōyō, when confronted with the problem of a character's internal psychology that could not be perceived from outside, could only resort to methods that revealed that psychology as if to an external observer, such as in this passage from *Newly Polished Mirror of Marriage*: "What are Oyuki's true feelings? Let's take out our magic mirror and reflect her innermost thoughts" (*MBZ* 16:216).[21] The problem here is not so much how a person comes to have a certain interiority, but rather how a person becomes aware of their own interiority. Shōyō shows no interest in the situational circumstances that force a person to such an awareness, and as a result he is forced to resort to feeble pretexts like this. Futabatei was the first to overcome this weakness.

Moreover, in Futabatei, a situational impasse leads to an impasse in the language that one uses to address others. Bunzō is unable to tell the other characters that he has been dismissed from his job, even though he knows that he must tell them. His fear of the disgusted look his aunt will surely give him causes the words to stick in his throat. His fear here, that his setback will be brought to light and that his aunt's family will reject him, gives birth to his interiority. The fact of his dismissal, which he is strongly aware must be communicated to others, is suppressed into silence when threatened by a real situational impediment, the probability of his aunt's displeasure and Honda's ridicule. At that moment, his internal language, a language entirely different from that which he would use to speak with others, becomes an object for his own consciousness. Futabatei captures the nature of this consciousness, developing a mode of expression that could convey the process by which the pressure of this consciousness can alter even a person's sensibility, the way that person perceives the external world. It was a decisive transformation in novelistic methods of expression.

After this point in *Ukigumo*, we find fewer and fewer expressions made from the point of view of the non-person narrator. The self-complacent ridicule and triumphant air that characterized it are subsequently transferred onto the spoken dialogue of characters like Honda, dialogue that impedes Bunzō's own ability to produce utterances. The *words* of his obstructed speech are thereby driven within, giving rise to his interiority. From this point, the expressions of the narrator (i.e., in passages of narrative description) unfold in adherence to

21. This passage and its relationship to Hirotsu Ryūrō are discussed at length in chapter nine.

Bunzō's psychology, making possible the psychologizing of external physical descriptions. Moreover, the low vulgarity that had initially characterized the mocking narrative tone (now carried on by Honda-like dialogue) is exposed and rendered into an object of criticism. In that sense, this Bunzō-oriented mode of expression constitutes a form of critical "knowledge" about sensibility, a knowledge that was achieved through a process of alienation from (and the acquiring of a critical stance toward) the mode of expression of the *gesaku*-like opening passage (and the Honda-like worldview that dominated it). At last, a reliable mode of expression for the I-sensibility had become possible. A writing style now existed that could honestly and straightforwardly express the real nature of the self of the *individual*. Kobyashi Hideo argued that the "individual" had to "become of profound human significance" ("Discourse on Fiction of the Self") before the I-novel could emerge, but we must invert Kobayashi Hideo's understanding. Historically, it was only after this mode of expression had been achieved that the appearance of novels depicting the individual's "profound human significance" became inevitable. Nakamura Mitsuo located the foundations of Futabatei's mode of expression in his study of Russian literature, a view that is now commonly accepted in histories of modern Japanese literature, but this interpretation too must be overturned. When we analyze *Ukigumo*'s mode of expression and see how it unifies the protagonist's mental situation with his (sensibility-determined) surroundings, we necessarily come face-to-face with the mode of being of the author himself, forced by the practice of his own mode of expression into an awareness of the problem of the individual, the problem of his own self.

But the acquisition of this mode of expression for Futabatei meant the abandonment of *Ukigumo* as an unfinished work. He would subsequently have to wander for many years before he could return to literature. In this, we see the problem of his method. There was a fatal flaw in the way he grasped sensibility as a negotiation between the reality of private circumstances (the I-situation) and sensibility-determined surroundings. In short, Futabatei was unable to achieve a critical "knowledge" that would allow him to objectify his own Bunzō-oriented mode of expression.

Chapter Four
"An Oddball Rich in Dreams":
Mori Ōgai and His Critics

Translated by Ayako Kano

*This chapter traces the continuing career of the non-person narra-
tor. In some works, characterized by a lack of any sense of sharing a
situation in common with the work's characters, as well as of any
interest in pursuing the actual nature of unfolding experience, it declined into a flippant self-exhibitionism, one that conveyed its sensibility primarily through witty expressions. But in other works from
the early 1890s, most notably Mori Ōgai's "Maihime," this non-person evolved into a person, more specifically, a first-person character
in fictional works—the narrator was now a character, visible to other
characters. Moreover, many of these works presented themselves as
autobiographical records. This made possible a new kind of fictional
plot, one centered not on external events but on the internal process
of self alienation, whereby one becomes increasingly conscious of
one's own sensibility. While this harbored inherent limitations in that
it tended to view the sensibility that arose through a sense of alienation from others as something innate and unique to the individual,
rather than as the product of a specific social situation, it also created new possibilities for a literature that found its drama in the processes of reflexive self-consciousness.*

As the attention paid to one's individual life reaches a certain intensity, one
begins to reflect on the self as it appears in everyday situations and scenes.
What becomes visible then is the figure of one's self primarily as something
tormented by a sense of estrangement from other people. Thus is born the idea
that the drama of one's life is rooted in this sensibility of estrangement.

In fact, this sense of estrangement from others should largely be attributed to one's situation and not necessarily to one's essential individuality. And
yet, it is also true that when it appears before our conscious awareness, it usu-

ally appears as if it were our essential individuality. Why? Because that sense of estrangement makes one a lonely person, set apart from others. This sense of estrangement or dissonance is difficult to communicate to others, and accordingly one feels burdened with a sense of an incommunicable individual difference.

The view that one is an unbalanced person, a person with many faults who cannot be accepted by others—such a view makes people hesitant and undermines their will. In the earliest modern novels of Japan written in the form of autobiographical memoirs, the protagonists (the "writers" of these autobiographical records) were young men of this type: for example, Seki Ōzan in Saganoya Omuro's *Tasteless* (*Ajikinashi*, 1888) and Ōta Toyotarō in Mori Ōgai's "Maihime" (Dancing Girl, 1890). Kidori Hannojō in his review essay "Maihime" (1890) criticized Ōgai's protagonist for being "weak of will and action, with no spirit, no sincerity, and therefore unhealthy in emotions" (*MBZ* 23:273). He lacks the sort of strong will that would have led him into conflict with social conditions. Kidori Hannojō (a pseudonym used by Ishibashi Ningetsu) elsewhere writes:

> Any novel that is worth being called a novel is constructed from the actions that arise out of a person's will and personality, as well as from the results of such actions [. . .] It would depict the conflict between the hero and objective fate. Due to this conflict, the hero might unknowingly go against the laws of nature; he might even disturb the order of the nation-state; or he might stumble and suffer and still find it impossible to extend his talents.
>
> "On Motive" ("Zaikaron," 1890)[1]

Seen in the light of this norm, Ōta Toyotarō lacked the qualifications to become a literary protagonist.

However, we must remember that "Maihime," though published under Ōgai's name, was written in the form of an autobiographical memoir by Ōta Toyotarō. There are aspects of the text that we cannot see unless we consider this fact. As Aizawa Kenkichi noted in "Letter to Kidori Hannojō" ("Kidori Hannojō ni atauru sho," 1890), defending the mode of expression used in "Maihime," these aspects become invisible to us when we read, as did Kidori Hannojō, only in terms of how the author explains the character of the protagonist.[2]

---

1. Reprinted in *Ishibashi Ningetsu zenshū*, vol. 3 (Tokyo: Yagi Shoten, 1995), 146–49. The passage before the ellipsis appears on 148; the passage after the ellipsis appears on 147.
2. Aizawa Kenkichi is the name of one of the characters who appears in "Maihime." Ōgai himself wrote this essay, which was published in Ōgai's journal, *Shigarami zōshi* 7 (April 25, 1890): 20–27. As we will see below, Kamei borrows a phrase from this essay, "an oddball rich in dreams" (24), for the title of this chapter.

If we generalize further, we can say this: the reason that Ōta, while trying to be kind to the weak and underprivileged, ends up hurting others as well as himself is that he is defeated by the denigrating self-image that is forced upon him by his sense of estrangement from others. He is defeated by that image, and thus he enters into "conflict"—to use Ishibashi Ningetsu's word—even with those whom he loves and who care for him. He then cannot help but blame himself even more. If he were to look back in reflection, he would see that this sensibility was the "motive"—Ishibashi Ningetsu uses this term to mean causality or plot line—weaving together the events of his life. Such a way of looking at the self and at life, however, had never been narrated before. And yet, wasn't this the true way of looking at one's self and life? What if one were to try to capture in writing this manner of self-reflection? A reader such as Hannojō, who searches for some necessary connection linking one event to another, might be dissatisfied by the fact that the hero lacks a strong-willed personality that could provide the motive for such a connection. But a human being lives and is moved by the self-image that arises through his or her involvement via sensibility with others. While trying to be oneself in dealing with others, one is constantly exposed to the threat of a negative revision of one's own internal self-image. Such a crisis often begins from a trivial experience at the level of sensibility, one so trivial that it hardly registers in other people's eyes. A trivial action can trigger a sense of estrangement from others, simultaneously altering one's sensibility towards one's own internal self-image and changing one's manner of dealing with others. The way in which one becomes consciously aware that this was indeed a significant incident for oneself cannot be seen unless we adhere to the standpoint of the person in question. A reading strategy that pursues only plot development will not allow us to understand a mode of expression that thematizes sensibility and the crisis of self-image.

Looking at this from the history of literary expressions, we see that prior to "Maihime," there existed no mode of writing that used the narrator's sensibility as the necessary motive force driving narrative development. The narrators of earlier literature, that is, narrators who do not appear as characters and who do not participate in incidents but are positioned immanent to the depicted scene, did not have the ability to generate plot developments through the medium of their sensibilities. We cannot say for certain that they inherently lacked such an ability, but it is clear that the authors of the time were unable to bestow such an ability onto their narrators. The transition occurred when this narrator was made into a character within the story, as a first-person narrator. To put it simply, thus began a method in which the narrator, as a character, writes about incidents that happened to him. It was a transition in expressive method that brought about a revolutionary change in human self-awareness.

How was this change effected? Before we look at concrete examples, let us examine the mode of expression in Kidori Hannojō's (Ishibashi Ningetsu's) "Princess Tsuyuko" ("Tsuyukohime," 1889). It might help our understanding, since "Kidori Hannojō" himself appears in the work—one of the characters in "Princess Tsuyuko," a comic sidekick, bears this name.

> Venturing out into the fields in spring to gather young buds; no pastime is as pleasurable as playing in the fields in the month of March, when the sun shines warmly and gently, the wind is like air warmed by a stove—until yesterday the wind was cold and severe to the skin, but today it mildly and pleasantly brushes the face; furthermore, the air is thoroughly perfumed from having passed among the blossoms on the trees—what details of care in creation!—if only one could bottle this air and put it on sale in times of frost bite and hypothermal winds, the profit would be much greater than that of selling ice water in summer—what cleverness in commercial calculation!—even birds start to frolic and almost forget where their nests are; the loveliness of horsetails that raise their buds through the soil though they might get trampled, the innocence of violets seduced by the continuing sunshine into blossoming early; if you look around you will see a vague mist hovering far away on the riverbank treetops: it must be that they are also beginning to flower. Where is this place? A small village not too far from Mukōjima! In this happy realm a troupe of women wander about picking young buds, and among them a lady of seventeen or eighteen years, a princess in long-sleeved kimono; is she a virgin? Of course! Is she a beauty? Of course! (*MBZ* 23:221)

This shamelessly frivolous tone of voice is of course a characteristic feature of the immanent non-person narrator, rather than being something unique to Ningetsu himself. This mode of writing had spread rapidly among young authors of the time, ever since Tsubouchi Shōyō and Futabatei Shimei had developed it.

But the self-consciousness of having to live the same situation as characters in the story, which had been the starting point for Tsubouchi Shōyō and Futabatei Shimei in conceiving this method, was not necessarily shared universally. If the necessity determining a certain methodology is not widely shared, such a technique must inevitably degenerate. This tendency is already visible in Yamada Bimyō's "Musashino" ("Musashino," 1887) and Ishibashi Shian's "A Maiden's Heart" ("Otomegokoro," 1889), but not to the extent that it would become visible in the works of Ishibashi Ningetsu.

Take, for example, the expression cited above from the opening of "Princess Tsuyuko." For the narrator, immanent to the depicted scene, the motivation behind this expression is clearly not to communicate accurately the real features of the object, but rather to display the narrator's own way of seeing and feeling, to engage in self-exhibition through clever analogies and witty bon mots. The frivolous simile of "the wind is like air warmed by a stove," the pedantry of "details of care in creation" and "times of frost bite and hypothermal winds": these could never mark the sensibility of a person trying to get closer to the object itself. Moreover, the passage "if only one could bottle this air [. . .] what cleverness in commercial calculation!" provides no help to the reader in understanding the object visually. It is as if the narrator wallows in these awkward analogies and associations for his own smug enjoyment, so that these expressions in the end lack any sense of necessity.

In any case, this narrator eventually turns his gaze to "faraway on the riverbank." What he now sees is "a troupe of women" and among them "a lady of seventeen or eighteen years, a princess in long-sleeved kimono." But to take a "princess in long-sleeved kimono" and to tack on questions and answers such as "Is she a virgin? Of course!" is, we must say, again a gesture of unnecessary self-exhibition. At the risk of becoming tedious, let us quote this narrator's frivolity a little further.

> Among them is a lady who stands out in the eyes of onlookers; if we see her from behind, she is slim and slender, with a long nape—her neck is thin and whiter than snow, standing tall and straight—that in itself makes us guess her beauty; if we see her from the front, she has an oval face, a complexion like a plum blossom blooming in the cold, mixing eight parts pure white with two parts pale red, and the way she keeps her tiny adorable lips sealed epitomizes the gracefulness of her whole body; but even when she laughs, those lips express the attractiveness of her whole body. You ask why? I'll tell you why: it's because within those blushing petals of her red lips, her teeth play hide and seek like gourd seeds; it's because each of her appropriately plump cheeks comes endowed with its own whirlpool of Naruto. (*MBZ* 23:221)

Of course, such expressions of flashy self-exhibition can also be found in Tsubouchi Shōyō and Futabatei Shimei. In this period, such excessive insistence beyond any necessity on the object's details had been initially advocated by Tsubouchi Shōyō as a way to go beyond the modes of expression characteristic of Edo *gesaku*. As he put it, novelists in Japan had hitherto "been content to rely on detailed illustrations to make up any descriptive deficiencies in their text, often not bothering with verbal depictions of people and scenery at all"; Shōyō thought this was a grave mistake: "Description needs as much detail as possible."[3] In other words, he was dissatisfied with works in which narrative description merely functions to provide stage directions for passages of dialogue, and tried to heighten the expressive value of narrative description itself by insisting that it depict in detail the visual aspects of the scene. His intention was to overcome the reliance on illustrations, or in other words, to muster the visual and image-evoking function of words themselves. It was then a very natural progression for authors to become especially conscious of the visual perspective from which a given scene is described.

It is true that in the *gesaku* works of Tamenaga Shunsui and Takizawa Bakin, many words are spent providing background explanations and interpretations, while there are surprisingly few visual descriptions of scenes. Moreover, much use is made of traditional literary techniques such as *kakekotoba* (puns) and *engo* (conventional verbal associations), so that visual clarity is lacking. Sometimes, unusually detailed descriptions are found, but these seem to have been written mainly for the purpose of giving instructions to the illustration artist. Tsubouchi Shōyō and his ilk tried to escape this manner of expression, and yet they carried on the tendency of indicating even the minutest of the object's details. Taking up one detail after another in this way meant struggling to produce clever analogies and tropes, polishing up one's descriptive verbiage. As long as one remains under the sway of such a mode of expression and consciousness, so-called nature description cannot come into being. This is evident from a glance at Shōyō's *The Temper of Students in Our Times*. In it, there are indeed some expressions containing detailed descriptions of physical settings, but the objects described are mostly parks and gardens already beautifully arranged by human hand; even when it does depict other objects, only settings that fit traditional aesthetic norms are chosen. Shōyō was unable to take up scenes that did not fit these norms. Futabatei Shimei was more advanced. He still used many expressions characterized by self-exhibition, but he also bore a desire to pursue the essence of the object, of the actual experienced event, so that expressions of a lived sensibility gradually came to predominate in his writing. He progressed to the point where the depicted setting as mediated by the sensibility of the narrator became an expression of the emotional situation of the characters.

Yet Yamada Bimyō and Ishibashi Ningetsu retreated from that position. Their less advanced position likely represents the general average for that time. Even Yamaguchi Toratarō, who was favorably disposed toward "Maihime,"

---

3. Translations adapted from Tsubouchi Shōyō, *The Essence of the Novel*, trans. Nanette Twine, *Occasional Papers*, no. 11 (Brisbane, Australia: Department of Japanese, University of Queensland, 1981), 101.

expressed his dissatisfaction with the work's descriptions: "Yet the author's pen does not succeed in capturing the figures of the characters, and they lack in decoration; readers will have difficulty guessing the features and clothing of the characters. It may be that the writer wanted to show that he deliberately hides some things, but this will probably not satisfy readers."[4]

Yamaguchi Toratarō was probably expecting the kind of descriptions found in the expression cited above from "Princess Tsuyuko." Let us compare that with the following passage from "Maihime" (1890):

> Just as I was walking past I noticed a young girl sobbing against the closed door of the church. She must have been about sixteen or seventeen. Her light golden hair flowed down from under the scarf around her head, and her dress was spotlessly clean. Surprised by my footsteps, she turned around. Only a poet could really do her justice. Her eyes were blue and clear, but filled with a wistful sadness. They were shaded by long eyelashes which half hid her tears. Why was it that in one glance over her shoulder she pierced the defenses of my heart?[5]

The expression here is simple and well organized. This organization is the result of the narrator having chosen from the scene only those aspects that made a strong impression on him. He has discarded all other details. The fact that at the moment he had had no time to notice such details may also be a reason, but it is primarily such experiences at the level of sensibility that determine the subsequent fate of the two characters. This means that he possessed a method that could relate the expression of the object that moved his sensibilities to the ineluctable unfolding of the depicted event, thus creating a relation of necessity between expression and its object. This was a decisive transition in the history of expressions, one that exceeded the grasp of Yamaguchi Toratarō.

If we return now once more to Ningetsu's "Princess Tsuyuko" and attempt to grasp the self-consciousness of its narrator from his narrative tone of self-exhibition, what characteristics do we see? When he feels the pleasant spring wind against his skin, he imagines "air warmed by a stove"; when he perceives the scent of the spring wind he speculates that it must have "passed among the blossoms on the trees." What we have here is a consciousness marked by a strong tendency to grasp sensibility through wit. We could see this as a variation on the mode of expression found, for example, in Yamada Bimyō's "Musashino":

---

4. Yamaguchi Toratarō, "Detailed critique of Maihime" ("Maihime saihyō"), *Shigarami zōshi* 4 (January 25, 1890): 46–50. This passage appears on 49.
5. Mori Ōgai, "Maihime (The Dancing Girl)," trans. Richard Bowering, *Monumenta Nipponica* 30.2 (1975): 151–66. This passage appears on 155.

> As the sun approaches the peaks of the mountains of Hakone, and
> begins *to spit out its* rays of scarlet *according to ritual*, the fields
> little by little gain an outline of pale orange, and the distant moun-
> tains also gradually turn purple *as if they had drunk poison.* (*MBZ*
> 23:3; emphasis Kamei's)

This kind of expression is rarely found in Edo-period *gesaku*. In them, it is more
common to find instead an expression that appeals directly to sensibility, to
which is then appended commentary on what the expression might mean. Accordingly, to avoid this, to pile intellectual interpretations onto the phenomena
before one's eyes, to use sophisticated expressions to describe them and to show
off one's pedantic knowledge: this was the "modernism" of the era of Ningetsu
and Bimyō. Their narrators are under the sway of this kind of modernist self-
consciousness. Permeated by that kind of self-awareness, the plot development
and themes in their works, too, necessarily had to turn to "modernism."

This was the Meiji 20s' equivalent of the Newly Arisen Artistic School.[6]
The essence of their *gesaku*-as-modernism was that the narrator would shoulder
none of the ethical task of pursuing the true meaning of the unfolding event that
was its object of perception.

We should note here that Ishibashi Ningetsu's "On Motive" and "On
Imagination and Reality" ("Sōjitsuron," 1890) contain some of the most sophisticated literary theories of the time and remain worth considering even today.
Moreover, while surprisingly many critics and researchers read "Maihime" only
in relation to incidents from Mori Ōgai's own life, Ningetsu (writing under the
name Kidori Hannojō) critiqued the story in the following terms:

> The design of 'Maihime' is to create a life condition in which it is
> impossible to have both love and fame, then to place in this condition
> a person who is timid and cowardly, a person with feelings of pity
> but lacking in courage and independence, then to show the relation-
> ship between this person and that condition [. . .] The writer makes
> Ōta discard love and choose fame; but I believe that he should have
> cast away fame and chosen love. ("Maihime," *MBZ* 23:272–73)

As a result, there are many who consider Ningetsu to be the winner in the literary debates over "Maihime." In his own fictional works, however, insofar as

---

6. The Newly Arisen Artistic School (*Shinkō geijutsu-ha*) was a diverse group of writers who
   emerged around 1930 to challenge the hegemony of Marxist literary theories and to promote
   various forms of experimental and modernist writing. Its diverse membership included such
   figures as Kawabata Yasunari (1899–1972), Nakamura Murao (1886–1949), and Hori Tatsuo
   (1904–53).

Ningetsu was unable to conquer the internal self-consciousness of being a modernist, he could not produce the kind of literature that would, in his words, "depict the conflict between the hero and objective fate." This limitation might have been partly due to the writer's youthful immaturity, but at the same time, when we see the formulaic nature of his theories of literature, we must ask whether his critical writings too were nothing more than another facet of this sort of modernism. It is certain, at least, that he did not derive his ideas from the actual problems he encountered in his own experiences. This is not a shortcoming limited to Ningetsu, however. Any literary criticism or scholarship that fails to grasp the concrete history of literary expressions specific to Japan—no matter whether it takes the perspective of comparative literature or civilization, or even those of traditionalism and nativism—cannot help but end up as mere "modernism."

But the modes of expression in this period were undergoing a gradual transformation at a level that Ishibashi Ningetsu could not perceive.

* * * * *

In my view, they were moving in two directions. First, there was the tendency that began with Yano Ryūkei's *Tale of the Floating Castle* (*Ukishiro monogatari*, 1890) and continued through Hara Hōitsuan's *Secret Politician* (*Anchū seijika*, 1890–91). The other tendency began with Kōda Rohan's *Encounter with a Skull* (*Tai dokuro*, 1890).

The non-person narrator, immanent to the depicted scene, now began to appear as a first-person narrator, one visible to other characters and one who participated in or witnessed the depicted incidents. The narrator "I" in *Tale of the Floating Castle* by coincidence ends up becoming a member of a group of émigré adventurers and participates in their project of establishing an idealistic republican government abroad. He himself is a mediocre and commonsensical young man, with few talents beyond a knack at writing. The reason the author chose such a mundane fellow for his narrator may have been to neutralize the fantastic aspects of the tale; nonetheless, the narrator is attracted to the personalities of the two leaders of the adventurers, comes to share their ideals, and as a result acquires an internal motivation sufficient to make him choose to participate in various incidents and to record them. The unfolding of events takes place on a level over which he has no control, yet his mode of expression attains a certain degree of necessity in that it adheres to his internal motivation. Thus the fundamental lack of motivation found in earlier texts like "Princess Tsuyuko" was on the verge of being overcome.

The only weakness of "I" in *Tale of the Floating Castle* is that since his internal motivation is formed only after he joins the group of émigré adventurers, he cannot function as their immanent critic. In his mode of expression, there is hardly any conflict between his sensibility or self-consciousness on the one hand, and the unfolding of events on the other: there is no dramatic structure embedded in the details of his expressions. In that respect, it represents only a small advance beyond the mode of expression of the non-person narrator. Hara Hōitsuan, however, had progressed a step further. The narrator "I" of his *Secret Politician* is a person who has come to Hokkaido on a mission.

> A single pair of eyes—there are limits to how one can describe a pair of eyes, no matter how hard one tries, not to mention a pair of eyelids that are closed. I am not skilled in the art of rhetoric, but even the most skilled in the art would never be able to communicate to the reader, merely by describing these closed eyelids, the entirety of feelings that arose in me in this single moment toward this blind man. And yet although it is utterly impossible, I shall nonetheless endeavor to describe them. His closed eyes seem to shine resplendently and more brightly than the unclosed eyes of a hundred men.
>
> There is no reason why closed eyes should shine; thus it must be that I had the sensations of surprised terror and trembling excitement, and thought his eyes were shining, and that these sensations were incited by their contrast with the other aspects of his appearance. He had a cane in his hand but he did not use it to probe the ground; he merely raised it in the air as if to play with it. He was taking the arm of another person, but he did not seem to be leaning on him in order to walk; his gait was assured. He did not seem hesitant either; his chest was thrust forward and his shoulders were squared. In other words, he did not have a single feature that a blind man ought to possess. In general, when a person does not have features that he ought to have, there is a certain sense of the bizarre. When a cripple does not look like a cripple, it gives rise to an indescribable sense of awe. What shocked and terrified me at first sight might not have been his closed eyes as much as the absence of the physical features that ought to have accompanied those eyes. (*MBZ* 26:286)

Such a struggle over expression seems bizarre. Someone calls to the protagonist out of the blue, then appears before him: this type of introduction had already been tried out in Tsubouchi Shōyō's *The Newly Polished Mirror of Marriage* (*Imotose kagami*, 1886). But in *Secret Politician*, the acts of meeting and seeing in themselves are given the form of an internal drama. Deep in the mountains far away from any village, the protagonist is hailed by two men who do not appear to be ordinary travelers. It may be quite natural that this meeting in itself seems dramatic. But even after the tension of "surprised terror" has subsided, the interior drama continues until the end. "I have a grand 'mission'; I must examine everything in detail; I shall not create incidents myself" (*MBZ* 26:322). Thus he strives to limit himself to the roles of observer and reporter. Yet, when he looks at himself he finds that "when I have no job to perform, I tend to become sometimes a thinker, sometimes a dreamer" (*MBZ* 26:323). This kind of internal conflict continues throughout the work. Even encounters with natural scenery inevitably incite this drama of self-consciousness.

On the one hand, there is his sensibility, which is immediately attracted to what is visible to the eye and audible to the ear; on the other hand there is the internal constraint of wanting to remain in the position of a reporter and fulfill his mission. Moreover, the objects of sensibility are two people who may well be crucial to that mission, so that he feels attracted to them. Yet at the same time his sensibility also awakens a sense of estrangement from them. The external world necessarily appears to him in a contradictory, conflicted guise. This is why when he tries to describe the external world, his expressions become bizarrely tangled, twisted, and he cannot help obsessively repeating questions to himself. It is only upon further reading that the reader begins to understand the internal circumstances behind this, but this kind of obsessive self-questioning has already begun in the first passage cited above, from almost the start of the tale.

One of the people encountered is a blind man. In trying to express his "surprised terror" upon realizing this fact, the narrator describes the closed eyes as seeming to "shine resplendently," but of course that is a contradiction in terms. Though it may truthfully describe the impression he received, as a phenomenon it is impossible. So the narrator begins to analyze this confused impression. He comes upon the idea that sensibility does not operate only in relation to objects directly in front of one's eyes; perhaps its movement is also entangled with conceptual images that are already sketched out in one's perception. This estrangement is different from what Ishibashi Ningetsu calls "conflict," but human beings often experience this kind of drama of sensibility, and this work is constructed as an expression of the unfolding of such a drama. "In general, when a person does not have features that he ought to have"—that is, when a blind man behaves in a manner that contradicts the preexisting concept of a blind man as helpless and unsure—the narrator feels a certain indescribable sense of awe. The concept is peeled away, and he is now forced to face the object directly. This is what I mean when I say that the process of seeing itself constitutes a drama. And this manner of pursuing the causality of sensibilities is of an entirely different nature from the witticisms of Yamada Bimyō and Ishibashi Ningetsu.

The protagonist eventually comes to think that these two men might enable him to fulfill his mission and travels together with them. They separate for a while, but later he helps the blind man cross the Straits of Tsugaru and witnesses a peasant uprising and its suppression. What, then, is his mission? We find out in the end that it is something very trivial, so trivial in fact that we may even suspect the author changed his mind about the plot midway through writing the novel. But the strange peculiarity of this work lies in the fact that this fits perfectly with the motif of the dramas of seeing and hearing that runs throughout this work. When we focus on its plot structure, we cannot deny that this work is imperfect. But this work is written above all by focusing on the estrangement of sensibility in the "I"; there are many scenes in which two contradictory impressions of the object appear at the same time, and these scenes in the end serve to underline the contradictory nature of the incident itself. The complexity of the shadowy figure who was once the leader of the rebellious peasants and is now an informant against them is expressed through the bizarre words and behavior of the blind Kensaku, who carries out the informant's instructions and then dies.

It could not, however, have been easy to continue writing in this tortuous manner, and it was in addition poorly matched to the tastes of the readers of the day. Either an interruption in the author's writing career or a literary failure was inevitable. But once this sort of speaking subject had appeared in a literary work, it could not help but affect other authors, altering the self-consciousness and expression of sensibility of their immanent narrators. Writers such as Kōda Rohan and Izumi Kyōka would progress so far as to mold the narrator's expressions of sensibility around his sense of estrangement from the perceived object, or even to make use of the narrator's power of visual hallucination.

* * * * *

The second tendency began with Saganoya Omuro's *Tasteless* and continued with Mori Ōgai's "Maihime" and Takase Bun'en's "Young Leaves" ("Wakaba," 1893). As I have already mentioned, this is a literature that takes as its theme estrangement from others and the transformation of one's internal self-image. For example:

> Attributing the fact that I neither drank nor played billiards with them to apparent stubbornness and self-restraint on my part, they ridiculed and envied me. But this was because they did not know me. How could anyone else know the reason for my behavior when I did not know it myself? *I felt like the leaves of the silk-tree which shrink and shy away when they are touched. I felt as unsure of myself as a young girl. Ever since my youth I had followed the advice of my elders and kept to the path of learning and obedience. If I had succeeded, it was not through being courageous.* ("Maihime," 154; italics Kamei's)

Life was pleasant even in the midst of poverty and Elis' love was hard to reject. Being so weak-willed I could make no decision there and then, so I merely promised to follow my friend's advice for a while, and try and break off the affair. *When it came to losing something close to me, I could resist my enemies, but never could refuse my friends.* ("Maihime," 161; italics Kamei's)

> Later letters [from Elis] seemed to be written in great distress [. . .] "When I travel home with you, she [Elis's mother] is talking of going to stay with some distant relatives who live on a farm near Stettin. If, as you say in your last letter, you are doing important work for the Minister, we can somehow manage the fare. How I long for the day you return to Berlin."
>
> It was only after reading this letter that I really understood my predicament. How could I have been so insensitive! *I had been proud to have made a decision about my own course of action and that of others unrelated to me.* But it had been made in entirely favorable rather than adverse conditions. When I tried to clarify my relationship with others, the emotions that I had formerly trusted became confused. ("Maihime," 162–63; italics Kamei's)

All of these are quotations from "Maihime." Kidori Hannojō cites the three italicized sections and attacks the contradiction among them, but if we read these passages in context, they are not necessarily contradictory. In other words, while Kidori Hannojō sees these types of expressions as being the author's explanation of the protagonist's character, we should realize that the first two passages consist of what Aizawa Kenkichi calls "self-commentary," that is, descriptions of self-recognition inserted by Ōta at the time he wrote down his autobiographical memoir. And the remaining third passage represents Ōta in the moment his self-image undergoes a decisive change, a change that triggers the negative self-objectification that will give rise to the sort of "self-commentary" found in the other two passages.

Perhaps, Ōta thinks, I am not the person I thought I was. This troubling thought comes to him when he is about to leave Japan for Germany: "I felt quite the hero until the ship left Yokohama, but then I found myself weeping uncontrollably" ("Maihime," 154). To borrow Herbert Read's vocabulary, the hard shell of "character" that had been formed through other-orientation is now broken, and the soft "personality" begins to emerge from underneath it. Ōta's memoir proceeds by focusing on the destiny that was created by that soft personality. But I think it is significant that his self-recognition—"I thought it strange at the time, but it was my true nature showing through" ("Maihime," 154)—was achieved not at the point when Ōta shed those tears, but only after he had experienced life in Germany. The novel weaves into the experiences of sensibility of that earlier time the later self-recognition from the time when the memoir is being written. Because many readers have failed to perceive this temporal structure, much discussion of "Maihime" hitherto has been subject to a simple mistake. At the time he began his life in Germany, all Ōta was aware of was the internal crisis of the shell of character breaking apart: "There grew within me a kind of uneasiness; it seemed as if my real self, which had been lying dormant deep down, was gradually appearing on the surface and threatening my former assumed self" ("Maihime," 153).

His rebellious words and actions toward his superiors were caused by this crisis. His "real self" consisted of his revulsion against his own other-orientation and his desire to be liberated in sensibility. And this was precisely why he could not play around in an other-oriented manner with the other Japanese students sent to Germany. His desire to be liberated in sensibility paradoxically resulted in his feeling estranged from their debauchery. For this, he was ostracized by the other students. But we must note here that he himself did not grasp the true reason for this at the time: "How could anyone else know the reason for my behavior when I did not know it myself?" When he looks back now, he realizes that it was due to his passive personality, and the phrase "I felt like the leaves of the silk-tree which shrink and shy away when they are touched" is, needless to say, a "self-commentary" added from the present moment in which he is writing his memoir.

We must say, however, judging from the unhappy ending of Ōta's love affair with Elis, that his locating its cause in the weakness of his own heart, as seen in such metaphors as "I felt like the leaves of the silk-tree" and "as unsure of myself as a young girl," amounts to nothing but self-pity. It is not that there is direct deception involved, but he glosses over his self-accusations with lyrical and sentimental metaphors. Moreover, such metaphors are not sufficient to explain his sense of estrangement from the other students. To use that estrangement to foreshadow the plot line and to portray himself as a victim—e.g., "The ridicule of the students was only to be expected, but it was stupid of them to be jealous of such a weak and pitiful mind" ("Maihime," 154)—is nothing but an avoidance of the truth of the matter. It was actually here that his "weak and pitiful mind" is to be found; Kidori Hannojō ought to have attacked him on this point.

Another thing we must note, however, is that after this, Ōta's self-expressions come to have an entirely personal, individualized hue. I have already cited the scene of encounter with Elis. Other authors of his time would have described this scene differently. Seeing a beautiful and delicate girl in a foreign country quietly "sobbing" and observing that her eyes were "blue and clear, but filled with a wistful sadness [and] shaded by long eyelashes which half hid her tears," they would never have used an expression like, "Why was it that in one glance over her shoulder she pierced the defenses of my heart?" Anyone would be expected to feel deep pity. In that sense, no other author would even have thought to question the universality of the narrator's sensibility. Other authors wrote under the presumption that their expressions were grounded in a commonly shared sensibility. That was the basis on which their other-oriented, self-exhibiting expressions were laid out. But in Ōta's case, he becomes aware of his sensibility as a result of suffering from a sense of estrangement from his peers and of being ostracized by them. In the end, it is the sensibility of a person who has been alienated in a lonely, isolated situation, the sensibility of one conscious of having a nature different from that of other people. In other words, while he actually does feel the same emotions as anyone else, he himself can only be aware of them as if they were the workings of a private sensibility. To repeat myself, his "weak and pitiful heart" was none other than his I-sensibility that was uncovered in this manner.

Weaving what he has uncovered into his past experiences, or finding new evidence of it in that past—this is how Ōta's self-reflection proceeds. Yamazaki Masakazu in his *Ōgai: The Fighting Patriarch* (*Ōgai tatakau kachō*, 1972) objects to readings of this work that find in it a literature of the birth and failure of the modern self. Though I agree with him on this point, I think it is utterly mistaken to read "fatherhood" in Ōta as Yamazaki does. Seeing Elis weep pitifully, he was moved by his own mental situation of loneliness. His behavior in protecting her was merely due to the fact that Elis's circumstances required it. To be kind to Elis was to console himself as well.

The decisive catastrophe begins when he receives a letter from Elis, while he is in Russia in the service of Count Amakata. The love between the two is shattered as he begins to see himself in a self-negating way. She anticipates that he will return to Japan and is resolved to go with him. Ōta, on the other hand, while happy that Count Amakata has a high level of trust in him, is not conscious of the implications for his future: "The gods might have known how this was connected to my hopes for the future, but I never gave it a thought" ("Maihime," 163). Instead, he learns of this possibility through Elis's letter, and at the same time realizes what great anxiety this prospect is causing in her: "It was only after reading this letter that I really understood my predicament. How could I have been so insensitive!" ("Maihime," 162). For the first time, Elis attempts to assert her own will; that is, for the first time she appears in Ōta's eyes as one bearing her own independent character, and as a result he is forced into an awareness of a blind-spot in his heart, a heart so obtuse in its relations with others: "When I tried to clarify my relationship with others, the emotions that I had formerly trusted became confused" ("Maihime," 163). Elis, spurred by anxiety, thus inadvertently incites in Ōta a desire to return home.

According to the testimony of Aizawa Kenkichi, when he read the memoir that Ōta wrote on the ship carrying him back to Japan, Aizawa was "only moved by the facts and was incapable of considering whether those lines should be published or not" ("Letter to Kidori Hannojō," 20). But, recently, a man named Ōgai had published it in *Kokumin no tomo* under the title "Maihime." Aizawa Kenkichi, needless to say, is the name of a character in "Maihime." The reason Ōgai used that name was to counter Ishibashi Ningetsu's use of the name of a character from "Princess Tsuyuko." In that same April 1890 issue of *Shigarami zōshi*, Ōgai published the essay "On Spoken and Written Language" ("Genbunron") under his real name, Mori Rintarō, and yet another essay, "Reading 'On Motive'" ("Doku zaikaron") under his pen name of Ōgai. In other words, he published his critique of Ningetsu's "On Motive" paired with a critique of Ningetsu's critique of "Maihime," yet he felt a need to distinguish between the names under which the various essays were published.

Following for the moment Ōgai's usage in nomenclature, we must note that "Maihime" was originally written in the form of Ōta's memoirs. Ōta himself declares at its beginning that "Not only do I still feel dissatisfied with my studies, but I have also learned how sad this transient life can be. I am now aware of the fallibility of human emotions, but in particular I realize what a fickle heart I have myself" ("Maihime," 151). Accordingly, we must read the subsequent memoir as the concrete unfolding of a comprehensive commentary.

Ōgai cites the example of Raisky, the protagonist in Goncharov's *The Precipice*, pointing out his habit of day-dreaming: "In one instant he imagines himself a poet; in another instant he imagines himself a painter; in yet another instant he imagines himself a sculptor" ("Letter to Kidori Hannojō," 24). Ōgai points out that Ōta belongs to the same type of human being, if not quite to the same extreme. The Ōta that we as readers perceive is nothing more than an ordinary, average young man. But as is the case with many persons, if we adhere to his internal self-image, we see the emergence of an "oddball rich in dreams" ("Letter to Kidori Hannojō," 24).

Mori Ōgai himself probably maintained the hard shell of other-oriented character his whole life. Could we say then that literature for him was something to satisfy those internal desires that could not be fulfilled otherwise in his other-oriented way of life? To a certain degree, this is probably true, but we must add that the process by which a human being becomes conscious of him or herself always involves a doubling, a supplementary image of the self as alienated from the self. Moreover, this process of becoming conscious is always attended by some affect, be it pain, satisfaction, or something else—i.e., there is a certain sensibility attached to that process, and here again the alienated sensibility intervenes. This alienated sensibility consists of the various demands of sensibility that must be repressed in order to protect the other-oriented character. In the case of Mori Ōgai, "Maihime" achieved autonomous existence as a literary work in the following manner: Ōta began as a character constructed only out of aspects drawn from Ōgai's supplemental self-alienated image, and this character was then further self-alienated by making him into the speaking subject (the writer of the memoir). This speaking subject was of course bestowed with the ability to become conscious of himself. What Ōgai insisted, through Aizawa Kenkichi's mouth, was that "Maihime" needs to be read as a drama of the unfolding of human self-consciousness. We can of course surmise that Ōgai's own sensibilities and experiences of self-image were to a certain extent projected in altered form in this depicted unfolding. But the mode of reading that he expected for "Maihime" was far beyond the capacities of Kidori Hannojō, and even later readers lacked a reading strategy that would allow them to understand its mode of expression.

*****

This is not to say that this method originated entirely with "Maihime." The "I" of Saganoya Omuro's *Tasteless* is a person who at a young age is abandoned by his mother and whose father dies. He is reared by a monk and eventually becomes a student of Izumi Jō, an early-Meiji Enlightenment thinker. He subsequently graduates from college and is sent to America for further study, becomes sick and returns to Japan and, realizing that he is near death, writes this work, looking back on his life.

As he looks back over his life, he realizes that he has often engaged in self-aggrandizing words and actions as a means of overcoming his unfortunate circumstances. His self-reproach for this is even more severe than that of Ōta in "Maihime." He tried to amaze his teachers and triumph over his classmates by grappling with grand questions like "What is the essence of the self?" (*MBZ* 17:209). At the time, he thought he had come up with answers that were fully capable of amazing others. Looking back on it now, however, it seems to him that such questions "did not arise from my heart; they were merely thoughts from books reflected onto the mirror of my brain" (*MBZ* 17:209). The movement of his heart to seek its own essence—that movement itself had been overwhelmed by an other-orientation. If that is so, he muses, perhaps vanity was the essence of his heart. He thus excavates "the hot blood of youth" (*MBZ* 17:209), which becomes "the target of self-scorn every time he thought back on it" (*MBZ* 17:217), especially the vanity that marked his internal self-image.

In his expressions, however, his emotions and the external scenery seem skillfully matched, as when he narrates the death of his teacher's daughter:

> The moon is full, and the night is melancholy, the sound of geese
> crossing the sky is like a medium that adds to the sadness; the wind
> blowing down from the eaves makes a rustling sound—it must be
> that the first leaf of the paulownia tree has fallen. (*MBZ* 17:221)

But in fact, all we have here is a case where a perfect background has been
selected in order to emphasize the emotions of the moment. In other words, he
did not yet have a method for making the description of the scenery a necessary
one, a method in which new motivations arise from out of the way in which the
scene is viewed and felt. The other weaknesses of the novel are related to this:
the failure to convey clearly the protagonist's sense of estrangement from his
classmates, and the resultant failure to trace realistically the critical change in
his internal self-image. Instead, the view of self at the point of writing the memoir is rather clumsily inserted into the depicted self-consciousness of boyhood.
It was "Maihime" that finally overcame these weaknesses.

And regardless of whether Mori Ōgai himself pursued its development,
after the appearance of his story, Japanese authors began to adopt this method
of developing their expressions of sensibility at a private, personal level. To be
conscious of one's self, to embrace an internal self-image, already amounts to
incorporating something excessive within one's self. If that is the case, something excessive is also added as a supplement to the way in which one sees or
feels an object. It is not that some unusual and strange sensibility is manifested
in the way that Elis appears to Ōta's eyes. But the strength of impression with
which her appearance pierces Ōta's heart must have been inexplicable to the
other students and even to his friend Aizawa Kenkichi. If that is so, then Ōta's
personal obsession, what we might call a fantastic, phantasmic aspect, was appended to his way of seeing. This probably had its basis in his internal self-
image. To repeat myself, it is not the case that Mori Ōgai himself was aware of
this point and developed it in his later novels, nor was it the case that the other
authors were consciously aware of and pursued this method in the terms in which
I have formulated it here. Yet we can still say that this method of expressing
sensibility from the level of an individuated human being, of expressing as private I-sensibilities even sensibilities that were widely shared, spread rapidly.

But this also meant that the weaknesses inherent in this method were
also carried on. When the self-pity of "I felt like the leaves of the silk-tree" or
the victim-speak of "such a weak and pitiful mind" became commonly understood as the authentic way to express the truth of the self in literature, these
became no more than pity-laden code-words for appealing to one's own circle.
Moreover, as sensibility began to be seen primarily as something private, this
gave rise to the belief that sensibility is unique and essential to the individual,
and therefore an innate quality that cannot be changed by the individual him-

self. To draw an internal self-image with self-pity and victim-mentality at its core, to affirm mutually with others that this indeed was the true figure of the author himself, to form thus an exclusionary world—this is the *bundan* as described by Itō Sei in his *Methods of the Novel* (*Shōsetsu no hōhō*, 1948).[7] While postwar writers have mostly overcome this kind of thinking, it has now spread to other realms. We can even say that it has become a kind of universal among Japanese people. The sort of consciousness that arises in Ōta when he reads Elis's letter, one of critically reflecting on one's "dull heart" and on the blind spots in one's relationships with others, does not come easily.

But I may be jumping ahead of myself. Our forefathers had barely become aware of the "oddball rich in dreams" existing within themselves. They had arrived at a point where they could begin to use that as the basis for extending and expanding various objectified visions and fantasies, into which they could even incorporate the tales told by the common people.

7. *Bundan* is the name given to the unofficial and yet highly organized world of literary circles in modern Japan, in which access to publication and public recognition were regulated in guild-like fashion. It has been widely studied by Itō and other scholars of modern Japanese literary history.

Chapter Five
The Words of the Other:
From Tamenaga Shunsui to Nakae Chōmin

TRANSLATED BY JOSEPH ESSERTIER

In this chapter, Kamei takes up the intersubjective nature of sensibility. He depicts the manner in which the speech of others can reorganize our own sensibility: consciously or not, we identify with the image of ourselves we detect in the words of others. In the Edo period fiction of Tamenaga Shunsui, we see examples of this happening, but there the resulting changes in sensibility (and sexual encounter) are cloaked in natural imagery, so that the newly transformed sensibility appears as if it were nature itself. In modern works, however, this same process is reconfigured into an ethical question, and taking responsibility for one's own sensibility emerged as a new possibility. But the first-person fictions that emerged around this new awakening to sensibility harbored another ethical failing: in focusing solely on one's own changing self-consciousness, they risked eliding that same process as it occurs in others. A process that began in the words of the other can easily end up silencing that other. Kamei suggests that this failing has repeatedly undermined oppositional political movements in Japan, starting with the People's Rights movement. This is not an inevitable result, however, and Kamei argues that Nakae Chōmin's Discourse by Three Drunkards on Government *and Ozaki Kōyō's* Two Nuns' Confessions of Love *demonstrate the possibility for a mode of expression that retains a place for the other even as it expresses the developing sensibility of self.*

The girl notices the friendly gaze directed at her, and she of course takes pleasure in it, but does not yet know how to play the coquette. Or rather, she cannot tell what it is about herself that is so attractive to the other. This causes her anxiety. As she shyly looks away and blushes, the girl hastily directs her self-reflexive consciousness toward her own appearance. As her body becomes an

87

object for her own internal visual intentionality, a kind of self-consciousness is illuminated all across it. It is a shaking of the senses, the awakening of sensibility. She wants to hide, and yet she also wants to be gazed at even more intently. This is what is meant by love.[1] It consists of an identification with the gaze of another, in short, of a self-reception at the level of sensibility that is mediated by that gaze.

Tamenaga Shunsui (1790–1843) understood this well. In order to introduce a number of relevant questions, I would first like to take up a passage from his *ninjōbon Nightingale in Spring* (*Harutsugedori*, 1838):

> Chōga: "Oh, you're just full of all kinds of excuses! Make up your mind." When he said this, rather than thinking of Chōga's words as a playful game, Otami thought them an actual expression of his love for her, and so she was happy and shy and became flustered, unable to make any reply. She could only mutter "Yes, yes," as she felt her face redden to the color of autumn maple leaves and the redness spread to her ears like the leaves of ivy,[2] coiled like ivy around him, to the eyes of a spellbound man, she wanted for nothing, her attitude that of an innocent girl in a state of rapture. He no longer missed the flowers of the pleasure quarters, having been completely taken by this young maiden. On the eighth day of September in the shade of an autumn evening, Chōga pushed open the storm door and washed his hands in the pot of water outside. The sky had suddenly cleared to reveal a melancholic evening moon. In his lover's robe, from the front of the dew-laden garden, he looked out into the distance beyond the hedge. A cold wind blew in spite of the autumn season. A mournful foxfire glowed at the edge of the forest. Chōga: "Otami." Otami: "Yes." At that, she came to the veranda and Chōga stood near her. He pointed toward the rice fields and spoke in a low voice, as if terrified. Chōga: "There, look over there."[3]

Supposedly, Nagai Kafū was deeply impressed by this scene, saying that he could never equal it.[4] It certainly displays a striking mode of expression.

1. Kamei here uses the word *koi* (love), which usually denotes a sexual relationship between man and woman, as opposed to the more platonic words *ai* or *ren'ai*, a word current in the Meiji period to describe the modern (and primarily Christian) notion of a spiritual love between man and woman. The word *koi* was widely used in *ninjōbon* and other Edo-period *gesaku* genres to describe passionate relationships between men and women.
2. "Autumn maple leaves" (both *momiji* and *kōyō* here) and "ivy" (*tsuta*) are *engo* (conventional associations) for the color red. This passage is written in the 7–5 rhythm used frequently in classical Japanese poetry and prose.
3. The text is reprinted in *Sharebon kokkeibon ninjōbon*, vol. 47 in *Nihon koten bungaku zenshū*, 51 vols. (Tokyo: Shōgakkan, 1971), 385–608. This passage appears on 412–13.
4. Nagai Kafū (1879–1959) was a modern novelist whose works, both fiction and non-fiction, frequently engaged with Edo-period *gesaku*.

Otami is a servant girl only sixteen years old. She could never have imagined that Chōga, well known for his exploits with women, would take an interest in her. In fact, Chōga, for his part, has only hired her to fill in for a maidservant who is ill. Nevertheless, one night after dark Chōga is about to leave for the Yoshiwara quarters when unexpectedly it begins to rain. Suddenly awakened to the charms of Otami as she bustles about looking after him, he cancels his plans to go out and instead instructs her to shut the outer storm doors.

At this point he launches into well-crafted words of wooing. He renders love into something natural, thereby heading off any possibility for ethical objections. In spite of his full awareness of her virginity, Chōga teases Otami, accusing her of being involved with other men. As he verbally toys with her feelings, he even offers her a gorgeous kimono that he has had made for Ohama, a geisha. The more that Otami resists Chōga's sexual innuendoes, the more she feels compelled to give voice to her own longing for him. This is not to say that she already had such feelings before this encounter. In fact, she desperately appeals to her purity and innocence:

> Tami: "Oh, is that what you think about me? If I am to be thought of in that way, I would rather die." She begins to sob, and Chōga sees this. Chōga: "There, there, don't cry. If it upsets you so much, I won't force you to answer. If you would rather die than reveal the names of your lovers, then it would be cruel to ask. Don't worry, I won't ask you about them anymore." Otami: "Oh, what shall I do? That's not what I'm saying. What I meant was that I would rather die than have you continue to suspect me [of having had previous sexual liaisons]."
> (*Nightingale*, 411)

But her words here sound like a vow of fidelity to Chōga, and pulled along by the force of her own spoken dialogue, in this instant Otami is awakened to the emotion of romantic love. It is nothing more than an imaginary emotion, a fiction projected by her reply to Chōga's challenge, but of course Otami is too flustered to realize this.

On top of this, the kimono Chōga forces Otami to try on is particularly luxuriant:

> . . . a delicate stripe pattern in a gray-indigo silk crepe. The cloth used inside the sleeves and hem was the same as that on the outside, and the inner lining of the kimono was of the finest crimson silk. The crest was a double Chinese bellflower embroidered with silk thread. On the hem were scattered delicate wisteria flowers of silver thread. The two undergarments were of a mauve Kyoto crepe and a white material dyed with a fallen-leaf pattern, and there was a full-length

embroidered *juban* underrobe. The decorative collar was made of white velvet with Mitsugorō stripes sewn into it with silver thread. The under-petticoat was made of finely woven white silk lined with the best crimson silk. The obi was nine inches wide and made of a blackish-brown silk plain-weave embroidered with black and purple threads cross-stitched into Mitsugorō stripes, and the two-faced *kuijira-awase* obi was of a pine-green weave embroidered in silk thread with tiny wisteria flowers, scattered across it every six or seven inches. (*Nightingale*, 407)

I myself cannot explicate the dense cultural meanings entrusted to every minute detail of this kimono. The only thing that I can be certain of is this: once she is made to wear the beautiful clothing of a geisha, Otami's sensibility will gradually take on a presentiment of approaching sexual union. Shunsui introduces this process in the form of a kind of nature description: the pattern of the kimono hem. And, in fact, what stops Chōga from going out for the evening is a sudden accident of nature, the rain. The opportunity for his discovery of Otami's charm is provided by nature, just as the lust that arises in Chōga as he seizes this opportunity is fulfilled under the sway of the man-made nature manifested in the kimono patterns. Otami, awakened to a presentiment of sexual love by the imaginary projection of romantic love evoked within her by her own response, can no longer resist when Chōga directly propositions her. It is as if this were the *natural* unfolding of her sensibility. The cruelty of Chōga, forcing a sexual encounter on a sixteen-year-old, is deftly covered up by this gorgeous, "natural" pattern. This is because nature, and accordingly the natural unfolding of sensibility too, are constructed here so as to leave no room for the intrusion of ethical considerations.

The first passage quoted above, in which Otami inadvertently finds herself in love with Chōga, follows this description of the kimono. As is clear even from a quick reading, what attracts Chōga is not her mind or her spirit, but her physical appearance. Otami knows this too. Indeed, perhaps that is why she feels "happy and shy." The burning glow that spreads through her body at the moment she realizes this is depicted by Shunsui through a series of visual images that adhere to Otami's own standpoint: "she felt her face redden to the color of autumn maple leaves and the redness spread to her ears like the leaves of ivy." In short, Otami herself is made conscious of her anticipation of sexual love in the form of certain natural images. Having been bestowed with this internalization of sensibility by the author, she is liberated from the burden of feeling that she has given herself up to the advances of the young hero. At the same time, these natural images—"she felt her face redden to the color of autumn maple leaves and the redness spread to her ears like the leaves of ivy"—also represent the figure of Otami as seen in the eyes of Chōga, and from this there very naturally occurs the change in perspective marked by the phrase "to the eyes of a spellbound man." This kind of deft change of subject positions within a single sentence has disappeared in modern prose. Indeed, the images used to depict Otami's charming appearance are not simply a matter of words, but actually change Chōga into a man "spellbound" to the bottom of his heart. In this sense, we can say that Otami's sensibility has spread to Chōga in turn. What we find portrayed here is this kind of intermingling of sensibilities.

A yoking together takes place at the level of sensibility, so that the reception of the other's passionate love itself becomes the self-reception of sensibility. This transforms the natural setting into a kind of symbol. Once their sexual love is consummated, Chōga opens the storm door and looks at the foxfire in the distance. It seems a symbol of the fire of sexual passion that was first ignited within Otami, only to spread and engulf Chōga too. Already, Chōga can no longer gaze at it alone, because it is now a symbolic nature that yokes together their two consciousnesses.

* * * * *

I may seem excessively fascinated with Shunsui's love scene. However, it is a fact that, even more than the authors of all the recently published theories of sensibility and the body, Shunsui had firmly grasped one of the secrets of sensibility. To wit, the one who takes the initiative in the wooing scene is without a doubt Chōga. This is not simply a matter of their status-based hierarchical relationship. In this scene the interest of the author Shunsui lies in how he can weave a virginal maiden such as Otami into his own characteristic pattern of romantic love, and the means by which he carries out this objective is Chōga's spoken dialogue. If, at the end of the conversation he devised, Otami had not been made to follow blindly in the direction laid out by that dialogue, not only would Chōga's wooing have ended in failure, but the author Shunsui too would have lost the means for sustaining development in the work. In this sense, it is possible to consider Otami the protagonist, at least within the confines of this scene, yet from beginning to end the one who dominates the conversation in the scene is Chōga.

If we can speak of a writing style that structures passages of spoken conversation, the writing style in this case is constructed in adherence to Chōga's spoken dialogue. Otami's sensibility is constructed in the form of her being woven into the flow of that dialogue. Accordingly, expressions such as "she felt her face redden to the color of autumn maple leaves and the redness spread to her ears like the leaves of ivy " represent Otami's internalization of this sensibility, and these expressions are moreover rendered nearly homogeneous with the descriptive expressions attributed to the author Shunsui—that is, with the writing style from the passages of narrative description (*ji no bun*). The ethical callousness of forcing a young girl like Otami into sexual union fades from view as Shunsui aestheticizes it under the pretext of a series of natural images, and in the end Otami submits to this writing style, acquiescing with a sense of both pleasure and shame. In this sense, the sensibility that is born here is, in one sense, an imaginary projection, and yet at the same time it is also something very real.

Now that we have confirmed this, we need to trace through the kind of qualitative changes that subsequently occurred in the modern Japanese novel. For example, there is the case of Yano Ryūkei's *An Illustrious Tale of States-manship* (*Keikoku bidan*, 1883–84), which we explored at length in chapter two. In it, Pelopidas comes to understand his own feelings for Leona in the following manner:

> Whatever thing, whatever deed she desired, he would devote his heart and soul to obtain, and while proclaiming this he watched her, enraptured by the beauty of her face and figure, a beauty apart from this world, a beauty that would put to shame even the spring flowers and the autumn moon. He had never thought about it until now, he wondered, so why should she stop his heart on this day of all days? Filled with sentiments of her goodness, a love was born in his heart. Thus, here he started to feel a love for her for the first time. (*MBZ* 15:37)

The process by which Pelopidas becomes aware of his own sensibility is rendered into an ethical problem, in that it takes the form of his gratitude for her saving his life. To say this differently, the possibility of sexual union is completely abstracted away here, which in turn renders impossible the rise of a narcissism that would attempt to naturalize sensibility by rendering it into a series of natural images.

The sense of an internal necessity that determines the unfolding of a novel depends on the manner in which the characters in the work become conscious of their own sensibilities. If we consider it in this way, there is no way that the internalization of sensibility seen in Otami or Chōga could have given rise to a problematization at the level of ethics. While the author Shunsui attempts in the work to actualize the common moralistic theme of "encourage the good and chastise the evil" (*kanzen chōaku*), in the end he is unable to render this into an internal necessity for the work's characters. The sensibility-based motivation that drives the work's characters and the author's overall moralistic theme end up like the relation of water to oil. In Takizawa Bakin's *The Story of Eight Virtuous Heroes* (*Nansō satomi hakkenden*, 1814–41), on the other hand, we find no expressions of internalized sensibility. But since a whole new set of theoretical considerations would be required to read and interpret it, I will omit it from the present discussion. As is clear from Tsubouchi Shōyō's preface to his translation of Bulwer-Lytton's *Rienzi* (*Gaisei shiden*, 1884), what Shōyō wanted to promote in modern literature was an internalization of sensibility such as is found in Shunsui's characters. What he wanted to expel was the antithetical moralism of "encourage the good and chastise the evil." Shōyō cites Bakin's *The Story of Eight Virtuous Heroes* as a representative work of this latter tendency. But even before Shōyō embarked on his own attempt to realize in practice his literary ideals, Yano Ryūkei in *An Illustrious Tale of Statesmanship* had achieved the structure of narrative development that would characterize modern literature.

When the process of becoming conscious of sensibility took on an ethical dimension, then for the first time a more spiritual, romantic love (*renai*) could be distinguished, away from scenes of purely sexual love (*seiai*). In other words, it became possible to take on self-consciously the burden of one's own sensibility, to pursue its ethical preservation. This is not a matter of some external constraint, as for example happens with the theme of "encourage the good and chastise the evil" in *The Story of Eight Virtuous Heroes*. Rather, it is a matter of taking responsibility for one's own sensibility, a sensibility that characters accept in the form of a self-discovery. Even more, it is an ethical obligation that characters accept toward their interlocutors of the opposite sex. It was in this direction that Ryūkei's mode of expression advanced, albeit by small steps.

That was as far as Ryūkei was able to go. While his novel is not written entirely in adherence to the sensibility of Pelopidas, the political goals of the author are voiced chiefly in the form of Pelopidas's spoken dialogue, so that in the end almost all of the work's conversation scenes are dominated by a manner of speaking that equates Pelopidas with the author. For example, Mellon, who is exiled to Athens, tries to plead the sad plight of his own country before the citizens of Athens. He yells out "Gentlemen, save our Thebes!" (*MZB* 15:23), but is unable to speak beyond this. He subsequently lapses into the following ludicrous situation:

> Waving his hands and stomping his feet in a manner utterly unknown to the dais of political debate, the man appeared desirous to speak. But in his inability to put together an argument, it seemed that all he could do was to face forward and take on new shades of red even deeper than his natural ruddiness, all the while emitting little puffs of steam from his brow. (*MBZ* 15:23)[5]

5. An abridged translation of *An Illustrious Tale of Statesmanship* can be found in John Mertz, "Meiji Political Novels and the Origins of Literary Modernity" (Ph.D. diss., Cornell University, 1993). Translations from the work here were produced in consultation with Mertz's versions.

Pelopidas then appears, saving Mellon from his dilemma and setting forth an eloquent "political argument" (*MBZ* 15:23). Thus, the author begins by depicting the brawny but tongue-tied Mellon, who is unable to propound the author's own "political argument," or, more precisely, the author's views as projected onto ancient Greek history. Only after this humorous image is established does Pelopidas come forth with his "political argument," offering a brilliant speech, so that his spoken dialogue comes to dominate the scene. In this work, then, the leading role is taken by a character who represents the aims of the author and who is able to muster *words that dominate the scene*. That is the primary distinction between characters employed in this work. They may engage in various debates, but their diction is never differentiated explicitly enough to convey a sense of each character's distinctive interiority. Accordingly, the work includes no scenes where conversation provokes changes in sensibility, even to the limited extent that this had been achieved previously with Otami in *Nightingale in Spring*. Ryūkei's characters are only able to behave in accordance with their predetermined *character* and are not able to experience a *personality* that would change and develop through the personal relationships depicted in the work.

When Tsubouchi Shōyō read Sanyūtei Enchō's *Strange Tale of the Peony Lantern* (*Kaidan botan dōrō*, 1884), as he noted in his preface to that work's second edition, he admired the way "it uses only everyday colloquial language throughout. It is not entirely lacking in elegant language, but it is not used to distraction, so that every phrase and sentence seems packed with impressive significance, and I felt just as if Hagiwara was right before my eyes, as if I was actually encountering the ghostly maiden Otsuyu" (*MBZ* 10:3). It was only natural that Shōyō would be dissatisfied with the mode of writing in *An Illustrious Tale of Statesmanship*. He had discovered that "everyday colloquial language" could produce a distinct, autonomous literary writing style. The individual personalities of the characters in a work could only be manifested through the intertwining of their spoken dialogue (their manners of speaking). An author who creates such a scene finds that this "everyday colloquial language" writing style necessarily becomes a kind of authorial self-limitation, a kind of substructure underlying the scene that manifests the characters' personal relationships, in particular the intertwining of their spoken dialogue. Shōyō fully understood this. And so, in this manner, the immanent non-person narrator became a methodological necessity. Unable to appear within the scene, the author was no longer permitted to dominate the interiors, that is, the spoken dialogue (manner of speaking) of the various characters.

Nevertheless, this method still had one troublesome problem to resolve. As I have touched on in earlier chapters, the immanent narrator depicts a certain setting and then has the various characters appear in it. To state this as a theoretical problem, one can argue, as Shōyō does in *Essence of the Novel* (*Shōsetsu shinzui*, 1885–86), that:

> There are two ways of describing a person's character. I shall call them the negative method and the positive method. The former, used by most Japanese novelists, indirectly makes a character's nature known through his speech and conduct rather than by stating it frankly.[6]

The setting sketched in by the narrator is not simply a stage backdrop for the action; the narrator must perceive it in the same way as do the characters. If this were not the case, the depicted setting would no longer fulfill the condition of being the environment lived out through the sensibilities of the various characters. However, when these two strands of perception (narrator's and character's) are merged as closely as possible, one of two things happens: either the narrator's language (the passages of narrative description) comes to dominate over the interior of the work's characters (their spoken dialogue), or vice versa. In either case, the result is that a specific persona comes to occupy the main role. In this manner, the depiction of the setting as perceived by a specific character takes on a methodological necessity for the work as a whole, but at the same time, the way that same setting appears to other characters is ignored, so that their sensibilities end up being excluded.

However rare it may be, the sharing in common of a particular setting should lead to a sympathetic rapport at the level of sensibility. But even in scenes where this seems likely, incompatibilities appear, as in the following passage from Book One of Futabatei Shimei's *Ukigumo* (*Drifting Clouds*, 1887–89). If we compare it to the scene where Chōga and Otami look out at the foxfire, its distinguishing characteristics will become even clearer.

> "The moon. It looks like it's rising right out of the bamboo grove. Look!"
> The cool moon rose, outlining the leaves of ten slim bamboo trees which stood in the corner of the garden. There was not a single cloud and its powerful, radiant, white light lit up the face of the sky. Glistening drops of light poured down to the earth below. At first the bamboo fence between the houses held back the moonbeams and they extended only halfway across the garden. As the moon rose in the sky, the moonbeams crept up the verandah and poured into the room.

6. Translation adapted from Tsubouchi Shōyō, *The Essence of the Novel*, trans. Nanette Twine, *Occasional Papers: Department of Japanese, University of Queensland*, no. 11 (Brisbane, Australia: Department of Japanese, University of Queensland, 1981), 101.

The water in the miniature garden there shimmered in the light; the windbell glittered and tinkled. Then the moonlight silhouetted the two young people and stole the brightness of the single lamp in the room. Finally, it climbed up the wall. Each time the cool, refreshing breezes blew, the shadows of the moonflowers clambering up the garden fence danced and fluttered, and pearls of dew clinging to the tips of lily leaves turned to fireflies and skipped away. With the rustling of wind through the foliage, excitement grew within the hearts of the young people. As the wind subsided, everything was hushed. The only sound was the chirping of insects gathered in the rush of the eaves. It was a beautiful scene, but Bunzō and Osei were so preoccupied with their own thoughts that they did not really see it.

"How lovely!"

Osei mouthed these words, smiled sweetly for no particular reason, and turned her head, pretending to gaze at the moon.[7]

Osei here sidesteps more than just Bunzō's emotions. This physical setting itself, or rather, the expectation of the reader that is evoked by it, meets with a certain evasion. For *Ukigumo*, this passage represents a somewhat uncharacteristic attempt to portray the setting in affectedly aestheticized terms, as we see, for example, in *Chance Encounters with Beautiful Women*. If Bunzō and Osei had actually fallen in love here, this setting would have subsequently changed into something symbolic for the two of them. It would have become a setting that caused them to experience an intermingling at the level of sensibility, one that would have yoked together their two consciousnesses so that even a simple mention of it would summon up between them the emotions felt at that time. But in fact they do not fall in love, and for Bunzō the setting can form only a painful memory: it becomes that which Osei manipulated in order to evade his longing. The mode of expression used here is likewise transformed into a degraded parody of that used to depict famous scenes in works such as *Chance Encounters with Beautiful Women*. In this sense, it is Osei who controls this scene, just as it is she who is most closely linked to the thoughts of the immanent narrator as he frustrates the expectations of the reader by cutting off this scene suddenly, having the two be interrupted before Bunzō can speak his vows of love for Osei.

In these chapters, I have again and again returned to *Ukigumo*. The reason is, of course, that so many types of experimentation with prose expression can be seen in it. As should be clear from the above example, however, the

7. All quotations from *Ukigumo* are adapted from the translation in Marleigh Grayer Ryan, *Japan's First Modern Novel:* Ukigumo *of Futabatei Shimei* (New York and London: Columbia University Press, 1967). This passage appears on 217–18.

thoughts of its immanent narrator frequently penetrate into the spoken dialogue of Osei and Honda Noboru, thereby dominating scenes that depict conversations, ridiculing Bunzō, causing him to stutter and mumble, and robbing him of his speech. And yet at the same time, the author's own most earnest and pressing ethical concerns are entrusted to this same Bunzō. This is why it is often difficult for us to know who the main character is, and the result is that the work leaves us with a confused image.

In order to overcome this methodological weakness, it was necessary to employ a first-person narrator who appeared as one of the characters in the work. I have already traced through this from a different angle in previous chapters. But, as I have also previously indicated, in the world produced under such a method, a world transformed to match the perceptions of an I-sensibility, the thoughts of other people are necessarily excluded. For example, as we saw in chapter four, in Ōgai's "Maihime," the process of becoming conscious of one's own sensibility—as seen in such expressions as "I felt like the leaves of the silk-tree which shrink and shy away when they are touched" and "I felt as unsure of myself as a young girl"[8]—represent Ōta Toyotarō's totalizing critique of himself formed in retrospect as he looks back on his time in Germany. The work unfolds, however, as if it were itself the materialization of this totalization. In its various scenes, the internalization of sensibility is never able to transcend the realm of a lyrical aestheticism—"the leaves of the silk tree," "as a young girl"—so that the self-cognition attained here always retains a certain vagueness and sentimentality:

> Her eyes were blue and clear, but filled with a wistful sadness. They were shaded by long eyelashes which half hid her tears. Why was it that in one glance over her shoulder she pierced the defenses of my heart? ("Maihime," 155)

The vector of a work's unfolding is determined by the way in which its characters became conscious of their own sensibilities. This is often true in our own lives as well. If, for example, we posit that Otami's internalization of sensibility in *Nightingale in Spring* was transformed to follow the (ethics-driven) pattern found in Pelopidas from *An Illustrious Example of Statemanship*, then the work's development would necessarily have followed a different course, and vice versa. In this sense, the moment Ōta's dawning awareness takes the form of a lyricism expressed through metaphors borrowed from nature, already

---

8. Translation from Mori Ogai, "Maihime (The Dancing Girl)," trans. Richard Bowering, *Monumenta Nipponica* 30.2 (1975): 151–66. These passages appear on 154.

from that point on, Elis's unhappy fate is prefigured in the amoral, unsympathetic ruthlessness implicit in that "natural" lyricism. The methodology of a first-person autobiographical memoir means precisely that the writing style of the narrator (of the autobiographical memoir) and the interior of the protagonist are identified with one another. Elis is utterly dominated within this mode of expression, which is unable to consider the question of how she internalizes her sensibility. In the end, she has to resort to writing a letter in order to appeal to her own subjectivity, but even the writing style of this letter is homogenized into that of the narrator/protagonist. The text of the letter is able to a certain extent to pierce the blind spot of the protagonist, but is ultimately incapable of causing a change in his thinking, and in the end, it finds itself woven into the protagonist's own internal conflict. In short, this was a method that deprived the other of the possibility for speech.

That is not all. The awakening to consciousness of one's own sensibility that I am discussing here is something that becomes at least partially an imaginary projection from the moment it is rendered into language, so that it is at the same time a matter of reality and a form of self-deception. As we saw in the preceding chapter, the first-person memoirist in Saganoya Omuro's *Tasteless*, Seki Ozan, is a young man with a keen ability for self-analysis, to the extent that he is able to perceive his own vanity. One day while tidying up the office of his teacher Izumi, a Civilization and Enlightenment thinker, he accidentally discovers a letter. The sender is a certain MM living in Switzerland, and we learn that "this MM, who is actually German, is in fact a well-known figure in Europe" (*MBZ* 17:231). The contents of the letter are left undisclosed, but we are able to gather a rough idea about them from expressions such as the following:

> Aah, my teacher conspired with this well-known figure, they had many secret plans! [. . .] However, while the French Revolution that set the capital city Paris afloat in a sea of blood happened as a result of the leadership of Robespierre, Danton, and Marat, wasn't it conceived in the womb of the fierce writings-in-blood of the school of Voltaire, Montesquieu, and Rousseau, which shaped the public opinion of that later generation? Aah, my teacher is not just a scholar of extensive knowledge and wisdom [. . .] However lofty this -ism might sound, if it became a real force in society it would become something truly dangerous. (*MBZ* 17:231)

Judging from the protagonist's shock, it seems that the doctrines propounded by MM are likely some form of communism. Izumi himself has previously been depicted as urging the need for solidarity with the lower-classes and for advocating freedom.

In any case, the memoirist "I" who reads this letter resolves that "to pervert public duty because of private feelings would be beneath my manly pride" (*MBZ* 17:231). The "I" here describes his affection for and his desire to repay his debt to his mentor Izumi as a matter of "private feelings." Thus "public duty" refers to his allegiance to the nation-state, to the preservation of the existing political order. Taking this position, he winds up regarding his ethical obligations and emotional attachments to Izumi as being "private feelings." In this, he neglects even to consider the political philosophy that he has supposedly inherited from Izumi, one that advocated befriending the poor and defending freedom. In short, the work covertly transforms the question of a change in "I"'s political philosophy into a problem of "private feelings" versus "public duty."

> I am so ashamed! Lately I am almost always aware of my existence, but never of the existence of others. I know my personal feelings, but not the feelings of others. I know the glory of respecting truth and am blind to the vanity of recklessly spouting off, with no regard for time or place, making a great show of "truth." [. . .] Thinking only that, for the sake of the nation-state and for the sake of truth, awakening a man of great learning to the errors of his beliefs was like Christ coming to save the world, I believed I was performing a distinguished service for the sake of splendid truth. I planned to do this great deed for my benefactor's sake and was unaware that I myself had fallen into a kind of vanity. Sitting at his feet, I announced that his thought deviated from the truth and that I would struggle to the death to make him abandon those false views. My teacher's eyes stared at me, transforming into a terrible glare that flashed at my face. (*MBZ* 17:232)

We find the picture of sincerity here in this moment of self-torture. But it is precisely this frank sincerity that betrays the presence of a crafty old fox: in the shadows behind this unsparing ethical reflection on his emotions lies concealed the reality of his own act of intellectual betrayal. Probably, he takes this course of action to escape the burden of his trespasses: his trepidation and guilty conscience at having stolen a glance at his mentor's private correspondence and the intellectual shock that the letter's contents send through him. Fabricating an equivalence between the "nation-state" and "truth" itself, he tries to dissuade his mentor, and he declares in retrospect that his motive was "a kind of vanity." In this situation, it is only too convenient for him to find fault for his actions in the psychological dimension. He declares the necessity of denying "private feelings" for the sake of "public duty." Under this pretext, which was rampant in the period, he self-rationalizes his betrayal of his debt to his intellectual mentor as a matter of "private feelings." As a result, he depicts a scene of discord that centers around private emotions—his mentor's displeasure and his own "vanity"—thereby allowing him to escape without having to touch on the problems of his own guilty conscience and intellectual apostasy.

Of course, this scene does include a serious attempt at unfolding a philosophical debate. But the memoirist "I" is so busy probing his own psyche that he manages to relate only a scant sampling of his mentor's words. In sum, the internal voice of the memoirist single-handedly dominates this scene, thereby abstracting away the words of his interlocutor. The methodology of first-person narration is well-suited for grasping the unfolding of self-consciousness, but it always carries the danger that one will overlook the same process occurring in the other. This problem is not limited to the realm of fiction writing. In our own interiors too, we often find, there dwells a scribbler of our own memoirs, one who at first glance seems ceaselessly engaged in unsparing and sincere psychological self-criticism, but who in reality functions to allow us to sidestep pressing philosophical problems and questions of responsibility. To the extent that this is true, the more we blame ourselves, the more we in fact console ourselves. To acknowledge one's childlike desire to be coddled or one's feelings of malice and dislike for others is not particularly difficult or painful. In many cases, giving voice to such feelings actually allows one to skip over an objective analysis of the real situation, and it can even function as a means for summoning up a sympathetic audience. This is one of the pathologies of modern language usage (writing styles), one that crosses all political and philosophical boundaries. Note that 1930s *tenkō* memoirs (including not just so-called "*tenkō* literature" but also the various confessional records of political activists who had committed *tenkō*) almost invariably employ this writing style.[9]

The tendency for employing a mode of narration that was capable only of awakening an awareness of one's own sensibility was created by the literature that I have discussed up to this point.

* * * * *

So far in this chapter, I have looked at a variety of works mainly from the perspective of their limitations, their negative aspects. That being so, we now need to look at possible sources in the period for overcoming those negative aspects,

---

9. *Tenkō* refers to the widespread phenomenon of political apostasy among Japanese left-wing intellectuals and activists in the 1930s, who under pressure renounced their political allegiances to Marxism and promised to discontinue subversive political activities, often as a condition for being released from prison. So many writers who committed *tenkō* subsequently went on to write literary accounts of it that a distinct genre of *tenkō* literature arose. The postwar period saw a lively debate as to the nature and significance of the *tenkō* phenomenon.

for setting into motion a different kind of transformation. This possibility was present, at least in trace quantities, in two works: from the lineage of the political novel there is Nakae Chōmin's *Discourse by Three Drunkards on Government* (*Sansuijin keirin mondō*, 1887), and from the realm of so-called "pure literature," Ozaki Kōyō's *Two Nuns' Confessions of Love* (*Ninin bikuni iro zange*, 1889).[10]

Some might object to my reading *Discourse by Three Drunkards on Government* as a novel. But with respect to the methodological question of how to weave the position of the other into one's own expressions, this work engaged in a remarkable experiment. It uses a question-and-answer format to explain in an easily digestible manner the various policies of the new era. Such an attempt had already been put into practice in so-called "Civilization and Enlightenment" pamphlets, including such early examples as Ogawa Tameji's "Questions and Answers on Enlightenment" ("Kaika mondō," 1874) and Matsuda Toshitari's "Rural Questions and Answers on Civilization" ("Bunmei inaka mondō," 1878). A similar attempt is found in Tsubouchi Shōyō's "Lectures of the Pure Administration Tea Shop" ("Hatsumō Kakumin Seijiyu kōshaku," 1882). Among works that tried to depict the different speaking styles of various ranks and classes was Kanagaki Robun's *Sitting Around the Stewpan* (*Aguranabe*, 1871), although the essence of that work lies not in conversation per se, but rather in its portrayal of drunken monologues. Other works also take the form of questions and answers, but they consist of nothing more than long one-sided speeches by which an advocate of Enlightenment dominates intellectually his unsophisticated audience. In fact, these works adopt the question-and-answer style only in a half-hearted fashion, and the manner in which their expressions force themselves onto the reader is even more objectionable than that of essays that directly preached the need for Civilization and Enlightenment.

On this point, the methodology of *Discourse by Three Drunkards on Government* was absolutely epoch-making. In the preface it introduces us to another oddball: "Master Nankai loves drinking and discussing politics."[11] Once this character is posited, it is through his eyes and ears that we encounter the

10. Nakae Chōmin (1847–1901) was a well-known political activist in the People's Rights movement. His *Discourse on Three Drunkards* presents a debate on contemporary political issues in the guise of a drunken conversation between three men, each of whom advocates a different position. Ozaki Kōyō (1867–1903) was the most prominent Japanese novelist of the 1890s. The leader of the Kenyūsha school of writers, his most famous work is *Golden Demon* (*Konjiki yasha*, 1897–1902). *Two Nuns' Confessions*, written in a style reminiscent of Ihara Saikaku (1642–93), helped set off the Saikaku Revival of the early 1890s; it was Kōyō's first work to achieve wide acclaim and established his reputation as the leading Japanese novelist of the day.

11. Translations from this work adapted from Nakae Chōmin, *A Discourse by Three Drunkards on Government*, trans. Nobuko Tsukui (New York: Weatherhill, 1984). This passage appears on 47.

various assertions made by the other two main characters, the Gentleman of Western Learning and the Champion. It is only when we readers consent to the playful mentality through which the political arguments are refracted, to what we can only call his drunkard's eccentricity (his dilettante's taste), that we become interested in lending them our ear—when, for example, we see that the arguments for abstract idealism made by the Gentleman of Western Learning themselves take the form of an abstraction. This is true even for the Champion when he criticizes this from a realistic standpoint: "A person like me is a kind of cancer within society. I pray that I may cut myself out so as not to harm the living flesh of the nation forever" (*Three Drunkards*, 114). Once this motif of self-sacrificing self-negation surfaces, we know that we are being presented with an utterly fanciful debate. All of the various assertions strike the reader with a persuasive force that derives from their realistic impracticability and from the loftiness of their theoretical speculations.

Not only this, the very names assigned to the other two, Champion and Gentleman of Western Learning, derive from their figures as seen through the drunken eyes of Master Nankai:

> One visitor was dressed completely in European style, from top to bottom—right down to his shoes. He had a straight nose, clear eyes, and a slim body. His motions were quick and his speech was distinct. This man appeared to be a philosopher who lived in a room of ideas; he breathed the air of moral principles and marched forward along the straight line of logic. He had a disdain for the winding path of reality. The other was a tall man with thick arms. His dark-skinned face, deep-set eyes, his outer robe with splashed patterns, and hakama indicated a man who loved grandeur and cherished adventure, a member of the society of champions who fish for the pleasures of fame with their lives as bait. (*Three Drunkards*, 49)

The observations made by these drunken eyes harbor a certain bantering tone. Thanks to this sensibility, we readers too are granted a certain margin for enjoyment, so that we become able to watch and listen to the responses of the other two with a sense of good-natured pleasure. In short, we achieve a degree of openness and receptivity toward the words of the other.

What is particularly interesting here is that the Gentleman of Western Learning speaks about his cognition of how the awakening to consciousness of sensibility ends up creating an invisible prop for the social system. He calls this invisible prop "a certain intangible tool" (*Three Drunkards*, 64). There is, for example, the ethic of "loyalty between sovereign and subject," a loyalty that "is not necessarily something that arises from an artificial self, for it is based on a combination of benevolence and gratitude" (*Three Drunkards*, 64). This loyalty between sovereign and subject is a conscious and systematic institutionaliza-tion of emotional bonds, but it does not take form solely as the norm of an artificially constructed self, of the self as a kind of legal fiction. It is created through an apparently natural intermingling of emotions: the benevolence that a sovereign feels for his subjects and their feelings of gratitude to him in turn. To this extent, it cannot easily be negated. However, if it tends excessively toward conscious and systematic institutionalization, then only those aspects that arise "from an artificial self" will remain functional, and the sensibility linking the people cannot but dry up or be rendered into something mechanical.

> Under these circumstances, the function of the brain gradually shrinks, and the complete human being is reduced to a mere digester of food. [. . .] The entire nation becomes a mere lump of slimy, jellylike flesh. (*Three Drunkards*, 66)

In order to break through this stagnation, one of course has to alter the way in which one becomes conscious of one's emotions.

As one can see, what he calls the "self" here (in Japanese, lit. "I" – *watakushi*) consists of a normative process of naming, whereby such apparently natural emotions as benevolence or gratitude are given specific names: "be-nevolence" or "gratitude." In other words, it consists of the aspect whereby one's coming to consciousness of these emotions takes place linguistically, through the linguistic norms that yoke one together with others. In this sense, the "I" is none other than language (spoken dialogue). When that language is brought under the sway of a systematic and institutionalized domination, it falls into decline:

> Life in a despotic country is like a brew without ferment; sediments at the bottom of a barrel. Consider, for example, the literature of a despotic country. Occasionally some work appears to be noteworthy, but closer scrutiny reveals that nothing new is produced in a thou-sand years, nothing unique among ten thousand works. The kinds of phenomena that would ordinarily appeal to an author's sight and hear-ing are, in these societies, merely sediments at the bottom of a barrel, and the author copies these phenomena with a spirit that is also a sediment. (*Three Drunkards*, 60)

Under such conditions, even the human body "becomes a mere lump of slimy, jellylike flesh." The only way to restore the totality of spirit and body is to permit a lively freedom to language.

The Gentleman of Western Learning is brought on stage in this manner and made to speak these ideas quite freely. He seems to have reached these conclusions intuitively, but in fact he hits closer to the essential question than do many of today's theories of corporeality or sensibility. This is because when contemporary writers try to record their own experiences of sensibility, their tone inherits the writing style (when seen at the level of expressive structure) of "Maihime" and the latter half of *Ukigumo*. Their writing style abides by a systematic institutionalization of sensibility, yet they remain unaware of its blind spot: that under it, only the private, personal, "I" dimension is available to conscious awareness. Nonetheless, these writers attempt to explicate the intersubjective nature of the body and sensibility. And if the Gentleman of Western Learning is depicted as having acquired a concept that strikes at this blind spot, this means that Master Nankai too must have the same concept. Here we can see the budding of a new kind of immanent "knowledge" of sensibility, a knowledge that the narrator of *Ukigumo* loses once he begins to adhere closely to the position of the protagonist Bunzō. Of course, even in *Three Drunkards*, we cannot call this a complete success. The three main characters are not distinguished by individualized manners of speaking; all of them are made to conform more or less to the writing style of Nakae Chōmin. While this is true, we do see a skillful deployment of tactics whereby their debate unfolds, one that follows out from an articulation of the impressions first received by Master Nankai. For example, the Champion criticizes the ideas of the Gentleman of Western Learning as being insane, whereupon Master Nankai declares, "Mr. Champion has aptly explored the inner workings of human nature and has described human pleasures well. He seems to have learned from psychologists' studies" (*Three Drunkards*, 98).

Master Nankai's praise for his grasp of "the inner workings of human nature" arises from the Champion's grasp of the following sort of concept in his critique of the Gentleman of Western Learning:

> Mr. Gentleman is obsessed with the idea that war is undesirable. He imagines the sufferings of soldiers exposed to wind and rain and believes that it is real. He imagines the pain of soldiers being scorched and thinks that it is real. But is this suffering real? Is this pain real? (*Three Drunkards*, 96)

Master Nankai appreciates the aptness of the Champion's conceptual method, one that proceeds by grasping the characteristics of sensibility manifested in the imaginings of the Gentleman of Western Learning and that is thereby able to relativize the basis of his argument. As for the sensibility of the Champion himself, it is manifested in his imagination of a battle scene:

> Imagine a vast plain with no houses within twenty-five miles. Surrounding the plain are undulating hills like a long row of folding

screens. The sky is clear and the wind calm; the morning sun shines on the frost. The field is covered with withered grass that breaks if one steps on a thin stem. (*Three Drunkards*, 97)

Beneath the idealism of the Gentleman of Western Learning we see a human-oriented, somewhat pessimistic sensibility, whereas in the scene of battle sketched out by the Champion, even its descriptions of the physical setting are aestheticized through an optimistic and heroic sensibility. The debate between the two advances as a confrontation between these different sensibilities, and as a question of the degree to which each is conscious of this difference.

We also encounter an entirely unexpected turnabout.

> The Champion laughed and said, "I see that you [the Gentleman of Western Learning] are a true believer in the element of novelty. You wish to adopt democracy and abolish the armed forces. I belong, of course, to the nostalgic element. I wish to save the country by military power. You know only how to fatten living flesh. I seek to remove the cancer for the good of the nation. Unless we remove the cancer, we cannot fatten the healthy flesh even if we want to."
>
> At this point the Gentleman asked, "How would you remove this cancer?"
>
> The Champion said, "I'd simply cut it out."
>
> The Gentleman grew impatient. "Don't talk nonsense. A cancer is a diseased part of the body and can therefore be cut out. But the nostalgic element pervades the entire body. How can it be cut out? Please stop joking."
>
> The champion replied, "A cancer is to be cut out; the nostalgic element is to be killed."
>
> "And how," asked the Gentleman, "can the nostalgic element be killed?"
>
> The Champion said, "We should drive them to war. [. . .] If the state issues an order and starts a war, two or three hundred thousand men will gather instantly under the military banner. A person like me is a kind of cancer within society. I pray that I may cut myself out so as not to harm the living flesh of the nation forever. (*Three Drunkards*, 114)

What is called the "element of novelty" is a desire for reform, and what is called the "nostalgic element" is a conservative mentality. The Champion distinguishes himself as being backward in comparison to the progressiveness of the Gentleman of Western Learning, but this is not merely an opposition between conservatism and reformism as a matter of political ideology. Even within a single political party or other organization, there exist both elements. For example, as the Champion argues, even among members of the progressive Jiyūtō (Liberal Party) there were many people

> who were warriors until only recently [and who] have now instantly become dignified politicians of the civilized world. But are they truly the politicians of civilization? They had originally cherished the ideal of dying in battle, but they found no outlet for it and became frustrated. When by chance they learned of democracy and liberty, they found in them something decisive and vehement, and joyfully thought, "These ideas resemble our ideal of dying in battle. We must exchange our ideal of dying in battle, which is a relic of the feudal system, for this democracy imported from foreign lands." (*Three Drunkards*, 109–10)

The Champion includes this group among his "nostalgic element." This was undoubtedly a painful criticism for many members of the old Liberal Party. But while the Champion calls them a "cancer," he also acknowledges that he himself is one of their number. There is nothing to do with this but cut it out, for the sake of achieving the goals of the nation-state and of the Gentleman of Western Learning.

It is important to note that this ethic of self-negation that we see in the Champion is not the result of his having been dominated or forcibly overcome by the language of the Gentleman of Western Learning. In fact, in his acknowledgment that the Gentleman's kind of visual intentionality will "fatten" the "living flesh" of the nation, he clearly affirms the theory of sensibility that forms one link in the notion of democracy advocated by the Gentleman. Moreover, it is the Champion who possesses a clear awareness of the difference between their tendencies at the level of sensibility. It is precisely because the Champion possesses this flexible power of understanding that he coins the phrase about the two "elements" in order to emphasize the difference between the two men and thereby is able for the sake of his interlocutor to construct an ethic of self-negation. Whether or not this methodology of self-negation was realistic is not our concern here. Rather, what is important is that this ethic of self-negation does not place an emotional burden on the other, because it is unfolded as a matter of subjectivity. We can see here that the Champion has a certain generosity of spirit. And, precisely because of this, the Gentleman of Western Learning remains uninhibited and free to voice even more scathing criticisms:

> But it is precisely monsters such as these that greatly hinder the progress of society. [. . .] Clearly, those champions who devise temporary and violent policies to deal with immediate situations harm the great plans of the nation for the next hundred years. (*Three Drunkards*, 116)

The two never arrive at a moment of mutual agreement in their argument. Yet, as we have seen, the work does portray a kind of internal negotiation, a negotiation conducted on the basis of a coming to awareness of the sensibility of the interlocutor, something not seen in previous works of literature. Probably the Gentleman of Western Learning was born as a result of Nakae Chōmin's critical objectification of his own feelings and ideals, which were closer to those of the Champion, ideals that could only be entrusted in self-negating fashion to the coming generation. The figure of Master Nankai then provided the mode of expression for this gloomy self-image, one that could only drown its sorrows in liquor.

At this point, it is probably unnecessary to go into detail about Kōyō's *Two Nuns' Confessions of Love.* A nun who is still quite young lives in a hermitage and another nun, who is also young, comes and begs to stay the night. The host nun wonders why such a girl should have ended up a nun: "I myself am twenty-one years old. She seems about two years younger. With such a pretty face, and at such a young age, ripe for marriage. Where does the seed of her enlightenment lie?" (*MBZ* 18:5). Then the perspectival locus shifts to the visiting nun's thoughts. "When the guest sees the host: Can this be the image of one who has been abandoned by the world? Can a person of this age be weary of the world? Is this the result of a fate like mine? I want to have her listen, I want to have her tell me. About myself, about herself." (*MBZ* 18:5). In this way, the thoughts of the two are in a kind of tacit agreement, and once they mutually disclose their life stories, it turns out that they are linked through their relations with the same man.

What we find here is an experiment with a particular mode of human negotiation, a mode in which one embraces the existence of one's interlocutor as a result of speaking with him or her. Yet, the author's powers of expression had not yet developed to the point where he could fully mobilize a unique, individualized speaking voice for each character. In the end, the contents of speech of the two nuns are subjected to the sensibility of the narrator as it is objectified in scenes of reminiscence. It was not until Kunikida Doppo appeared that this weakness was finally overcome. The mode of writing that characterized works such as *Three Drunkards* ended up being nothing more than an isolated experiment carried out here and there during this period.

* * * * *

This, however, is not to say that there were no attempts to resolve the weak points found in Saganoya Omuro's *Tasteless* and Mori Ōgai's "Maihime." We see such an attempt in, for example, Kōda Rohan's works, including *The Buddha of Art* (*Fūryū butsu*, 1889), *Venomous Coral Lips* (*Dokushushin*, 1890), and *Encounter with a Skull* (*Tai dokoro*, 1890).

The bearers of these narratives (the main characters) are all self-consciously eccentric, oddballs out of step with the trends of their times. The monk Shuun in *Buddha of Art* resolves that he must "dispel a part of the deep-seated anger inside me from when my plasterworks were looked down on by others, as arrogant as foreigners" (*MBZ* 25:3). "In a world where there are railroads," he nonetheless chooses "the difficulties of religious austerities". (*MBZ* 25:3) and sets out on foot for a religious pilgrimage along the Kiso Road. Along the way he stays at an inn in Suhara and encounters the young woman Otatsu, whom he rescues from wretched circumstances. But when it comes time for them to marry, her father, a successful high-level bureaucrat of the Meiji government, suddenly appears, and Shuun ends up being betrayed by Otatsu. In terms of plot, we can see that this narrative moves in exactly the opposite direction from that of "Maihime."

Moreover, the speaking tone of the narrator here, who is immanent to the world of the work, is marked by an ability to utilize skillfully Buddhist vocabulary softened by informal slang. This tone produces a superb effect: one after another, long passages of individualized spoken dialogue by various characters are brought out from it. What I mean by "brought out" here is, to look at it another way, that this tone achieves the effect of weaving into itself the existence of the other. If we consider this in terms of the personal relationships depicted in the work, Shuun is made to shoulder responsibility for Otatsu's fate precisely in the way his expressions are unfolded as interwoven with the voice of the immanent narrator (even as we note that this result is precisely what the old man at the inn had suggested).

Shuun of course has no reason to dislike Otatsu. Yet when Otatsu is suddenly taken away, he begins to hear unfamiliar words in her place. "Everything you have said is very true, but a person cannot be split in two and since there is no chance that Otatsu will go back to selling pickles again, what you want to do is impossible" (*MBZ* 25:15). This strange voice is marked by an intimate tone, but mainly it voices a quibbling that is nothing more than the egoism of the ruling class. Moreover, it consists of spoken dialogue that seems foreign to the speaking tone of the immanent narrator. Accordingly, the tone of speech here becomes tangled and confused.

> In this floating world even a ferocious tiger resents the distant position of a monkey in the trees who makes light of him. If some lofty office or title was attached to my name, it would make that Tahara bow so deeply that the tatami floormats would leave deep marks on his forehead, make him speak in respectful tones. To kowtow before a viscount, to worship him as an "honorable son-in-law"—how regrettable, in this day of equality between the four classes, to distinguish between men as if one were dirt and the other heaven![12] To

---

12. During the Edo period, virtually all Japanese were divided into four hereditary classes or status groups, which were ranked hierarchically: warrior, peasant, artisan, and merchant. One of the

appraise Shuun cheaply, to try to clamp his lips shut with hundred- or ten-thousand-yen bills: this was a grudge that ran into the millions! [. . . .]

Growing thinner and thinner, finally falling ill, persecuted by love and wrung with sadness, too weak to take heart: [he is] haunted by strange dreams—legs tangled in duckweed as he is mired in a bog, or again, walking along a mossy road laden with dew, a chilly shudder as leeches fall on [his] neck. When [he] awakes, [he] comes to suspect that even the light of the sun has grown weaker [. . .] [He] is half-asleep during the day and sometimes raves deliriously; when [he] sees the faces of others, [he] neither jokes nor grins. When the world is gradually turning to spring and the wind blows peacefully across the blue sky, the treetops throw off their snow garments, the icicles on the houses have suddenly disappeared, and the white spots mottling the eaves gradually vanish. When the southern-exposed straw roofs show their faces not seen since last year, even old men with blurry eyes rejoice, "Now there's something I've missed." The water is warm and the grass is budding. "Seen any hawks yet?" and "How about pheasants?" and then they race ahead to rumors about river trout, while the young people dash about just as spirited as their horses, and yet in their midst [he] seems to be suffering from an unseasonable melancholy. (*MBZ* 25:16)

In the original Japanese version of this passage, it is nearly impossible to tell what parts of it belong to the voice of the immanent narrator and what parts consist of Shuun's inner monologue. Originally, Shuun was a young Buddhist monk who deliberately turned his back on the trends of the new age and set off on foot into the Kiso Mountains as a kind of ascetic religious training. What appeals to this self-awareness of being an eccentric oddball is Otatsu, a lovely young lady selling a local variety of pickles. When asked, she says that she is the daughter of a geisha who fell into unfortunate circumstances due to the war that led to the Meiji Restoration. Otatsu too is a woman fated to struggle against the trends of the new age, making her existence one not easily forsaken by a youth bearing the sort of self-consciousness that marks Shuun. As for the process by which Shuun becomes conscious of his own sensibility, the immanent narrator takes charge and brings out from within itself the speaking tone of the old man from the inn, which depicts Otatsu's circumstances. In this way, the necessity of Shuun and Otatsu being united is skillfully developed within the

---

first acts of the new Meiji government was to abolish these class distinctions and declare equality between the four classes (although new forms of discrimination and hierarchy were also immediately introduced).

very structure of expression. Nevertheless, the world on which Shuun had turned his back ends up taking its revenge on him. Otatsu launches onto the social mainstream of the day, leaving Shuun behind. This was probably a reflection of the sense of tension toward the new period that existed within the self-consciousness of the author, Kōda Rohan. The disruption caused by the new Meiji authorities affects not only Shuun: the immanent narrator and the old man at the inn too are made to produce words attacking the falsity of the ideal of the new age, "equality between the four classes." The self-serving language of the new authorities forces itself onto the common people, who are unable to check or resist it, and their subsequent rage and confusion are given expression here in dramatic form.

Shuun has been rendered incapable of enjoying the natural scenery. Otatsu at the level of sensibility should have shared that scenery in common with him, but she has deserted him. As a result, any possibility of him achieving an aesthetic sensibility toward nature is foreclosed. From this point on in the history of expressions, whenever a person driven into a situation like Shuun's tries to depict nature, that depiction will necessarily be marked by a certain distortion. The nature unfolded there will necessarily be a fantastic, hallucinatory nature, one completely different from the clarity and aestheticality of the nature seen by a person capable of riding the trends of the times. The age of a new mode of expression, one partially realized by Kitamura Tōkoku and then more fully realized by Izumi Kyōka, was soon to arrive.

Another thing that is important to note here is that, in spite of Shuun's unhappy destiny, his self-consciousness never collapses. What is necessary to this self-consciousness is not the image of Otatsu, the lofty wife of the Viscount Iwanuma, but rather that of Otatsu, the impoverished pickle seller, and so he proceeds to carve a sculpture in that image.[13] This may well mark an obsession that even Shuun himself would acknowledge as a blind delusion. Nonetheless, it represents a movement in the opposite direction from that of Ōta in "Maihime," who while giving in to the temptation offered by his friend Aizawa Kenkichi, engages in spiteful recriminations against both his friend and himself—thereby falling into an unmanly collapse of ego, which in turns drives the unfortunate Elis into even more desperate straits. Shuun demonstrates that there are those for whom self-consciousness can assert its legitimacy only by means of a blind delusion. Such people endure the pain of a sensibility that is incapable of self-enjoyment and can establish only an estranged relationship with the objects they create. And yet they find that they have no choice but to go on creating.

13. In the final scene of the story, Shuun carves a sculpture in the image of Otatsu, a sculpture that magically seems to come to life.

Chapter Six
The Structure of Rage:
The Polyphonic Fiction of Higuchi Ichiyō

TRANSLATED BY JOSHUA YOUNG

Here Kamei turns to works from the 1890s that seem to step back from the progressive narrative of Civilization and Enlightenment that marked the works discussed hitherto. Not only do these works focus on social groups marginalized and alienated under the rise of capitalism, in their writing style they reject the modernizing genbun itchi *style and make no attempt to unite their expressions through a single, unifying self-consciousness. But whereas previous studies have dealt with these works as atavistic throwbacks to Edo-period* gesaku *writing styles, Kamei argues that their unique style requires a new method of reading. He notes a resemblance between these works and the "polyphonic" style that Bakhtin discovered in Dostoevsky, but notes that in the latter, polyphony emerges from the breakdown of a previously established self-consciousness. In the works discussed here, such a preexisting coherent subject cannot be presumed. Instead, their mode of expression stands suspended halfway to the sort of awakened self-consciousness found in the works of Futabatei or Tsubouchi. In Higuchi Ichiyō's "Child's Play," we find not a coherent narrator, but rather a speaking voice suspended between worlds, one interpenetrated by the words of others: it is a "nomadic half-speaker" that attaches itself to various characters and is possessed by their voices. As a result, unlike the narrators in Futabatei or Tsubouchi, this voice, by weaving the words of the various characters into the flow of its own narrative descriptions, is able to capture the interior emotions of those characters. Moreover, it becomes a medium through which passions can flow back and forth between various characters, bringing them into dialogue even when there is no direct contact between them. Rather than capturing the drama of emerging self-consciousness, Ichiyō's work captures the drama of polyphony, the clashing of multiple voices and sensibilities.*

111

As if bewitched, people writing novels began to turn their gaze upon worlds detested and shunned by petty bourgeoisie thinking. Such is the trend that took hold in the 1890s, especially the latter half of that decade, and that continued on into the early 1900s.

The novels of this period portray, for example, the world of the rough women who engage in prostitution, or the world of a woman abandoned deep in the snowy mountains and whose skull relates to a passing young man the story of her wretched life: the worlds, in other words, found in Higuchi Ichiyō's "Troubled Waters" ("Nigorie," 1894) and Kōda Rohan's *Encounter with a Skull* (*Engaien*, later retitled *Tai dokuro*, 1890). Similarly, writers such as Hirotsu Ryūrō and Oguri Fuyō liked to depict the lifestyles of the urban lower classes, including portrayals of siblings driven into doomed, incestuous love relationships by irrational social prejudice (discriminatory consciousness).[1] That a similar tendency exists in the works of Izumi Kyōka goes without saying. Even Masaoka Shiki, though the work was not published until after his death, wrote *"Higan Lilies"* ("Manjushage," ca. 1897), a kind of ghost tale in which the flower-peddler daughter of a snake charmer brandishes a mysterious power to exact revenge on the hero on the day of his wedding to another woman.

To approach this from another angle, we can say that the women who appear in these works in most cases are made to bear some sort of social taboo. These women with bewitching features in fact were made to symbolize the prohibitions that defined the everyday thinking of the petty bourgeoisie. The resentment and pride of these ostracized women form the core of the dramatic constructions of these novels.

I am not sure why such a trend arose. If we look at it in terms of literary history, it seems that the political novels of the 1880s, which had imaginatively depicted dramas carried along by the ideals and spirit of men, gave way to novels constructed around women's sensibilities and passions. Futabatei Shimei's *Ukigumo* and Mori Ōgai's "Maihime" and "The Courier" ("Fumizukai," 1891) mark the turning point in this history. In a sense, this trend also represented a revival of the so-called poison-woman stories that were popular around 1880. In terms of the socio-political situation, we can say that with the growth of Japanese capitalism, civil society was produced only unevenly, thereby bring-

---

1. Kamei is alluding in particular to two stories that depict ill-fated romances involving members of the *burakumin* pariah group, Hirotsu Ryūrō's "What Sin?" ("Nan no tsumi," 1903) and Oguri Fūyō's "Night Face Powder" ("Neoshiroi," 1896). The latter suggests an incestuous relationship between a brother and sister. For a more detailed discussion of discrimination and works depicting burakumin characters, including the Masaoka Shiki story discussed immediately below, see chapter eleven.

ing about the problem of the lower classes who were left behind or alienated from the development of civil society. Eventually, this group—that part of society portrayed in the works I have mentioned above—came to be saddled with the greater part of the social contradictions inherent in that development process. The underlying causes behind this literary trend cannot be understood without bringing all these points together into some sort of synthesis.

However, such an approach could still not explain the strange powers of attraction and fascination that we find in the works themselves. We should note that the thinking of the characters within these works for the most part does not extend beyond their everyday personal relations; they are closed off to the so-called larger situation. When we consider the authors, too, we find that their critical historical consciousness was not very finely honed. At the least, we can say that these works were not written with social criticism as a self-conscious motif. Why these writers felt compelled to approach women's sentiments and passions is another point that is difficult to explain. And it is for these sorts of reasons that the critics and scholars who have hitherto examined this literature have in the end done nothing more than point out a residual "*gesaku* consciousness" in these writers and treat this era as a low point in the history of modern literature.

Yet, unexpectedly, it may well be the very opaque nature of these works, that is, their mixture of modern and *gesaku* forms of consciousness, that holds the secret of their creation. When we look at this in terms of writing style, it is true that the modes of expression in both Ichiyō and Rohan represent a kind of regression. Their writing lacks a consistency of self-consciousness of clearly individualized persons, not only in the *words* (spoken dialogue) of the characters, but even in the passages of authorial narrative description. Instead, other voices continually intrude, like water seeping into marshland, disrupting any attempt to attain a clear grasp and evaluation of the object (objective) world. Moreover, we find in their writing something different from the *gesaku*-like tone of a narrator who is conscious of a close-at-hand audience (auditor), such as we noted in Tsubouchi Shōyō's *The Temper of Students in Our Times* or Futabatei's *Ukigumo*. The mode of expression here corresponds in one aspect to what Mikhail Bakhtin in his *Problems of Dostoevsky's Poetics* calls polyphonic (multivocal) expression, but there is a decisive difference: here, we are dealing in terms of an only half-awakened state of self-consciousness. This is not to say that Ichiyō and Rohan were unaware of individual consciousness; on the contrary, each unmistakably took pride in his or her own individuality. Yet as soon as they entered the topos of expression, that individuality found itself somehow transformed by some other thing, so that the "self," which ought to be objectified within their expressions, stops halfway through the process of attaining the status of a speaking subject. This inclination is particularly pronounced in Ichiyō's works.

In the case of Dostoevsky's works, a stable, secure self-consciousness is made to undergo suffering. That self-consciousness is possessed by doubts about its "self" and upon reaching a moment of total exhaustion it discovers an other within itself, or again, it achieves—though not without conflict—a reconciliation with the *words* of the other. This process was developed into a methodological principle in Dostoevsky's writing style. In the expressions of Ichiyō and Rohan, however, we find a mode of writing that belongs to people whose self-consciousness has yet to be seized by doubt, which is precisely why they were able to take pride in their own individuality. But this was also the reason why they were unable to achieve a consistency of consciousness in the narrators that are immanent to their expressions.

In short, we must improvise a new methodology if we want to explain the particularities of these works. Having resigned ourselves to this fact, let us set out to reread these works. In doing so, we will encounter many crucial problems that demand a fundamental reconsideration of our view of literature. Our examination of these problems will also lead us to reconsider the degree of validity of the currently hegemonic methodology that focuses on interpretation within the limits of a single literary work (*sakuhinron*) and of the adequacy of the various humanistic concepts that underlie that methodology.

* * * * *

To consider this problem of women's sentiment and sensibility, I shall first take up the works of Higuchi Ichiyō. The following is from the opening passage of "Child's Play" ("Takekurabe," 1895–96). Note the abrupt presentation of a quite chilling world.

> Most of the people here, in fact, have some connection with the quarter. The menfolk do odd jobs at the less dignified houses. You can hear them in the evenings jiggling their shoe-check tags before they leave for work, and you'll see them putting on their jackets when most men take them off. Wives rub good-luck flints behind them to protect their men from harm. Could this be the final parting? It's a dangerous business. Innocent bystanders get killed when there's a brawl in one of the houses. And look out if you ever foil the double suicide of a courtesan and her lover! Yet off the husbands go to risk their lives each night. So strange to see how they treat this life-threatening work as fun and games. Daughters too are involved in the quarter: here, a serving girl in one of the great establishments; there, an escort plying back and forth between the teahouse and the brothel.

They bustle along with their shop's lantern, an advertisement for all to see. But what will become of these girls once they have graduated from their present course of training? They see nothing funny about the work, it's grand and gala, as if they were performing on a fine wooden stage. Then one day before they know it they have reached the age of thirty, trim and tidy in the cotton coats with matching dresses and their sensible dark blue stockings. They carry their little packages under their arms, and we know what these are without asking. Stomp, stomp, they go with the heels of their sandals—they're in an awful hurry—and the flimsy drawbridges flop down across the ditch. "We'll leave it here at the back," they say, setting down their bundles, "it's too far round to the front." So they are needle-women now, apparently. Customs here are indeed a little different. You won't find many women who tie their sashes neatly behind their waists. It's one thing to see a woman of a certain age who favors gaudy patterns, or a sash cut immoderately wide. It's quite another to see these barefaced girls of fifteen or sixteen, all decked out in flashy clothes and blowing on bladder cherries, which everybody knows are used as contraceptives, but that's what kind of neighborhood it is. . . .[2]

This narrator is evading, holding at arm's length, the world depicted in this passage. Perhaps we can say that this occurs because the doubling of the self that takes place in the author has yet to reach the stage of a clear split, so that there is a constant wavering between the stances of critic and apologist.

We see few residents in this scene who maintain an orderly or honest way of life. There are no people who make a respectable living; most exist on the fringes, trying to piece together a livelihood on the leavings of the pleasure quarters. Yet they close their eyes to the wretchedness of this existence and earnestly live out their miserable roles. The introduction to this world notes that "daughters too are involved in the quarter: here, a serving girl in one of the great establishments; there, an escort plying back and forth between the teahouse and the brothel. They bustle along with their shop's lantern, an advertisement for all to see. But what will become of these girls once they have graduated from their present course of training? [. . .] It's one thing to see a woman of a certain age who favors gaudy patterns, or a sash cut immoderately wide. It's quite another to see these barefaced girls of fifteen or sixteen, all decked out in flashy clothes and blowing on bladder cherries, which everybody knows are

2. This and all other quotations from "Child's Play" are adapted from Robert Danly's translation of the story as it appears in Robert Lyons Danly, *In the Shade of the Spring Leaves* (New York: W.W. Norton, 1981), 254–87. This passage appears on pp. 254–55. The story has also been translated by Edward Seidensticker under the title "Growing Up" in Donald Keene, ed., *Modern Japanese Literature* (New York: Grove Press, 1956), 70–110.

used as contraceptives." Obviously the narrator is conscious at this point of the gaze of an outsider, or else the narrator herself (more accurately, itself) steps into the position of an outsider. The outsider that is assumed here is most likely the kind of person who, since the Edo period, had taken it as a virtue to maintain domestic discipline in keeping with one's social rank and class. Among such people, a rigid distinction was maintained between respectable and inferior occupations, and of course only those people who belonged to the former category were regarded as leading a proper way of life. It seems likely that Higuchi Ichiyō herself bore this type of sensibility.

In that sense, the structure of expression in this work takes the form of an introduction for outsiders to a certain world, a world that seemingly could not be affirmed when viewed from the evaluative axis of an outsider who sides with the bourgeois social order. However, this introduction is certainly not intended to reform anyone's view of humanity. Following the critical "what will become of these girls once they have graduated from their present course of training?" comes the assertion, "they see nothing strange about the work, to them it's grand and gala, as if they were performing on a fine wooden stage." And to balance the censure of "to see these barefaced girls of fifteen or sixteen, all decked out in flashy clothes and blowing on bladder cherries, which everybody knows are used as contraceptives," there is at least the apologetic "But that's what kind of neighborhood it is." So even while this narrator is mediated through an outsider's gaze, she often also reverts to the position of a person who belongs to this world of the pleasure quarters. Yet the degree of self-assertion made from that position—that is, the sense of living in common with the people of the pleasure quarters and sharing their fate—is never particularly strong.

As we can see from the scene where Midori has a passing lady minstrel sing a popular song of love gone wrong ("Child's Play," 272), the perspective of the narrator in these cases is probably closest to that of the wife at the paper store.

The frequent use of the ambivalent word "*okashii*" (funny/strange/unusual)[3] arises out of the ambiguity of this position and its doubled perspective.

> "Your old man's a 'horse,' isn't he? Isn't he?" The blood rushes to the defendant's face. The poor boy—he'd rather die than admit his father collected bills for a brothel. And then there are the favorite

---

3. Danley has, quite legitimately, used various different expressions to render the original word "*okashii*," which as Kamei notes occurs repeatedly in the first part of the story. In the translated passages, we have inserted the word in parentheses where it occurs.

sons of the big shots of the quarter, who grow up in lodgings at some
remove, free to feign a noble birth. They sport the latest prep-school
cap, they have a look of leisure, and they wear their European clothes
with style and panache. All the same, it's amusing [*okashii*] to watch
the others curry favor. "Young master, young master," they call them,
when "spoiled brat" would do. ("Child's Play" 256)

Certainly for the children in question, but even to the eyes of an outsider,
this matter cannot be very "amusing." Yet the writing seems deliberately to amuse
itself in depicting this incredibly wretched and cruel spectacle. Or, again:

Most of the people here, in fact, have some connection with the
quarter. The menfolk do odd jobs at the less dignified houses. You
can hear them in the evenings jiggling their shoe-check tags before
they leave for work, and you'll see them putting on their jackets when
most men take them off. Wives rub good-luck flints behind them to
protect their men from harm. Could this be the final parting? It's a
dangerous business. Innocent bystanders get killed when there's a
brawl in one of the houses. And look out if you ever foil the double
suicide of a courtesan and her lover! Yet off the husbands go to risk
their lives each night; so strange [*okashii*] to see this life-threatening
work as fun and games.

The expression "innocent bystanders get killed when there's a brawl in
one of the houses" is taken from either Kawatake Shinshichi III's kabuki,
Kagotsurube: Sobering Up in the Quarter (*Kagotsurube sato no eizame*, 1888)
or else from an anonymous Edo-period factual novel, *Hero of the Three Cities:
Kagotsurube* (*Santo yueiden: Kagotsurube*).[4] Such dangerous incidents no longer
occurred in Ichiyō's time, so the expression here presents a highly theatrical
temperament, that of one who goes off to work acting as if it were to a truly life-
threatening hell. In fact, however, all this narrator has done is to borrow a line
from Kawatake's popular play and use this allusion to define the temperament
of the pleasure quarter people. Having done so, the narrator then declares
"strange" the sight of these people going off to work as if "it were fun and
games." In other words, while she feigns to touch upon the daily emotional life
of the people who work in this area, in fact, the narrator only amuses herself
with the discrepancy between her own theatrical allusion and reality. In the end,

4. Higuchi Ichiyō, *Zenshū Higuchi Ichiyō*, 4 vols. (Tokyo: Shōgakkan, 1979), 2:8n5. See also
Danly, *In the Shade of the Spring Leaves*, 324n6. An abbreviated English version of
Kagotsurube is available in Donald Richie and Miyoko Watanabe, trans., *The Grand Kabuki:
Libretto* (New York: Program Publishing Company, 1960), 15–27.

she only toys with the emotions of the people of the quarter, thereby obscuring any possibility for serious ethical judgment.

Previously I described this world as "chilling." It goes without saying that I include in that assessment this stance of the narrator.

* * * * *

The result of this mode of writing is that the characters who appear in "Child's Play" are deprived of any consciousness capable of focusing on what lies outside their own small world. The writing style does not permit a self-critical self-consciousness to awaken within them. Instead, the mode of expression here covers over their consciousness with emotions that derive from the narrator's allusions. The central characters are of course children, but they perform the appearances and feelings of adults with remarkable precocity:

> Mother Meng would be scandalized at the speed with which they learn to mimic all the famous clowns; why, there's not a one of them who can't do Rohachi and Eiki. They hear their performances praised, and that night the smart alecks repeat their rounds. It starts at the age of seven or eight, this audacity, and by the time they're fifteen! Towels from the evening bath dangle from their shoulders, and the latest song, in a nasal twang of disrespect, dribbles from the corner of their lips. ("Child's Play," 255)

They are, so to speak, half-grown-up children, or grown-ups in the guise of children.

It is true that they perform a caricature of adult life, but they themselves are not aware of this fact. These diminutive adults are made to perform in its purest form the highly theatrical temperament that the narrator associated via her theatrical allusion with the people of the quarter.

Representative of this is Chōkichi, like a child sent from heaven expressly to reveal the character of this area.

> The Festival of Senzoku Shrine was set for the twentieth of August, and not a block would there be without a float of its own jostling for glory. Over the ditch and up the side of the embankment they charge: all the young men, pushing, pulling, bent on taking the quarter. The heart beats faster at the mere thought of it. And keep an eye, mind you, on the young ones – once they get wind of what the older boys are up to. Matching kimonos for the whole gang are only the beginning. The saucy things they dream up *will give you goose bumps.* The back-street gang, as they preferred to call themselves, had Chōkichi for their leader. He was the fire chief's son—sixteen and full of it. He

hadn't walked without his chest puffed out since the day he started policing the fall festival with his father: baton swinging, belt low around the hips, sneering whenever he answered. *The firemen's wives all griped among themselves*: if he weren't the chief's boy, he'd never get away with it. Selfish Chōkichi saw to it that he always got his way. He stretched his side-street influence wider than it really went. But then there is Shōta, the leader of the main-street gang. Shōta is three years younger than me, but he is the son of Tanaka, the pawn-broker; his family has money, people like him [. . . .] With his band of admirers—even some grown-ups numbered among them—for the last two years Shōta's plans for the festival have flowered more luxu-riantly than the efforts of our gang. It has been no contest, and, if I lose again this year, all my threats—"Who do you think you're deal-ing with? Chōkichi from the back streets, that's who!"—will no longer garner even enough members for a swimming team at the Benten ditch [. . . .] Now the festival is only two days away. More and more my losing colors are showing through. Something must be done! If I could just see that Shōta got a little egg on his face, it wouldn't mat-ter if I myself lost an eye or a limb. If I could just recruit the likes of Ushi, the son of the rickshawman, and Ben, whose family makes hair ribbons, and Yasuke, the toymaker's boy. . . . ("Child's Play," 256–57; italics Kamei's)

The mode of expression here is the same as in the opening passage. First there is an introduction to the Senzoku shrine festival for an outsider who is presumed not to know: "it's enough to give you goose bumps. . . ." Then, it assumes an insider's voice, that of the local firemen's wives, to comment on Chōkichi's detestable strutting.

And yet, in this passage, the ambiguous term "funny" doesn't appear at all. Its figure is erased. That is to say, to a certain degree the sense of belonging to this world has been strengthened. If the characters here were adults, no mat-ter how much the narrator might favor a certain temperament and muster theat-rical allusions to figure the characters, in the end such a staging would inevita-bly come into conflict with reality. But with a child like Chōkichi, who wants nothing better than to walk the rounds with his father, whose whole existence is caught up in copying the manners of his hot tempered firecrew-chief father, we have a character able to act out to the letter the tenor of the narrator's allusion. Note, for example, the highly theatrical manner in which the passage stirs up his fighting spirit: "More and more my losing colors are showing. Something must be done! If only I could see that Shōta got a little egg on his face, it wouldn't matter if I myself lost an eye or a limb. . . ."

Even so, the passion attributed to Chōkichi's position still seems ex-cessive and exaggerated. To speak in terms of dramatic formula, his is the role of hated spoiler who interferes in the romance between the courtesan Midori and the wealthy young Shōta. That this despised villain is the first character to appear in the story suggests in advance that events will develop only to the extent that his passion (rage) entwines the other characters. We are presented with a person of exaggerated intensity, one who considers a trifling tussle over the festival procession as a challenge to his honor; without that energy, the drama of this narrative would not come to life.

In that sense, Chōkichi is the driving force in this narrative; he is the only character to embody a dramatic passion. But to put this another way, we can also say that the narrator of this work has yet to acquire a methodology for constructing a novel that would center on the reactions to events that she herself has witnessed. In short, she does not possess a method that would depict the object world in relation to transformations in self-consciousness. For this reason, she can only move the story along by resorting to the passion of a highly theatrical villain as the fulcrum of dramatic development.

So far I have been speaking of the narrator and have avoided the term "author." I have already explained my reasons for this, but here, perhaps we should think of this more rigorously in terms of a nomadic half-speaker, one who attaches herself freely to other characters within the work.

As is clear from the passage quoted above, the speaker constantly jumps from one person's perspective to another, all the while unfolding her expressions by overlaying her own voice onto the *words* of those people. The "gripes" of the firemen's wives, if we extract only their direct spoken dialogue, consist solely of the *words* "if he weren't the chief's boy, he'd never get away with it." But in the passage that comes just before this, we can already detect the perspective and even the *words* of the firemen's wives: "he hadn't walked without his chest puffed out since the day he started policing the fall festival with his father: baton swinging, belt low around the hips, sneering whenever he answered." And the ripples of their gripe-filled expressions continue to spread out through the subsequent pronouncement that "selfish Chōkichi saw to it that he always got his way. He stretched his side-street influence wider than it really went." At this point, she abruptly switches to the standpoint of Chōkichi and his emotional expressions (*hyōshutsu*): "But then there is Shōta, the leader of the main-street gang. Shōta is three years younger than me, but he is the son of Tanaka, the pawnbroker; his family has money, people like him. . . ."

Let me add a short aside on this passage. In the Shōgakkan version of Ichiyō's complete works, this passage—"But then there is Shōta. . . ."—is punctuated to indicate that it belongs to the narrative descriptive voice of the author. Certainly, the layout of this edition is easy to understand, and the explanatory notes are quite useful (they informed me, for example, of the connection with *Kagotsurube*). But in the matter of this quoted section, I chose to use the original version of the text as it first appeared in magazine form, ignoring the annotations produced by the Shōgakkan editors, including revamped paragraphs and punctuation and the placement of quotation marks to distinguish spoken dialogue and internal soliloquies from their contexts. I have cut out these devices simply because I fear they erase the special characteristics of writing style in this work.

If we look at it from the standpoint of the author, this half-speaker who continually attaches onto other voices functions something like a transmitter that permits varying degrees of modulation. In one seamless flow of narration, she proceeds by adjusting the modulation, selecting, one after another, voices of appropriate wavelengths, or what in physics are called stationary waves. This is not necessarily something unique to Ichiyō; other works, including Rohan's *Five-Story Pagoda*, use this same mode of writing. In terms of the history of modes of expression, it is an important characteristic of early 1890's prose, but few writers had the knack with it that Ichiyō demonstrated. Chōkichi's internal *words* start out, "But then there is Shōta, the leader of the main-street gang," and then are modulated into a highly theatrical mannerism: "More and more my losing colors are showing. Something must be done!" It is not difficult to detect in the spoken dialogue that latently dominates Chōkichi's everyday speech, for example, lines reminiscent of characters from Takeshiba Kisui's play *The Match in Harmony* (*Kami no megumi wagō no torikumi*, 1890),[5] such as Tatsugorō, or better yet, Kamesaemon of Rogetsu-chō. Chōkichi hears these lines of spoken dialogue inside his head and they provoke a change in his attitude: "Ah, and better still: him. Yeah, that guy. Fujimoto-No. He'd have a good idea or two" ("Child's Play," 257). Referring to Nobu via the street-tough *words* "Fujimoto-No," as Seki Ryōichi has pointed out,[6] lends this a tone of rough bravado, so that it expresses (*hyōshutsu*) Chōkichi's ardor. When he is face to face with Nobu, of course, he doesn't use this manner of address. Fujimoto Nobuyuki of Ryūge Temple at first balks at Chōkichi's entreaties, but soon he gets into the spirit of the matter. "And if that happens, I'll wrap Shōta around my little finger. Nobu's reticence had already been forgotten. He opened his desk drawer

---

5. Takeshiba Kisui (1847–1923) was a prominent kabuki playwright. A disciple of Kawatake Mokuami, he became resident playwright for the Meiji-za theater in 1895. *The Match in Harmony*, also known as *The Fight of Megumi* (*Megumi no kenka*), tells the story of a dispute in and around the Shinagawa pleasure quarter between a gang of local firemen and some sumo wrestlers. The introductory scene was apparently written by Kawatake Shinshichi (who wrote *Kagotsurube*) and several parts are thought to have been composed by Kawatake Mokuami. In an earlier kabuki version of the same story written by Mokuami and premiered in 1872, one of the lead characters is named Chōkichi.

6. *Zenshū Higuchi Ichiyō*, 2:11n14.

and showed Chōkichi the prized Kokaji dagger his father had brought him from Kyoto. Say, that'll really cut!, Chōkichi admired. Look out—careful how you wave that thing" ("Child's Play," 259).

The line "that'll really cut!" echoes a line of dialogue spoken by Sano Jirōzaemon in the kabuki version of *Kagotsurube*: "but this sword looks like it'll really cut!"[7] The sword called Kagotsurube bears an evil curse: if one keeps it hidden and never draws it out, then it will not haunt that person. If, however, one deigns to draw it from its sheath, then without fail that person will fall into some tragic mishap that will not end until blood has been spilled. Jirōzaemon, knowing this, unsheathes the sword to whet it, whereupon he becomes embroiled in a bloody catastrophe. The scene of Chōkichi and Nobu thus overlaps with the kabuki scene and the story behind it, and hence the *words* of caution that seem to slip out unexpectedly at the end of the above passage: "Look out—careful how you wave that thing." It goes without saying that these *words* belong to the nomadic half-speaker herself.

If this is so, what kind of relationship exists between this nomadic half-speaker and the author of the work? Or rather, what sort of position does the author hold in relation to the work?

The editors of the Shōgakkan edition see these *words*, "Look out . . . ," as representing "Ichiyō's feelings."[8] Of course we cannot simply say that this is wrong. However, if we proceed without assuming the existence of a narrator immanent to the work (a distinct and unified speaking subject), it becomes possible to read them as belonging to Nobu. To wit, having been carried away by the situation, he suddenly senses the danger and renders into *words* the impulsive act of drawing the dagger.

Fundamentally speaking, the author and the speaking subject that is objectified within a work must be distinguished from one another. This speaking subject produces its expressions in its capacity as what I have called the non-person narrator—a speaking subject that possesses self-consciousness as an individuated person but does not appear as a character in the work. Eventually this type of speaking subject evolved into another type, that of the first-person reporter. If we look at it in terms of this history of development, the nomadic half-speaker that occurs in Ichiyō's "Child's Play" represents a step backward, in that she lacks a clear consistency of self-consciousness. However, the non-person narrators who appear in Tsubouchi Shōyō's *The Temper of Stu-*

---

7. Kikuchi Akira, ed., *Kagotsurube sato no eizame/Kami no megumi wago no torikumi: kabuki on suteiji* 7 (Tokyo: Hakusuisha, 1986), 87.
8. *Zenshū Higuchi Ichiyō*, 2:12n12.

dents in Our Times and Futabatei Shimei's *Ukigumo* go no further than to make satirical allusions and observations regarding the external features of the characters; they lack the consistency of consciousness required to produce expressions that adhered to the characters' so-called interiorities. Ichiyō, on the other hand, had progressed to the point of developing a form that, by performing one after another the *words* of any number of characters, all within a single continuous stream of narration, was able to suggest via allusion the various characters' emotions. What seemed like a regressive form was in fact progressive.

In trying to come to an understanding of the reasons for this phenomenon, I have in the two years between my writing the previous chapter and this one, belatedly though it may be, looked at Bakhtin's discussion of Dostoevsky. I have also been reading the theoretical works of structuralists, as well as Noguchi Takehiko's *The Japanese Language in Fiction* (*Shōsetsu no Nihongo*, 1980), Karatani Kōjin's *Origins of Modern Japanese Literature* (*Nihon kindai bungaku no kigen*, 1980) and several volumes by Hasumi Shigehiko.[9] These works have been a rich source of ideas. But to speak for the moment in terms of Bakhtin's work, he deals only with the relations between the author and the characters in the work, or the reciprocal relations among the various characters. As we know from Miura Tsutomu's work, this must come up short as a theory of literary construction because it fails to consider the decisive role of the narrator – as, for example, the non-person narrator. In other words, it overlooks the delicate construction process that occurs when the author's own ideas about structure and plot negotiate the expressions of the non-person narrator who is immanent to the depicted world.

Furthermore, while pursuing in previous chapters the problem of the expression of sensibility, I came up with a way of approaching the material that seems to correspond to Bakhtin's analysis of what he calls monologic writing. But in my approach, I came to the realization that in the works I studied, a new "knowledge" of sensibility had arisen out from the writing style used to represent passages of spoken dialogue. With this realization, I was able to account for the struggle over *words* between characters and the generation of an "interior" writing style, as well as the relationships of domination that structured passages of spoken dialogue. When viewed from that standpoint, it seems that my approach allowed me to address a number of questions that are dealt with incompletely or not at all in Bakhtin's work and in that of the other critics I mentioned just now. I eventually intend to deal with those various points, but first of all I want to take up the matter of what Bakhtin calls monologic writing.

9. These works are discussed at length in chapter twelve.

Bakhtin uses the concept of monologic writing in the following manner:

> Thus Vyacheslav Ivanov, having arrived at a profound and correct definition of Dostoevsky's fundamental principle—the affirmation of someone else's "I" not as an object but as another subject—proceeded to monologize this principle, that is, he incorporated it into a monologically formulated authorial worldview and perceived it as merely one of the interesting themes in a world represented from the point of view of a monologic authorial consciousness.[10]

Though this does not necessarily refer only to works written in the first-person soliloquy form, we can say that the representative monologic novels of the era around 1890 include Tōkai Sanshi's *Chance Encounters with Beautiful Women* and Mori Ōgai's "Maihime."

> The weakening or destruction of a monologic context occurs only when there is a coming together of two utterances equally and directly oriented toward a referential object. Two discourses equally and directly oriented toward a referential object within the limits of a single context cannot exist side by side without intersecting dialogically, regardless of whether they confirm, mutually supplement, or (conversely) contradict one another, or find themselves in some other dialogic relationship (that of question and answer, for example). *Two equally weighted discourses on one and the same theme, once having come together, must inevitably orient themselves to one another.* Two embodied meanings cannot lie side by side like two objects—they must come into inner contact; that is, they must enter into a semantic bond. (*Dostoevsky*, 188–89; emphasis Kamei's)[11]

From this point of view, the language of "Child's Play" can be seen as an example of "the weakening or destruction of the monologic context." What is crucial here, however, is the sentence that I have emphasized.

But this is not simply a matter of the "weakening or destruction" of a "Maihime"—like (monologic) style of writing. In fact, if we look at Shōyō's *The Temper of Students in Our Times* or Futabatei's *Ukigumo*, we see the reverse: movement toward a monologic mode of expression. The non-person nar-

---

10. Mikail Bakhtin, *Problems of Dostoevsky's Poetics*, trans. Caryl Emerson (Minneapolis: University of Minnesota Press, 1984), 11.

11. In the Japanese translation of Bakhtin's work, this quote reads somewhat differently, particularly the sentence that Kamei has emphasized. A literal English translation of the Japanese sentence would read, "Even when two words of equal weight have simply encountered one another through their relation to a single theme, this inevitably results in the reciprocal objectification of one another."

rators who occur in these works, because they only poke satirical fun at and invoke *gesaku*-like allusions to depict the external aspect of the characters, are unable to relate directly to the humanistic ideas and internal motifs that the author uses to structure the work. Instead, the ideas and motifs of the author are manifested primarily in statements made by the works' central characters. It is true that the non-person narrators in these works sometimes give the impression of polyphony, when, for example, they portray the external speech characteristics of the various characters—what kinds of things attract their attention, what kind of vocabulary they like to use, the manner in which they speak. That impression is particularly strong in the first two books of *Ukigumo*. But once a specific character (Bunzō) comes to occupy the position of the author's internal progeny and alter ego (i.e., becomes the protagonist or perspectival character), it marks the beginning of the transformation of the work into a monologic world.

In comparison to those narrators, the nomadic half-speaker of "Child's Play" takes from the start a form more directly connected to the author's central motifs. This was probably the methodology that Shōyō and Futabatei were aiming for. It is not so completely monologic as the form we find in "Maihime," and this in-between quality allows it to produce a richly multivocal writing style. Let us return once again to the opening passage. In terms of plot and composition, the structuring idea that Ichiyō chooses is this world where,

> It's a long way round to the front of the quarter, where the trailing branches of the willow tree bid farewell to the nighttime revelers and the bawdyhouse lights flicker in the moat, dark as the dye that blackens the smiles of the Yoshiwara beauties. From the third-floor rooms of the lofty houses the all but palpable music and laughter spill down into the side street. Who knows how these great establishments prosper? The rickshaws pull up night and day. They call this part of town beyond the quarter "in front of Daion Temple." The name may sound a little saintly, but those who live in the area will tell you it's a lively place. ("Child's Play," 254)

I have already touched on the fact that the nomadic half-speaker who looks upon this world is situated as one of "those who live in the area," in particular as occupying a position like that of the firemen's wives. Thanks to this setup, it becomes possible to repeatedly bring in the *words* of unnamed others, even those not necessarily directly present in the work. But the flip side of this is that the author assumes the position of an outsider. Hence we have the double-faced stance of both criticism and apologetics with regard to local customs—particularly the manners of the children—that in turn gives rise to an internally conflicted structure.

This being so, what mode of human consciousness does this writing style visually intend to depict? That is to say, what is the structuring idea of this work in terms of composition and plot? I believe that it is the sentiment of rage (*kuchioshisa* or *kuyashisa*).

> Off she went to the shrine among the paddy fields. She rang the bell, shaped like the great mouth of a crocodile, and clasped her hands in supplication. And what were they for, these prayers of hers? She walked through the fields with her head downcast, to and from the shrine. Shōta saw her from a distance and called out as he ran toward her. He tugged at her sleeve: "Midori, I'm sorry about last night." "That's all right. It wasn't your fault." "But they were after me. If Grandmother hadn't come, I wouldn't have left. And then they wouldn't have beaten up Sangorō the way they did. I went to see him this morning. He was crying and furious [*kuyashigatta*]. I got angry [*kuyashii*] just listening to him talk about it. Chōkichi threw his sandal at you, didn't he? Damn him, anyway! There are limits to what even he can get away with. But I hope you're not mad at me, Midori. I didn't run away from him. I gulped my food down as fast as I could and was just on my way back when Grandmother said I had to watch the house while she went for her bath. That's when all the commotion must have started. Honest, I didn't know anything about it." He apologized as if the crime were his, not Chōkichi's. "Does it hurt?" Shōta examined Midori's forehead. ("Child's Play," 265–66)[12]

Rage spreads out like ripples in water among the various children, and the cause of it all is Chōkichi's grudge. As I pointed out earlier in the passage that first introduces Chōkichi, he is depicted from the beginning as conceited, in perfect accord with the firemen's wives' complaints: "The firemen's wives all griped among themselves: if he weren't the chief's boy, he'd never get away with it. Selfish Chōkichi saw to it that he always got his way. He stretched his side-street influence wider than it really went. But then there is Shōta, the leader of the main-street gang." That is to say, it is in full awareness of the griping of the wives, or rather in reaction to it, that Chōkichi tries to strut his smart-aleck nature, and it is from this that expressions arise that give shape to his feelings. His internal *words* in this context take the form of a resistance against the griping *words* of the firemen's wives, or, perhaps we should say the form of an attempt to transcend them. In short, throughout the work and with unexpected frequency, sharp criticisms from a wife-like point of view are cast against the

---

12. Following Danly's translation, we have used quotation marks here to set off passages of dialogue. In Ichiyō's original (and in Kamei's citation of that original), no such punctuation is used.

speech acts of the children and the way of life of their parents. But once these sharp *words* reach the point of provoking feelings of rage, they suddenly disappear. Only the sentiment of rage remains, maintained in all its purity.

Thus, we find a form whereby first Chōkichi's rage is depicted, whereupon this feeling envelops Nobu and then finally invades the play space of Midori and Shōtarō. Sangorō, a back-street kid who joins Shōtarō's main street gang, gets the worst of it all. "I hate you [*kuyashii*], I hate you, I hate you, I hate you! Damn you, Chōkichi! You bastard. Damn you! Damn you, Bunji! Damn you Ushimatsu![13] Why don't you just kill me? Come on. Just try and kill me. I'm Sangorō and maybe it's not so easy! Even if you did kill me, even if I turned into a ghost, I'd haunt you for the rest of your lives. Remember that, Chōkichi!" ("Child's Play," 265). With the word *kuyashii* repeated four times, what a striking instance of rage this is! Yet once again we can hear an echo of dialogue from the kabuki *Kagotsurube*, namely Osei's "if you're going to kill me because I'm in the way, just do it. Don't think it'll end here though. Your wife and children will go to hell. I'll return to kill. Think of that. [. . .] Go ahead and kill me, why don't you just slaughter me?"[14]

In contrast, the rage felt by Shōtarō is that of one whose docility as his grandmother's pet has worked against him. No one has any reason to hate him, but nonetheless Chōkichi takes him as an enemy. When Chōkichi makes his attack, however, Shōtarō happens to be absent. Thus Shōtarō is made to feel he has done wrong by Midori and Sangorō, who were inadvertently embroiled in what was really his fight. He is caught between the one-sided hatred of his adversary and the wrong of having no way to redeem himself to his friends; such is Shōtarō's rage.

The resentment of these children gradually turns into rage at the unjust state of affairs that they encounter. But Midori's rage has something more to it, a different aspect. With Chōkichi, Sangorō or Shōtarō, their rage at least is directed at an actual adversary. That is, there exists for them some specific other with whom their words can undergo mutual relativization, someone against whom they can direct their resentment. But Midori's case is different; her rage is rooted in her very situation. As an outsider to this area, she carries the burden of the past: "Ever since [the owner of the Daikokuya house] had come to their home in the provinces to appraise her older sister, Midori and her parents had found

13. "Kuyashii, kuyashii, kuyashii, kuyashii. Chōkichi-me . . ."
14. Osei is a former geisha whom Jirozaemon's father, Jirobei, marries but then turns out into the street when she gets sick. Later Jirobei and Osei meet by chance and he kills her. This part of play (the first four acts) is generally not performed today and is omitted from most modern published versions.

themselves here at the Daikokuya. They had packed up their belongings, along with her sister, to seek their fortunes in the city" ("Child's Play," 259).

> From the day after the festival, Midori came to school no more. She could wash the mud from her face, but the shame could not be scrubbed away so easily. They sat together side by side at school—Chōkichi's gang, and the main-street gang—and one might have expected that they could get along. But there had always been a sharp division. It was the act of a coward to attack me, a weak, defenseless girl. Everyone knew Chōkichi was as violent and as stupid as they come. But if he hadn't had Nobu backing him, he could never have behaved so brazenly. And that Nobu! In front of others he pretended to be gentle and wise, but a look behind the scenes would reveal that he was the one pulling all the strings. Midori didn't care if he was ahead of her in school, or how good his grades were. So what if he was the young master of Ryuge Temple! She, after all, was Midori of Daikokuya, and not beholden to him in the slightest. She had never borrowed a single sheet of paper. So who were they to call her a tramp, or those other names Chōkichi used? [. . .] Her parents were mere caretakers for the master's house, but her sister was Ōmaki of the Daikokuya. She didn't have to take insults from the likes of Chōkichi. And too bad for him if the little priest wanted to be mean to her. Midori had enough of school. She was born stubborn and was not about to suffer anyone's contempt. That day she broke her pencils and threw away her ink; she would spend her time playing with her real friends. She wasn't going to need her abacus or her books. ("Child's Play," 269)

When her older sister was sold into the pleasure quarter, Midori and her parents drifted to this neighborhood. Regardless of the actual state of their appearance or property, they must have felt as if they had fallen to the level of beggars. Even the child Midori is caught up in this refraction into the position of an outsider, and from this is born her perverse tendency to defend her own pride by hiding behind the image of her sister as a high-ranking courtesan. To compensate for her outsider position, she excessively identifies herself with and conforms to the local temperament. And though she comes to reign over the other children like a queen, Nobu's existence continues to weigh on her mind. This is because her own sense of alienation—"New to the city, Midori had bristled when the other girls made fun of her, calling her a country girl for wearing a lavender collar with her lined kimono" ("Child's Play," 260)—allows her to intuit the (admittedly somewhat different) refraction that Nobu undergoes as the butt of nasty jokes: "His classmates liked to tease him. 'Here this is your line of work,' they would laugh, stringing up a dead cat. 'How about offering last rites?'" ("Child's Play," 256). And beyond this, there is the question of who really holds power in this neighborhood. Midori as outsider cannot help but try to sniff out who is really in charge "behind the scenes." Chōkichi's violence is a small matter. Even if she were able to get back at Chōkichi, that would not assuage her refracted rage. Her enmity leaps beyond Chōkichi to imagine the mean ignobility of Nobu who, she has no doubt, "pulls the strings behind the scenes."

Seki Ryōichi points out that since it still ought to be summer vacation, the line "From the day after the festival, Midori came to school no more" probably represents an oversight on the part of the author. That may be so, but we must also remember that school was supposed to be a place of equality and fairness, one free of discrimination: "They sat side by side at school—Chōkichi's [back-street] gang and the main-street gang—and one might have expected that they could get along." Midori's rage here at being wounded—"me, a weak, defenseless girl"—is so deep as to reveal to her the falsity of this sham policy. She resolves to refuse this logic of the school, which in the end is nothing more than a fiction.

Midori thinks she detects scorn lurking in the gaze of the other neighborhood children: *when all is said and done, she will end up a prostitute.* If that is so, how much better to adopt the disposition of a famous courtesan, to triumph over her old companions by becoming a great courtesan who lies far beyond their reach. But in the *words* of the passage I quoted above, we also hear the echo of another voice, one that transcends this kind of theatrical expression (*hyōshutsu*) of sentiment.

As is the case with Chōkichi and the others, here too the nomadic half-speaker quite literally adheres to Midori's own rage. But in fact here the two perspectives are even more tightly linked. From the beginning the nomadic half-speaker relates sympathetically to Midori's feelings: "Midori stopped going to school [...] but the shame [*kuyashi*] could not be scrubbed away so easily." In the case of Chōkichi and the other characters, their *words* of rage do not appear except through their own spoken lines of dialogue. That is, their spoken lines (and their individual feelings of rage) arise dialogically, in correspondence or response to those of other characters who address the same theme. They have a reciprocally objectifying relationship; in Bakhtin's words, they "must inevitably orient themselves to one another." Their case serves to highlight the contrast with Midori's, in which the fundamental relation is with the nomadic half-speaker herself, a relation that summons up from the author a variety of directly emotive *words*.

The following is a passage from Ichiyō's diary. This passage was not incorporated directly into "Child's Play," but the sensitivity to shame that it manifests certainly shows that she bore an emotionality that could easily turn to self-destructive despair.

There was a time when I desperately wanted our house to prosper and his [Nishimura Sennosuke's] to fall into ruin. When we moved, he seemed to be plotting to look dignified and be benevolent since we were poor. [. . .] But if I think it through, he is certainly my enemy. Well if he's going to be an enemy, it might as well be to the bitter end. Does he think the two remaining daughters of the Higuchi house have no pride, no guts? We're not some sheep in the street. We don't have to look over our shoulders listening for the enemy. You have to die sometime in this empty world. Are we supposed to bow our heads before the likes of Sennosuke? (July 25, 1893)[15]

In "Child's Play," once the focus turns to Midori's rage, the author's original structuring idea loses its line of development. Chōkichi and Shōtarō's rage are initially rendered absolute vis-à-vis the firemen's wives' critical viewpoint, but once separated from that immediate setting, they are situated in a relationship of reciprocal objectification. If Midori's rage too were confined to this same dimension, it would likely have led her to some kind of highly theatrical catastrophe. In fact, Ichiyō constructed a different work, "Troubled Waters" ("Nigorie," 1895), by placing a Midori-type passion in an adult woman in an even more desperate situation and tracing through the inevitably catastrophic end. Historically we know that Ichiyō wrote up through the eighth chapter of "Child's Play," where Midori's feelings suddenly explode and she exhibits a ferocity that shocks even Shōtarō, whereupon Ichiyō stopped and started writing "Troubled Waters."[16] It seems that Ichiyō was unable to bring this young girl Midori to a final self-destructive catastrophe.

After this break, the story line of "Child's Play" unfolds in accord with the temporality of everyday life. Chōkichi apologizes for his violence and for not heeding Nobu's orders, and "Within a week Sangorō's wounds healed and his *rage* cooled. He was ready to forget what he'd been *angry* about" ("Child's Play," 276; emphasis Kamei's). What governs these changes in attitude is the progress of the seasons:

Then the autumn holidays are over. Here and there a red dragonfly bobs above the rice fields. Before long quail will be calling out along the moat. Mornings and evenings, the breeze blows cold. At the sundries shop, pocket warmers now take the place of mosquito incense. It's sad, somehow, that faint sound of the mortar grinding flour at Tamura's, over by the bridge. ("Child's Play," 276)

15. *Higuchi Ichiyō zenshū*, 4 vols. (Tokyo: Chikuma Shobō, 1974–94), 3:307.
16. In Danly's translation, the break occurs following the lines, "Even for Midori, the proposal was ambitious. 'Don't overdo it, girl,' Shōta muttered" ("Child's Play," 272).

Along with that natural change comes a natural, physiological change in Midori, too, as she begins to show the signs of adult womanhood. This leads to a change in her sensibility as well. Her rage is replaced by bitterness, and then that bitterness too is dissolved in the routine of daily life, as all the passion and fury of the summer's events flow away on the current of nature's time.

Only Midori's unease with Nobu remains. This uneasiness that replaces her dissolved rage at first turns into a kind of anxiety and then becomes a feeling that resembles love. But Nobu is as reserved as ever and shows no sign of reciprocating, of reciprocally objectifying, Midori's feelings. While the outsider Midori overcompensates by trying to adopt the temperament of the neighborhood, Nobu is ashamed of his own family and of the neighborhood and harbors a secret desire to get away from them.

Having bestowed on these two characters distinct visual intentionalities, which have no possibility for reciprocal contact with one another, the author sets up a scene where they meet. This is the famous rainy day scene, where the thong of Nobu's clog breaks. The work's immanent narrator traces the emotions of the two and tries to connect their feelings by means of a common referential object (the Yūzen crepe):

> There—she hurled the [Yūzen crepe] rag outside the lattice without saying anything. Nobu pretended not to notice. Oh! He was his same old nasty self! It crushed her, the tears welled up. Why did he have to be so mean? Why didn't he just tell her what it was? It made her sick. But her mother kept calling. It was no use. She started for the house. After all, why should she be sentimental? She wasn't going to let him see Midori eat humble pie. He heard her walk away; his eyes wandered after the sound. There the scarlet scrap of Yūzen silk lay in the rain, its pattern of red maple leaves near enough to touch. Odd, how her one gesture *moved him with its generosity*, and yet he could not bring himself to reach out and take the cloth. He *stared at it with an empty feeling of futility*. ("Child's Play," 281; emphasis Kamei's)

At first glance it seems as if this expression gives equal weight to the emotions of the two, but in fact the narration takes Midori's emotions, abandoned together with the Yūzen crepe, and transfers them into Nobu. This is clear from the fact that the *words* that I have emphasized originally derive from Midori's emotive structure. Nobu, glancing back, catches sight of the Yūzen crepe and makes no effort to look after Midori's figure. And this scene is not unique in that way: there are no instances anywhere in the story of Nobu's internal *words* depicting how he visually intends Midori.

Despite these aspects, most discussions of "Child's Play" have understood these two people to be mutually and equally in love, and in a certain sense the author herself was not fully aware of the true structure of the mode of expression we've just looked at. This is clear from the story's conclusion:

> One frosty morning, a paper narcissus lay inside the gate. No one knew what it was doing there, but Midori took a fancy to it, for some reason, and she put it in a bud vase. It was perfect, she thought, and yet almost sad in its crisp, solitary shape. That same day—she wasn't sure exactly where—Midori heard of Nobu's plans. Tomorrow he was leaving for the seminary. The color of his robes would never be the same. ("Child's Play," 287)

In terms of actions, Nobu returns to the scene of their meeting and re-enacts it in reverse. But in terms of mode of expression, this latter scene in no way repeats the earlier one.

* * * * *

This analysis of "Child's Play" has taken longer than I expected, but of course my interest lies mainly with the first half of the story. Rage itself is a compositional motif shared by many writers of the time. The question is, how was that motif actually structured? Limiting our discussion to just Ichiyō's works, we should look not only at "Child's Play," but also at "Troubled Waters," which arose out of the change in structure found in the former's first half. In that the compositional structure of "Troubled Waters" visually intends a dramatic catastrophe, the theory of composition presented in Yoshimoto Takaaki's *What is beauty for language?* (*Gengo ni totte, bi to wa nani ka*, 1965) is relevant, in particular his concepts of "dramatic thought" and "compositional thought."[17] We need to consider these matters more carefully before we reach any definite conclusions, but for the time being let me just say the following. Rage, at least in "Child's Play," is the emotion of people entirely caught up in their private I-situation. Never aware of the pettiness and comedy of their state of affairs, they wager their whole existence in embodying the outrageous absurdity of their situation. This gives rise to behavior and sentiments that seem so unacceptable in terms of the public value judgments of the era.

If such a process were depicted in the adult world, the protagonist would be ridiculed by the people around her, goading her into the idea that it was her persecuted destiny to have been forced into such a position. And she would

---

17. Yoshimoto Takaaki, *Gengo ni totte, bi to wa nani ka*, 2 vols. (Tokyo: Keisō Shobō, 1965), esp. 2:501–26. See also Kamei's discussion of this work in his introduction to this translation.

have to be set in a situation completely closed off from relations with others. If that were not the case, the protagonist would never try to liberate herself from her persecuted destiny by some sort of self-destructive act, but rather would choose compromise.

In the works I am examining here, there seems no room for compromise. Or even if there were, it seems preferable to become a person scorned. Such is the compositional idea behind, for example, Ozaki Kōyō's *Golden Demon* (*Konjiki yasha*, 1897–1903). With "Child's Play," Ichiyō participates in the tendency of this era, when so many works of this type were written. She does so by borrowing the world of children, who lack the necessity for compromise that marks adults. And yet, in touching on Midori's rage, she summoned up a deeper and more desperate emotion from within. This is the emotion of a woman who is not allowed to compromise even if she wants to. The only escape open to such a woman is to remove herself from the human world. The initial conception for "Troubled Waters" probably came much earlier, but it seems that Ichiyō only latched onto the governing compositional idea for the story at this point in time, midway through writing "Child's Play." Yet in "Child's Play" itself, the catastrophe takes a different form. Since no thought of liberation from his persecuted destiny is depicted in Nobu, a final catastrophe is avoided, an avoidance that takes the form of the apparent appearance of a reciprocal objectification (an emotional response) to Midori's frustrated feelings of love for Nobu. Most likely the author herself was not aware of this subtle difference between the structure of her expressions and the work's plot composition. In that sense this work gives us an important clue to the relationship between drama and the novel.

In short, there is something that is not found in drama, but that is inescapable for the novel. It is something that comes into conflict with the *words* of the various characters, that reacts subtly to the author's compositional process, that even clashes with the nature of the expressions in the work. This something is the narrator immanent to the work. Even the structure of which structuralism speaks cannot be understood without taking it into account.

Chapter Seven
Shinjū as Misdeed: Love Suicides in Higuchi Ichiyō and Chikamatsu Monzaemon

TRANSLATED BY LEWIS HARRINGTON

In this chapter, Kamei traces through literary portrayals of suicide, from the passion-driven double suicides of Edo-period theater to the suicides of modern, alienated individuals in late Meiji fiction such as Shimazaki Tōson's Spring *and Natsume Sōseki's* Kokoro. *Kamei argues that these novels arose out of a critical reaction to a wave of earlier fiction that narrated love suicides, including Higuchi Ichiyō's "Troubled Waters" and Hirotsu Ryūrō's* The Love Suicides at Imado. *In examining the "philosophy of suicide" harbored by Ichiyō's story, Kamei argues that the key lies in its mobilization of a second-person narrator. The flow of narration moves seamlessly between various characters' voices (especially since no punctuation is used to distinguish between speakers), weaving their distinct tones into the narration, yet also at the same time maintaining a distanced, effaced position. A dynamic tension between ground (narrative description) and figure (spoken dialogue) is maintained throughout, a technique whose origin Kamei traces to the Edo-period* jōruri *puppet plays of Chikamatsu Monzaemon. Further ties to Edo-period theatrical genres are brought out through a comparison of Ichiyō's appropriation of the different modes for relating body to voice that characterized* jōruri *and kabuki. Kamei concludes that what emerges in Ichiyō's heroine is an embodied sensibility that perceives itself as an offense against the social order, but that nonetheless commits itself wholly to that offense, finally to the point of self-destruction.*

Most likely, Genshichi asked Oriki to die with him and Oriki was unable to refuse. At least, Higuchi Ichiyō's "Troubled Waters" ("Nigorie," 1895) is written in a manner to allow such a reading.¹ As Maeda Ai has vividly analyzed, this is because in Oriki's feeling of ostracization, as if she had been completely cut off from this world, there is certainly "already the portent of a wretched death."²

In the case of Hirotsu Ryūrō's *The Love Suicides at Imado* (*Imado shinjū*, 1896), on the other hand, it is most likely the courtesan Yoshizato who proposes the double suicide.³ With the man she loves having returned to his hometown, Yoshizato lies crying in a room when Zenkichi enters. Zenkichi is a customer whom Yoshizato has repeatedly rejected. Zenkichi says he is visiting her for the last time; even if he wanted to, he will not be able to visit her again; and that being the case, he pleads, will she not be with him for just one night?⁴ Most likely Yoshizato intuits a certain resolve in Zenkichi's words and allows him to stay in the brothel. She sells her clothes, borrows as much as money as she can from her friends in order to pay off Zenkichi's bills, and finally throws herself into the Sumida River together with him.

What a truly miserable way to die!

Death is the only way for the man, Zenkichi, to transcend his oafishness. For the woman, however, the point is not that she loves this man, but rather that she is reduced to such dire circumstances that all she can do is intensify her own unhappiness by surrendering herself to his oafishness. That she has to be accompanied in death by a man she has hated makes her death all the more wretched.

But why did works that described such abject love suicides reach a peak in this age? If such works as Izumi Kyōka's *Noble Blood, Heroic Blood* (*Giketsu kyōketsu*, 1894) and "The Operating Room" ("Gekashitsu," 1895) are also counted, then the end of the third decade of Meiji, that is, the mid-1890s, is certainly the age of love-suicide literature. It is also clear from such works as Natsume Sōseki's "Dew on the Shallots" ("Kairōkō," 1905) and "The Heredity of Taste" ("Shumi no iden," 1906) that a critical transformation of that plot device was a central motif for the literary world in the latter half of Meiji 30s.

---

1. The conclusion of "Troubled Waters" is ambiguous. Both Oriki, a prized courtesan, and Genshichi, a long-time customer who has declined in the world largely due to the patronage he has lavished on her, are found dead, an apparent double suicide, but Oriki's corpse has been stabbed in the back, as if she had perhaps tried to flee.

2. Maeda Ai, *Higuchi Ichiyō no sekai* (Tokyo: Chikuma Shobō, 1989), 208.

3. Hirotsu Ryūrō (1861–1928) was an important mid-Meiji novelist, associated with the Ken'yūsha group led by Ozaki Kōyō. Hirotsu is known as the creator of the "tragic novel" (*hisan shōsetsu*) genre through such works as *Cross-Eyed Den* (*Heme-den*, 1895) and *Black Lizard* (*Kurotokage*, 1895). *The Love Suicides at Imado* is his best-known work.

4. Zenkichi has bankrupted his family business in his previously unsuccessful pursuit of Yoshizato and has now even sent his wife back to her parents, suggesting that he has decided upon a desperate course of action.

In my understanding, it was Shimazaki Tōson's *Spring* (*Haru*, 1908) that effected a crucial transformation in the portrayal of suicide.[5] When viewed as a work that portrays Kitamura Tōkoku's tragic death (suicide) as an intellectual problem, it undoubtedly has certain shortcomings. It is doubtful whether Tōson understood even half of Tōkoku's philosophy. But the point I would like to concentrate on is how *Spring* is written as if Aoki (Tōkoku) proposes the suicide of his entire family because of the strained circumstances of their lives. "Aah, you're a lost cause [*haibokusha*], and I'm a lost cause, too. How about it? Should we do it? Together, you and me. . . ." (*MBZ* 69:106). While the crux of this proposal lies in Aoki's belief that they are all lost causes, his wife Misao does not think of herself in this way. "If we didn't have kids, well then, I wouldn't care how things ended up [. . . .] Haven't I suffered enough for your sake, don't I sacrifice everything just to obey your words? Isn't that enough?" (*MBZ* 69:106). For Genshichi in "Troubled Waters" and Zenkichi in *The Love Suicides at Imado*, it is the breakup of their families that triggers their love suicides. But in Aoki's case, it is the opposite: bound up in the logic of household-and-home, he dies a wretched death *within* the family. After his death, Aoki's family refuses to probe the reasons behind the suicide, dismissing it with such comments as "From that time on, Father was crazy" and "Well, even I don't understand" (*MBZ* 69:128). Nonetheless, precisely because that is the case, his suicide must have had a new philosophical meaning. That is to say, the suicide of a person unable to find anyone to share his feelings of being a "lost cause" and who dies a wretched death even within the family corresponds, in terms of the structure of the novel, to a new philosophy: the philosophy of one who dies what is literally an *individual* death, having found no one willing to take up his proposal (his *words*).

That being the case, in the earlier love-suicide fiction, there must also be a corresponding philosophy of the love suicide. The deaths chosen by the men and women in "Troubled Waters" and *The Love Suicides at Imado* are not overtly tied to any particular philosophy, at least in the usual sense of the term. In terms of literary history, following up on the transformation that Tōson's *Spring* effected, Natsume Sōseki in *Kokoro* (1914) advances a new philosophy of suicide: suicide as ethical self-judgment. Moreover, Sōseki understands that everyone shares the potential for being driven to a tragic death within the family, a knowledge that enables him to portray with such a delicate hand the actual

---

5. *Spring* is an autobiographical novel that depicts Tōson's days as a member of the youthful Romantic school of writers and poets of the mid 1890s. One of its central incidents, as Kamei discusses below, is the suicide of the group's leader, the charismatic Aoki, modeled after Kitamura Tōkoku (1868–94). Following this shock, the novel's protagonist (modeled after Tōson) flirts with the idea of suicide, but finally resolves instead to struggle on and find some meaningful way to live out his own life.

circumstances of modern domestic life. The suicide of Sensei in *Kokoro* accordingly is made into an ethical question, not only in its motives, but in that it carefully excludes any element that could lead to its being interpreted as a death whose cause lies within the family. Sensei's suicide, thus, is planned so as not to burden in any way the remaining members of the family. In that sense, its philosophy of suicide is at the same time a philosophy of the family.

After Tōson's portrayal of the problem within the world of the intellectual classes, the shock value of lower-class love suicides of the type seen in "Troubled Waters" and *The Love Suicides at Imado* abruptly faded. Of course, even in love suicides, a human being can only die an individual death. Nevertheless, in these works we encounter something astonishing: at that time, it was thought reasonable not only for characters to desire someone else to accompany them in death, but also for them to find someone who would actually fulfill that desire. If we could extract the philosophical meaning of the consciousness that marked this earlier form of human relations, it would help clarify the true nature of the literature of Sōseki and others who pursued a critical objectification of it and thereby created a new philosophy of suicide.

One key for solving this problem lies in the notion of being "a lost cause" that was rejected by Aoki's wife in *Spring*. Genshichi and Zenkichi, both "lost causes" in the sense of being unable to maintain their families and households, seek fellow travelers for their self-punishment in prostitutes, women alienated from the norms of domestic life, the roles of bearing and raising children. And these prostitutes are in fact posited as the root cause of the destruction of the families of Genshichi and Zenkichi. If that is the case, then what kind of beings are Oriki and Yoshizato?

In her writing style, Higuchi Ichiyō makes clear that they are beings who can live only in the world of the second-person.

* * * * *

In a rare move, Ichiyō opens "Troubled Waters" by describing the characters' voices. While I do not know the extent to which this was a consciously chosen methodology, this mode of writing does result in the birth of a characteristically second-person writing style, one that continually invokes the presence of a "you."

What is first heard in the work is the coquettish voice of a woman trying to stop men in a vulgarly frank tone of voice, a "harangue" marked by an exaggerated familiarity.[6] The men, however, run off to the public bath, and as

---

6. All quotations from "Troubled Waters" are adapted from the translation of the story that appears in Robert Lyons Danly, *In the Shade of Spring Leaves* (New York: W.W. Norton, 1992), 218–40. The passage discussed here appears on 218.

the woman then enters the shop, stepping over its threshold, she angrily grumbles, "They won't come back later. They've no intention of coming. Once they get married, that's the end of it." Then, from inside the shop, another woman says "Otaka, you're really talkative, aren't you," and this launches us into a depiction of the world of the women inside the shop. Note that the author limits her perspective of expression to the inside of the shop, delineating a mode of life that can be seen and heard only within its threshold.

But this is not the only limitation the author imposes on herself.

> "I suppose I'll have to stand out in front again tonight, trying to snare a customer. What kind of life is this?" In a fit of anger, she sat down in front of the shop and kicked at the earthen floor with her sandals. She was a woman of perhaps twenty-seven, perhaps thirty. She had plucked her eyebrows and painted a dark line in their place and had outlined her widow's peak in black. A thick layer of powder covered her face. Her lips were rouged a shade of crimson so deep they lost their charm and suggested more a man-eating dog than a courtesan. ("Troubled Waters," 218)

This is a portrayal of the woman called Otaka. But when the narrator, who is immanent to the depicted scene, portrays Otaka's manner of speaking, the narrator's own manner of speaking—that is, the tone of voice in the passages of narrative description (*ji no bun*)—becomes homogenized with Otaka's. This narrator, who critically depicts with an ironic eye the women of the shop, takes on the same meddlesome and bitter tone of voice that marks the other women. The narrator, of course, does not appear as a character in the scene, but her mode of expression is like that of, for example, a woman hired as kitchen-help who gazes with a critical eye at the goings on.

> The house was a two-story building twelve-feet wide in front. A festival lantern hung beneath the eaves, and a little pile of salt, good for luck, invoked prosperity. Bottles of one of the better brands of saké lined the shelf above the bar, but whether there was anything in them was another question. Now and then came busy sounds of someone starting a fire in the clay stove in the kitchen. At best, one might expect a chowder or a stew, served up by the lady who owned the place, although, according to the sign in front, the house aspired to the status of a full-fledged restaurant. What on earth would they do if someone actually came and ordered something? They could hardly claim to have just run out of their entire stock. Nor would it do to fall back on the excuse that they were only in the business of entertaining men. A good thing people seemed to know better! No one was boorish enough to order any side dishes. ("Troubled Waters," 219)

This passage introduces the inner conditions of the shop with an ironic eye, showing how they are engaged in a rather dubious business, but the mode of expression itself negotiates some dubious territory. This is because the tone that appears here is like that of a woman who, conscious of the gaze of outsiders, has objectified the situation of her own kind, and who accordingly addresses her coworkers with a mixture of self-scorn. We can call this a second-person writing style. Even passages of narrative description are written under a conception that internally sketches in the existence of an interlocutor, and thus the manner of speaking of Otaka and the others can be incorporated into those passages quite realistically. Or, to put it differently, the narrator relates to the voices of others as if she were one of them, but she also always retains her objectifying consciousness as an external, effaced narrator.

Moreover, and this is an important point, the second-person writing style by its nature must be written entirely in *words* of agreement or repulsion. That is, expressions of sensibility-determined value judgments are frequent, and they function together with the emotional manner of speaking of the characters to force the characters' consciousnesses to attend to the dialogical relations that exist in the present moment (in the *here and now*). The following is a representative example of this type of expression; note that Ichiyō here is also clearly announcing her idea for the work's plot and composition.

> Otaka looked at her [Oriki] as if remembering something. "Oriki—" She scratched the base of her hairdo with a copper bodkin *kanzashi.* "Did you mail the letter?"
>
> "Mm," she answered absent-mindedly. "But he still isn't going to come. I was just being polite," Oriki laughed.
>
> "Who are you kidding? You took all that paper to write to him. And two stamps on the envelope! Don't tell me you were just being civil. You've known him ever since Akasaka, haven't you? So what if you've had your misunderstandings? You can't afford to break with him. It's up to you. Why don't you make more of an effort and try to keep him? You can't treat people that way and expect to do all right."
>
> "Thanks for the advice, but he's not my type. You'd better get used to it—there's nothing between us." She talked as if the topics were of no concern to her.
>
> "You astonish me," Otaka laughed. "You're as selfish as a grand lady. Ah, but me—there's no hope for me," she sighed, reaching for her fan to cool her feet. "I used to be a flower of a girl. . . ."
>
> From the window she could see men passing in front of the shops. Calls of solicitation vied with each other in the night. ("Troubled Waters," 219)[7]

7. In the original Japanese text, as is typical in Ichiyō's writing style, in this passage there are no quotation marks to distinguish the characters' and narrator's voices from one another, nor any paragraph breaks. See the discussion of punctuation in Ichiyō in chapter six.

It seems that Oriki, before falling to the level of this seedy restaurant of illicit prostitution, was a geisha in Akasaka. Her fresh, fashionable appearance, with her "hair, just washed and done up in a great Shimada chignon knotted with a twist of new straw" ("Troubled Waters," 218), is a lingering trace of that past prosperity, but probably more than that a display of the self-conceit of someone who takes pride in such things. The playboy Yūki Tomonosuke is probably attracted by this, Oriki's status as a heterogeneous element. Oriki's haughtiness is revealed by the fact that she only speaks her true feelings to a wealthy customer like Yūki. Herein lies the necessity for his appearance. The popular geisha, blessed with a wealthy and handsome customer, coolly drives away the broken Genshichi—this is the role of an Akasaka geisha, but Oriki performs it in this dubious restaurant located in a newly developed area on the fringes of the city. In this setup, where a character's career drags her down to the position of an outsider in lower-class society, we can of course see the self-reflection of Ichiyō herself.[8]

It is just as important to note also that in the conversation quoted above, Oriki and Otaka speak about exactly the same matter, but in quite different ways.

The object of the conversation between the two is the customer Oriki has known "ever since Akasaka." Regarding techniques of holding onto customers, their ways of thinking are utterly antithetical. What Otaka says is, for a woman of this profession, very commonsensical, and in that respect it demonstrates a shrewd appraisal of the motives behind the letter Oriki wrote. While Oriki's response to Otaka on the surface seems to speak of her dislike for the customer she has known her "ever since Akasaka," it actually demonstrates how she attends to and reacts against Otaka's commonsensical advice. In that sense, Otaka's *words* manifest a common ground (the hidden truth) shared by the women, against which Oriki's *words* are spoken and thereby highlighted as the showy bluster of her heart (her vanity and shows of courage).

That showy bluster is, ultimately, self-scornful. Thus, as the common ground grows more dominant, Oriki loses her vanity and pluck. That change appears clearly in the unfolding of expressions in chapter five of the story, which begins by alluding to an *uramibushi* (song of ill-will):

> White demons, someone had dubbed them. And, in fact, there was an air of the nether reaches to it all. Even those who appeared guileless were ready to drive a man into a pool of blood, or chase the customer up the side of a mountain of needles. If they enticed men with their soft voices, they could also sound as shrill as a pheasant being swallowed by a snake. ("Troubled Waters," 230)

8. During her short life, Higuchi Ichiyō experienced the fall of her family from respected samurai status to utter poverty.

In folk songs (e.g., the song "Utaura" contained in the *Collection of Recitations and Songs Ancient and Modern*), this sort of listing of images related to Buddhist notions of hell—the mountain of needles, the pond of blood—is used to describe the terrifying world that prostitutes would encounter after death.[9] But here this is reversed, and it is the restaurant women themselves who are figured as the devils in a this-worldly hell. This, of course, is portrayed as being in part the self-consciousness of the restaurant women themselves, so that the passage continues:

> Still, these girls had once spent the same ten months in the womb as everybody else—when they were small, they too clung to their mothers' breasts and were fondled and coaxed to babble their first words; when they were offered their choice of money or candy, like any other child they held their hand for the sweets. In the trade, one did not look for an honest woman; one girl in a hundred shed tears of true love for a man. . . . ("Troubled Waters," 230)

What arises here is a narrative voice that sounds as if it belongs to one of Oriki's coworkers, so that it can immediately follow the above passage by entering into a grumbling entreaty, an exclamation that in the original Japanese simply flows out of the above, marked off by neither quotation marks nor a new sentence—beginning: "hey listen to me, what about Tatsu, the dyer" ("Troubled Waters," 230). One restaurant women feels sad about the dishonesty of customers, while another who has a child sobs, "Ah, today is the sixteenth, the Day of Souls [. . . .] I certainly didn't choose this profession lightly, but I suppose my boy despises me for it" ("Troubled Waters," 230–31). While these grumblings belong to women other than Oriki, they unfold as one continuous stream of language in the original Japanese, with no sentence or paragraph breaks or quotation marks to distinguish between speakers. As a result, Oriki's desire for death is realized in a form that brings into Oriki all the complaints of the others. As we saw in the previously discussed scene, Otaka speaks the commonsense of the professional woman in the unadorned manner of being-in-itself, whereas Oriki stands outside and therefore objectifies that commonsense. In fact, however, the *words* of Otaka and others provide the opportunity for making Oriki's vanity visible and, in the end, for crushing it.

---

9. *Collection of Recitations and Songs Ancient and Modern* (*Ginkyoku kokin taizen*) is an Edo-period collection of popular ballads. It is reprinted in Fujita Tokutarō, ed., *Kōchū Nihon bungaku ruijū: kindai kayō shū* (Tokyo: Hakubunkan, 1929), 350–432. "Utaura" appears on 393–94, although this version is missing the last several lines from the version that Kamei cites below.

This unique method for developing plot through mode of expression cannot be grasped through a reading strategy that brackets the characters' spoken dialogue between quotation marks. While this might present difficulties for a structuralist methodology, if we attempt a faithful reading of Ichiyō's original text in which spoken dialogue is woven seamlessly into passages of narrative description, we should be able to see how the opportunity for *words* exists even within passages of narrative description, and likewise how a relationship between ground (background information) and figure (conspicuous emotional expressions [*hyōshutsu*]) exists even in the lines of dialogue spoken by various characters.

* * * * *

This type of relationship between ground and figure was quite common in Edo-period literature. I was reminded of this problem by Yoshimoto Takaaki's essay "On the Theory of Construction" ("Kōseiron") in his *What is Beauty for Language?* (*Gengo ni totte bi to wa nani ka*, 1965).[10] Allow me to quote from Chikamatsu Monzaemon's *jōruri* puppet play, *Kagekiyo Victorious* (*Shusse Kagekiyo*, 1686).[11] The courtesan Akoya, spurred on by jealousy, reveals Kagekiyo's hiding place to the Rokuhara military authorities. Learning that Kagekiyo has been captured, she goes to apologize, bringing their two children Iyaishi and Iyawaka, but Kagekiyo stubbornly refuses to forgive her.

> (Ground) [Akoya] So no matter how much I beg your forgiveness, you refuse to listen?
> (Speech) [Kagekiyo] Shut up! Shut up! I cannot stand the sight of you, go home this instant. I no longer love any of you!
> (Ground) [Akoya] Oh, having outlived you in this way, is there anywhere I can call home? Oh my children, even though your mother knows she has erred and is trying to apologize, did you hear what your merciless father said? With your father and my husband thinking us his enemies, even you children have no reason to go on living. From now on, don't think that you had a father. You are the children of this mother only. If I too go on living and my disrepute over straying from the true path spreads, I will regret it even after I die. So children, die with me and apologize in the next world.

10. Yoshimoto Takaaki, *Gengo ni totte bi to wa nani ka*, 2 vols. (Tokyo: Keisō Shobō, 1965).
11. Chikamatsu Monzaemon (1653–1724) is widely recognized as the greatest playwright of the *jōruri* puppet theatre genre. It should be noted that in *jōruri* performances, all spoken dialogue is voiced by a chanter who sits at the side of the stage, sometimes adopting the voice of one of the puppet characters, sometimes speaking in his own voice as narrator, but weaving all the voices into a single flow of narration.

(Speech) Oh, master Kagekiyo, see the depths of my deceitless heart!

(Ground) Pulling Iyaishi near, drawing her dagger with a swoosh, and saying *namu amida butsu*, she stabs Iyaishi. Iyawaka is surprised and cries out, *No, no, I'm not my mother's child. Father, help!*, and he runs up and presses his face into the lattice of his father's cage. [Akoya] *What a cowardly thing to do*, and she pulls him near. He bursts out, putting his hands together, [Iyakawa] *Please forgive me, please go easy on me. From tomorrow I'll behave and we can shave the top of my head for my* mage *hairstyle. We can even burn* moxa *on my skin. What an evil mother. Father, help!*, and so he cries at the top of his lungs.

(Ground) [Akoya] *Oh, it is reasonable to not want to die. However, you are not murdered by your mother, but rather you are murdered by your father who should save you. Look at that, your older brother also died quietly, and if you and your mother do not die, we have no excuse before your father. Although it is unfortunate, please try to understand*, she advises and Iyawaka is persuaded, *If that is the case, then let us die together*. And having said *Father, good-bye*, he approaches his brother's corpse, firm in his resolve to die, and looks up at his mother. But Akoya becomes dizzy trying to decide where to stab her son, loses her strength and falls down writhing in sadness. [Akoya] *Yes, but there is already no use. Consider this your fate from a previous life and do not begrudge your mother. I will follow you in death, namu amida*, and with that she stabs Iyawaka through the chest. And saying *Well, master Kagekiyo, with this please dispel your grudge against me. Please welcome them into the Pure Land, merciful Buddha*, she presses the sword against her throat and falls on top of the corpses of her sons, the lives of a mother and her children having been lost. What a truly hopeless scene![12]

What astonishing hatred!

In *jōruri* scripts, "ground" (*ji*) did not as such signify what we would call narrative description (*ji no bun*), just as "speech" (*shi*) did not necessarily signify lines of spoken dialogue. Moreover, it seems that there was consider-

---

12. *Shusse Kagekiyo* is reprinted in Chikamatsu Monzaemon, *Chikamatsu shū*, vol. 16 of *Kanshō Nihon no koten*, ed. Hara Michio (Tokyo: Shogaku Tosho, 1982). This passage appears on 92–94. In the original Japanese, there are no paragraph breaks in this passage. The words in parentheses here appear in superscript annotations in the original; they (along with other annotations that are omitted here) indicate how the ensuing lines should be chanted in performance. Also, in this translation, italics and character names in brackets have been added here for clarity's sake; there are no equivalent markers in the Japanese text. It is precisely the flexible ambiguity of this style (which the markers in the English translation unfortunately undermine) that Kamei is highlighting here.

able variation from period to period in the relation between the two terms. If, however, we provisionally permit ourselves to apply modern novelistic distinctions to these terms, "speech" would refer to the other-oriented *words* of the characters—the hailings and answerings of utterances exchanged between the characters themselves, or the verbal attacks and censures they direct toward their interlocutors. On the other hand, "ground" would refer to expressions made from the position of the narrator, depicting the movements and spoken lines of the characters, or more precisely, of the puppets enacting those characters. When *words* appear within "ground," they often represent the act of recounting something to one's own self or, when that is not the case, the manifestation of some emotion so urgent that it does not allow for the adoption of the sort of other-directed tone that characterizes "speech."

An opportunity for *words* is present in any human action. *Words* are mediated by, born out from corporeality. At least, we can say that this type of expression consciousness existed among the authors of *jōruri* plays. The mode of writing of the modern novel, by contrast, brackets out spoken dialogue within quotation marks. These take the form of other-directed utterances made from the standpoint of the characters themselves, utterances from which embodiedness is almost entirely abstracted away. On the other hand, corporeality itself, that from which the *words* have been abstracted, is confined to passages of narrative description that portray the expressions and actions of the characters from the standpoint of the writer (more properly, the immanent narrator). In this sense, we can say that in Edo-period modes of expression, the degree of mutual alienation between *words* and body was quite small.

The reason for this likely lies in the mode of performing through the manipulation of puppets. The chanter/narrator, while indicating the actions through his descriptive expressions, breathes emotional life into the puppets. Or rather, the narrator comes to possess the puppets corporeally. Chikamatsu described the circumstances of this as follows:

> *Jōruri* differs from other forms of fiction in that, since it is primarily concerned with puppets, the words should all be living things in which action is the most important feature. [. . .] Once when I was young and reading a story about the court, I came across a passage that told how, on the occasion of a festival, a heavy snow had fallen and piled up. An order was then given to a guard to clear away the snow from an orange tree. When this happened, the pine tree next to it, apparently resentful that its boughs were bent with snow, recoiled its branches. This was a stroke of the pen which gave life to the inanimate tree. It did so because the spectacle of the pine tree, resentful that the snow had been cleared from the orange tree, recoiling its branches itself and shaking off the snow which bends it down, is one

which creates the feeling of a living, moving thing. Is that not so?
From this model I learned how to put life into my *jōruri*.[13]

If that is the case, then what exactly is a puppet? Of course *jōruri* puppets had
their origins as magic ritual objects, but by Chikamatsu's time they had probably already lost their folk religious meaning. Whatever the case, a "lifeless
wooden puppet," i.e., a human who has been estranged from life and turned into
a *thing*, was for Chikamatsu precisely the indispensable condition for summoning up "a variety of emotions" (*Souvenir*, 437). Through the mediation of the
visual intentionality of the "lifeless wooden puppet," he tried to sketch internally the embodied self-image of the characters placed in that scene. According
to Yoshimoto Takaaki, when this is achieved within linguistic expressions, a
mode of expression is born "that transcends the dimension of narrated content
to such an extent that the characters who appear thusly in the dimension of the
act of narrating begin to exist, within the ideas of the authors and within the
drama of language itself, as images of fully living human beings who maintain
their totality in acting of their own volition and in relating to others" (Yoshimoto,
What is Beauty for Language? 2:470).

Words are born in tandem with an image of the body. Chikamatsu in
particular worked hard to give expression to this in the case of women.

> To be precise, many things are said by the female characters which
> real women could not utter. Such things fall under the heading of art;
> it is because they say what could not come from a real woman's lips
> that their true emotions are disclosed. If in such cases the author were
> to model his character on the ways of a real woman and conceal her
> feelings, it would permit no pleasure in the work. (*Souvenir*, 438)

If that is the case, then for Chikamatsu, what exactly is a woman? Among the
people in this world, it is she who is most thoroughly reified into a *thing*, so that
she invites only tragedy if she tries to act on her own volition. Otane in *The
Drum of the Waves of Horikawa* (*Horikawa namitsuzumi*, 1706), while washing
clothes with her younger sister Ofuji, reflects upon the loneliness of sleeping
alone while her husband is away:

> (Ground) [Otane]: Aah, Ofuji. (Speech): No matter what, always serve
> your master in such a way as to please him. (Ground): Forget about
> men. That's what I've learned the hard way. Because Master Hikokurō

---

13. Chikamatsu's words are quoted in the preface to *Souvenir from Naniwa* (*Naniwa miyage*, 1738)
    by Hozumi Ikan (1692–1769). Quotations from the work here are adapted from the transla-
    tion by Donald Keene in Ryusaku Tsunoda, Wm. Theodore de Bary, and Donald Keene, eds.,
    Sources of Japanese Tradition, vol. 1 (New York: Columbia University Press, 1958), 437–40.
    This passage appears on 437.

and I were a couple that had a relationship before we were married, when we did get married we were happy beyond words. (Speech): The sadness of being married to a low-level samurai; his being held hostage in Edo every other year. Even when he is back home in this province, he is stuck in the castle everyday. Ten nights a month he has guard duty. Making love like a married couple, how long has it been since we did it?[14]

In carelessly speaking these scandalous words, which violate the norms of modesty and self-control and which no real samurai wife could have uttered, Otane inadvertently ignites her own passion, the first step toward her tragic ending.

In the case of *Kagekiyo Victorious*, the prostitute Akoya, upon seeing a letter from Kagekiyo's official wife, is pierced by a sense of humiliation that ordinarily she would have been able to suppress:

> How bitter I feel, how angry, spiteful, envious! If in love social status makes no difference, then how dare they call me a prostitute? Even if I am a prostitute, the real wife is the one who has the children. Don't they know this? While I don't bear a grudge towards her, I feel bitter for having cared so much, for having loved, for having exhausted my affections. What I cannot forgive is that beast of a man, that philanderer. Oh, my resentment! Oh, how inexcusable! (*Kagekiyo*, 59–60)

This rage drives Akoya into a corner, in which excuses and apologies are useless. Akoya appeals to Kagekiyo: "Even so, my jealousy is a result of how much I love you, my master. Jealousy is something that all women feel" (*Kagekiyo*, 81). But he refuses to listen. If that is the case, perhaps in the very act of thinking that "in love social status makes no difference," Akoya has already overstepped the bounds of her status as a prostitute. At this point, Akoya has already resolved to die. She pleads earnestly: "Please forgive me for everything. If you would tell me once more in this world that you forgive me, it would give me the strength to commit suicide, it would be proof that I didn't betray you out of viciousness" (*Kagekiyo*, 81). Kagekiyo, however, not only refuses her request but even vows his hatred of their two children: "When I think that you two were born from the womb of that vicious woman, I end up hating even you two" (*Kagekiyo*, 86).

It is a situation so full of hatred that Kagekiyo refuses Akoya even the pretext that would give her strength to commit suicide. Akoya has no recourse but to use tragedy to expose the mercilessness of Kagekiyo's stance. She stabs

---

14. Chikamatsu Monzaemon, *Chikamatsu Monzaemon shū* 1, vol. 43 in *Nihon koten bungaku zenshū*, 51 vols. (Tokyo: Shōgakkan, 1971), 233–34.

their son to death as he tries to flee, desperately imploring his father for help. Akoya is driven to kill her children out of hatred for her relationship with Kagekiyo: "You are not murdered by your mother, but rather you are murdered by your father who should save you." This same rage brings about her own death too. It is as if the only possible end that can result from making female characters say "things which real women could not utter" is a tragedy that befalls the female characters themselves.

Everything begins with scandalous speech—"things which real women could not utter." But a reflective consciousness that could elevate the emotional charge unleashed by those words into the realm of the ethical never arises. Therein lies the cause of the tragedy of Akoya and other female characters like her. This reflects the limitations of Chikamatsu's dramatic modus operandi. The consciousness of expression of the narrator here is unable to distance itself from the internally generated body image (and the *words* that arise from it) and hence is unable to establish a viewpoint that could objectify the scene in its entirety. The contradictions and lack of integration that arise between the various scenes is probably also due to this.

Seeing Akoya kill his children in order to spite him and then kill herself, "Kagekiyo cries and writhes with screams, but already there is nothing he can do. *Are there no gods or buddhas in this world? Somehow please forgive me. Oh, my children. Oh, my wife*, says Kagekiyo, who could be mistaken for a demon as he raises his voice and cries out" (*Kagekiyo*, 94). Shortly thereafter, however, upon the appearance of Akoya's brother Jūzō, Kagekiyo, in a feat of unbelievable strength, breaks out of his cage and overpowers him. This type of a development could not occur in the world of novels. If Kagekiyo was in possession of such strength, why was he reduced to impotent screams and writhing inside the cage as he watched his helpless children murdered before his eyes? If this were a novel, the author himself would have had to entertain this doubt.

But what if Chikamatsu had been able to situate an immanent narrator within this scene? Of course, this supposition can really only apply to prose narratives, but let us here try to read Chikamatsu's play in the mode of "drama as language," after the manner of Yoshimoto Takaaki. Such a narrator would portray the tragedy of Akoya and her children, and next, of course, would shift its line of vision to Kagekiyo, who has just witnessed the murder of his young and helpless children. Regardless of whether or not it would directly manifest this in its expressions, this gaze would inevitably include an ethical critique of Kagekiyo's stubbornness. How would Kagekiyo respond to this ethical questioning? Of course, there is no reason to expect Kagekiyo would answer directly to the questioning of the narrator, who while being immanent to the depicted scene would not appear directly as one of the work's characters. Nonetheless, as Kagekiyo faces Jūzō, he would necessarily be portrayed as a person tormented by his own ruthlessness, yet as one who must still search for some grounds for self-justification. In Chikamatsu's play, however, his reaction to Jūzō is depicted as follows: "Kagekiyo cackles with laughter. *Hey, you blockhead, don't you know that they* [Akoya and her children] *died because of their sadness caused by your greediness? On top of that, just what do you mean by calling me a samurai beast?*" (*Kagekiyo*, 102). In a novelistic world mediated by an immanent narrator, Kagekiyo could not possibly denounce Jūzō in such a flippant tone.

The history of the Edo-period novel, from Ueda Akinari to Takizawa Bakin, is the history of how the immanent narrator came to structure realistically the spatial relationships of the various characters.[15] It is simultaneously a history of the strengthening of the moralistic tenor of the questioning that was inherent in the narrator's perspective. This is especially so in Bakin's works, where all of the characters are forced into making self-justificatory long-winded speeches. The grounds for those justifications sometimes extend to karmic causal relations that stretch across several generations. The immanent narrator retains the memory even of past events that have been forgotten by the characters themselves, and the various characters, as if forced to answer to the narrator's questioning, are made to produce speech and actions that seek to avow their own consistency and constancy. The modern novel dissolved this moralistic tenor and thereby acquired a more objective perspective. It accordingly enhanced its ability to pursue the essence of human existence in all its variety. Be that as it may, it is clear from this history that without the immanent narrator, the more rigorous grasp of spatial structure and the temporal expansion of the characters' consciousnesses could not have arisen. The various characters who appeared in Saikaku's late seventeenth century works, for example, still lacked a consciousness that would lead them to strive for consistency in their speech and actions. The lack of a clear organic structure in Saikaku's works, which are nothing more than a series of largely unrelated short episodes strung together, also comes from this.[16]

15. Ueda Akinari (1734–1809) wrote in a number of prose fiction genres, including *yomihon* and *ukiyozōshi*. He is best known for *Tales of Moonlight and Rain* (*Ugetsu monogatari*, 1768) and *A Tale of Spring Rain* (*Harusame monogatari*, 1808), both collections of ghost stories. Takizawa Bakin (1767–1848) wrote numerous works of fiction in the *yomihon* and *kusazōshi* genres. His heroic tale, *The Story of Eight Virtuous Heroes* (*Nansō satomi hakkenden*, 1814–41) is one of the most famous works of late Edo fiction and continued to enjoy wide popularity well into the Meiji period.
16. Ihara Saikaku (1642–93) was a popular writer of *ukiyozōshi* fiction. His best known works include *The Life of an Amorous Woman* (*Kōshoku ichidai onna*, 1686) and *Five Women Who Chose Love* (*Kōshoku gonin onna*, 1686).

In *Kagekiyo Victorious* as well, Kagekiyo, who until now has been sobbing loudly inside his cage, suddenly "cackles with laughter," inveighs against
Jūzō, and then breaks out of the cage. His stubbornness toward Akoya and her
children instantly changes into a violent passion directed at Jūzō. In this sense,
the lack of consistency between scenes in *Kagekiyo Victorious* represents not
only a problem inherent to the genre of *jōruri*, but also this era's historical limitations in terms of development of narrative form. Certainly, as Yoshimoto argues, we see here the appearance of a new technique in narrative development,
one in which "on their own, the characters speak and establish mutual relationships, and it is by these means that the situation moves forward" (Yoshimoto,
What is Beauty for Language? 2:465). But there is one important point missing
from this reading: Yoshimoto is unable to problematize the fact that the characters here still lack any relationship to themselves, any being-for-itself relationship. Let me put this more precisely. In both Akoya here and in Otane from
Drum of the Waves of Horikawa, we find the bare beginnings of a relationship
with the self. But they are unable to break out of the form of relational consciousness that is characteristic of second-person narration, and so they never
reach a level of self-reflection at which they could produce their own ethicality.
Hence, Akoya can only lament, "How dare they call me a prostitute? Even if I
am a prostitute, the real wife is the one who has the children," and Otane likewise declares, "Forget about men. That's what I've learned the hard way."
Kagekiyo and Hikokurō (Otane's husband), in contrast, are backed by the whole
system of institutionalized ethical norms and are not troubled by the least doubt
about their own conduct. Hence, it is inevitable that Akoya and Otane will meet
defeat.

Yoshimoto Takaaki grasps this point in the following manner:

> Cornered by Kagekiyo, who is backed by Confucian ethics and hence
> remains implacable, Akoya acts as if she has *no choice* but to kill her
> children and then herself. She does not die because she acknowledges
> and submits to Kagekiyo's ethics; she dies rather out of sheer petty
> spite: "You are not murdered by your mother, but rather by your fa-
> ther who should save you" [. . . .] It is Akoya and Iyawaka, killed by
> his mother as he cries and screams, who on the surface seem to die in
> the service of doctrine. But in this scene the [this-worldly, vulgar]
> pettiness of the mother and Iyawaka conflicts with and prevails over
> Kagekiyo's Confucian ethics. It serves as an unmistakable proclama-
> tion of the universality of the petty ethics of Edo-period townspeople
> society. (Yoshimoto, *What is Beauty for Language?* 2:520)

This is an important remark for understanding the essence of drama in
Chikamatsu. When we adhere to the works themselves, however, we find that

Akoya and Otane are able to render their own acts to consciousness only as careless mistakes. Because they accept this form of consciousness in their relation to themselves (a budding self-consciousness), they inevitably lose out to the official, institutionalized ethics of Kagekiyo and Hikokurō, which are foreign to that type of consciousness, and they are left no choice but to expose the heartlessness of those ethics through acts of suicide. If we pursue this further and locate the ethical core of the philosophy they represent, it lies precisely in the absolute nature of their defeats. Yoshimoto Takaaki, in the end, lacks a methodology that could grasp literary style at the level of the immanent narrator, and for that reason, even in his history of modern expressions (*hyōshutsu*) in *What is Beauty for Language?*, he can approach expressive structure only at the level of the author. His analysis is relatively valid for works appearing after the latter half of the Meiji 30s, that is, after around 1902, when expressions that depended on an "I"-sensibility came into general use. But for earlier works, his arguments are marked by arbitrariness and his readings quickly fall apart when we examine alternative passages from the same works he discusses. That he ended writing separately both a history of expression (*hyōshutsu*) and a theory of plot construction, the former as a history of the modern novel and the latter extending to Edo-period drama, is likely also due to his failure to consider the role of the immanent narrator.

* * * * *

But in Ichiyō's "Troubled Waters," it is Genshichi's wife Ohatsu who finds herself cornered. Having endured and sacrificed so much for her husband, she is tormented day after day by the same painful question: Why isn't he in the least concerned about their family? In a fit of anger, she throws away the cake that Oriki has bought for Ohatsu's son Takichirō. When Genshichi cannot forgive this spiteful act, she responds as follows:

> "It was wrong of me. Forgive me. I shouldn't have thrown the cake away, after Oriki was kind enough to give it to us. It was wrong. You're right—for the things I've said about Oriki, I'm the one who's a demon. I'll never say anything bad about her again, ever. I'll never mention her after this, I swear. I'll never gossip about her, so please don't divorce me [. . . .] Even if you hate me, at least consider Takichi. Please. I'm sorry Genshichi." She bowed down on the floor and wept. "No, it won't work." He looked toward the wall, with no intention of listening to any further argument. He had never been so cruel. Was this what happens to a man when a woman bewitches him? Not only was he prepared to cause her anguish, for all she knew he might let their adored son starve to death. No amount of begging or apologiz-

ing was going to save the marriage, but she might at least still save the child. "Takichi, Takichi," she called. "Who do you like? Your father or your mother?" ("Troubled Waters," 239)

She cannot believe that the true reason for their plight lies in the role she plays as a thoughtful, devoted wife. When she voices hatred for Oriki, it takes the form of scolding the child for his lack of good sense. When she tries to head off divorce, the reason she gives is again the child: "at least consider Takichi. Please." She does not think her position as a wife so unstable that she would have to defend herself against Oriki by asserting, as did Chikamatsu's Akoya, that "in love social status makes no difference" and that "the real wife is the one who has the children."

In that sense, Ohatsu is in the same position as Aoki's wife in *Spring*. Aoki is rebuffed when he suggests double suicide to his wife: "Aah, you're a lost cause, and I'm a lost cause, too. How about it? Should we do it? Together, you and me. . . ." If Genshichi approached Ohatsu in the same way, her reply would probably have been the same as that of Aoki's wife. Although Ohatsu has a husband, she does not think of him as a love partner. And while she can countenance the existence of a wife who leaves her husband because of his failures as a provider, she cannot conceive of a husband who would abandon his wife because of her supposed inadequacies as a woman.

In the end, Ohatsu takes the child and leaves. But what is distinctive here is that, at least in passages that portray the household of Ohatsu and Genshichi, the mode of expression of the narrative description takes a neutral stance. Seen in terms of the history of expression, Ichiyō's expression foreshadows the historical process of the shift away from an *oral style* that used judgmental language manifesting sympathy, revulsion, or irony, and toward the non-emotional, judgment-neutral, *written style* of what would be called naturalism. While the immanent narrator's *words* of course adhere at times to Ohatsu's standpoint and at other times to Genshichi's emotions, nowhere are they melded into the spoken dialogue of Ohatsu and Genshichi so that they cannot be clearly delineated from one another. In other words, in these passages, the characters' spoken dialogue is completely bracketed off from the *words* of narrative description. Correspondingly, the third-person objectivity of the narrative description is strengthened. This characteristic becomes clear when we contrast the mode of description in the passage introduced above, describing the world of Oriki and her fellow prostitutes at the restaurant Kikunoi, with that in the following expression:

On the outskirts of the new quarter, where a narrow alley ran between the greengrocer's and the hairdresser's shops, the eaves hung so close together that the passageway all but had its own roof, and the space between the crowded tenements on each side of the lane was so tight that on a rainy day one could scarcely open an umbrella. Missing sewer covers left gaping holes in the middle of the road. It was not an easy path to navigate. At the end of the road stood a rubbish pile and a small, ramshackle house. The rain shutters no longer closed properly, and the place looked quite unsafe. It did, however, have both a front and a back door, unlike the other houses in the alley. Removed as it was, fortunately, from the center of town, it boasted a porch some three-feet wide, which overlooked an empty lot in back. There, weeds grew with abandon and begonias and China asters and bean vines entwined themselves around a makeshift bamboo fence. It was here that Oriki's Genshichi lived. ("Troubled Waters," 227)

Here, the narrator's bantering, ironic commentary that characterized the earlier passage has almost entirely disappeared. Moreover, when Ohatsu's external appearance is subsequently portrayed, it is described with the same objectivity. In a sense, this could be called a refinement in the mode of expression of modern prose, but the spoken dialogue that appears in this kind of narrative description will inevitably be haunted by a sense of estrangement.

Ohatsu's sole desire is for Genshichi to awaken from his infatuation with Oriki and devote himself to his work, raising the capital necessary to restart his former business. Precisely because of this, the people of the tenement-house slum are mindful of the poverty of Genshichi's family and refrain from offering the usual gifts of rice cakes or dumplings at the time of the spring and autumnal equinoxes, knowing that they cannot afford to reciprocate. This makes things even more unbearable for Ohatsu, yet although she often complains, she of course tries with all her might to pluck up Genshichi's spirits. It does not dawn on her, however, that her acting the part of the devoted wife is Genshichi's heaviest burden. That is to say, Ohatsu's consciousness is entirely occupied by thoughts of public opinion and the restoration of the family business. She lacks any ability to consider matters in the manner of the second-person, with its characteristic embodiedness. She lacks any thought of what Genshichi might mean to her as a man or what she as a woman might mean to him. Naturally, any conversation between the married couple must end at cross-purposes.

On this point, Ohatsu's plight contrasts strikingly with the tragedy of Akoya. Akoya's cognition of reality never expands to transcend the realm of her embodied consciousness. Because she lacks a commonsensical, worldly sense of reality that could restrain her corporeal passions, Akoya falls into a painful plight: even her own children demand that she return them to their father. Ohatsu, conversely, acts out the public ideal of the wise wife who suffers in order to restore the family business. Although Ohatsu momentarily lost self-control when she sees the cake her child has received from Oriki, upon learning of her husband's anger, she immediately admits that she is in the wrong and apologizes by portraying herself as a bad woman. Of course it is not the case that she has committed any unforgivable wrongs, and she is confident that her son would choose her over her husband.

This ideal-driven self-sacrifice and self-persecution reminds us of typical characters in a kabuki play, as opposed to those in *jōruri*. The characters in kabuki strive to remain loyal to some ideal associated with their role, an effort that, due to their inability to divulge their true motivation to others, invites unexpected misunderstandings. Hence, their surface oafish behavior often conceals a hidden ideal that, when at last revealed, leads to the restoration of their honor. Naturally, there are also cases when they really do engage in unmitigated oafish behavior, but, even in such cases, what seems at a glance to be a useless suicide that tries to atone for that behavior often ends up becoming, after one thing leads to another, the distant cause for a happy ending. That is to say, if "Troubled Waters" were a kabuki drama, it would begin with the scene of the marital separation of Genshichi and Ohatsu. Genshichi would harbor a hidden ambition, or again, he would be visited by a certain dramatic change of heart, and in the end would return to Ohatsu and their son. But the resemblance between this story and the kabuki extends beyond the motivations of the characters: even the mode of writing in the story's depiction of Genshichi's household is reminiscent of a kabuki script. The passages of narrative description restrict themselves to the explanatory role of stage directions, so that forward movement in this tragedy of a couple who fail to understand one another is accomplished solely through the lines of spoken dialogue they exchange.

To again borrow Yoshimoto Takaaki's ideas, here "the spoken dialogues occurring between the characters, which drive the dramatic progression, are already bracketed out, and passages of narrative description now serve only to string them together" (Yoshimoto, *What is Beauty for Language?* 2:528). Yoshimoto grasps this mode of expression in the following manner:

> Puppeteering, or the manipulation of the puppets, whether or not one considers the religious origins of the puppets as magical objects à la Origuchi Shinobu, has a doubled nature: human beings dialogue with each other behind the puppets, and at the same time they self-externalize that dialogue onto the puppets. [. . .] However, when the language of *jōruri* begins using a mode of expression that brackets spoken conversation between quotation marks, the acting agent is no longer a puppet but a human being. Through the appearance of the flesh-and-blood performer, the drama for the first time must inevitably attain a certain totalization. This is the terminal point at which

Chikamatsu's conception of *jōruri* arrived in less than half a century. This terminus also harbored implicitly a necessary switch to kabuki drama [in which puppets were replaced by human actors] (Yoshimoto, *What is Beauty for Language?* 2:528–29)

In my understanding, this means that the *words* that were separated from actions in a process of mutual alienation within the "ground" passages of *jōruri* were in kabuki re-constituted as exchanges of other-oriented "speech." Those exchanges now took place on a level governed by the hidden motivation, the character role-ideal from which corporeality has been abstracted away. While the actions of characters are of course indicated in the stage directions and performed by the actors, the most dramatically tense scenes are constituted through the gap between the "speech" representing the character's hidden ideal and the painful actions arising out of the need to constrain his or her true feelings. Or again, we find a mode of expression constituted through a duality of deceitful "speech" that seeks to divert others' attention, and actions or poses that convey the unspeakable hidden ideal. In either case, the crux of dramatic development is sought in a rupture between *words* and body, and when a situation arises in which the two can be united, the dramatic contradiction comes to closure. Only a living human being could carry out this complex dramatic process.

Ichiyō's "Troubled Waters," however, ends with the divorce of Genshichi and Ohatsu. Ichiyō herself here smashes the kabuki-style schema, a schema also found in her story "Child's Play." She abandons the final moment of unification, in which *words* are restored to body. With this, Ichiyō denied the restoration of Genshichi's reputation and family, the ending that the majority of her readers had likely anticipated. In a way, she playfully invokes her readers' horizon of expectation. Three rumors concerning the love suicide of Genshichi and Oriki are introduced in the conclusion to "Troubled Waters." While scholars have busily debated which of the three rumors best conveys Ichiyō's intention, in fact all three were possible within the horizon of expectation that Ichiyō posited. Even the possibility of a restoration of Genshichi's honor, including the posthumous repose of his soul, is indicated, however faintly, in the following rumor: "He, on the other hand, did a splendid job of it! Hari-kiri and the whole business. Who would have thought he had it in him? Ever since the days he lost his bedding shop, at least. But he died like a man. Went out in a blaze of glory" ("Troubled Waters," 240).

On the other hand, I have already touched upon how Oriki was a being in whom were gathered the thoughts and feelings of the women of the Kikunoi. While the sections that focus on Ohatsu are kabuki-like, the expressions that center on Oriki are more like *jōruri*, although this difference is of course not absolute. Note the symbolism involved in having Oriki's existential agony repeatedly expressed (*hyōshutsu*) through the corporeal suffering of headaches. Her headaches probably derive from her worries:

> She hated it! She hated! She felt almost delirious and leaned against a tree at the side of the road. "I'm afraid to cross to the other side; I'm afraid to stay where I am." It was her song, the echo of her voice, but where was it coming from? "I have no choice," she whispered. "I will have to cross the bridge by myself. My father fell treading it. They say my grandfather stumbled, too. I was born under the curse [*urami*] of many generations, and there are things I have to undergo before I die. [. . .] Sometimes I wonder if I've lost all sense of kindness and decency. No, I mustn't think such things. It won't do me any good. With my station in life and my calling and my fate, I'm not an ordinary person anymore. It's a mistake to think that I am. It only adds to my suffering. ("Troubled Waters," 232)

While the "curse" (or "grudge": *urami*) of many generations, according to what Oriki tells Yūki a little later, signifies a curse of misfortune passed down through many generations, we can also sense here the nuance of having borne the curse or grudge of society (*seken*), since just before this comes the passage in which the grief and grudges of the women of the Kikunoi are written so as to flow directly into Oriki. Here, the passage echoes the grieving voice in the previously cited an Edo-period folk song, "Utaura":

> If I close my eyes for a while and look back on the past, my old friends are all dead. If I use my fingers to count the dead, many kinsmen have passed away. Time passes, things change. Nowadays, what goes on forever? People stay but I go away. No one is constant. The Three Worlds are without peace, like a burning house. Even a heavenly saint must suffer and die, all the worse for the lowly and poor, whose sins cannot be light. [. . .] Since the fault arises with myself, my heart's demon torments me and I suffer. Resentment [*urami*] piles up on the mountain of sexual passion. The circle of karma keeps turning. The more I think about it, the angrier I get. Pierced by the sword, the path of Asura titans. Fallen one by the other on the ground and destroyed in a moment. The more I think about it, the angrier I get. The name I had in this world is blown away. My name is buried in the snow of a winter storm; it disappears and is no more.

Why has the singer of these lyrics fallen into this living hell? It is not because she has committed some unforgivable wrong. After long thought she still fails to come up with an answer, and so at last she has no choice but to understand this as the result of fate and karma from a previous life. The very fact of having been born into such a base and poverty-stricken position must be punishment for some crime that she is not aware of. When she comes to this conclusion, the result is that her own "heart's demon" torments her even more. Here there is no longer any distinction between cursing and being cursed, between bearing a grudge and being the target of a grudge. This type of abject sensibility borne by prostitutes since the Edo period flows in Oriki, too, carried into her via the immanent narrator.

I have already touched upon how Oriki is set up as a heterogeneous element even among the restaurant women at the Kikunoi, a princess among commoners. A kabuki-like conceptual idea flows even through Oriki's teasing banter: "My ambitions are as grand as those of Ōtomo Kuronushi, who wanted to rule the entire world" ("Troubled Waters," 221). However, just as in "Child's Play," we find a nomadic half-speaker set in the interior of the Kikunoi, one who continuously picks up the worried *speech* of the restaurant women in a second-person feminine tone of speech reminiscent of a kitchen maid. (Note by contrast how the immanent narrator in the scenes depicting Genshichi's family is de-feminized and rendered neutral.) The flow of this nomadic half-speaker molds Oriki's sensibility, and she is finally rendered into a self-conscious being. Whereas the restaurant women's feelings are of a second-person type, meaning they are unable to transcend simple embodied consciousness, Oriki's self-consciousness as mediated through the narrative description has no choice but to feel more and more strongly a self-tormenting sense of being closed off from the world. "Sometimes I wonder if I've lost all sense of kindness and decency. No, I mustn't think such things. It won't do me any good. With my station in life and my calling and my fate. . . ." ("Troubled Waters," 232).

One of the main points in Yoshimoto Takaaki's reading of Chikamatsu's plays is to find in Akoya and Otane's petty and oafish behavior (such misdeeds as informing on others, committing adultery, etc.) the key to dramatic development. Leaving aside whether or not we agree with Yoshimoto's assertion that this vulgar, worldly behavior ultimately triumphs over official ethical doctrine in such scenes, it is certain that Chikamatsu's philosophy of drama cannot be grasped without this point. Akoya and Otane reproach themselves for their misdeeds and die before their honor can be restored. In Oriki's case, however, even in the absence of any specific misdeed, the painful conditions of the present world are rendered despairingly inescapable and absolute. No matter what she might say by way of explanation or vindication, there is no reason to expect society would listen, and so Oriki in despair defiantly embraces the dishonor of being a restaurant woman at an illicit brothel. That is to say, her attitude and sentiment in and of themselves constitute her misdeed, her revolt against the social order. Ichiyō, having carried the matter through to this point, no longer has any need to manufacture further dramatic events. As with Midori in "Child's

Play," Oriki's sentiment no longer has any concrete object, and all that remains is to portray the collapse of Genshichi's family after he succumbs to the flames of Oriki's despairing passion. At the conclusion, having driven Genshichi to ruin, all that Oriki can do is cast her lot with him in a love suicide.

In rendering Oriki's passion absolute, so that by itself it constituted a misdeed, Ichiyō realized the most profound human philosophy possible in the 1890s. While that absolutization arose as a result of the positing of an immanent narrator, Ichiyō's writing style also utilized elements from *jōruri*, allowing her simultaneously to excavate a sensibility of tragic women that had existed since the Edo period.

Ichiyō herself may have encountered a psychological crisis in which her passions themselves seemed misdeeds. If so, it was likely a passion that could bring only conflict with the norms of the family, and what created it was the situation of the petty bourgeois intellectual, who can only gaze skeptically at any attempt to provide an explanation for circumstances. The sense of being a lost cause as a flesh-and-blood woman that arose from this situation is sketched out as Oriki's misdeed, and it eventually provides the willing receptacle for Genshichi's proposal. In the face of the situation of the petty bourgeois intellectual, one that tries to attain self-exhibition through ideal-laden *words*, she attained the "outrageous words" of passion that a real woman was not allowed to speak. And having attained those "outrageous words" through her own embodiedness, she buries herself in them. To connect this with the previous chapter, there is a type of institutionalized sensibility that we are apt to understand as being our private "I"-sensibility. Furthermore, in the depths of its embodiedness there lies submerged a sensibility of shared suffering, what might be called the communality of hell. For human beings dragged down by a shared suffering, the only salvation lies in being buried together, like lovers in a double suicide. This astonishing attempt was carried out on the level of narration: not by bracketing the lines of spoken dialogue between quotation marks, but rather by weaving them into the flow of narrative description.

Chapter Eight
The Burdens of Ethicality: Izumi Kyōka and the Emergence of the Split Subject

TRANSLATED BY JOSEPH MURPHY

In this chapter, Kamei turns to the fantastic world of the writer Izumi Kyōka, using it to identify a blind spot in structuralist literary theory. Comparing three versions of the manuscript for the story Noble Blood, Heroic Blood, *Kamei traces the experiments in composition and form that Kyōka carried out. In particular, he focuses on the modes of intersubjective recognition the various versions of the work solicit from their readers. He traces through the process whereby the heroine of the story at first comes to inhabit a certain attitude, that of a stereotypical character-type, a dissolute "iron lady," that inheres in certain expressions she uses, but then achieves a self-reflexive awareness of that sensibility through her relation with the work's hero. This unfolding drama of self-consciousness eventually awakens in her a sense of ethicality, a need to take responsibility for her own sensibility, which allows her to transcend the "iron lady" character type. Kamei also examines the writing style Kyōka developed to portray passages of direct spoken dialogue, arguing that much of the pleasure of and driving force behind the narrative derives from Kyōka's skillful handling of these expressions, an aspect of writing style that would subsequently be lost to readers accustomed to the protocols of "realism" that came to dominate modern fiction in Japan, as a visually oriented mimesis elbowed out an orally oriented mimesis as the dominant technique. Kyōka uses the device to solicit contemporary readers' interest, but then transcends it and his readers' horizon of expectations by shifting the direction of the plot toward an ultimately ethical resolution of its central problem, one in which the characters take on an unpredictable life of their own, having transcended the domination of authorial intent of character type.*

Textual correlations done by Mita Hideaki and Koshino Itaru of the two extant handwritten manuscripts of Izumi Kyōka's *Noble Blood, Heroic Blood* (*Giketsu kyōketsu*, 1894) make it clear that the hand of Ozaki Kōyō intervened fairly heavily before the work reached the form in which we know it today. This assistance went well beyond the suggestions and proofreading one would expect of an editor.

Strictly speaking, it is perhaps only *Blind Justice* (*Kohanji*, the title of the earlier manuscripts) that can be called Kyōka's work. *Noble Blood, Heroic Blood*, however, has been treated up to the present as a Kyōka story. Be that as it may, this study is not aiming for the type of author-centered inquiry (*sakkaron*) that would look to clarify the essentially "Kyōka-esque," but rather for some understanding of the way individual works solicited recognition from their contemporaries. Hence, we may set aside the question of whether *Noble Blood, Heroic Blood* was in fact something closer to a collaboration and retain the term "Kyōka" in the sense in which it has come to signify the author of a particular group of texts that includes *Noble Blood, Heroic Blood*. Keeping in mind the work of earlier scholars, I would like to explore this process of revision, raising questions about the problem of conception and structure, as well as the autonomy of the writer and the active contribution of the reader.

In concrete terms, then, what is the point from which we can begin to read out the stakes in this solicitation of recognition from contemporary readers? As our first example, let's take a passage not from the manuscripts, but from the work as it appeared in print (hereafter, *Noble Blood, Heroic Blood*). In this passage Taki no Shiraito (the stage name for the heroine Mizushima Tomo) makes conspicuous use of double entendre to launch a surprise attack on her interlocutor. Or perhaps it would be better to say she is made to bear the refracted self-consciousness incorporated in that mode of usage.

> "Kin-san," she called familiarly.
> The coachman was taken by surprise. Meeting this beautiful woman, fresh under the moonlight, and here she knows my name. Coachmen aren't the type to be taken by surprise either. The first thing that came to his mind was, well maybe here I am face to face with one of those foxes and badgers I never believed in anyway. His head was positively spinning.
> "You're really heartless, you know. What kind of a man forgets a woman that he's held in his own arms."
> "Held in his arms? Me??"
> "That's right, you held me tight."
> "Where?"
> "Right where it counts!"
> Shiraito passed a sleeve over her face and smiled coyly.
> The coachman was lost in dark deliberation, but after a while he straightened and announced,

"I have no recollection of embracing you, but sure enough, I seem to have seen you somewhere before."

"'Seems,' nothing. On the coach from Takaoka that time you were racing the rickshaw runners, you held me tight all the way from this side of Isurugi. I'm the woman who rode on the horse with you."

"Oh! That's right." The coachman clapped his hands and shouted. Shiraito was startled by his intensity.

"Well, well. It all seems to be coming back to you now."

"Yeah, I remember now. Um hmm, I've got it."

A smile crept to the coachman's lips, and he clapped his hands again. (*MBZ* 21:11)

This passage comes from the night scene on Tenjinbashi in Kanazawa, where the two meet for the second time.

Whether it is the very first draft or not I do not know, but in what appears to be the earliest of the surviving manuscripts—we'll call it the grass manuscript—this conversation couldn't possibly have taken place.[1] There, the competition between the horse-drawn carriage and the rickshaw-men appears in pretty much the form we know it today, but in the grass manuscript, when the carriage overturns after the coachman tries to jump a washed-out bridge, the coachman simply jumps on a horse and rides away.[2] The woman for her part, "wrapped up the cash in a sheet of tissue paper, licked the tip of her little finger and drew it across her moistened lips and wrote in lipstick 'A Token of My Appreciation—For the Repair Fees.' She left the parcel in the coach and walked away without a second look." In the second handwritten manuscript—hereafter *Blind Justice*—we find the scene as it appears in *Noble Blood, Heroic Blood*, the coachman unhitches the horses, and "holding the woman close, went flying off at a gallop." However, in this version, when they meet again, the woman simply says, "So, how have you been?" just as in the grass manuscript, and

1. Since Kamei wrote this chapter, an even earlier manuscript has been uncovered. In Matsumura Tomomi, "*Giketsu kyōketsu* no henyō—Kōyō kaisaku wo megutte," *Nihon kindai bungaku* 31 (1984): 29–43, the various versions are designated "A" (the newly discovered version), "B" (the grass manuscript discussed here) and "C" (*Kohanji*). The first two were handwritten by Kyōka in Kanazawa, the former being a draft of the manuscript finally sent to Kōyō in Tokyo, while "C" is virtually rewritten in Kōyō's hand. The finished story was serialized in the *Yomiuri* newspaper under the title "A Certain Someone" (*Nanigashi*) from November 1 to November 30, 1894. Various manuscript versions of the story have been published in facsimile form (with no page numbers) in Izumi Kyōka, *Jihitsu kōhon Giketsu kyōketsu* (Tokyo: Iwanami Shoten, 1986).

2. In both versions, the story opens in Takaoka, where rickshaw pullers are tying to lure customers away from the horse-drawn coach by promising to get to the next town faster. Shiraito has raised the stakes by promising to up the coachman's fee if he can beat the rickshawmen to Isurugi.

there is none of the tendentious wordplay on "the woman you held in your arms." The author at this stage seemed rather to have an aversion to making a clear suggestion of sexual relations. The woman asks, "Do you remember at all?" and the coachman replies *coolly*, "No, I don't remember." Following this, the *Blind Justice* author tacks on the following words of approval:

> This was a coachman who placed the greatest weight on the simplest promise, on fulfilling one's duty. As long as this was so, it was nothing to be wondered at that he would fail to recall a woman he had held close to his own flesh. There are those who style themselves red-blooded, and ride a wave of pointless passions and feverishly interfere in matters outside their proper purview, mounting the dais for a day-long harangue, the shopkeeper discourses on military matters, the farmer expostulates legal opinions, the workman weighs in on politics, or, to take it to the extreme, saving a woman who has tossed herself in the drink, robbing from the rich and giving to the poor, throwing stones at dogs, etc. I say as long as one forges straight down the path with diligence, glancing neither left nor right, let us call that benevolence, let us call that noble. . . .

And so on.

It is his own carriage boy who has made the ridiculous wager with the passengers, so there is nothing else to be done but carry through with it, and when the carriage breaks down the coachman is duty-bound to take up the woman in his arms and fulfill the pact on horseback. That the feel and the visage of the woman would slip from his memory should come as no surprise. While noting his sense of duty, the author also takes time to censure those who would frivolously boast of such things as benevolence or righteousness. In both manuscripts, the modifier "cool and indifferent" (*reizen to*) appears again and again in characterizing the coachman. This would appear to be a way to construct the character as a young man successful at subjugating the hot-blooded passions that might incline one to deviate from appointed duties.

In *Noble Blood, Heroic Blood* as it eventually appears in print, however, the above authorial explication is pared away, and the problems of righteousness and nobility are brought center stage in the work's title. The woman transforms in a stroke the distance separating her from the coachman to familiarity through her *words* connoting sexual relations (the equivalent of the scandalous words spoken by female characters in Chikamatsu's puppet plays[3]). This marks a substantial shift in the conception of the work.

---

3. See chapter seven.

Particularly important here is the way the verb "to hold" (*daku* or *idaku*: lit., "to embrace"; the verb also functions as a euphemism for sexual relations) works through the passage to effect what in structuralism is called a code shift. Yuri Lotman lays out the relation between a sign and its meaning, the possibility of reversal in the usual relation between the form of a sign (signifier) and its semantic content (signified): "Thus in a language lesson the teacher, speaking to students who do not know English, points to a table and says, 'Table.' Here things become the signs of a metalanguage, and words are their content."[4] Borrowing this terminology, we may say that the woman takes a euphemism for the sexual act as a sign in itself and purposely eludes the original meaning (content). Giving meaning the slip, of course, is a roundabout way of transmitting the content impressionistically. So at the same time the coachman can discern the meaning content, he also understands the *false information* of the encoded sexual allusion as a joke. What the reader absorbs, though, does not end simply at that. To again borrow Lotman's language:

> Consider the words *est'*—*rat* ["to eat"—"to stuff yourself"] and *spat'*—*dryzat'* ["to sleep"—"to be dead to the world."] On the level of a message indifferent to stylistic coloring, the words in the first pair (and in the second) are equivalent. But if the message includes, for example, information regarding the attitude of the speaker toward the activity of the object, then the words are not equivalent. (Lotman, 46)

The only information we can discern from the locution of this passage in the story is that this is a woman who enjoys verbalizing her relation to men in the *words* of sexual activity, or that she uses these kinds of *words* when attempting to bridge an estranged relation. The device succeeds and the reserve between the two quickly melts away.

That, however, is not enough to constitute a code shift. What is crucial here is that the woman herself, within this device, has been *brought into relation with her own self*: she becomes conscious of herself as a being that can only effect an approach to the coachman through sexual euphemisms. That is to say, the code through which the woman relates to herself undergoes a transformation, a recoding. The coachman is able to understand both the content and the play of the message the woman transmits, and their conversation progresses to the level of personal matters and mundane worldly chatter. Even as the conversation tends to the mundane, however, within the woman's interior relational consciousness, a self-conception as a sexual being now haunts her, emerging in

---

4. Jurij Lotman, *The Structure of the Artistic Text*, trans. Ronald Vroon (Ann Arbor: Michigan Slavic Contributions, 1977), 35.

even her most trivial gestures. She asks to borrow the coachman's pipe and while cleaning the stem interrogates him with such lines as, "So, you're a widower?" and "Oh, but you must have any number of lovers. . . ," precisely the techniques a courtesan uses on a first-time customer. Ultimately, she learns of his aspirations to higher education, proposes that she assist him with school fees, and they once again announce their names to each other. The man announces himself as Murakoshi Kinya. It falls to the woman now to make clear her own position, and she is submitted to the following refraction:

> "So, where did you say you were located?"
> "That way," the gorgeous woman pointed to a hut on the riverbed.
> The coachman looked off in that direction,
> "What do you mean, that way?"
> "The sideshow tent," Shiraito let slip an ethereal smile.
> "The sideshow tent, that's odd."
> The coachman suppressed the astonishment he felt in his heart. He was under no misconception that this was the daughter of a fine family. It seemed a bit more likely that he had spied out a monster that had been in the mountains or sea for five hundred years. But really, that she would be part of a band of itinerant show people living in a tent by the riverside, well that really took him by surprise. Nevertheless he feigned indifference. Shiraito saw through his feelings, and made light of herself.
> "Extremely odd, wouldn't you say?" (*MBZ* 21:16)

Like the scene with the pipe, this conversation is absent from the earlier drafts and first appears in the final published version. Her status as a riverside beggar made clear now, she cannot help but feel contempt even in his very nonchalance. Coupled with the aforementioned self-perception, the image of the lowest class of prostitute pierces her consciousness. That their second meeting takes place at the riverbed, a site conventionally associated with impurity, ostracization, and prostitution, only intensifies this effect: "Shiraito saw through his feelings, and made light of herself."

> "Do you play the shamisen there?"
> "It's worse than that. I'm a headliner."
> The coachman let slip not the slightest hint of condescension,
> "Really? A headliner! What's your claim to fame?"
> "I'm a water magician. Let's leave it at that, shall we, really, you're embarrassing me."
> The coachman only got more earnest.
> "The star water magician? Hahaa, you mean you're the one that's been getting raves lately . . ."
> All the while he was gazing at her. Shiraito blushed all of a sudden and turned her face.

"Really, that's quite enough. Go easy on me, will you?" (*MBZ* 21:16)

Though she has just offered to support him through university with her own funds, because of the mere fact that she is an itinerant performer it is Shiraito who feels cheap, who thinks she should be apologizing. This refraction ultimately generates her so-called interiority and opens up an ethical dimension. Though for now this youth who announces himself as Murakoshi Kinya is nothing more than an unemployed masterless samurai, considering what the future holds after his education in Tokyo, the distance between them will likely grow wider and wider. And perhaps the time will come when a patron like herself will become a liability or burden. Even if her partner makes no issue of this, the time will surely come when she herself cannot help but feel it. Shiraito's offer of assistance was itself a kind of casual suggestion, a proposal that arose out of her *words* themselves.

> She has no parents, no siblings, no lover, so every penny of her earnings has to be used up on herself. [. . .] Scattering twenty for every ten that comes in, she spent the gold pieces as soon as she made them. Part of the reason, though, is she'd never known difficulty in making money in the first place. (*MBZ* 21:18)

Relying solely on her art, she had lived until that time without restraint, and with just that temperament she hit on the idea of playing patron herself. When asked what she wants in return, she surprises her partner with a graceless request, "You know what my fondest hope is? I want you to be real nice to me." Of course we find here a certain declaration of goodwill as a member of the opposite sex, but note how this is also a manner of speaking that always allows itself to be taken as a joke, one that solicitously permits the interlocutor to accept the proffered goodwill with no fear of entangling obligations. "Hey, do you really need to make such a dreadful face? Nobody's saying make me your wife. I'm just saying not to treat me like a stranger, that I want you to think of me like a relation from now on" (*MBZ* 21:15).

With this "iron-lady" temperament[5] Shiraito comes to behave toward him like an older sister, but along with the sharp consciousness of her ignoble

---

5. "Temperament" (*kishitsu* or *katagi*) refers to a stock character-type; *katagi-mono* was a late-Edo and early-Meiji genre of humorous fictional works that presented catalogs of various stereotypical character-types. Kamei here and in subsequent chapters will trace the breakdown in Meiji fiction of the *katagi* notion of "character" and the rise in its place of the modern notion of "personality."

circumstances, there arises in her an ethicality born of inferiority. That is to say, there arises her powerful sense of loyalty, such as we saw in the love-suicide works examined in chapter seven. I may seem to be belaboring this point, but to understand the intervening circumstances I'd like to compare the mode of expression in *Blind Justice* with that in the published version of *Noble Blood, Heroic Blood.* In the former, Shiraito's name is Mizushima Otama, while the coachman is called Hanyū Sōnosuke.

> If there were no such thing as obligation, getting through life would be a rather more smooth process; however, our lives will not likely be free anytime soon of obligation, consequently are not free of responsibility. We bring about this obligation and responsibility through pacts between self and other,
> Born in Niigata of Echigo-kuni, Otama came with a full measure of that beauty and grace that typifies the women of that land, and moreover as an expert water magician she never failed to bring accolades wherever her company played, hence the manager gave her what was really an extravagant salary. Moreover, as she herself said she has no parents, no brothers and sisters, and all alone in this world she is free to dispose of every penny of that income exactly as she pleases. But this she throws away, shows no pleasure in an aristocratic lifestyle. Quite the contrary, it's living the simple, average life, or perhaps more to the point, the life of the lower classes that seems to suit her fancy, and when they're on the road she doesn't seek out an inn, if she can just have a place to curl up in the circus tent she doesn't give a care to word or deed or anything at all, she lives her own life, defiant, dissolute, loose and free,
> Now, however, that she's taken on the obligation of sponsoring Hanyū Sōnosuke's studies in Tokyo, as well as the living expenses of his aged mother in Takaoka, this spirited woman has passed this year and some days applying herself resolutely and in the execution of her pledge, (*Blind Justice*)[6]

> She found no joy in the high-class life, but rather leaned toward the lot of lower class society by choice, and she neither chased after fashion nor pursued extravagance in ornamentation. She was beyond common to the point of becoming an iron lady [*tekka*]. On average, women of the iron lady type are without exception on the royal road to dirty dealings, sin, and perdition. Shiraito's temperament as an iron lady, on the other hand, sprang from naivete, and was a pure and unsullied thing.
> She'd passed these many years in peace and tranquillity, brandishing this temperament just exactly as she pleased. Now, however,

6. There are no indentations to mark paragraphs in the original Japanese, and even paragraphs end in commas, not periods.

things had changed. Murakoshi Kinya, taking her at her word, was away studying in Tokyo. His mother was sitting poised at the table, awaiting word of his success. Shiraito was now the head of a household, responsible every month for their support and sustenance.

The course was clear, the Taki no Shiraito of old had to restrain that wantonness, reign in that spirit, and become the upstanding wife Otomo. She became the thrifty and self-sacrificing housewife, who if it was for the sake of her charge would coil up rock, twist iron and fold over the unfoldable bamboo joint, all for the sake of her charge. In carrying out that charge, while yet preserving the vigor of the Taki no Shiraito of old, her spirit strained and sweated as Murakoshi Otomo and no other. And so passed a full three years. (*Noble Blood, Heroic Blood, MBZ* 21:18)

What governs Shiraito in the earlier *Blind Justice* version is "duty" and "pacts between self and other." Of course, that isn't all, but at least one can say that in terms set by the actual expressions used, she is bound by "duty." This forms the groundwork in *Noble Blood, Heroic Blood* as well, though in the expressions used there, what governs her, or rather what sustains her in her "strain and sweat," is a consciousness of "responsibility," the imaginary projected self-consciousness of being "the upstanding wife Otomo," of being "Murakoshi Otomo and no other."

Another way of putting this would be to say that from the pact "between self and other" was born a "pact with oneself," a metamorphosis into a consistent interior ethicality over and above a sense of duty, one that put in check her temperament as an "iron lady" and transformed her into "the thrifty and self-sacrificing housewife." The more refracted her feelings in regard to her own circumstances and the more acute her feeling of inferiority toward Murakoshi Kinya, the more necessary it was for her to accept as her own personal ethicality the position of a "head of a household with responsibilities" and to sacrifice herself, as if it was her own heart's desire, to the fictional projection of being "the upstanding wife Otomo" and the "spirit" of "Murakoshi Otomo and no other." It goes without saying that the poignant fulfillment of her self-consciousness as a sexual being is entrusted to this self-sacrificing devotion. When I somewhat high-handedly forced Lotman's theory onto the *word* "embrace" above, it was in fact because I wanted to show that one can't grasp this kind of code shift within a character—the emergence of self-consciousness, for example, and the structural change in expression that accompanies it—using a conventional structuralist methodology.

As a form, the novel would appear to be outside the scope of Lotman's work, which deals chiefly with poetic expressions. The perspective of Todorov and Ducrot's *Encyclopedic Dictionary of the Sciences of Language*, though, does allow for Shiraito's "embrace" to be classed as connotative language in one sense:

> ... if it is the level of expression that is a language in its own right, we are confronting a connotative language. Connotation is found in fact, in Hjelmslev's view, when the signifying element is the actual utilization of a given language. When Stendahl uses an Italian word, the signifier is not simply the term employed, but the fact that in order to express a certain idea, the author decided to take recourse to Italian, which recourse has as its signified a certain idea of passion and of liberty that is linked, for Stendahl, to Italy. The natural languages, in their literary usage, provide a ready example of connotative language, since in this usage the signifier is less the word chosen than the fact of having chosen it.[7]

When we juxtapose this with Lotman's notion discussed earlier that "the message includes, for example, information regarding the attitude of the speaker toward the activity of the object," the limitations introduced by structuralism's dependence on information theory become clear. To be sure, the theorization of reading from the side of reception (the function of the reader) was an epoch-making event, but what this perspective lacks is recognition of the fact that these aspects—"less the word chosen than the fact of having chosen it" (such as the term "embrace" with its sexual connotations) or "information regarding the attitude of the speaker"—rebound back onto that speaker, the character in the work. The code shift in self-consciousness that accompanies this in turn rebounds back onto the author, who in order to produce expressions necessarily undergoes an ideational doubling of his own self. The reactions to the code shift by the work's character ripple out to affect the author's own conceptions and the cognition and expressions of the narrator who is rendered immanent to the work. The new understanding of characters born from that process gives rise, for example, to critical assessments of a sort not present in *Blind Justice*, such as the assertion that Shiraito is "beyond common [*heiminteki*, lit., 'commoner-like'] to the point of becoming an iron lady." As if in reaction to this change in the assessment of Shiraito's character, the author's conception of "commoner" (*heimin*) also undergoes a transformation and deepening, a process that mediates the reevaluation of Shiraito's "iron lady" temperament as something "sprung

7. Oswald Ducrot and Tzvetan Todorov, *Encyclopedic Dictionary of the Sciences of Language*, trans. Catherine Porter (Baltimore: John Hopkins University Press, 1979), 23–24. The work was originally published as *Dictionnaire encyclopedique des sciences langage* (Paris: Editions de Seuil, 1972) and was translated into Japanese in 1975 as *Gengo riron shōjiten* by Takita Fumihiko et al.

from naivete [. . .] a pure and unsullied thing." In other words the "iron lady" temperament that is initially definitive of Shiraito's characterization is delimited, and what arises in the wake of this are expressions that depict her internalization of an ethic of responsibility and her restraining of her own self-indulgent and wanton behavior. Within the romance-like overall structure of the work, it is this unfolding of the protagonist's own self-regulating mental autonomy (consciousness of self), that gives the reader the impression that this is a modern novel.

This shift in the work's conception naturally affects the story's resolution as well. In both the grass manuscript and *Blind Justice*, Hanyū Sōnosuke returns from Tokyo as a magistrate and is put in charge of examining Shiraito, who has refused to admit the fact that she was assaulted by the circus knife-thrower and robbed of her money. The knife-thrower's counsel points out the "personal nature" of Hanyū's relation to the woman and calls for "His Honor to yield the bench to another magistrate":

> Smiling coolly, as if waking from a dream, Sōnosuke quietly turned his gaze on the counsel, and then as he turned to take in Otama's pale visage an indescribably pained expression came over his face, but in an instant his usual demeanor returned and he calmly picked up the butcher knife lying on the table as evidence and plunged it into his right eye, and before anyone realized what was happening switched hands and stabbed it through his left eye, and making no effort to wipe the blood coursing out of the wounds, he turned on the counsel, 'so you say you can't judge someone you're intimate with, well there are no friends, no relations, nothing in the eyes of this official,' spitting out the words with a ferocious determination. (*Blind Justice*)

The provisional title given to the manuscript at this stage, *Blind Justice*, is likely a thematization of this climax. Upon seeing this act of cruel ferocity, Shiraito confesses not only that she was attacked and robbed, also but that she herself has committed larceny and murder. Sōnosuke hands down a sentence of death and then kills himself that night.

In the *Noble Blood, Heroic Blood* version, though, the dramatic tension does not come from being subjected to the gaze of the spectators and the lawyer who exposes their relationship, but rather is enacted entirely within the dimension of the couple's relational consciousness. The defendant's counsel is given no role whatsoever in driving them into a corner (although he is indeed present in the scene), nor does Murakoshi Kinya perform the highly theatrical act of putting out his eyes. Instead, what drives Shiraito to confess are the *words* of Kinya, standing in the role of prosecutor. Or more precisely, on meeting Kinya in the courtroom, Shiraito is forced to recognize her position, a relation to Kinya many times more wretched than the poignant disparity she had foreseen at the start of their relation. At that point, she is already driven into a corner psychologically.

> Until that time, she had thought of him in her heart as simply a coachman with some promise. [. . .] In a certain sense, she had felt she should hold the position of dominance over him. However now, brought face to face with assistant special prosecutor Murakoshi Kinya, she felt she didn't have the right to touch a hair on his head. Aah, magnificent, grand-hearted Taki no Shiraito! Until that moment she couldn't have imagined herself reduced to that state in front of a man. (*Noble Blood, Heroic Blood, MBZ* 21:27)

Kinya's interrogation cruelly jabs at her sense of inferiority:

> Is this Taki no Shiraito not an artist of major stature? To utter a falsehood, even in jest would be a disgrace to the name. [. . .] If this official were the patron of such an artist, from the present day forward I would withdraw my affection without regret, would not spit in her direction if we met in the street. If I were a patron of long-standing, though, before severing my ties I would counsel her in no uncertain terms, never to give voice to cowardly lies, even at the cost of her life. (*Noble Blood, Heroic Blood, MBZ* 21:28)

By using such *words* as "patron" he connotes a relation known only to the two of them, appealing to Shiraito's sense of honor and communicating his desire that she not damage his respect for her. It is doubtful, though, that anything could have played more painfully on Shiraito's sense of inferiority than these *words*, with the hint of withdrawn affection concealed behind their ostensible expression of good intentions. The only avenue open to her at this point is to protect her honor and, in the guise of cooperating with Kinya in his duties, to carry out with utmost rigor her own ethic of responsibility. At the same time, this fulfills at the level of ideals her self-consciousness as a sexual being.

Kinya charges Shiraito with murder, and on the day the death sentence is handed down he kills himself.

This is of course a kind of double-suicide. From the moment she becomes wrapped up in her own personal ethic through the mediation of the imaginary projection provided by the suggestion of sexual relations, Shiraito's emotions are already of a nature that cannot find satisfaction in Kinya. Well aware of this, she pushes through to its denouement her self-sacrificing devotion, and the man, caught in the contradiction between his obligation to her and his public duties, dies as well. In this sense, the work is constructed so that in sacrificing themselves to passions that cannot achieve fulfillment in any specific object, they seem to achieve a sort of mutual objectification. It is a characteristic of works of this period, one that it shares with Higuchi Ichiyō's "Troubled Waters."

* * * * *

This reading, though, relies on the comparison of successive manuscripts, something to which the contemporary reading public did not have access. And with the exception of scholars specializing in Kyōka, one can probably say the same for readers today.

According to Lotman, when an author writes, he or she is aware that there were other possibilities in actualizing a work, but the reader is prone to think that the form in which a work appears is the only way it could have been written. In other words, in a text perceived as artistically complete, it is thought that nothing could have been left to chance. Of course, when we read and compare the grass manuscript, *Blind Justice* and *Noble Blood, Heroic Blood*, we see differences in quality among them, but all three must be called variants of a *single work*. Particularly in the case of *Noble Blood, Heroic Blood*, where we can detect additions from Kōyō's pen, this sense is all the stronger. That is not to say that this *single work*, the invariant that lies behind the three variants, actually exists. It can only be inferred from the three versions. The question of the shape of the work by which the writer solicited the recognition of his readers needs to be posed from this perspective as well.

The following passages are similar not just in terms of plot events, but also, more concretely, in the expressions they use, expressions for which the author evidently felt some attachment. They all come from an incident occurring early in the story, the race between the horse-drawn carriage and the rickshaw drivers on the road from Tsugaru.

> The old man turned again to the coach driver "Hey, young master there, these horse-drawn carriages, they don't flip over now, do they?" he asked in alarm, "What do I know?" he coolly replied, "if you hit a rut, they'll roll over" (grass manuscript)

> Turning again to the coach driver, "I say, young master coach driver, these horse-drawn carriages, they don't flip over now, do they?" the old man asked in alarm, "What do I know?" he artlessly replied without so much as looking back, "if you hit a rut, they'll roll over." (*Blind Justice*)[8]

8. There is little change in the wording between the grass manuscript and *Blind Justice* versions; however, a number of words written in *hiragana* in the former are rendered with Chinese characters in the latter.

The old man straightened up stiff as a board,

"I say there, pardon me. That must have quite hurt. Please do pardon me. Good gracious, I'm just not cut out for this. I say, coachman! Young man! These horse-drawn carriages don't flip over now, do they?"

Without so much as a glance behind, the coachman drove the horses on harder,

"What do I know? If the horse trips, then that's that." (*Noble Blood, Heroic Blood, MBZ* 21:5)

The following three passages take place just before Shiraito and the coachman meet for the second time on a bridge in Kanazawa. Here Shiraito has left the sideshow tent and is walking out on the riverbed to enjoy the cool of the evening.

The lady mounted the bridge and touched her hand to her hair all done up in a young lady's style, "Oh, I've had it with this, this is really a pain," she said, roughly letting it down and then teasing herself she muttered, "hmm, what a fool I am," drew her hair up into a bundle, passed over it a boxwood comb which she then inserted sideways to pin it into place, and a refreshing feeling shone in her face (grass manuscript)

Otama mounted the bridge and touched her hand to her hair all done up in a young lady's style, "Oh, I've had it with this, this is really a pain," she said, roughly letting it down and then teasing herself she muttered, "I'm so bored by it all, hmm, what a fool I am," and at that she drew her hair up into a bundle, pinned it into place sideways with a comb, and then for the first time a refreshed feeling shone in her face (*Blind Justice*)

At last she reached the bridge. The sound of her azuma-geta clogs tripped the silence reigning between heaven and earth, and echoed click-clack up to the moon. Amused by the sound, she made them sound louder, and when she reached the middle of the bridge raised her left hand to the hair styled high on her head,

"Oh, I've had it with this, this is really a pain!" she said, roughly letting it down and drawing it nimbly into a knot.

"Aah, that feels better. What's the point in a takashimada hairstyle and heavy makeup at twenty-four?" (*Noble Blood, Heroic Blood, MBZ* 21:10)

Just to be on the safe side, let me also give an example of a passage persistently adhered to in both manuscripts, but which was edited completely out of the published version.

And then one of the associate judges said, "If it was just a question of the money never getting to its destination we could let you off with a warning, but a person's life is involved here, can you not distinguish the gravity of the two?" Otama shot back insolently, "Money? Where money's concerned it's all small change to me, and as for people's affairs, I'm only concerned with my own, and as for this knife-throwing bastard I couldn't care less," and the associate judge just sat there silently, his face crimson with anger. (*Blind Justice*)

Because the expression is virtually identical, I omit the quotation from the grass manuscript.

I deliberately chose passages that don't bear heavy thematic content, hence ones that are apt to be overlooked. It should be clear from these few examples, though, that the author's interest consistently lies with capturing the tang and bite of rough-and-tumble spoken dialogue. The coachman's blunt dismissal of the old man's concerns in the first example probably indicates his anger at the distasteful sight of people who, having just goaded him into a competition with the rickshaw pullers, now get all flustered when he complies and the carriage begins to bounce and rock. But the spoken dialogue here transcends that situation-specific motivation and evokes a certain pleasure of its own – the stern savor of carrying out to the letter the pledge transacted half in jest between the sideboy and the passengers, and the bite of turning that act of ultra-fidelity into an ever-so-slightly cruel act of retaliation for their self-centeredness. This pleasure gives rise in the reader to a sense of goodwill toward the coachman and a positive estimation of his character. It's likely that same feeling of pleasure turned around and summoned up a reaction in the author as well, so that the old man's *words*, in the progression from "Hey, young master there" to "I say, young master coach driver" to "I say, coachman! My good young man!" imply a successive devaluation of the old man's position in the course of revision.

It goes without saying that character dialogue is at the same time the self-expression of the author. In his *The Japanese Language in Fiction*[9] (*Shōsetsu no Nihongo*), Noguchi Takehiko divides discourse in the novel into four categories (dialogue, representation, description, intervention) and theorizes the relative degree of authorial self-reference in each. Noguchi writes that "in dialogue, because the enunciations belong to the work's characters themselves, we may regard the level of [authorial] self-reference as zero" (Noguchi, 59), but it is doubtful he could sustain this position in the light of his own experience with actual works. It is precisely because these "enunciations belong to the work's characters themselves" that the author can achieve a high degree of self-refer-

9. Noguchi Takehiko, *Shōsetsu no Nihongo*, vol. 13 of *Nihongo no sekai*, 16 vols. (Tokyo: Chūō Kōronsha, 1980–86).

ence in the tone of these objective enunciations (the characters' enunciations). It is when such enunciations evoke meanings that transcend the specific context—or when these evoked meanings elicit reactions that in turn enrich the context-specific meaning—that the reader recognizes a text as literary (artistic).

So what, we may ask, are the passengers' reactions to the coachman's blunt dismissal of their concerns?

> The old man blinked and muttered, "Ee, what kind of a fool thing, we're supposed to feel at ease here?" and the coachman turned around his way, "If it's safety you're after, then you should walk," *he said with a cool smile, and the lady stole a look at his face.* (grass manuscript; italics Kamei's)

> When the old man blinked and muttered in amazement, "Ee, what kind of a fool thing, how are we supposed to feel at ease like this," the coachman turned around for the first time, "If you can't feel safe like this, then you should walk," *he said with a cool smile, and the lady stole a look at his face, a smile creeping to her lips too.* (*Blind Justice*; italics Kamei's)

> "Ee, what kind of a fool thing is that? How are we supposed to feel at ease here?" The old man muttered in amazement and the coachman looked back for the first time
> "If you can't feel safe like this, feel free to walk on your own."
> "Oh yeah, right, thanks a lot."
> The old man stole an angry glance at the coachman's face. [. . .] But when the situation became desperate, the only one with eyes to see his trustworthiness was this young beauty. All the other passengers were in a most unsightly uproar and confusion, calling out to their gods dead and living. Now this young beauty, all the while this ruckus was going on, she kept her eyes fixed on the coachman. (*Noble Blood, Heroic Blood, MBZ* 21:5)

In these three variants, the old man is rebuffed by the coachman in successively more humiliating terms, while conversely the woman's expressions of sympathy, goodwill and trust toward the coachman are successively strengthened.[10] A corresponding reserve of goodwill and positive feeling toward the woman is thereby solicited from the reader.

10. The progressions Kamei is seeing from manuscript to manuscript depend on a sensitivity to Meiji period context, nuances of style, and the definition of relative position in Japanese through honorifics and speech levels (even though, or perhaps especially because, spoken dialogue in this section of the story is not elaborately marked). It is difficult to capture in translation the nuanced sense of progression, though we have attempted to make clear that subtle shifts in expression are at work.

The scenes under consideration here all seem to correspond to what Noguchi calls representation: "incidents occurring in the novel are described as if they were occurring before one's own eyes" (Noguchi, *Shōsetsu no Nihongo,* 58). Noguchi's supplementary explanation that "it is, from beginning to end, the character's actions that come to the fore" (Noguchi, 59) brings to mind mainly the italicized portions of the previous passages. Yet within these passages, expressions such as "but when the situation became desperate" (which in *Noble Blood, Heroic Blood* replaces the italicized passages from the earlier variants) approach Noguchi's category of description, where "narrated events are compressed, abbreviated, and given in explanatory form" (Noguchi, 59). Similarly, the embedded bit of ironic humor, "calling out to their gods dead and living," would seem to correspond to intervention, where "the author and/or narrator add comments of their own" (Noguchi, 58). However, as one can see in tracing through the process of revision, these instances of description and intervention that follow "but when the situation became desperate" render into an even more concrete form what was achieved in the earlier *Blind Justice* with the representation "and the lady stole a look at his face, a smile creeping into her lips too." As a result, the woman's sympathy is elevated into full-blown trust. They are ultimately nothing other than the deliberate materialization of the author's self-referentiality achieved in relation to the coachman's spoken dialogue.

Noguchi maintains that "the base point of the perspective that obtains between the reader and the fictional characters is fixed as the exact reverse of the relative degree of self-reference in these four categories of fictional discourse. The more the author brings himself forward within the composition, the farther readers find themselves distanced from the characters. Conversely, the more the author allows the characters to narrate themselves, the closer the reader is drawn to those characters" (Noguchi, 59). But even if we set aside the process of revision and take up only the expressions found in *Noble Blood, Heroic Blood,* we find no support for this assertion. Continuing to press the point, we may come to question the concept of "degree of self-reference" itself, and we may question the lack of clarity in the concept of "perspective" here, in that it does not clearly delineate between its visual, temporal, or psychological senses. But one can at least maintain that there are cases where the author's self-referentiality varies in direct proportion with the perspectival configuration of the reader (vis-à-vis the fictional characters), and that one would have to agree with Noguchi that "it is precisely because mechanisms exist for modulating the distance between the two that novelistic language can be novelistic language" (Noguchi, 59).

Moving on to the scene where Shiraito goes out to enjoy the cool of the evening, we may discern an invariant to which the writer adheres in all cases,

Shiraito's rough disentangling of her takashimada hairstyle and her subsequent murmuring of, "Oh this is uncomfortable, I really need to get out of this." The line of dialogue that follows is revised successively from "hmm, what a fool I am" to "I'm so bored by it all, hmm, what a fool I am," and finally "Aah, that feels better. What's the point in a takashimada hairstyle and heavy makeup at twenty-four?" She carries here a certain indefinable resentment at her circumstances. The reader will discern that her impenitent sundering of the symbol of her lot in life, the takashimada hairstyle,[11] becomes a motif in her later actions, but the writer's investment in the scene itself perhaps lies rather in the cavalier haughtiness of her spoken dialogue. Her violent feelings with regard to the circumstances in which she is unwillingly placed harbor an impulse toward self-destruction. Her haughtiness, already hinted at in the extravagance of the tip she raises for the coachman and in a scene where she steps down from the water juggling stage mid-performance, without a thought to the spectators, is transformed via these lines of spoken dialogue into her own passion. This tone of bravado was likely the catalyst that led the author, too, to these passions. This is where we begin to find the image of Shiraito enshrouded in the visage of the "poison woman."[12] Her pledge to support the coachman, and her resolution in executing the pledge also bring out this haughtiness and obstinacy. After being violated by the knife-thrower and robbed of the money she'd saved for Kinya's final tuition payment, her transformation into a poison woman becomes clear: "'Hmmh?' She took up the knife with no particular thought and held it aloft, peering at it. An uncanny glow stole into her eyes, a kind of darkness shrouded her visage, and the color of her face shifted imperceptibly" (Grass manuscript; the passage is virtually identical in *Blind Justice*). And when she seeks a fleeting pleasure by challenging the associate judge's interrogation with the rebellious words, "Money? Where money's concerned it's all small change to me," we see her constructing herself into a person who invites only contempt.

In the scene where she goes out to enjoy the cool of the evening, though, the question of what it is about herself that troubles her is given concrete objectification in another line of dialogue: "Aah, that feels better. What's the point in a takashimada hairstyle and heavy makeup at twenty-four?" Furthermore, the expression of this for-itself sensibility evident in the enjoyment she derives from the sound of her *geta* is transformed into an expression appended at the level of

11. In the Meiji period, this hairstyle indicated a young unmarried woman.
12. Kamei uses the word *dokufuteki*, or "poison-woman-like," referring to a genre of serialized reportage wildly popular in the 1870s and 80s, fact-based yet sensationalized accounts of notorious murderesses. These women often were portrayed as ruthless exploiters of the revolutionary changes underway in the Meiji social landscape. They were also often, like Shiraito, associated with outcaste groups and portrayed as being sexually promiscuous.

narrative description (*ji no bun*). This self-objectification becomes a harbinger of the splitting of self that will occur in the word "embrace," and it ultimately develops, through her assumption to ethicality, into something capable of checking her rebelliousness and poison-woman fatalism.

The author presents it in this form to the reader. Setting aside the process of revision and looking only at this form, in the context of the surrounding expressions the cavalier attitude and the aggressive relation of self to other embodied in Shiraito's spoken dialogue do not give a pronounced impression of haughtiness. Nevertheless, the impression lingers at least to the extent that it is necessary to reaffirm that her "iron lady" temperament is "sprung from naivete, and was a pure and unsullied thing." This impression produces discord in the unfolding of the relational consciousness I have analyzed here, leading to an expansion in the scope of mutual complementary recognition of human existence. The following passage from Lotman is relevant here:

> . . . the relation between the accidental and the systemic in an artistic text has a different meaning for sender and receiver. In receiving an artistic message whose text obliges him to work out a code for deciphering that message, the receiver constructs a model. In this way systems may arise which will organize the fortuitous elements of a text and give them meaning. Thus the quantity of meaningful structural elements may increase in the passage from sender to receiver. This is one aspect of the complex, little-studied ability of an artistic text to amass information. (Lotman, *Structure of the Artistic Text*, 25)

In the eyes of a reader accustomed to novels written since late Meiji, that is, after the rise of naturalism and the notion of "realism" that has dominated modern literature in Japan, it is likely that the unfolding of a relational consciousness will seem significant here, while the rough, raffish tone of the spoken dialogue—"Oh, I've had it with this, this is really a pain!"—will seem a merely contingent element. It will appear to be nothing more than a pretext setting up her subsequent self-scorn, "what's the point at twenty-four." But this spoken dialogue, which to the "perception" of today's reader might appear only as a pretext, was for the author an essential invariant, one that he stuck with throughout the process of revision. It is, however, downgraded to the level of an object for Shiraito's self-negating self-consciousness (her sense of inferiority), and it is linked with her invariant and invariable temperament, the temperament that drives her to an unhappy fate.

Seen from this perspective, the story of *Noble Blood, Heroic Blood* seems a romance.[13] A haughty, street-wise woman with the air of a femme-fatale

---

13. Kamei uses the Japanese term *denki* (adventure tale, romance) here and provides the pronunciation gloss *roman*.

poison wife pledges financial support to a youth whose naive impulsiveness attracts her, and in the end she is judged by the same youth when she is drawn into a crime. This is likely the form through which contemporary readers sought to take in its artistic message. Yet it seems that there was also another level of development, one that constantly interfered with and produced discord with the reader's expectations, thereby producing an entirely unforeseen impression: her ethical devotion to the youth without expectation of recompense, its subsequent failure, and her final service to the boy in the form of her self-sacrificing confession. It may seem odd to us today, but the author's invariant emphasis in the first half of the story lies with the woman's headstrong capriciousness (the extravagance of her tipping, her disregard for her audience, etc.), and this was unquestionably perceived by contemporary readers as a device employed deliberately by the author. Of course, such readers were unaware that this had remained an invariant through multiple versions of the manuscript. But even in the conversation added to the work in the final *Noble Blood, Heroic Blood* version, Shiraito is made to point out her own headstrong caprice in a self-exhibitionary manner:

> "No reason in particular. I just want to set you up with a little allowance."
> "That's sheer insanity!"
> "Insanity, eh? I'm guess I am insane, so why don't you let yourself go, too, and indulge my desires? Eh, Kin-san? What do you say?" (*Noble Blood, Heroic Blood, MBZ* 21:14).

Readers likely perceived Shiraito's rough undoing of her hairstyle and the spoken dialogue she muttered then as being part of this same line of development. Having captured their interest by means of her unpredictable and headstrong verbal sallies, the author shifts strategies in the second half, drawing the woman into a series of unforeseeable situations, so that by the final scene, in a completely unpredictable face-to-face confrontation, tremendous anticipation is generated as to what this woman's reaction will be. This literary device is similar to what the Russian Formalists called "baring the technique" (*dénudation*) and in the clarity with which the reader is made to perceive the technique, this mode of writing is able to bring into play an unpredictability of a completely different order.

From the perspectives of literary and intellectual history, the important point here is that this device effected a transformation of mood into will power, of haughty pride into an ethic. If we think just at the surface level of abstract dictionary meanings, mood would seem an antonym of will power, and it would be difficult to find in haughtiness a synonym for ethicality. However, it is possible to situate haughtiness within the range covered by the idea of will power, which then provides the mediation that makes it possible to connect it to ethicality. In a word, the revisions of *Noble Blood, Heroic Blood* took place following that sort of process. While sticking to devices that solicited the reader's interest along the axis of mood, the work was infused with a seeking after an ethicality that would transcend those devices, a seeking after something worth sacrificing oneself to. It is because of this structure that Kyōka's work from this period came to be called "concept novels."[14]

If the work had simply followed the form of earlier stories and plays, there would need to be some sort of concealed motive or cause that would explain Shiraito's goodwill and charity. There would have to be, for example, the revelation of the kind of hidden identity or motive that one finds with the character Oriki in Ichiyō's "Troubled Waters": "You know Ōtomo Kuronushi, who wanted the whole wide world? That's me."[15] However, Oriki is in such wretched circumstances that her unpredictability consists only of jests like this one, pathetic attempts to divert her attention from her plight. The unpredictability of Shiraito is of an entirely different order. In her case, it is the coachman who possesses the hidden identity or motive (he is the son of a samurai family and aspires to an education), while she herself is denied the kind of secret that would permit her to carry out a self-rationalization or self-aestheticization of her own speech and actions. And precisely because she is this kind of woman, she is sensitive to the presence in the man of what she herself lacks, and yet can only grasp her motive for offering to help him as being "insanity," a whim that arises because "To tell you the truth, I just love the way students talk" (*MBZ* 21:14)— that is, as a caprice that arises out of her mood and feelings. In the end, she then has no choice but to carry through in an ideal manner her own self-sacrificing devotion. For contemporary readers who felt a sense of crisis over the diminishing possibilities for advancement in the new modern society or felt a weakening basis for the self-rationalization and aestheticization of their own actions, perhaps Shiraito's way of living provided a self-dramatization that summoned up an almost perilous sense of empathy. Only the subsequent suicide of the man could bring some sense of meaningfulness to her tragic fate.

It is not the case, however, that the author had already firmly grasped this kind of dramatic philosophy from the start, in his initial conception for the

14. Concept novels (*kannen shōsetsu*; also sometimes translated "problem novels") is the name of a genre of mid-Meiji works, including the Kyōka story here, which were perceived to revolve around the working out of a specific intellectual or ethical problem.
15. See the discussion of this story in chapter seven. The quotation from "Troubled Waters" is from the translation of the story that appears in Robert Lyons Danly, *In the Shade of Spring Leaves* (New York: W.W. Norton, 1992), 218–40. This passage appears on 221.

work. I have heretofore been using as a convenience the term "author" in dealing with the grass manuscript and *Blind Justice*, but as is clear from the expressions quoted above, in those two earlier versions, lines of spoken dialogue are mostly embedded within passages of narrative description (*ji no bun*), which are generally dominated by (what we may call) exposition of the author's own thinking. As one example we can cite the author's approving discourse on duty that follows after the exchange where Shiraito asks the young man, "Don't you remember me?," and he replies *coolly*, "No, I do not." This, if anything, is a prime example of what Noguchi Takehiko calls authorial intervention. But in this mode of writing, such interventions occur even within the characters' spoken dialogue. In *Blind Justice* we find the following passage:

> "You mean to refuse? That's really weak, worrying about whether you can pay it back, or can't pay it back. It's not like you, it's so indecisive. Just make your intentions clear, that's all you need to do. If your goal is to worry yourself about whether you should let me know or not let me know, there's no point in even getting started here."

The speaker here is Shiraito, who is trying to convince the vacillating coachman to accept her assistance. The narrator then continues, "What a pleasure to convince him!," as if Shiraito in her attempt to persuade the youth had become the author's mouthpiece. The author here seems overly eager to push the story forward. In sum, Kyōka had not yet mastered the methodology he would describe in later years:

> I don't start writing with a fixed idea in mind, so there's no particular plan of action either. I just leave it up to the free interplay of the man and woman. So, let's say there's a woman, thoroughly skilled, and a man who in no uncertain terms refuses to do something, and the question is whether she can manage to convince him or not. It's all in the woman's methods of persuasion, and the way she talks. If she is awkward in convincing him and gets rebuffed, well then I have her get rebuffed and write the rest accordingly. On the other hand if she does it well and gets the man to behave the way she wants, then I develop the story that way.[16]

But by the final revision, *Noble Blood, Heroic Blood*, Kyōka had made great strides toward mastering this methodology.

16. "Leaving It Up To Them" ("Mukō makase," 1908), in *Kyōka zenshū*, vol. 28 (Tokyo: Iwanami Shoten, 1973–76), 698–701.

In that sense, there are other possible modes of authorial self-reference. On the one hand, we can find authorial intervention (self-reference) even in characters' spoken dialogue, while at the same time we can have a uniquely dialogic style for writing conversations, in which everything is "left to the free interplay of the man and woman." The reason I've focused so insistently on the work of Noguchi Takehiko is that I perceive a blind spot in the structuralism on which he relies. Of course Noguchi too discusses on occasion the distinction between author and narrator, but because he has not rigorously theorized this point, when it comes down to concrete analysis as in his discussion of Kyōka's "Grass Labyrinth" ("Kusa meikyū," 1908) and "Ghost with Hidden Eyebrows" ("Mayu kakushi no rei," 1924), he mixes them indiscriminately. Only this allows him to conclude that, "Kyōka's act of enunciation no longer had any need to show itself in the story world" (Noguchi, *Shōsetsu no Nihongo*, 224). This is likely a result of his having hit on the idea of the "implied author" from Wayne Booth's *Rhetoric of Fiction* and Roger Fowler's *Linguistics and the Novel*, but having gone no further than an initial infatuation, he fails to grasp either theoretically or concretely the way the concept works itself out in the unfolding of a mode of expression. In Lotman's *Universe of the Mind: A Semiotic Theory of Culture* we do find the notion of "autocommunication," but there the concept of "implied author" is absent, and again there is no grasp of the kind of "autocommunication" that occurs within the characters themselves, or of the way that incites corresponding reactions on the part of the author or narrator, the very aspects that I have stressed here.[17]

In the grass manuscript and *Blind Justice*, lines of spoken dialogue are indeed bracketed within quotation marks, but they are still embedded within passages of narrative description and they frequently become proxies for the author's opinions. By comparison, in *Noble Blood, Heroic Blood* they are set off on separate lines and indented, thereby heightening their autonomy. This was Kyōka's praxis of the "free interplay of the man and woman." Through this concern for autonomy, in Shiraito's case, for example, *words* emerge that effect in her a new relationship to herself, giving rise to the characteristic conversational style we see in her banter. I will take up the question of the writing style used for conversations again, but what I want to call attention to here once more is how adherence to the spirited *words* of the coachman expands the scope of the descriptiveness of the narrative description, just as it heightens the distinct individuality of the various characters' spoken dialogue through mutual contrast. In other words, the overt explication of authorial ideas and the transfor-

17. See the discussion of Lotman's "autocommunication" in chapter nine.

mation of characters into authorial mouthpieces is eliminated, and a world of expression is created through the mediation of a subject of expression (the narrator) who is immanent to the depicted scene and relatively independent from the author. And through this the reader's scope of empathy is expanded. We have already observed the concrete path along which this mode of expression developed. The lack of this sort of perspective is also the reason, in my judgment, that Yoshimoto Takaaki's theory of literary composition could not develop to include the novel and had to stop at the stage reached by Edo-period drama.[18]

Kyōka's work broke through the literary and intellectual limitations of his age when he produced a new mode of expression, one characterized by an immanent narrator able to objectify the unfolding of the characters' self-consciousness in both of its aspects, spoken dialogue and interiority. It was an achievement that had the power to obviate any need for overt explication of authorial opinions. Herein lies the distinguishing characteristic of what we now call the concept novel.

18. See chapter seven.

Chapter Nine
The Self-Destructing World of Significance:
Inner Speech in Izumi Kyōka and Hirotsu Ryūrō

TRANSLATED BY ROBERT STEEN AND MICHAEL BOURDAGHS

In Lotman's and Vygotsky's classic theories of subject formation and language acquisition, the final stage is reached when the child develops the capacity for inner speech—that is, when it uses the language it has acquired from the world outside to address itself, in the form of a private, memorandum-like code understandable only to the self. Here, Kamei traces the appearance of inner speech in the literary expressions of Izumi Kyōka and Hirotsu Ryūrō. Through a close reading of the title and expressions in Kyōka's "X Praying-Mantis Blowfish Railroad," Kamei locates a mosaic-like form, a kind of private language that thwarts conventional expectations, that deliberately occludes closure and forces each reader to negotiate the text on his or her own terms. What emerges is a new technique for portraying "realistically" the psychology of subjects: not internal monologue, but rather spoken dialogue that manifests through its use of the opaque codes of autocommunication a deeper strata of psychological meaning and that disrupts the syntactical expectations of ordinary conversation.

At the time Izumi Kyōka was writing "X Praying-Mantis Blowfish Railroad" ("X kamakiri fugu tetsudō," 1896–97), he seems to have been struggling with formal aspects of the novel. To borrow from the parlance of structuralism, Kyōka's predicament can be characterized as a situation in which the inner speech of the author and his characters was beginning to interfere with and erode the formal conventions that had hitherto governed the composition of fiction. Kyōka, however, regarded this as a challenge, and his struggle to address these formal difficulties would bring an unprecedented degree of freedom to the modern Japanese novel. By staging a confrontation between a mode of expression that focused on the egocentrism of inner speech and the popular, everyday ethic of his readership (and the expectations about fiction that accorded with it), Kyōka launched a methodology that deliberately unraveled the fabric of that ethic. The conclusion of a work would no longer necessarily coincide with the resolution of its thematic content, nor would its structure necessarily provide semantic closure. This mode of writing, a kind of breakdown in conventional compositional techniques, causes the reader to trace repeatedly through the labyrinth of an enigmatic diegetic space; it encourages the reader to negotiate his or her own version of the work's subjective theme and to endow the world of the work with his or her own version of semantic closure.

"Inner speech" as I use the term here does not refer to what is often called interior monologue or descriptions of interiority. As I will explain more concretely below, one of the reasons I have chosen to employ this notion is that it allows me to revise structuralist theory in ways that render it more productive.

Even the curious title of the story, "X Praying-Mantis Blowfish Railroad," is in a certain sense a kind of inner speech.[1] The title provides not the theme of the work, but rather *words* that function like a secret code, produced according to the private whims of the author.

The "X" in the title refers to a novel authored by Hatakeyama Sugako under her pen name, Shūran. Sugako pays a visit to Shinako, an old school friend who was once like a sister to Sugako, but who now as the wife of Yamashina leads a miserable life in a slum tenement. As Sugako says to her, Shinako was

> without parents and raised by your uncle since you were a young girl, and when your relatives told you to do it, you married your husband, making no complaints. [. . .] Once you were married to him, he was your husband and master. No matter how far your fortunes might sink, what could you possibly say? ("X," 95)

Shinako's husband then barges in on their conversation. He tells her that he has bought a blowfish to eat with his family—a delicacy whose poison might well kill them all—but at a railroad crossing he has bumped into what he thought was a policeman and threw the blowfish away in his panic to escape.

At this point the young officer whom the husband has mistaken for a policeman approaches them on horseback. It is Sugako's younger brother. The husband flees a second time. The young officer then takes Shinako's child on a horseback ride to a nearby field. When the child starts to cry, the officer shows him a praying mantis in hopes of distracting the child and calming him down.

1. The story is reprinted *Kyōka zenshū*, 29 vols. (Tokyo: Iwanami Shoten, 1973–76), 3:87–112.

Sugako in the meanwhile, worried over the child's well being (Shinako has expressed strong dislike for her son), arranges to adopt him. At the story's end, Shinako is on duty as a railroad-crossing attendant, and the main characters assemble at the station.

> A train thundered toward them. Nobutsura [Shinako's son] leapt from Sugako's lap, startled by the noise. "Mommy, mommy," he cried as he ran toward his mother across the tracks, his kimono sash flying in the wind. Sugako's face whitened as she sprung for the boy and grabbed him. Moments later the train came to a complete stop.
> Sugako breathed a deep sigh of relief and lifted the child above her head, without a thought of the people around her, the blue signal flag still fluttering in Shinako's hand. The train coming to a halt, her eyes filled with overwhelming emotion, but Shinako turned her face away, gazed at intently. The young officer, the palms of his tightly clutched fists sweaty from worry for Nobutsura, recovered his composure and reached for his pocket watch. As soon as it clicked open he set off across the field of tall pampas grass, grabbing handfuls of reed as he went.
> The train began to move again, with Sugako and the child now aboard. As the autumn day's sun began to set, darkness fell on the nearby woods. In the desolate field, holding the folded blue flag, lingering in silence, Shinako, her cold gaze fixed on it, on the railroad tracks stretching east to west alongside the rows of pampas grass, the blowfish that lay split open nearby. ("X," 112)

Kyōka arrived at his title for the story by arbitrarily assembling several words chosen from the story. This flew in the face of the standard practice of choosing a title that symbolizes the theme of the story. Furthermore, in the work itself, at the moment the words of this assemblage have finally all made their appearance, just at that moment of completion the various characters disperse, leaving to go their separate ways.

What is the author trying to say here? Even in stories where the author's message is unclear, more often than not the reader finishes the story without noticing the ambiguity. But in this case, Kyōka seems deliberately to devise a technique that will elicit confusion in the reader. He presents us with three contrastive pairs:

> A1: A woman who once showed great promise, but whose hopes have been snuffed out and who has fallen on hard times (Shinako)
> B1: A woman who has become a successful writer despite her lack of talent, and who retains the temperament of a young maiden (Sugako)
> A2: The cruelty of a child's biological mother (Shinako)
> B2: The kindness of the woman (stepmother) who adopts that child (Sugako)

A3: The ignorant, peevish husband (Yamashina)
B3: The gallant and wise young officer (Sugako's brother)

One can imagine any number of possible narratives in which the B characters could rescue the A characters from their plight without injuring their pride and perhaps even restoring their pride along the way. Whether such a narrative took the route of depicting either social problems or the dramatic unfolding of deep psychology, once the above sort of clearly contrasted pairings had been recognized, readers would conventionally expect a conclusion that would somehow rescue the A characters from their plight.

There are certainly moments in the story where such an expectation is at least partially fulfilled, as when Sugako rescues Nobutsura from the train. Yet note that here, it is only the child who is rescued. Not only are the characters from the A group left unrescued, but A1 and A2 undergo no transformation at all. On the contrary, A2 remains consistently antagonistic toward B2's common sense. But this does not necessarily signify an attempt by Kyōka to depict the failure of the B characters' efforts to help the A characters, that is, the proposing of a simple antithesis to the conventional expected resolution. If such was Kyōka's plan, he would have structured the work around a clearer depiction of the spiritual blows suffered by the B characters.

In fact, the starker the contrast between the pairs, the stronger the conscious sense of ambiguity we derive from our inability to distinguish between resolution and nonresolution, between thesis and antithesis, in the work's composition. A similar ambiguity can be found in the details of the expressions that appear in the story. If we rearrange the closing line of the story, we find that it is constructed around the following main clause:

C: Shinako, her cold gaze was fixed on it, the blowfish that lay split open nearby.

In contrast, we can extract a second sentence, also embedded in mosaic-like fashion, among the actual sentences that close the story:

D: Shinako, in the desolate field, holding the folded blue flag, lingered in silence on the railroad tracks, stretching east to west, alongside the rows of pampas grass.

This, too, could be broken up into two distinct sentences, (D1) "The railroad tracks stretched east to west, alongside the rows of pampas grass," and (D2) "Shinako, holding the folded blue flag, lingered in silence in the desolate field." Expression C, too, in terms of semantic content, could be rewritten as (C1) "Shinako's cold gaze was fixed on the blowfish that lay split open nearby."

In fact, for clarity in meaning and visual description, the passage could perhaps best have been written in the order D1-D2-C1:

> The railroad tracks stretched east to west, alongside the rows of pampas grass. Shinako, holding the folded blue flag, lingered in silence in the desolate field. [Her] cold gaze was fixed on the blowfish that lay split open nearby.

Such a mode of writing would be chosen in cases where it was necessary to grasp the object from a specific, stable point of view.

Yet Kyōka, while in semantic terms subtracting nothing that is found in that D1-D2-C1 form, chooses instead to disperse the perspectival center between the blowfish and Shinako, for which the clauses D1 and D2 respectively become participial rhetorical figures in the original Japanese. This impedes the reader's ability to understand the semantic content of the passage. On top of this, he transforms the semantic grammatical subjects of these two clauses, Shinako and the blowfish, into rhetorical figures—the synecdochal "cold gaze" and the indefinite pronoun "it." In the end, a floating "cold gaze" is fixed on an indefinite "it," a syntactical structure that seems deliberately to deconstruct or evacuate any meaning from Shinako's act of gazing. An even more extreme example of this is found in the same passage: "The train coming to a halt, her [Sugako's] eyes filled with overwhelming emotion, but Shinako turned her face away, gazed at intently." Again, we find a similar mosaic-like structure in this expression, combining four distinct events and perspectival focuses: the train stopping, Sugako's eyes filled with overwhelming emotion, Shinako turning away to avoid this gaze, and Sugako watching intently the turned-away Shinako. The effect of condensing these four into a single sentence is to efface the actual grammatical subject (Sugako) and to effect an emptying of the act of seeing by hollowing out any semantic content from its object.

What we see in these is a kind of radical condensation, one that takes its most radical form in the work's title. X, praying mantis, blowfish, and railroad tracks: four nouns that, of course, are directly tied to the work's content. Yet when they are strung together as if they formed a title, they lose not only any mutual semantic interrelation as nouns, but also virtually all semantic relation to the work's content. Just as Sugako's novel is given only the title "X," a title devoid of any semantic content, so too the praying mantis is never narrated so as to bestow on it any unique meaning as an object in relation to the interiority of the officer or the boy, and likewise with the blowfish to the husband and the railroad tracks for Shinako. Rather, we have here an author who creates his title by choosing objects that have deliberately been deprived of meaning. Yet this is not to imply that this title was meaningless for the author. In choosing a

title that has some connection with the work's content yet which is deliberately
evacuated of any clear significance, we have a meaning that is understandable
only to the author himself, a kind of private memorandum. Note also that in
Japanese, this title is highly rhythmical in a 4-4-2-4 pattern: E-k-ku-su, ka-ma-
ki-ri, fu-gu, te-tsu-do-u. What we have here, then, is the totality presented by a
literary work condensed into several words that are understood only by the author himself, *words* that moreover contain a strong sense of rhythm. It is precisely this sort of expression that the structuralist Yuri Lotman calls "inner
speech" or "autocommunication."

While I have some reservations about Lotman's theories, for the time
being I will employ his ideas in order to highlight the point I am trying to make
here. In the story we are considering here, we find one character whose very
origin seems to lie in what we might call a Kyōka-esque "inner speech."

> "But not as much as this." The wife [Shinako] looked down at
> her side. A beautiful, fair-skinned boy lay face up there, the faded
> red pillowcover rat bitten, its stuffing spilling out. The sleeping child
> twitched its eyelids ever so slightly as it faintly snored. Looking down
> at it, she sighed and continued, "Yes, my education has caused me
> only trouble, my book learning has only brought me grief—but not
> as much as this boy has. Nothing could be the bother he is. I swear,
> nothing on earth could cause as much trouble as he does."
> Sugako gently slipped her warm right arm beneath the pillow,
> cradling the sleeping boy's head. [. . .] "Please stop talking such non-
> sense. It's all nonsense, he's beautiful. How old is he? Three?"
> "No, he's five. He doesn't get enough to eat, and he seems to shrink
> and grow smaller every month," came the reply, eyes blinking.
> "Oh, but that makes him all the more darling. The apple of your
> eye. All the fat is off of him, he's solid as a rock." She put her mouth
> up next to his ear, but then didn't know what to call him. "What do
> you call him? His name, what do you call him?"
> The wife spat out, "That boy doesn't deserve a name, he's
> worthless."
> "But what do you call him?"
> [. . .]
> Laughing slightly, "It's *Shinko*. We call him *Shinko*."
> "Shinko. How odd."
> "It suits him."
> Sugako drew closer. The two looked at each other. "I wonder, is
> there really such a name?"
> "No." ("X," 96–99)

A frightening conversation. This is not the usual false humility shown by parents when speaking about their children. "Shinko" is the Chinese (*on*) pronun-

ciation for the characters that form the child's real name, Nobutsura. Ordinarily, we might consider this a term of affection, a diminutive form of a child's name such as Japanese parents often use. But Shinako's manner of speaking contains no trace of that sort of affection. Her disgust at even the simple act of speaking his name gives birth to this "Shinko," a contemptuous form of "inner speech" that makes clear her desire to avoid speaking that *word*. Therefore, she is unable to keep up her end of the everyday, commonplace conversation that Sugako tries to carry on with her.

To say that someone's child is darling is a commonplace norm of polite conversation. Under the then-current conventional expectations, the reason an author would include such a conversation in a work is to provide a pretext for revealing the mother's desire for her child to achieve success in the world, even if that success is denied to the mother herself. Hence, under this convention, the reason for the existence of the B characters would be clear. Yet Shinako refuses to carry out her expected role in this conversation. Her calling the boy a "bother" is perhaps not so unexpected, but her subsequent remarks—that the boy grows smaller every month, that he doesn't deserve to even have a name—are *words* that utterly reject maternity, words that baffle her interlocutor and derail the flow of the conversation, so that it flounders through the final lines of dialogue from the passage quoted above. Sugako's *words* never go beyond the ordinary etiquette of social conversation; through them, she painstakingly tries to bring Shinako's feelings out into the open. But Shinako's remarks, which remain at the level of egocentric inner speech, nullify Sugako's efforts. At the same time, they bring about a crucial transformation in the writing style that was used in novels to represent spoken conversations. What is achieved here, at least in Kyōka's works, is not a depiction of a character's *interiority* through internal monologue, but instead the introduction of spoken utterances that deliberately refuse the dialogism of language. This new writing style for depicting conversation seems on the surface level to render the conversation virtually meaningless, yet it allows for the revelation of a latent deeper meaning. This technique would subsequently be employed to even greater effect by Natsume Sōseki.

Ultimately, as Shinako responds to Sugako's inquiry, she sinks deeper and deeper into an autocommunication that takes as its visually intentional object the silent child. If we trace the path of her remarks—from calling the child a "bother" to saying it doesn't get enough to eat and grows smaller every month to finally saying it doesn't even need a name—we see that Shinako's desire is ultimately to turn back time and effect the erasure of the child's existence.

In that sense, the primary conflict in this work is between mother and child. Shinako displaces her awareness of this, an awareness reached through this process of autocommunication, onto the blowfish.

> "Sugako, there is poison here [in the blowfish and in her married life], see? Awful, awful poison—that is what I want to say. It's awful even to look at, and when you eat it, a chill runs through you as you wonder if it might take your very life. Understand? And so when my husband eats it, I think, well, if he's going to be poisoned, then we might as well die together, so I eat it too." ("X," 108–9)

While cursing the fate of her marriage in these *words* of warped love, she conveys an irresistible longing for destructive, ruinous evil. The scene that symbolizes the rescue of the child, defenseless against this murderous desire for evil, is the work's conclusion. Sugako and the child flee together on the train, and Shinako is left staring at the cruel figure of the poison that festers within.

When we look at the work in this way, it is clear that its spoken dialogue, which takes as its keynote Shinako's "inner speech," provides the means of setting the A and B characters in opposition. And, while the child is rescued from the A characters by the B characters, the conflict between the good intentions and kindness of the B characters and the poisonous brutality of the mother is left unresolved for the reader. This sort of avoidance of neat resolutions is also symbolized by the structure of expressions that we looked at above, where the B1-D2-C1 expression is reassembled in mosaic-like fashion, thereby hollowing out its meaning, at least on the surface level.

As I have already mentioned, the notion of "inner speech" is borrowed from Lotman. As might be expected from a semiotician, Lotman is interested in the status of signs in what he calls autocommunication. Autocommunication refers to communication that can be described schematically as passing along an "I-I" axis, unlike message communication, which passes along an "I-you" axis. The example of a diary comes to mind immediately, but Lotman is more interested in such signs as personal memorandums, signs intended to jog the memory. Such memos use an abbreviated style and are often rendered in the form of a code. Lotman focuses on the principles that govern such abbreviations.

> The tendency of words in an 'I-I' language to become reduced is to be seen in the abbreviations we use in notes to ourselves. In the final analysis the words in these notes become indices which can be deciphered only if one knows what has been written. [. . .] The index-words which are formed as a result of this reduction have a tendency to iso-rhythmicality. It is a feature of the syntax of this type of speech that it does not form completed sentences, but tends to be an unfinalized chain of rhythmical repetitions. [. . .] [T]he immanent and unconscious activating laws of autocommunication reveal structural features which we usually observe in poetic texts.[2]

2. Yuri Lotman, *Universe of the Mind: A Semiotic Theory of Culture* (Bloomington: Indiana University Press, 1990), 26–27.

But when we create our own system of abbreviation, we do not merely leave things out. We also add vocal sounds, *words* that bear no direct relation to the initial meaning (the so-called "signified"), and thanks to these our own understanding comes to include newly accrued meanings and nuances. It is unlikely that Lotman was ignorant of this linguistic phenomenon, whereby non-semantic phonic aspects are added or subtracted, but his failure to consider this problem seriously undermines the persuasiveness of his theory.

But before we take up this issue, we must first consider the relation of I-I speech to L.S. Vygotsky's notion of "inner speech." Lotman quotes from Vygotsky:

> The essential difference between inner speech and external speech is the absence of vocalization.
> Inner speech is dumb, soundless speech. This is its main distinguishing feature. But the evolution of egocentric speech tends in this direction towards the gradual increase of this feature. [. . .] The fact that this feature develops gradually, that egocentric speech can be distinguished by its function and structure before vocalization, demonstrates only what we have made the basis of our hypothesis about inner speech, namely that inner speech develops not *by the outer weakening of its phonic aspect, passing from speech to whisper and from whisper to silent speech*, but by its functional and structural demarcation from external speech; for it moves from external speech to egocentric speech, and from egocentric speech to inner speech. (Lotman, 25–26; italics Kamei's)[3]

This is a rather difficult passage. Vygotsky is developing his ideas here through a critical reading of Piaget. Where does Piaget's thinking appear in this passage? Since Vygotsky has not included a citation, for clarity's sake I have italicized the portion that summarizes Piaget's thought. Lotman also uses Vygotsky's summary in the above passage without citing Piaget directly, and if we go back to Piaget's original argument, we see that both Lotman and Vygotsky misunderstand and oversimplify it. But I will refrain from examining that issue in depth here. In sum, for Vygotsky, whereas external speech of course refers to language that is actually vocalized, *words* actually spoken aloud, inner speech is not necessarily unvoiced language, or language minus sound. Neither is it merely verbal memory (the lines of a poem that have been memorized by rote, for example). Rather, it is a "language to oneself" that requires active, subjective

---

3. Lotman here cites the original Russian version of Vygotsky's work. Many similar passages detailing Vygotsky's critique of Piaget can be found in the adapted English translation, L.S. Vygotsky, *Thought and Language*, trans. Eugenia Hanfmann and Gertrude Vakar (Cambridge, MA: Massachusetts Institute of Technology Press, 1962).

thought and effort, so that it is not a matter of whether or not it is actually voiced. This is how Vygotsky understands "inner speech."

But how is this inner speech acquired?

The utterances of a child at the preschool stage can be roughly divided into social language and egocentric language. Egocentric language refers to *words* spoken when, for example, a child thinks aloud. The child here makes no attempt to enter into the perspective of an interlocutor. This type of language occupies an extremely large proportion of a child's utterances. Piaget's argues that such *words* function to bring a certain cadence or rhythm to the child's thoughts or individual activities. In essence, he considers this to be no other than a sign of the child's shift from syncretism to egocentrism. This kind of *words* begins to decrease beginning in the school years:

> . . . a large portion of childish talk points to a certain egocentrism of thought itself, the more so as in addition to the words with which he marks the rhythm of his own action, there must be an enormous number of thoughts which the child keeps to himself, because he is unable to express them. And these thoughts are inexpressible precisely because they lack the means which are fostered only by the desire to communicate with others, and to enter into their point of view.[4]

Implicit in Piaget's theory is the notion that egocentric language is a step in a process that leads finally to social language. Vygotsky's criticism arises from this. He cautions that egocentric language should not be confused with egocentrism as it is conceived in psychoanalysis and kindred fields. This is indeed a crucial point. Let us examine Piaget's description of egocentric language's external characteristics. First, it takes the form of collective monologue. That is, it appears not when the child is alone, but precisely when the child is in a group of children engaged in similar activities. Second, this group monologue is accompanied by the fantasy of understanding. That is, the child thinks that his own egocentric language, which is not directed at anybody in particular, is understood by those around him. Third, this speech to oneself has exactly the same external features as social language; it is not an utterance to oneself made in a whispered voice. But could it not be said that these characteristics actually indicate that self-directed speech is not yet completely separated from other-directed language? If so, this would mean that social language is primary. This is the gist of Vygotsky's critique. If we put it this way, the appearance of ego-

---

4. Jean Piaget, *Judgment and Reasoning in the Child*, trans. Marjorie Warden (London: Routledge, 1928), 206.

centric language signals a stage at which egocentrism is still not yet firmly established, although it indicates the beginning of its establishment, which means that the establishment of egocentrism comes with internalization of egocentric language, that it arises in tandem with the development of "inner speech."

This revisionary view of egocentrism, a reversal of values, leads to a new understanding of the characteristics of egocentric language. A tendency toward stressing only predicates in syntax (a tendency to retain the predicate and related words but to abbreviate away the grammatical subject and words related to it) can be cited as one distinctive feature of egocentric language. But this should be regarded not merely as underdeveloped syntax, but as something possessing its own autonomous function and structure. Having understood this, we arrive at a new approach to the nature of inner speech. For example, Lemaitre studied a twelve-year-old who condensed the phrase "Les montagnes de la Suisse sont belles" ("The mountains of Switzerland are beautiful") to "L,mdSsb" because that brought to mind the contour of the mountains that lay behind the phrase.[5] Here the phonetic dimension of a set of *words* is reduced to the first letter of each, so that the total phrase is condensed and rendered into a single index-like word. Relating this inner speech form to the tendency to stress only predicates in egocentric language, Vygotsky argues a number of points: that the sense of a word always surpasses its conventional meaning, that in combinations or agglutinations of linguistic elements the strongest accent is always placed on the main root or concept, and that the senses of words that have been combined together flow into and influence one another (Vygotsky, *Thought and Language*, 146–48).

Obviously, this form is close to being a private idiom. This is where Lotman sees a link to I-I language, but what I find suggestive is the idea that there is an inner speech that is of a different nature from so-called interior monologue. This provides us with a valuable tool for thinking about the writing style used to portray spoken conversations.

If we quickly review modern Japanese literary history, we will likely conclude that the first modern work to experiment consciously with methods for the direct depiction of interiority was Tsubouchi Shōyō's *The Newly Polished Mirror of Marriage* (*Imotose kagami*, 1886). In Tsubouchi's view of interiority we find a cognition very like that of Piaget, that is, of *words* minus sound. Note the following two examples from the work:

---

5. Vygotsky cites A. Lemaitre, "Observations sur le langage intérieur des enfants," *Archives de Psychology* 4 (1905).

There's just something strange about the child. Is she depressed? Is she happy? I for one haven't the faintest idea. She's such a sore loser. I mean, going off to marry Tanuma. She seems to be happy about it on the inside, but doesn't want people to know. I wonder if she's just playing the innocent. (*MBZ* 16:216)

With even more determination I went to Mother and told her my gut feelings. Should I refuse the marriage proposal? No, no, don't turn down Mr. Tanuma. It's not that there is some special reason, but if I rashly turn down Tanuma, the next proposal might not come so easily. . . . I may end up having to go *there*. (*MBZ* 16:216)

The first quote is from a "private monologue, spoken after returning to her room" (*MBZ* 16:216) of Okama, Oyuki's wet nurse. As for the second, the narrator sets it up in the following manner: "What are Oyuki's true feelings? Let's take out our magic mirror and reflect her innermost thoughts" (*MBZ* 16:216). It is possible, it seems, to depict a spoken monologue directly, but in order to know inner thoughts a special tool called a "magic mirror" is needed. In other words, Shōyō seems to have persisted in the cognition that, even in the case of fictional characters that he himself had created, another person's interior could not be known directly. Nothing distinguishes Okama's monologue from the sort of grumblings she might speak to a close friend, just as there is nothing about the form of Oyuki's thoughts that distinguishes them from Okama's monologue. But toward the end of the depiction of Oyuki's inner thoughts, we learn that she harbors a secret: "I would hate it if people said that I fell for Misawa's manliness, so I have restrained myself and pretended not to care [. . . .] I still regret what I've done, but it is him I really love" (*MBZ* 16:217). For that very reason, her thoughts must remain voiceless and are bestowed with a tendency toward I-I language.

And so it was that Japanese literature acquired a new image of the human being, in which the emotions of the self were psychologized. Even if the work had omitted its depictions of Okama's monologue and Oyuki's internal soliloquy, and even if it had omitted its passages of internal description of the hero, Misawa Tatsuzō, passages that usually begin with such phrases as "he felt deeply in his heart that . . ." and "he himself thought . . . ," it would not be difficult to guess at their feelings, given the way events unfold in this work. Because the secrets revealed in these sorts of psychological developments contain little that is surprising, in a sense such passages seem unnecessary and forced. We can speculate that the intent of the author who deliberately created such scenes of internal soliloquy was to show a mode of human existence in which a person's psychology is produced through dialogues with an interior self.

However, the internal soliloquies in this work hardly depart at all in either syntax or semantic structure from the forms used in external speech. It was Hirotsu Ryūrō's *Women's Participation in Politics is Just a Dream* (*Joshi sansei shinchūrō*, 1887) that made the next step, developing a mode of expression that would represent "inner speech" in its characteristic form.

> First time met him, wouldn't it be wonderful if he was a member of our party . . . that's what I thought . . . every time we met, my feelings of love—aahh . . . Misao, Matsuyama Misao, so envious of her . . . she must be so happy—aahh . . . no no, mustn't think that. If Hisamatsu was a political enemy . . . no, it can't be, it can't be . . . he seems a little sleepy. Is he sleepy from yesterday's reception? . . . aahh, they say that not being free is painful . . . even a devoted suffragette . . . it's not that I don't see their point or can't take their advice . . . but to accept such a complete opponent . . . that Naniwa Times newspaper . . . *Hisamatsu . . . that editorial . . . the painfulness of love . . . a queer thing . . . so happy . . . Misao is so happy . . . in suffrage, no free choice . . . justice only for men . . . Hisamatsu, such . . . an editorial . . . happiness . . . to be free to . . .* Misao . . . Times . . . suffrage . . . rights . . . justice . . . freedom . . . Hisa . . . ma . . . tsu . . . Hisa . . . ma . . . (*MBZ* 19:132, italics Kamei's)

This is an interior soliloquy by the suffragette Satoko after she learns in a newspaper that Hisamatsu, a leader in the People's Rights movement whom she trusts and respects, holds views contrary to her own. In the confusion that follows this shock, she discovers that she loves Hisamatsu. If we supplement what is left out in the ellipses in the original, the flow of her feelings would perhaps go something like this:

> even a devoted suffragette . . . it's not that I don't see their point or can't take their advice . . . but to accept such a complete opponent . . . that Naniwa Times newspaper . . . Hisamatsu [we thought he would be our supporter] . . . [that he of all people would write] that editorial . . . [but] the painfulness of love . . . a queer thing . . . [I should hate him, but I don't, in fact this makes me all the happier] so happy . . . Misao is so happy . . . in suffrage [no, in love], no free choice . . .

As her turmoil intensifies, even the fact that Hisamatsu has written an anti-suffrage editorial is blanketed over by her feelings.

> justice only for men . . . Hisamatsu, [did you, of all people, have to write] such . . . an editorial . . . [this feeling of] happiness . . . [I want] to be free to [reveal it] . . . [oh, but then there's] Misao . . .

This is, of course, only my imaginary reconstruction, but it seems likely that the psychological turmoil condensed into the language of this passage is something along these lines. In short, we have here an outstanding example of interior description, one that predates the more famous examples found in the latter books of Futabatei Shimei's *Ukigumo*.

Satoko subsequently drops to sleep, almost as if she has fainted, and dreams about an encounter with Hisamatsu. In the dream, Hisamatsu speaks words of support for women's suffrage.

> (Satoko) Ah, what a relief. When I read that editorial . . . I was so angry that my breast nearly burst at the thought of you writing a thing like that. (Hisamatsu) Oh yes, I agree. I felt the same way. (Satoko) So it was all a lie . . . but, Hisamatsu? (Hisamatsu) Yes. What is it? (Satoko) It's about Misao. (Hisamatsu) Yes? (Satoko) When do you think she will be getting married? (Hisamatsu) I have no idea. (Satoko) Ho ho. You? No idea? (Hisamatsu) I honestly don't know. (Satoko) There you go again. How silly! (Hisamatsu) I admit it, she and I have become very close, but as for being engaged, certainly not. . . . (Satoko) Honestly? (Hisamatsu) Hisamatsu tells no lies! (Satoko) That . . . look over there—the riverbank by the Court of Appeals . . . a lady, a lady like Misao, ah, Misao . . . I can't see her anymore . . . oh, but from the Court of Appeals . . . a woman in shackles . . . a policeman is escorting her away to court . . . what could she have done? A political offense. But there was nothing in the papers about it. [. . .] Oh, we've come to Nakanoshima Park. . . . Tsuyako is there. Oh! Ho ho! You are in the boat with Misao. . . . aah, what a pleasant view . . . that organ music—where is it coming from? (*MBZ* 19:133)

This is the conversation that takes place in her dream. If we omit the nametags that identify the speaking subject for each line of dialogue, a style of polyphonic interior monologue emerges in which one internally exchanges *words* with an other. Through this dialogic monologue, Satoko's wishes seem fulfilled, but once she hears from Hisamatsu the words that make her happy, she twice suddenly changes the subject, as if she were flustered ("it was all a lie . . . but, Hisamatsu?" and "That . . . look over there"). Her anxiety about the reality that conflicts with her dream-fantasy seeps through to influence her egocentric dialogic monologue.

It is also important to note that when Satoko hears Hisamatsu deny his engagement to Misao, the image that appears is of Misao under arrest, followed immediately by the image of Misao and Hisamatsu together in a boat at Nakanoshima Park. Misao and Satoko had been close friends. But in the dream unleashed by the editorial, an editorial that can only be called Hisamatsu's betrayal of Satoko, Misao is bestowed with an antinomic semantic structure: Satoko on the one hand wishes to distance herself from Misao (a betrayal of their friendship), while on the other hand, she must exercise loyal self-restraint and wish Misao happiness. In previous political novels, the typical pattern was to have a talented youth and beautiful heroine struggle together for the same political objectives, with the novel reaching its conclusion as the two simultaneously realize their love for one another and attain their political goal. This work belongs to the tradition of the political novel, but here the talented youth Hisamatsu is made to take a "realistic" attitude (he argues that extending voting rights to women is premature), a position whose impact is presented from Satoko's point of view. As a result, it brings the major indices that predominated in the political novel—for example "rights," "freedom," and "love"—into conflict with one another, thereby bringing about a change in their meanings. One instance of this sort of change can be found in the above scene, where the symbol of loyal friendship, Misao (whose very name means "fidelity") is imbued with the meaning of betrayal. In the end, Satoko disappears after going mad in the face of the following combination of events: Misao and Hisamatsu's engagement, Misao's shift to opposing women's suffrage, and the denial of woman's suffrage by the Diet.

The name "Hisamatsu" was a favorite of political novelists because its Chinese characters bear the meaning of enduring hardship and remaining faithful. As we have seen, "Misao" corresponds to this. "Satoko," on the other hand, implies clarity of thought and wisdom. But note that in this novel, all of these names are turned on their head. They are, in a sense, transformed into language with a self-contradictory semantic structure.

Not only that. In the dream conversation quoted above, on the surface it appears that political solidarity is being linked to love, but at a deeper level the scene is dominated by anxiety and a sense of foreboding about the likely actual outcome (political disagreement and romantic failure). I would like to refer to this way of developing dialogue as the conversational writing style (*kaiwa buntai*). By this, I mean a kind of unfolding whereby an exchange of *words* between several people comes to disclose a certain unspoken, deeper meaning. This style reached its truest form in the works of Kunikida Doppo and Natsume Sōseki, but the writers who opened the way for this style of writing were Hirotsu Ryūrō and Izumi Kyōka.

Of course, this is only a rough analogy, but if we say that the internal monologues found in Shōyō's *The Newly Polished Mirror of Marriage* represent a Piaget-like mode of expression, then in Ryūrō's *Women's Participation in Politics is Just a Dream* we have a mode of expression that corresponds to Vygotsky's "inner speech."

* * * * *

The following is a passage from Kyōka 's "Scroll Six" ("Roku no maki," 1896):

> Seeing me nod, Millard nodded back.
>
> "Uesugi, I'm wearing a mother's clothing now. Mother, okay? You don't have a mother, so here, now you have a mother here. You don't need to cry anymore. I don't have a mother either, but now I am the mother, so I have a mother, so I don't need to cry anymore either. Now, you become me, Millard, and I become the mother, and when you are Uesugi, I'll be your mother too. That's how we should pretend. Today is April Fool's Day, and you played a trick on me this morning. I suppose you don't really want a mother like this, but you should play along, even if you don't mean it."
>
> After saying she was my mother, her cheeks flushed, her eyes glowed, her eyebrows twitched, and her shoulders shook. She suddenly stood up from her chair, drew near me and took up my hand.
>
> Takatsu laughed and patted my head.
>
> "This big boy is a crybaby. Wait I'll bring you some sweets."
>
> Still laughing, he quickly left the room.
>
> Millard seemed very agitated and stared intently at my face.
>
> "Millard!" she exclaimed and kissed the face of this pitiable child.
>
> Her cool hair brushed my cheek, and I could hardly restrain the beating of my dancing heart. (*MBZ* 21:131)

The series of linked works that begins with "Scroll One" ("Ichi no maki," 1896) and concludes with "Scroll of the Vow" ("Chikai no maki," 1897) comprise a fictitious autobiographical novel, the supposed childhood memoirs of Uesugi Shinji. The story begins in Kanazawa, while he attends Eiwa Gakkō, a mission school where one of his teachers is the young Millard. She is particularly fond of Shinji for his intelligence, but when he commits a blunder when a foreign missionary observes her class, she is disgraced. Finding herself ostracized by xenophobic jingoists, she eventually flees to Tokyo. Shinji too, with Millard's encouragement, enrolls in a school in Tokyo. His mother is dead, and he has developed something like a maternal bond of affection with Muraya Hide, an older woman. As for Millard's mother, she is Japanese, but her whereabouts are unknown.

It is easy to see that the word "mother" as used by Millard in the above scene is entrusted with a double meaning. She performs the role of her own mother, and at the same time imitates Shinji's mother, and by switching Shinji into Millard herself, she reveals her true feelings, which are something more than pure maternal love. The artifice of this form, though, allows her to erase any consciousness of having committed a sin, as she stresses that it is all an April Fool's Day prank.

As we saw in Kyōka's *Noble Blood, Heroic Blood* and "X Praying-Mantis Blowfish Railroad," here too we find the important compositional transformations achieved through the spoken dialogue of some character who speaks *words* that have become a sort of private code. It is as if *words* that had become autonomous from external speech and which possessed a unique semantic structure had leapt out directly to appear in a scene of external speech, without waiting for the appearance of a mode of expression developed through the process of internal monologue, such as we saw in *Women's Participation in Politics is Just a Dream*. Such *words* produce an unexpected shock in the consciousness of the interlocutor, forcing him or her to decipher the code and finally imposing a dramatic vector onto their mutual emotions.

This mode of writing meant that the spoken dialogue of characters in Kyōka's fiction necessarily had to be bracketed off from the lines of narrative description (*ji no bun*). Moreover, this meant that passages of narrative description would now be influenced by this conversational writing style, while in other cases we see the narrative description conflicting with and adopting a critical stance toward the spoken dialogue of a work's characters. Impacted by Millard's spoken dialogue, the infantile feelings of the "I" here (i.e., the narrator Shinji who exists at a later moment of recollection) give rise in him to expressions characteristic of feminine speech and babytalk: "Takatsu laughed and patted my head." This flows quite naturally into Takatsu's line: "This big boy is a crybaby." We also see the mode of writing in which the narrative description adopts a critical stance toward spoken dialogue in many places in Kyōka's "Poor People's Club" ("Hinmin kurabu," 1895). In contrast to the raffish iron-lady-like dialogue of the heroine Otan, the narrative description adopts the refined language of the aristocratic classes, whereas in depicting the scene of an attempted suicide by the steward of an aristocratic family, it adopts a cold, sardonic tone closer to Otan's perspective:

> From the start, the man had intended to overwhelm Otan with his life's wisdom in this farce, but in letting her witness he missed the mark in wanting to make her cry, and the momentum slipped away so that he did not have to carry out this historical drama. He suffered a slight wound, and saying that he didn't want to get lockjaw, he smeared it with Taikodai medicinal salve, but with every step he took, his stomach muscles rippled, so that he limped along crying out "Ouch! Ouch!" You should applaud his determination (even if it was all idiotic).[6]

The last sentence here—"You should applaud his determination (even if it was all idiotic)"—is an expression that manifests simultaneously the

6. *Kyōka zenshū*, 2: 160.

consciousnesses of both the narrator, immanent to the depicted scene, and the author.

The development of Vygotsky's "inner speech" is achieved through the increasing independence of the *words* one speaks to oneself from those that one directs at other people. Accordingly, with its development there should come an increasingly conscious awareness that the *words* one speaks to others are a social language. But Vygotsky showed no particular interest in the effect "inner speech" might have on the situation of external speech. He went no further than to point out that behind spoken *words* there lies the internal "subtext" they hold for their utterer, so that the psychological and grammatical syntaxes of a given phrase did not always match.

Of course, this insight alone already harbored rich possibilities. While we might not go so far as to declare this one of the sources for the theory of transformational generative grammar, at the very least we can say that it provided an important foundation for the reception and exploration of that theory by Soviet scholars. Let us look again at the expressions found at the conclusion of "X Praying-Mantis Blowfish Railroad." Let us say that the author's psychological theme or subject at this moment was the image of Shinako, lingering in the field of pampas grass through which the railroad runs. The psychological theme for Shinako, on the other hand, is the blowfish that lies split open on the ground.

If this theme is to be manifested through the eyes of the nonperson narrator, who is immanent to the depicted scene (the perspectival character who cannot show his own figure), then likely the passage would have used an expression such as C1. But this expression would fail to weave into itself adequately Shinako's own psychological theme. This psychological theme naturally includes Shinako's failure to look toward the child that Sugako was taking away, bringing an even stronger stress to the expression that depicts the blowfish, the direct object of her psychological theme. The result is C, the text's actual expression. In sum, the narrator's gaze is first turned toward Shinako, and then, as if her eyes were a kind of reflecting mirror, toward the blowfish, so that her eyes are rendered into its theme: "her cold gaze fixed on it." We can recognize the same type of syntax a few lines earlier: "her eyes filled with overwhelming emotion, but Shinako turns her face away, gazed at intently." In cases where the psychological theme of a character in the work is stressed, the narrator's focus centers on the eyes that are gazing at the object correlate of that psychology, be it the blowfish or Shinako's face. It is for this reason that the grammatical subject is abbreviated (or rendered into a participial rhetorical figure) and a syntax that stresses only the predicate is selected. This is the distinctive writing style used in the narrative description in this work. By considering Vygotsky's notion that psychological syntax and grammatical syntax do not necessarily match, we can contrast the text's syntax with the common-sense, conventional form that is normal grammatical syntax, and thereby grasp the means used to foreground the psychological theme. In Kyōka's case, we are able to detect a form in which the psychological syntax of the work's characters is overlaid onto the narrator's grammar.

My dissatisfaction with Lotman's work, as mentioned in the previous chapter, arises from the fact that his notion of autocommunication deals only with the relationship between author and work, and neglects the autocommunication of characters appearing within the work. In this sense, there is a blind spot in its theory of the structure of the novel. For example, in the scene of the second quote from "X Praying-Mantis Blowfish Railroad," Sugako's spoken dialogue consists entirely of conventional, other-oriented language, but Shinako's response in something like I-I language utterly demolishes that language and its norms. Sugako's spoken dialogue, looked at on the level of everyday conversation, consists of a message that takes up only the positive aspects of reality and tries to establish and sustain psychological contact. In previously existing novelistic technique, the purpose for deliberately including such flat, boring *words*, "natural language," in a work could only have been as a device to elicit from Shinako the expected *words* of maternal affection expressing concern for her child's future. In sum, when they encountered such a scene within this novel, contemporary readers must have anticipated a mode of expression that called for decoding in terms of this sort of supplementary code of commonsense. But in fact, the doubly significant spoken dialogue of Sugako is rendered invalid by Shinako's "inner speech"-like dialogue; it is rendered into nonsense. The grammar of conversation—complementing the child, asking its age and name—is transformed through the mediation of Shinako's negating, anti-semantic spoken dialogue into a unique conversational writing style. With this complication of the copular relationship that is a conversation, the doubly significant semantic aspect of their conversation is undermined and transformed.

Lotman's work is of significance to me in that it paves the way for this sort of approach. Shinako's spoken dialogue, her significance-destroying refusals to engage in dialogue, are in fact laced with a powerful meaning, a semantic function so strong that it tends to absorb into itself all surrounding semantic value. Its most concentrated prototype can be found in her response to Sugako's agitated "I wonder, is there really such a name?" Shinako's negation, her "no," summons up volumes of psychological content, yet ironically its own semantic content is a blank. We see a similar effect later in the story with the "it" of "the blowfish that lay split open nearby." This calls to mind the iso-rhythmicality of "inner speech" or the refrains found in poetic expressions, in which some meaningless sound or *word* is added on, thereby intensifying the emotional significance.

But for what sort of historical tendency did Kyōka's mode of expression serve as a metaphor? It figured the coming of an age when would people speak and act according to their own individual "inner speech," when the world's basic structure of significance, its primary framework for making meaning, had begun to crumble away.

Chapter Ten
The Demon of *Katagi*:
Possession and Character in Kōda Rohan

Translated by Michael Bourdaghs

Here Kamei continues his exploration of the styles used to depict spoken dialogue. Taking up the works of Kōda Rohan, Kamei argues that they are organized not so much around a visual as around an aural sensibility: they aim to portray realistically the speaking tone of others, rather than their interiorities. This is a characteristic they inherit from the katagi *works of Edo literature, works that provided humorous catalogs of various character types found in particular social worlds. By carrying through the logic of the* katagi *genre to its extreme, Kamei argues, so that* katagi *amounted almost to a kind of demonic possession, Rohan brought the genre to its own self-destruction. His characters are driven by their obsessions to break through the constraints that define their positions in society. This paved the way for the new ideas of personality and individuality that would dominate subsequent realist and naturalist fiction in Japan. But these later movements lack the possibility for self-relativization and for criticizing everyday social norms that was inherent in Rohan's mode of expression, and it is this lost possibility that Kamei aims to resurrect here. Rohan also enables a critique of Bakhtin and Vološinov's theory of ideology. Whereas their notion of linguistic dialogism enabled them to transcend the structuralism of Saussure's* langue, *when they attempt to connect linguistics to ideology and meaning, they presume a rigid system of behavioral norms, and are unable to theorize how subjects might be able to achieve awareness of and thereby relativize those norms.*

"Rohan" was not particularly concerned with (visual) description, and at times even stopped functioning as a narrator. Instead, "Rohan" was inclined to concentrate his attention on his ears, to focus on the *words* of others and through them to reveal their consciousnesses: he was more an auditor (*kikite*) than a narrator (*katarite*). And what this "Rohan" mainly tried to represent was the other's manner of speaking.

The "Rohan" that I am referring to is the Rohan who appears as a character in the works of Kōda Rohan.[1]

Moreover, by "reveal," I do not mean providing a glimpse into some verbally inexpressible internal psychology. "Without knowing why, I sat down on a stool at a shop selling chestnut rice, a local specialty, and began to worry: the existence of specters in the heart, like the phantom *hahaki* trees in the mountains, is always a mystery; here I wanted to enlist the aid of the *genbun itchi* writers" ("The Buddha of Art" ["Fūryū butsu," 1889]) (*MBZ* 25:12). *Genbun itchi* is a writing style that delves into the secrets of the heart. Kōda Rohan himself seems to think so, as he frequently uses playful expressions similar to this. But he himself had no intention of seeking after such an object or writing style. Rather, he produces this "Rohan" immanent to the depicted world for the purpose of representing consciousness as it was manifested in the particular tone and manner of speaking that characterized the spoken dialogue of the other. As can been seen in "Tales of Daily Life" ("Higurashi monogatari," 1890), his works objectify even *genbun itchi* as one style among others, placing it alongside those others and thereby relativizing it.

My purpose in this chapter is to draw out the possibilities that were immanent in this unique method and that were lost in the literature of a later period. First, however, I would like to explore the singularity of this auditor "Rohan" at greater length.

The "Rohan" of "Encounter with a Skull" ("Tai dokuro," 1890) gets lost while walking through the mountains near Nikkō. He then hears the story of a secret romance from a beautiful woman who lives alone in a rustic mountain hut. The "Rohan" of "The Wandering Balladeer" ("Tsuji jōruri," 1891) hears about the checkered life of the pot maker Dōni from another character, Kyōunrō.[2] It is clear that the main narrators in these works are the beautiful woman and Kyōunrō, whereas "Rohan" appears to have no other function but as a listener. As a device within the work, he performs the role of narrator only briefly, to describe the setting and introduce the circumstances that led to his hearing the long tales.

1. Many of the fictional works by Kōda Rohan (1867–1947), who along with Ozaki Kōyō dominated the literary scene of 1890s Japan, feature a narrator name "Rohan."
2. A translation of "Encounter with a Skull" is included in Rohan Kōda, *Pagoda, Skull and Samurai: Three Stories by Rohan Kōda*, trans. Chieko Mulhern (Rutland, VT: Charles E. Tuttle, 1985), 111–47. No English translation of "The Wandering Balladeer" is available; the Japanese text is reprinted in *MBZ* 25:35–53.

Nonetheless, it would be a mistake to think of this "Rohan" as being a purely neutral auditor.

"Rohan" himself is aware of his own perversely curious character type (*katagi*) and in fact is possessed of a strongly marked manner of speaking, as if to make this fact plain to both himself and others.[3] The tales of the mountain woman and of Kyōunrō unfold in the form of being drawn out by this characteristic tone. In other words, he has a manner of speaking that reveals his own character type to himself, one that moreover in and of itself tends to stir him out of his own feelings of boredom, and it is precisely because of this that he is able to grasp with a high degree of sensitivity the tone of his interlocutor's narrative, as well as that of the dialogue spoken by the characters who appear in that narrative. "Rohan" (i.e., his *words*) rarely intervenes in the midst of his interlocutor's narrative, yet as a device for sensitively capturing its tone, he does make an evaluative contribution. If we turn our attention to this aspect, we should be able to detect an unfolding that occurs on a level different from that of the narrated content.

Of course, this "Rohan" does not make a direct appearance in all of Rohan's works. But, for example, the curiosity-driven man who travels from Maebashi to hear the mysterious tale of the beautiful woman who lives in the mountains of Akagi in *Venomous Coral Lips* (*Dokushushin*, 1890) clearly is nothing more than a variation on this "Rohan." Moreover, even in works where this sort of auditor does not directly appear, we can locate numerous expressions in which a "Rohan"-esque ear is clearly rendered immanent.

* * * * *

This method, however, disappeared from the stream of modern literature, along with the view of human existence, *katagi*, that it had visually intended to depict. What rose to replace these were modern views of human life, such as personality and individuality, along with new ideas of expression, including a stress on neutral perspective and on objective description that suppressed any critical judgment (via evaluative words).

In most versions of literary history, this shift is recorded as a triumph, an overcoming of the former by the latter. *Katagi* is seen as consisting of stock

---

3. *Katagi*, usually translated "character," refers to a standard literary device used in Edo and early Meiji literature, particularly works of the genre *katagimono* such as Ejima Kiseki's *Characters of Worldly Young Men* (*Seken musuko katagi*, 1715) or Tsubouchi Shōyō's *The Temper of Students in Our Times* (*Tōsei shosei katagi*, 1885–86). The genre is structured around humorous portrayals of particular character-types that were supposed to be common in society, including close attention to the manners of speaking that characterized these types.

figures, indicating a premodern mode of cognition. Even though the expressive forms associated with this genre had a unique charm, in the end this was nothing more than the convoluted interest produced by an affectation that distorted the phenomenal aspect of the object world, by a writing style with a pronounced tendency to foreground its own particular point of view or manner of listening. That is to say, its denial is taken as an inevitable step in the course of the establishment of modern literature.

There is undoubtedly a certain logic to this view. Ironically, in a period that saw the rise of a demand for something like modern literature, Rohan himself in a sense played a role in proving its inevitability by negative example: he loyally pushed ahead with the *katagi* mode of writing until he brought the genre to its own self-destruction. Having said this, my purpose in discussing Rohan here is not to confirm this version of literary history. To reject the rhetorical refraction of the phenomenal aspect (and the *gesaku* style that aimed at producing interest through this refraction) and to approach the truth of the object world: when the naturalism movement began under the banner of this idea, it of course was straining to give birth to a new mode of being for the subject. Yet there was virtually no awareness that this new mode of being was itself in fact nothing more than one system, a *langue*. The demand for (a standard of) objectivity in point of view and for naturalness of sensibility, the demand for that which would make possible the appearance of the objective truth of the object world—to say it more pointedly, the self-confidence and pride that underlay this demand—buried such an awareness. As a result, what was born out of this was a mode of writing that prided itself on the truthfulness of its objectified subject (the essence of the author himself) and on the objectivity of this objectifying consciousness (the objective self). Along the way, this process produced a variety of positions, from Tayama Katai's flat description to Iwano Hōmei's one-dimensional description, but what it represented was nothing more than the character (type)[4] of the author, blindly self-affirmed as being (the objectification of) subjective truth.

If this is so, when we relativize this sort of literature by means of Rohan's *katagi* works, what particular qualities does each display? *Katagi* too is merely one mental system, one style of sensibility. Yet it does not lose its conscious awareness of itself as a system – more than that, it takes pride in this. *The Five-Storied Pagoda* (*Gojū no tō*, 1891–92) provides a good example of this.

---

4. Kamei here uses the same Chinese characters that are used for *katagi* (character type), but gives them the more common pronunciation gloss of *kishitsu*, usually translated as "character" or "temperament." The effect of this play on language is to highlight how the naturalist construction of the author was blind to the fact that it, no less than the *katagi* of earlier literary writing, was not absolute, but rather one of many possible modes of expression.

Early on in this work, acknowledged as the masterpiece of Rohan's early period, we find a narrative passage introducing the wife of the head carpenter.

> Her handsome, almost staunch eyebrows were shaved off, an indication that she was married, leaving an appealing suggestion of bluish green, like the brilliant color of mountains after rain. Her nose was straight, and her sharply etched eyes tilted upwards. She was plainly made up, her freshly washed hair rolled up into a severe chignon held tightly in place by a large hairpin, a strip of paper its only trimming. (21)[5]

From this external description, the reader learns something about the woman's past life and her temperament. Her careless treatment of her "black, lustrous hair," which was at the time as important to a woman as her own life and which for this woman had undoubtedly been her pride and joy, displays an irritability characteristic of the "iron lady" *katagi* we saw earlier with Taki no Shiraito in Izumi Kyōka's *Noble Blood, Heroic Blood*.

Yet this woman, Genta's wife Okichi, has now escaped from the world of the "water trade" (unlike Shiraito) and "her choice of pattern was not without taste, but her finery consisted of nothing better than a quilted kimono of double-strand fabric with a satin collar, quite devoid of any touch of brightness" (22). An eagerness shows in how she "dressed as though she gave no thought to her appearance, but rather as if she took pride in her upright character" (22), and this self-consciousness seems to be forcing the woman to adopt the appearance of the *katagi* of the perfect wife or of the respected elder sister. The following passage shows this aspect clearly (because the mode of expression here lacks any clear sentence endings, the quotation is a bit long):

> Except for the distant sounds of the maid doing the dishes in the kitchen, the house was still as the woman bit off and spat out the tip of a toothpick with which her tongue had been idly toying [. . .] and she pulled toward herself, using the tortoise-shell pipe in her right hand, a pretty inlaid-wood tobacco box, apparently a souvenir from some who had stopped off at Hakone on a pilgrimage to Afuri Shrine, then puffed leisurely on the pipe and let the smoke out slowly, so that it seemed to be rising from an incense stick, and abruptly she heaved an involuntary sigh: in the end, my husband will probably get the

---

5. Translation adapted from *The Five-Storied Pagoda* in Rohan Kōda, *Pagoda, Skull and Samurai: Three Stories by Rohan Kōda*, trans. Chieko Mulhern (Rutland, VT: Charles E. Tuttle, 1985). In particular, we have adapted Mulhern's translations in an attempt to reproduce those features of Rohan's writing style that are particularly relevant to Kamei's analysis.

job, but how annoying of *that Nossori* to set himself up against him, forgetting his own lowly station as well as the gratitude he owes us for having employed him last year; he fawns on the Abbot unabashedly in his attempt to get his hands on this job, and from what Seikichi tells me, even if the Abbot should be inclined to play favorites, the parishioners and donors are not likely to let such an important job go to an unknown—but there is little doubt of our ultimate success, though, and Nossori is so obviously doomed to fail—the likes of him could never handle a project of this magnitude, let alone find a crew willing to take orders from him, and nevertheless, I do wish my husband would come home soon, smiling and telling me that he has received the contract after all—he seems to have found an unusual challenge in this work, I'm dying to take on this precious project—never mind material gains, I want to hear people say, Genta of Kawagoe built the five-storied pagoda of Kannō Temple, splendid!, how well done!, spoken with so much enthusiasm, and if someone else should snatch this job from him now, he'd surely lose his temper and fly into a fine rage; he'd have more than enough reason for such an outburst; I couldn't possibly find any way to mollify him; well, I hope he returns soon, in good spirits—the silent thoughts of her wifely *katagi*. . . . (22–23)

The passage that describes the woman's thoughts, that is, the passage that begins "in the end, my husband will probably" and concludes "I hope he returns soon, in good spirits" at first glance appears to be an interior monologue.

But in the interior monologue forms of expression that Tsubouchi Shōyō consciously experimented with and that were further developed by Hirotsu Ryūrō and Futabatei Shimei, there is a shared mode of depiction. To put it simply, in such works, interior monologue is a form of expression that peers into the emotions surrounding some secret that cannot be spoken aloud to others. Accordingly, this form doesn't merely express the contents of the secret. Rather, the situation of having to suppress *words* (of needing to keep one's mouth shut) results in a disruption and shattering of the coherence of ordinary internal thought; consequently, there is a deep stratum of thoughts and feelings of which even the person in question is unaware, and it is this deep stratum that this form of expression renders manifest via a stream of word fragments. It was for this reason that the alienated human consciousness depicted was necessarily pregnant with the unique mental realm known as the *interior*. But in contrast, the thoughts of Genta's wife quoted above are not marked by this (situationally alienated) consciousness of a secret. Her thoughts are from the start given in the form of externally oriented *words*, so that if there were a friendly "someone to keep her company" (21) at her side, she would likely have spoken them out loud to that person without any alteration.

We might call the principle that is at work here that of the semiexpressed (*jun-hyōshutsu-teki*) thought. One posits one's self as "someone to keep [me] company," thereby doubling one's self and allowing one's thoughts to unfold in a dialogic manner toward a certain decision. Moreover, one's own internal *words* are expressed for oneself in a form that is dialogically bound up with the *words* of the other who is imagined within this process of thinking.

This form of expression is not necessarily Rohan's own creation. We can find its prototype in such earlier works as Takizawa Bakin's *Handsome Youths of Our Time, a Record* (*Kinseisetsu bishōnen roku*, 1828–48) or even earlier in such *kanazōshi* as the anonymous *Uraminosuke* (ca. 1612) and *The Tale of Tsuyudono* (*Tsuyodono monogatari*, ca. 1624). Clearly, indirect discourse is a traditional form of expression used throughout the history of Japanese fiction. I use the concept of indirect discourse here as defined by Mikhail Bakhtin and V.N. Vološinov:

> The linguistic essence of indirect discourse [. . .] consists in the analytical transmission of someone's speech. An analysis simultaneous with and inseparable from transmission constitutes the obligatory hallmark of all modifications of indirect discourse whatever. [. . .] Thus, for example, the direct utterance, "Well done! What an achievement!" cannot be registered in indirect discourse as, "He said that well done and what an achievement." Rather, we expect: "He said that that had been done very well and was a real achievement." Or: "He said, delightedly, that that had been done well and was a real achievement."[6]

In the way it analyzes our utterances not through a simple, formal grammatical explanation, but rather fundamentally from the standpoint of their dialogue and conflict with the *words* of others, this approach is very productive. For example, in the previous quotation of Okichi's thoughts, the *words* of Seikichi and Genta are recollected (cited, transmitted), so that at first glance this appears to be direct discourse. For example, "I'm dying to take on this precious project— never mind material gains, I want to hear people say, Genta of Kawagoe built the five-storied pagoda of Kannō Temple, Splendid!, how well done!" But the words that immediately follow this ("spoken with so much enthusiasm, and if someone else should snatch this job from him now, he'd surely lose his temper and fly into a fine rage") are expressions of the wife's analysis and interpreta-

---

6. V.N. Vološinov, *Marxism and the Philosophy of Language*, trans. Ladislav Matejka and I.R. Titunik (Cambridge, MA: Harvard University Press, 1973), 128–29.

tion of the tone of her husband's *words*. Moreover, even within the *words* that the wife recollects (cites), we can locate a similar mode of expression, one that includes her analysis and interpretation. For example, "this precious project" is couched in this explanatory form of expression.

In the case of Seikichi's *words*, a comparison with the lines spoken by him when he next appears makes it clear that here a supplementation or transformation has occurred in the expressions as transmitted by Okichi in her interior monologue. Yet even with this transformation, the tone of Genta's and Seikichi's spoken dialogue remains—in fact, perhaps Okichi in her analysis and interpretation has supplemented the tones to make them sound all the more like Genta and Seikichi—so that they have not been completely absorbed and assimilated into the woman's own characteristic manner of using *words*.

In this explanation, my analysis of the woman's semiexpressed thoughts has taken them as belonging to the narrative description (*ji no bun*) of the work, but be that as it may, the *words* of some other quoted in the above manner are what Bakhtin and Vološinov call indirect discourse. This technique was in fact widely used in the Meiji 20s, and abundant examples of it can be seen in works by, for example, Higuchi Ichiyō. In chapter six, I expressed my reservations about the punctuation system adopted in the Shōgakkan edition of Ichiyō's collected works, precisely because it seems to me that in too many cases, the *words* of characters that are transmitted via indirect discourse were instead enclosed within quotation marks, as if they were direct discourse.

In fact, the characteristics of expression particular to a given period are remarkably subtle and difficult to understand for persons of a later age. To make matters worse, the thoughts of the woman quoted above, the indirect discourse carried on inside her, does not take the form of *words* that were spoken aloud. That being the case, what relation does this passage have to the passages of ordinary narrative description, that is, to passages narrated by "Rohan"?

The concrete mode of being for this type of expression is to achieve a situational objectivity (relativization or self-objectification) with regard to one's own feelings.

> Bunzō was completely miserable and certainly not in the mood for looking at flower displays. [. . .] Watching their excitement, he was reminded over and over of his own predicament and gave off a sigh as damp as the sky during the summer rains. He was utterly despondent.

> How very depressing. It was depressing to see how yesterday, when Osei had asked "Are you going too?" and he had answered that he wasn't, her "Oh, really?" was so casual and untroubled. Bunzō felt that if she really wanted him to go, she should have insisted on it.

Then, if he had continued to refuse, he wanted her to say "If you aren't going with, then I won't go either."

"Aren't you just jealous?" he asked himself, trying to be reasonable. But her reaction continued to bother him . . . an uneasy mind.

Not wanting to go and not wanting to stay home, he felt sulky and displeased.[7]

This scene appears near the beginning of the second volume of Futabatei Shimei's *Ukigumo*. Here, the passage from "How very depressing" to "an uneasy mind" is comparable to the previous passage depicting Okichi's thoughts.

The reason that I see this as the expression of Bunzō's thoughts is that in the earlier conversation being recalled here, only Osei's *words* are bracketed off as spoken dialogue, whereas Bunzō's *words* from that time are dissolved into his present-moment reaction toward Osei (i.e., toward her spoken dialogue). Yet in the narrator (the speaker of the background narrative description) who is immanent within the scene, we find a somewhat satirical perspective (or tone): "Watching their excitement, he was reminded over and over of his own predicament and gave off a sigh as damp as the sky during the summer rains. He was utterly despondent." This perspective is capable to a certain extent of entering into Bunzō's thoughts, as it objectifies him in a third-person manner with the expression "Bunzō felt." This objectification next shifts to take the form of Bunzō's own self-objectification, giving birth to the emotional self-analysis that begins with the words, "Aren't you just jealous?" In other words, the narrator's tone sketches in the emotional state of the work's characters, but this tone is then absorbed into that state and finally it is transformed into the characters' own *words* (ideas). If we look at this transformation of tone in terms of the unfolding story of *Ukigumo*, we see that whereas previously Bunzō has been captive to his own emotions, this provides the opportunity for him to become more self-critical toward his own emotions.

In contrast, in Okichi from "Pagoda," we find no evidence of a self-critical stance toward her own emotions. This is because "Rohan," who is immanent to the scene, refrains from adopting the perspective and expressions (and tone) of a narrator and instead enters into the emotions and (tone of) *words* of Okichi. Yet this is not to say that there is nothing in common between these two narrative techniques. As a hypothesis, let us presume that Okichi really

7. Translations adapted here from Marleigh Grayer Ryan, *Japan's First Modern Novel: "Ukigumo" of Futabatei Shimei* (New York: Columbia University Press, 1965), 259–60.

does give voice to her thoughts, mutters them out loud as *words*. In the case of Bunzō, this would include the blunt, "heated" *word* "Damn!" with which he tries to sweep away his fantasies.[8] In the case of Okichi, the *words* centered around the phrase "*that Nossori*," which "Rohan" deliberately highlights with superscript markings, seem likely to have been muttered aloud. For example, she could have spoken them along the lines of, "that Nossori, how dare one of the day-laborer carpenters that we are good enough to hire set himself up in business as our competitor—doesn't it make your blood boil?"

What this demonstrates is that, whether in *Ukigumo* or in *Pagoda*, the semiexpressed thought is a form of expression that attempts to unfold via an internal self-objectification the situational reasons for emotions that could easily have been voiced as straightforward spoken dialogue. In that this represents the achievement of a situational objectivization (a structuralization) that occurs as one's (probably muttered) *words* are summoned up (semicited) internally, it is interior speech in the form of indirect discourse. And if we think of it as consisting of *words* quoted within the narrator's expressions—that is, as belonging to passages of narrative description—then it is an indirect discourse form of interior speech (indirect) discourse.

What is important here is that the initial emotion is analyzed and interpreted through this technique, so that its motivation is transferred to a different register. The displeasure marked by the words "*that Nossori*" serves to recall the *words* of Seikichi, which thereby leads to an objectivity toward the situation and a mollifying of the original feeling. What occurs after this is that Okichi thinks of the position of her husband, troubled by Nossori, who lacks ability and commonsense, and how her husband would feel if he had a job stolen from him, and these considerations lead her to feel a doubled displeasure. She feels a doubled displeasure because it is not simply a matter of having one's job stolen by some other person, but also of the sense of humiliation at being outwitted by someone as low ranking as Nossori. Of course, this feeling represents a change in register from her displeasure toward Nossori to that of her husband's, and it is via this that she legitimates her own unilateral belittling of Nossori.

The more the woman's worrying is directed toward the standpoint and feelings of her husband, the more it strengthens the self-exhibiting tone in her interior speech of her role as a loyal wife—for example, "well, I hope he returns soon, in good spirits—the silent thoughts of her wifely *katagi*. . . ." From this point on, the woman increasingly grows happy or angry for her husband's sake,

---

8. This passage occurs immediately after the one quoted above: "surprise, chagrin, and anger filled him, and finally with the heated word 'Damn!' he threatened himself and cursed his stupidity, but those devilish worms inside him again . . . yes, again . . ." (*Ukigumo*, 260).

at times even going too far, so that she is forced to pawn a precious memento of her aunt's to settle matters.[9] The "Rohan" who listens to and cites the *words* of her expressions of emotion is generally careful to note in them the pride characteristic of a wifely or sisterly *katagi*. That is to say, it is in the form of the self-exhibition of *katagi* that "Rohan" analyzes and interprets the tone of Okichi's semiexpressed thoughts.

* * * * *

Once again, I have spent a great deal of time analyzing the details of a specific expression.

Yet this woman, in fact, does not carry great significance in terms of the work's overall subject matter. Nor could we call her a semiprotagonist; hers is merely a supporting role. This being so, it may seem that have I plunged my blade too far into a nonvital spot, and yet, in fact, I do want to place emphasis on this mode of writing, which sets a supporting player at the beginning of the work and which bestows on this ostensibly minor character a form of consciousness that holds up even under detailed analysis from the perspective of a theory of expression.

It is via Okichi's thoughts that readers obtain their basic information on the relations between characters and the work's central event. Okichi's worries solicit the reader's suspense. Yet, on the other hand, Okichi harbors no sense of unease regarding the mode of being of her own feelings. To her, it is Nossori who owes "gratitude" for their having employed him last year, who forgets "his own lowly station" and who has "set himself up against" his master. To Okichi, her feeling of wrath, the displeasure that arises from being bitten in the hand by the dog she fed, is an exceedingly appropriate and natural feeling. Why in the world would a man like Nossori even think about attempting the construction of a five-storied pagoda, and why in the world would a person like the Abbot even considering lending an ear to such a proposition? These things simply make no sense to Okichi.

That her feelings are supported by popular commonsense, that they form a kind of shared mental system, becomes clear when we compare Okichi's thoughts to those of Onami, Nossori's wife.

---

9. Okichi pawns a cherished kimono to raise funds to help Seikichi travel out of the city until the furor over his attack on Nossori (an attack at least partially stirred up by Okichi's own spiteful remarks to Seikichi about Nossori) has died down and her husband can make appropriate apologies.

I'm beginning to hate sewing! If only my husband's wits were half as sharp as his trade skill, we would be spared such dire poverty. "Wasting a treasure in hand" goes the saying. He's merely a journeyman for all his talent, a petty carpenter doomed to obscurity. How vexing that he should be given even a mortifying nickname—Nossori, Slowpoke—by his colleagues, to be made the butt of their ridicule. I can't help but fret, yet he's totally unperturbed by it all. It's frustrating to watch him. This time, however, something happened to him. As soon as he heard about the five-storied-pagoda project of Kannō Temple, a fever gripped him. Selfishly unmindful of his lowly station and the wishes of the Master, to whom we are so deeply indebted, he's trying to get the contract for himself. When even I, his own wife, can't help but feel that he's overstepping his bounds, what must others think of him? Worse yet, the Master must be outraged, cursing him as that damned Nossori, and Madame Okichi must think he's an ingrate. . . . (27–28)

Onami believes in her husband's skills as a craftsman. Moreover, she cannot bear his meek acceptance of the insulting nickname, Nossori. Because the job in question is one that has suddenly roused her husband into action, she also feels that she "can't resist dreaming—may he win . . ." (28). Yet, as is clear from the above quotation, her husband's dream seems "selfish"; what is more, Onami cannot affirm even his desire to be allowed to fulfill his dream. Seen through the light of popular commonsense and of the ethics of the artisan's world, even his desire cannot be treated as legitimate.

In this sense, Onami is caught up in the same mental system as is Okichi. The only difference is that in this mental system, Okichi is in a position where she can feel confidence in her own propriety, so that she can also recollect her husband's desire as something legitimate: "Never mind material gains, I want to hear people say, Genta of Kawagoe built the five-storied pagoda of Kannō Temple, Splendid!, how well done!, spoken with so much enthusiasm." Of course, Nossori is equally unmotivated by mercenary greed. Onami's inability to cognize his wish as anything but "selfish" arises from her lack of any perspective (or freedom to conceive things differently) that would permit her to legitimate it. With pathetic servility, she ends up filling a role that supports from behind the legitimacy of the mental system that Okichi exemplifies.

Okichi or Onami: whose thoughts should be placed at the beginning of the work? Higuchi Ichiyō's "Troubled Waters," which opens with troubled thoughts similar to those of Onami, is a work that successfully exposes the cruelty of the mental system that yokes together self and other. But in this period, that mode of writing was highly exceptional. In *Pagoda*, Rohan clearly reveals a method of expression for opening passages that puts readers at their ease. If the reader felt a sense of alienation from Okichi's mode of feeling, or felt re-

pulsed by it, the work would lose much of its literary interest, but such an occurrence seems highly improbable. When readers react to the opening by concluding that Okichi's thoughts are not unreasonable for someone in her position, they are already half assimilated into this mental system, and through this
assimilation they likely form an expectation as to how her worries will be resolved. That is to say, as the narrative begins, by arousing these expectations
and this sense of unease, it presents the emotional basis of this unease and expectations in a form in which they are readily acknowledged as being legitimate. This is the key to the story's success.[10]

Incidentally, the method of opening the narrative with a description of
idle conversation by some third-party bystander has been used as far back as
such works as Sanyutei Enchō's *The Strange Tale of the Peony Lantern* (*Kaidan
botan tōryū*, 1884). It was also widely used in political novels such as Sudō
Nansui's *The Local Self-Government* (*Ryokusadan*, 1886) and Suehiro Tetchō's
Plum Blossoms in the Snow (*Setchūbai*, 1886). Book One of Futabatei's *Ukigumo*,
although it does not begin with idle conversation per se, can be seen as one
variation on this style with its deployment of a non-person narrator characterized by idle talk similar to that of a bystander. Works like Kunikida Doppo's
"Meat and Potatoes" ("Gyūniku to bareisho," 1901) and Natsume Sōseki's "Two
Hundred Tenth Day" ("Nihyaku tōka," 1906) gave birth to an entirely new fictional genre by splitting off this passage of idle conversation into an independent work. In the process of developing this style, experiments such as Izumi
Kyōka's "X Praying-Mantis Blowfish Railroad" ("X kamakiri fugu tetsudō,"
1896–97) were indispensable, as I discussed in the previous chapter. While they
were not entirely successful, such earlier works as Suehiro Tetchō's *An Account
of Twenty-Three Years into the Future* (*Nijūsannen mirai ki,* 1886) also represent early forerunners of this style.

Why was it necessary to begin with a description of idle conversation?
The Local Self-Government and *Plum Blossoms in the Snow* are works that as
political novels attempt to depict as realistically as possible the actual state of
human emotions, in concert with Tsubouchi Shōyō's argument in *Essence of the
Novel* (*Shōsetsu shinzui*, 1885–86). Their purpose was to awaken interest in
popular reform movements and thereby help realize an enlightened political
situation. In order to draw their writing style close to popular, everyday concerns, they began with descriptions of the *words* of popular conversation and

---

10. In other words, Kamei argues that the story's interest lies in the way it sets up a certain expectation and then, with Nossori's unexpected success in fulfilling his supposedly illegitimate
desire to build the pagoda, undermines it. This will be developed at greater length below.

then used those as the basis for constructing the *words* of the narrator as well. This did not represent the birth of a critical perspective on the political situation (and movement) that was based on popular ideas, but rather the arranging of popular *words* into a specific mental system.

The persons who appear in these scenes of idle conversation at the beginning of works are, of course, never named. They are understood as being the anonymous populace, or at best as the educated masses. This is an important point in this method: this anonymous consciousness characteristic of everyday life is projected as constituting popular opinion. To rephrase this, it is through everyday *words* (i.e., *parole*) that a mental system (*langue*), a mode of reception for the political/ideological state of affairs is being prepared. Once the main narrative begins, the characters from the prefatory scene of idle conversation generally disappear from the work, so that as a technique of composition, this device marks an unsophisticated, artless intrusion—and yet it was used over a long period in a wide variety of forms. This was because the efficacy of *words* (*parole*), as noted above, was understood and acknowledged. The vulgarity of this *parole* and of the perspective of idle conversation that functioned in this way would be critically exposed in such works as Kosugi Tengai's *Popular Song* (*Hayari uta*, 1902) and Tayama Katai's *Life* (*Sei*, 1908) through the very plot composition of these works themselves. *Popular Song* opens with a scene of gossiping farmers and, following the climax of its tragedy, closes with the introduction of a coarse popular song. Yet while the tragedy that is sandwiched between these two seems in its external form to be on the same level as irresponsible gossip or popular songs, it also exhibits a deep sincerity toward human life that cannot be so easily dismissed. Likewise, Katai's *Life* opens with conversation at a public bath. While a number of men out of a sort of irresponsible curiosity gossip about a neighborhood family that is about to bring in a new daughter-in-law as the second wife for its son, a young man sitting in one corner of the tub walks out, a hurt look on his face. He is the son of the family being gossiped about, and the narrator's perspective too moves on together with this youth, entering into the house of the family in question, whereupon the work launches into its main story. The mode of expression here clearly does not originate from the gossip-like perspective. The introduction of that earlier style here represents a deliberate attempt to reproduce the most primitive form of the existing style in order to destroy it. The compositional structure of this work itself serves to stress that in order to pursue the truth of the object world, one must distance oneself from the obscene irresponsibility of the consciousness of anonymous everyday life. This could not have occurred, however, without the previous step of objectifying in a critical light the anonymous conversation that was projected as possessing the legitimacy of popular opinion, a step accomplished in such works by Izumi Kyōka as *Reserve Soldier* (*Yobihei*, 1894) and *Dispatch from Hai-cheng* (*Haijō hatsuden*, 1896).

If we try to situate *Pagoda* within this history of opening-passage styles, its unique quality becomes all the more apparent. Tsubouchi Shōyō in *The Wife* (*Saikun*, 1896) had already experimented with an opening that channels interest toward the work's world through the sensibility of a supporting character, the heroine's maid, but it is Okichi in *Pagoda* who is provided with a reality of consciousness that bears up under a detailed analysis, and her subsequent conversation with Seikichi provides an orientation for the emotive evaluation of the state of affairs troubling her. Okichi's indirect discourse internal speech has the function of firmly establishing anonymous public opinion as a mental system, as a *langue* that yokes together the work's readers and characters. Readers are then given a second opportunity to sense how unyielding this anonymous public opinion is in the pressure that Onami feels.

* * * * *

In this manner, the *katagi* depicted by Rohan amounted to a mental system, a self-legitimating *langue* rooted in the latent background of anonymous public opinion. What makes Rohan unique is his ability to describe how that which drives a *katagi* to crisis is nothing other than one aspect of the *katagi* itself. On this point, there is a decisive difference between Rohan and such writers as Aeba Kōson and Ozaki Kōyō.[11]

But before I explore this, I would like to briefly address the theoretical issue at stake in Okichi's semiexpressed thoughts. Bakhtin and Vološinov would call this the "upper strata of behavioral ideology."

> What usually is called "creative individuality" is nothing but the expression of a particular person's basic, firmly grounded, and consistent line of social orientation. This concerns primarily the uppermost, fully structured strata of inner speech (behavioral ideology), each of whose terms and intonations have gone through the stage of expression and have, so to speak, passed the test of expression. Thus what is involved here are words, intonations, and inner-word gestures that have undergone the experience of outward expression on a more or less ample social scale and have acquired, as it were, a high social polish and luster by the effect of reactions and responses, resistance or support, on the part of the social audience. (Vološinov, 93)

---

11. Aeba Kōson (1855–1922) was particularly prominent in the 1880s for such *gesaku*-like works as *The Character of Modern Merchants* (*Tōsei akindo katagi*, 1886).

Bakhtin and Vološinov criticize theories that take so-called inner *words* to be nothing more than an individualistic interiority, and stress instead the need to grasp them as an internal struggle with the *words* of others, or as internal dialogue. They argue that even "an utterance still in the process of generation 'in the soul'" reflects its real social situation, being one link in "we-experience" (Vološinov, 87). My analyses above of internal speech start from this perspective, and it seems persuasive in the case of Okichi from *Pagoda*. Her thought level is clearly formed as an utterance consisting of words "that have acquired, as it were, a high social polish and luster by the effect of reactions and responses, resistance or support, on the part of the social audience" so that it can be understood via the following formulation: "*The ideological sign is made viable by its psychic implementation just as much as psychic implementation is made viable by its ideological impletion*" (Vološinov, 39). If we take up the passage from *Ukigumo* quoted above, Noguchi Takehiko in *The Japanese Language in Fiction* calls it the half-monologue style because its expression partially adheres to the interior of the protagonist, but we must avoid this sort of oversimplification.[12]

Nonetheless, Okichi and Bunzō's inner speech does not simply consist of the undigested interiorization of utterances (external language or spoken dialogue), be they of self or other. As Bakhtin and Vološinov anticipated, utterances that are contained within inner speech undergo a change in tone and a shift in motivation. In contrast to Vygotsky's view of "inner speech" as tending toward a simplification and rhythmification of external speech, here it takes the form of a situational supplementation carried out by a consciousness that reexamines the meaning of *words*. This supplementation, however, is sometimes apt to take the form of a one-sided distortion of or a too-hasty assumption about the real situation. This is because the consciousness that undertakes this supplementation is not entirely free from the emotional tone of the original utterance (i.e., of its *words*), and moreover because the supplementation is conducted with an eye (either sympathetic or antipathetic) toward anonymous popular opinion.

In general terms, we can say that the function of this situational supplementation reflects how in comparison "to an established ideology," the upper strata of behavioral ideology are "a great deal more mobile and sensitive" (Vološinov, 92). But it is another question whether or not we can always say that

> Here, precisely, is where those creative energies build up through
> whose agency partial or radical restructuring of ideological systems

---

12. Noguchi's work, *Shōsetsu no Nihongo*, vol. 13 of *Nihongo no sekai*, 16 vols. (Tokyo: Chūō Kōronsha, 1980–86), is discussed at greater length in chapters eight and twelve.

comes about. Newly emerging social forces find ideological expression and take shape first in these upper strata of behavioral ideology before they can succeed in dominating the arena of some organized, official ideology. (Vološinov, 92)

This is related to Bakhtin and Vološinov's view of *words* as being ideological signs:

Everything ideological possesses *meaning*: it represents, depicts, or stands for something lying outside itself. In other words, it is a *sign*. *Without signs there is no ideology*. (Vološinov, 9)

As long as we adopt this view, we cannot properly evaluate cases in which internal *words* veer away from the mode of ideologically (semiotically) reflecting reality (i.e., possessing meaning). In fact, Bakhtin and Vološinov dismiss "the lower strata of behavioral ideology" as being "erratic experiences" that lie "on the borders of the normal and the pathological" and as lacking "a socially grounded and stable audience"; they evaluate them only in negative terms: "To this stratum, consequently, belong all those vague and undeveloped experiences, thoughts, and idle, accidental words that flash across our minds" (Vološinov, 92).

In the end, they appear not to want to acknowledge any value in a consciousness that is not oriented toward some sort of mental system, toward some institutionalized ideological system. Onami in *Pagoda* is yoked to the same mental system as Okichi, and so long as this is so, she can only experience her desire ("I can't resist dreaming either—may he win . . .") as an unjustifiable, alienated emotion. Her sense of unease at "what must others think of him" represents a self-awareness of the lack of any "socially grounded and stable audience" that would lend a sympathetic ear to her husband's desires. This sort of emotion must seem "idle" even to the consciousness of the person who holds it, and in fact she can only express this thought via a stream of incoherent "idle, accidental words": "I can't resist dreaming either—may he win, but if only the Master would be gracious enough not to be vexed too much by it; I don't think it could happen . . ." (*Pagoda*, 28). Bakhtin and Vološinov maintain that in "the lower strata of behavioral ideology, the biological-biographical factor does, of course, play a crucial role" (Vološinov, 93). On the face of it, this is of course undeniable, yet there are also cases in which an emotion that is robbed of any foundation for self-legitimation is driven down to this level, split between hope and fear, lacking any focal point that would determine one's attitude toward it, so that in the end the emotion is transformed into bodily pain: "Oh, all this worrying gives me a headache! [. . .] I ought to stop right this minute—oh, my head!" (*Pagoda*, 28). This approaches what Bakhtin and Vološinov call an "I-experience."

Nonetheless, this remains one mode of engaging in dialogue or struggle with the *words* of an other. Dialogue or struggle can be viewed from a different perspective as consisting of the reflection and refraction of the *words* of the other. When Onami fears "what must others think of him?," it is not the case that she is completely unable to guess what others will say; rather it is because she is all too able to anticipate their comments that she avoids becoming conscious of (i.e., directly quoting) them and instead refracts them into this sort of *words*. In this sense, *words* that are uttered by somebody necessarily include both the reflection and refraction of some object *and* the reflection and refraction of some other's words. To abstract away this somebody (the uttering subject) and take up only its *words* is also to abstract away this doubled reflection and refraction (as well as its object). It is through such an act that Saussure's so-called *langue* is discovered. This *langue* is nothing more than an abstraction; Bakhtin and Vološinov's criticism on this point is very apt:

> The speaker's subjective consciousness does not in the least operate with language as *a system of normatively identical forms*. [. . .] In point of fact, the speaker's focus of attention is brought about in line with the particular, concrete utterance he is making. [. . .] For him, the center of gravity lies not in the identity of the form but in that new and concrete meaning it acquires in the particular context. (italics added; 67–68)

This is because *langue* amounts to a set of norms in the sense described by the passage italicized above. Yet Bakhtin and Vološinov themselves in defining human consciousness, especially when they take up what they term the "lower strata," seem to have forgotten the viewpoint of this doubled reflection and refraction.

Onami fears anonymous popular opinion. The *words* she anticipates are indirectly reflected and refracted into the form of fear, so that Onami without being conscious of it has begun to objectify popular opinion. "Worse yet, the Master must be outraged, cursing him as that damned Nossori, and Madame Okichi must think he's an ingrate. . . ." In this form, she reflects and refracts the *words* of the Master and Okichi that she anticipates, and at the same time she also makes them reflect the mental system (systems of duty and social obligation) that she shares with others:

> I don't think it could happen, but what if the job does fall into my husband's hands? I'm afraid to think how angry the Master and Ma-

dame would be! Oh, all this worrying gives me a headache! (*Pagoda*, 28)

Onami's thoughts become confused and lose coherence, and *words* that reflect unease and pain increase in frequency as her form of expression approaches that of a monologue. Popular opinion and her sense of being oppressed by the social system that she is yoked into are refracted and reflected into physical pain.

In the end, what Bakhtin and Vološinov call the "new and concrete meaning" that a speaking subject intends comes back to *langue*; it is nothing more than a variation of *langue*.

> A definite and unitary meaning, a unitary significance, is a property belonging to any utterance *as a whole*. Let us call the significance of a whole utterance its *theme*. (Vološinov, 99)

And yet,

> Together with the theme, or rather, within the theme, there is also the *meaning* that belongs to an utterance. By meaning, as distinguished from theme, we understand all those aspects of the utterance that are *reproducible* and *self-identical* in all instances of repetition. (Vološinov, 100)

In this instance, Bakhtin and Vološinov's employ "meaning" to the same effect as Saussure's *langue*, which they ostensibly reject. In their inability to distinguish theoretically between systematic norms and the *words* that use those norms as a medium in order to express the subject's cognition, Bakhtin and Vološinov are in the same boat as Saussure. "Meaning, in essence, means nothing; it only possesses potentiality—the possibility of having a meaning within a concrete theme" (Vološinov, 101). This *meaning* is synonymous with *norm*, yet when they declare that theme "is the *upper, actual limit of linguistic significance*" and that meaning "is the *lower limit* of linguistic significance" (Vološinov, 101), *meaning* is taken as belonging to the category of *expression*. As is clear from the stipulation quoted above, that "[e]verything ideological possesses *meaning*: it represents, depicts, or stands for something lying outside itself" (Vološinov, 9), what they refer to as ideological signs are, in short, norms. In this light, it seems that "behavioural ideology" amounts to behavioral norms, so that while they may have located a weak point in Saussure's view of *langue*, in fact they are only able to evaluate the individual concrete utterance (expression) in terms of something that reproduces (belongs to) some preexisting mental system or *langue*. On this point, Bakhtin and Vološinov are in complicity with structuralism.

Having pointed out this shortcoming, I would like to further develop the viewpoint of dialogue and struggle with the *words* of an other. To repeat, dialogue and struggle here are taken as being the reflection and refraction of the (anticipated) *words* of an other. In order to produce a theory of analysis of the novel, it seems necessary to re-investigate from this viewpoint the various functions of a message, particularly such concepts as the expressive and prosodic features, which Roman Jakobson elucidated in *Fundamentals of Language.*[13] It is likewise with what linguists call connotative linguistics, and to simply re-phrase this as "the emotive value of words" (Noguchi Takehiko) is not to advance the analysis to any significant degree. Moreover, such a viewpoint overlooks the theories of expression of such figures as Miura Tsutomu and Yoshimoto Takaaki. It is clear that Bakhtin and Vološinov have provided us with an extremely productive perspective.

Okichi's thoughts demonstrate a sense of confidence toward anonymous popular opinion and its mental system. Onami's thoughts take the form of an expression that reflects and refracts Okichi's *words* into an alienated emotion that arises even as she is yoked to the same system.

In *Pagoda*, the main actors in the story are, of course, Genta and Nossori, and yet the patterns of their thoughts amount to extensions of those of Okichi and Onami, respectively. Yet these two male characters stand in a position of needing to bring those thoughts to a conclusion, and here the *words* of the Abbot of Kannō Temple intervene. The fable that the Abbot tells the two men in itself possesses no deep significance; there are any number of similar tales among the *shingaku* parables that were current in the Edo period.[14] Yet it also functions to demonstrate that the Abbot alone possesses ideas that are different from those of the general public (anonymous popular opinion), a transcendence that lends symbolic backing to his rank as an Abbot. In reflected and refracted form, the fable is then woven into the thoughts of Genta and Nossori.

> No need for you to worry, the compassionate Abbot will let me be a man of honor when all is said and done, ha ha ha, you see, Okichi, being kind to a younger brother makes me a good elder brother, doesn't it? Sometimes one must share one's meal with a hungry man even if one finds it somewhat painful. [. . .] Aah, he who controls his temper, now that's a man, a true man indeed, just as the Abbot says, and the

13. Roman Jakobson and Morris Halle, *Fundamentals of Language* (The Hague: Mouton, 1956).
14. *Shingaku*, "Teachings of the Heart," was a school of ethical and religious thought loosely based on Buddhist and Confucian precepts and popular among commoners in the late Edo period. The parable related by the Abbot in *Pagoda* concerns two brothers who learn the necessity of brotherly love through a miraculous occurrence.

Abbot never lies; I loathe to give up even half of the job on which my heart is set, it pains me, but I must be the elder brother—Okichi, I intend to split the pagoda job with Nossori—a commendably meek man, aren't I? Commend me, Okichi, the entire matter is too dis-heartening, so at least let me hear you commend me, ha ha ha—with-out amusement he laughed absurdly loudly, and Okichi was unable to fathom her husband's true feelings. . . . (*Pagoda*, 49)

From the tone of the first half of this passage, it is clear that Genta believes that the contract for this job was rightfully his. Based on his past record and reputa-tion, he is the one with the qualifications and the right to take on this job. This self-assurance is further buttressed by his confidence that the world at large sees matters in the same way, allowing him to clearly exhibit the generosity of the sort characterized by such phrases as "never mind material gains" (23). Yet when the Abbot summons the two men, although Genta expects the Abbot to rebuke Nossori for his excessive desire and to urge him to withdraw and resign himself to his lot, what he encounters instead is the fable hinting that the two should reach an amicable compromise on the matter. For Genta, this is a vexing result.

Whether or not the Abbot was conscious of it, his treatment of the two men as equals already bespeaks, in and of itself, the absence of any legitimate foundation to Genta's self-assurance and self-confidence. Genta, however, is unaware of these deeper implications. He remains unaware, yet having encoun-tered the Abbot's *words*, he has no choice but to restrain his own unwillingness by adopting the form of a magnanimous generosity of spirit worthy of a master carpenter. Likening himself to an elder brother, he refracts the Abbot's fable through the metaphor of how "one must share one's meal with a hungry man even if one finds it somewhat painful," thereby preserving his own self-respect, and it is out of this self-serving conception that he decides to "to split the pa-goda job with Nossori." This reflects the *katagi* of a master carpenter, one un-able to free himself from behaving in a manner that is always determined by society's anticipated reaction. "Aah, he who controls his temper, now that's a man, a true man indeed": his expression is made to reflect in advance the antici-pated words of praise from society regarding his own good grace. Yet, as "Rohan" does not fail to hear, a hollow echo undercuts this self-exhibition of manliness: "without amusement he laughed absurdly loudly."

Genta's compromise, however, meets with Nossori's rejection. As Genta makes his offer, he explains that he does not "rely on the opinions of others" and that he is not "demanding [Nossori's] gratitude now" (*Pagoda*, 53). But Nossori's reluctant refusal punctures this pretense: "Giving me half the job seems charitable, but it's actually heartless. I won't accept it. I can't. As much as I want to build the pagoda, I've already given up the idea" (56). Genta makes the above explanations based on the presumption that Nossori will accept the proposal with tears of gratitude. But having met with the refusal, which takes the form of a refraction of Genta's proposed compromise through Nossori's standpoint, he is forced to reveal his own vanity:

> Do you think I'd jump at the chance to take over the whole job? I'd be ashamed to face the Abbot if I did! Furthermore, I couldn't fling to the wind my manly sense of honor that I've worked so hard to polish up. (57)

He ends up ceding the job to Nossori and then, when Genta tries to lend Nossori his own private plans for the project, he once again meets with rejection.

In one sense, Genta by refracting and reflecting the *words* of the Abbot is able to overcome the line of thought represented by Okichi and become a genuine man of honor, a paragon of manliness. This is acknowledged by the Abbot, so that in the end Genta finds himself bestowed with honor. But this view grasps the work in terms of its content alone, whereas a focus on Genta's spoken dialogue reveals that this is invariably undermined by the sort of hollow tone we have noted above.

Why is it necessary for Genta to be driven by Nossori in this manner? I don't have adequate space to quote Nossori's *words*, but to summarize briefly, what drives Nossori forward is a desire for liberation that arises from a *katagi* that harbors an impulse toward self-destruction. Because he makes his living as a carpenter, he would like just once to have the opportunity to fully utilize his skills on some highly prized project. This *katagi* of a craftsman becomes obstinate, to the point where the ethical duties of the carpenter's guild and Genta's kindness become a source of vexation, and Nossori himself is aware that in his overly ambitious dream "I forgot my place" (*Pagoda*, 46). To give up on the project, as if it had been a bad dream, is more suited to his station. And yet, "If I only live and die as if in a dream, deplored even by my own wife as a worthless husband, that will be that; now that I've abandoned my ambition, I feel wretched and resentful toward life and the cruel world" (46). When he thinks about how he is treated as a fool and about his regrets at having to surrender the project because it is beyond his station, his *katagi* as a craftsman becomes all the more pronounced. At the point where he has barely managed to check his regret, Genta arrives, bearing his well-meant proposal, but Nossori's sense of regret is so strong that it forces him to shake off that goodwill.

> I may employ helpers, but I refuse to get advice about my work, just as I would not presume to offer advice while employed to help some-

one else. If I alone am responsible for a job, I can arrange the bracing
of square supports or the balancing of beams just the way I want. I'll
be damned if I'll accept anyone's instructions on the smallest feature
of my work. I want to be wholly responsible for both the merits and
the flaws. [. . .] I don't want to be a parasite in another's work, any
more than I want to have one involved in my own work. (64)

What we find here already exceeds the ordinary *katagi* of the unreasonable master
artist. Nossori enunciates a stubborn will that dares to attempt an impossible
project and to take on all responsibilities for it himself, an enunciation that reso-
nates with a resolve for self-destruction in case of failure.

Nossori is burdened with the *katagi* of a craftsman who possesses superior skills yet is untalented in making a living, and in order to liberate himself
from the afflictions of this world, he deliberately drives himself into a situation
in which there are scant expectations for success, daring even to turn his back
on Genta's kindness. This feeling lacks any basis for self-legitimation, and Genta
acknowledges this, taking to the offensive in a form that ignores both popular
opinion and the ethical system of *giri* (duty) and *ninjō* (human passions). Being
a fellow carpenter, Genta too must acknowledge Nossori's *katagi* as a craftsman. As master carpenter, in the end Genta has no choice but to understand and
accept. Okichi, not restrained in this manner, is yoked along with Onami in the
mental system (*langue*) that consists of popular commonsense and the *giri*/*ninjō*
ethical system of the craftsmen guilds. Genta anticipates that he and Nossori are
likewise yoked together in such a system, yet that system is unable to extend
control over Nossori, whose self-sacrificing devotion to his work evidences a
katagi-as-character-type that has changed into a *katagi*-as-monomania. To borrow Bakhtin and Vološinov's phrase, here "behavioral ideology upper level"
gives birth via self-alienation to the "lower level," which in turn ends up puncturing the upper level's imaginary projection.

* * * * *

Originally, *katagi* consisted of styles of sensibility or mental systems constructed
according to status or trade. It was Ozaki Kōyō who worked to refine them,
portraying people as styles, as if to depict nature via stylized forms. Rohan depicts people who are possessed by *katagi* as if it were a demon of some sort.
Among the various modes of possession, there is the Genta type, a type that
aims at perfectly realizing a particular mental system; on the peripheries of this
mode we find Okichi with her wifely *katagi*, Seikichi with his Edokko *katagi*,
and Eiji with his pride in his chivalrous spirit. We find another mode of possession in the case of Nossori and his single-minded devotion to bringing his project

to perfect completion. The protagonist of Rohan's "A Sword" ("Ikkōken," 1890) also belongs to this type. Rohan seems to have been very interested in the unrelenting, demonic impulse that characterizes this latter type. We can detect this in the portrayals of Dōni from "The Wandering Balladeer" ("Tsuji jōruri," 1891) and "Surprise Gunshot" ("Nemimi deppō," 1891) and in Hikoemon from "The Whaler" ("Isanatori," 1891). In these instances, we find depicted the pure consistency of possession itself, in which the protagonist necessarily casts off his status or trade and sets off on an ordeal of a journey that is like a journey through hell.

What is essential here is that in each of these cases, the characters are given *words* (parole) that reveal the fact of possession itself to them. In the narrative technique used by "Rohan," the auditor acts as a latent force that encourages this self-awareness. In this way, Rohan's works become a topos of the struggle that characterizes *words* (as well as the self-consciousness that is opened up through *words*), so that the orientation that is characteristic of Okichi's interior dialogue at the opening of *Pagoda*, the orientation of her internal *words* toward a mental system (*langue*) shared by both Okichi and the reader, is destroyed by Nossori. In the way in which the anonymous popular opinion used in the work's opening in order to draw in the reader is relativized through the subsequent development of the work, we find here a precursor of such works as Kosugi Tengai's *Popular Song* and Tayama Katai's *Life*. In "The Whaler," it is through the process of narrating his own past that Hikoemon becomes aware of a demon, a "something that, good or evil, is constantly setting me into motion" (*MBZ* 25:127). Rohan's protagonists are marked by an air of self-contempt, a sense of shame toward their demons, but after the rise of naturalism, these demons would be taken as the inner nature of the human being.

But in literature that claims to provide objective description and that rejects the mode of writing that places anonymous, idle conversation at the opening because it is too similar to premodern *gesaku*, characters can no longer function to relativize the perspective or *words* of the "author." That perspective is positioned in a separate dimension as possessing objectivity vis-à-vis the subjectivity of the various characters, because the functioning of its *words* has been transformed: expunged of all *katagi-* and *gesaku*-like refractions, those *words* now function solely to provide a supposedly true reflection of the object world. To put it more precisely, this is because a consciousness of expression that exalts only this function became dominant. In the mode of writing characteristic of the I-novel, which posits a semantic equivalence between author and narrator, the viewpoint and *words* of the other (characters) have been forced into the position of object for the gaze, deprived of any autonomous existence outside of that gaze. In fact, this is a mode of writing that would take Okichi's thoughts just as they were and make them into the work's entire world. It is buried under a consciousness of expression that prides itself on manifesting the truth of the author (and his everyday world), and it represents a weakening of the self-aware-ness that characterized the earlier ideology-oriented works that visually intended a particular mental system (*langue*). In the new tendency, what ultimately as-sesses the truth value of the object world and objectified author (as mediated by the narrator) was yet another new ideology: the *nature* that was discovered by breaking through the sheath of everyday behavioral ideology.

Rohan's works, which in certain aspects paved the way for this ten-dency, also provide us with an effective method for both relativizing and criti-cizing it.

Chapter Eleven
Discrimination and the Crisis of Seeing: Prejudices of Landscape in Shimazaki Tōson, Masaoka Shiki, and Uchimura Kanzō

TRANSLATED BY ANTONIA SAXON

In this chapter, the political stakes for Kamei's phenomenology come into clearer focus, as do the grounds of his conflicts with such critics as Karatani Kōjin and Hasumi Shigehiko. Kamei here explores the ways in which the new sensibilities reconfigured intersubjective relations – including those between mainstream and marginalized social groups. Kamei links new forms of visual sensibility to social prejudice as he explores a variety of Meiji period works that revolve around characters from Japan's burakumin *outcaste community. Kamei traces the rise of a new visual mode of depicting nature and notes a variety of forms that it took, including that found in Shimazaki Tōson's* Broken Commandment, *where highly visual nature description exists side-by-side with paranoid hallucinatory visions; the actively temporalized haiku of "lived experience" that Masaoka Shiki sought in his advocacy of sketching from nature; and the nature descriptions found in the essays of Uchimura Kanzō, where we find a mode of expression that refuses to separate observed nature from the observing subject: both are one in God to the Christian Kanzō. What emerges in all of these is a dynamic relation between the gaze and its object, one in which both take an active role. When this relationship takes the form of a struggle for domination, what emerges is a paranoid, discriminatory gaze that fears possession at the hands of its demonized object. It was precisely this sense of alienation that Uchimura saw as man's original sin, an understanding that sharply distinguishes his understanding of nature from that of his contemporaries.*

On the evening he is first seized by the impulse to reveal the secret of his identity, Ushimatsu—the hero of Shimazaki Tōson's *Broken Commandment (Hakai,*

1906)—hears the voice of his father calling to him.[1] It is "a voice like that of a father seeking out the soul of his child" (*Commandment*, 64). If we look at the deep structure of the story, we see that at this moment the broken commandment is equated with the deed of patricide itself.

In fact, Ushimatsu conceives the idea of writing a confessional letter to Inoko Rentarō amidst the confusion of this auditory hallucination. In this sense, the appearance of the father's voice just before this impulse arises suggests a premonition of Ushimatsu's budding desire to confess. At any rate, at the very moment that Ushimatsu hears the terrifying voice, his father, working in the pastures in Nishinoiri, is gored to death by a bull.

As the reader is no doubt aware, there is an associative code that links the name of the hero, Ushimatsu (*ushi* means cow), to the bull (*tane-ushi*). The command he has been raised with—"keep our secret always, never forget what it cost your father to raise our family this far" (*Commandment*, 64)—is now just a millstone around his neck; he wants only to live as an ordinary human being. Yet to disobey the commandment is to destroy utterly his father's design for their futures. From a psychoanalytic point of view, hearing the illusory voice is a premonitory act of self-regulation against the breaking of the commandment. In terms of the deep structure of the novel, the bull represents the wish to kill the father, that is, to break the commandment.

The associative link between the bull and the hero with the bovine name can be seen also in the expression used to describe the eyes of the bull. Ushimatsu, after attending his father's funeral, looks at the bull that has been brought to the abattoir for slaughter. The bull has "great eyes, dimmed with a faint purplish mist" that "seemed to glare at the bystanders" (*Commandment*, 111). Tōson seems to have attached special significance to this image: note the "great purple eyes" of the stallion in the story "Straw Sandals" ("Warazōri," 1902) that "glitter" as it runs toward a mare (*MBZ* 69:377). If we search further back, we find the horse in the poem "Yosaku's Horse" ("Yosaku no uma," 1895) that "rages/his

---

1. Ushimatsu's secret is that he is a *burakumin*, a member of Japan's outcaste group (known in 1906 by such discriminatory labels as *eta* or New Commoners). At his father's command, Ushimatsu has concealed his origins and as a result avoided discrimination, allowing him to achieve success as a schoolteacher. Over the course of the novel, Ushimatsu's secret gradually leaks out, and he increasingly desires to reveal his identity, particularly to his mentor, Inoko Rentarō, a *burakumin* political activist who openly campaigns against discrimination. At the novel's climax, following the deaths of both his father and his mentor Rentarō, Ushimatsu confesses his identity to his students and teaching colleagues and subsequently emigrates to Texas. An English translation is available: Shimazaki Tōson, *The Broken Commandment*, trans. Kenneth Strong (Tokyo: University of Tokyo Press, 1974). All quotations from the novel below are adapted from this translation.

eyes/the color of deep purple flames."[2] The image appears again in the poem "Song in the Prime of Life" ("Sōnen no uta," 1901): "the brave horse rages," and "in his eyes, too/hot fire from his heart spews purple" (*TZ*1:246–47). Tōson used this metaphor of an awakening wildness in beasts of burden (the quality symbolized by "purple eyes") to describe the passion of wanting to live freely, to break through worldly conventions and restraints ("commandments"). Of course, the bull that actually does break free of its restraints and kills the father must be punished.

Nonetheless, the bull, who seems "to glare at the bystanders" with impressive composure when brought to the site of his punishment/slaughter, also becomes a metaphor for the image of the father that the son carries within himself. Even a cursory reading of the expressions used in this passage reveals this, so I will omit a detailed explication here. We see therefore that father and son are united in the figure of the bull. What is more, Tōson has the bull killed by precisely those people from whom both father and son would separate themselves—the burakumin.

> Working under him as slaughterers were ten young men, all of them obviously "New Commoners," and poor, brutish specimens at that, marked out by the colour of their skin. "Outcast" might have been branded on each coarse red face. Some stared at the visitors with the glazed, half-wit expression common among the lowest class of New Commoners. Some shrank timidly away after a furtive glance in their direction. . . . (*Commandment*, 109)

The contrast with the slaughterers makes the bull's serene countenance stand out all the more remarkably. Clearly, the mode of expression here, which adheres to Ushimatsu's sensibility, contains within it the deep revulsion with which he in fact regards these men. By transferring the punishment for his own dark patricidal passions onto these "poor, brutish specimens," "the lowest class of New Commoners," Ushimatsu is able to preserve his hopes for the future by adopting a distilled, purified form of personhood. This is the deep structure that underlies *Broken Commandment.*

* * * * *

Exposing the discriminatory consciousness hidden within Ushimatsu, however, is not my primary aim here. We have seen how associative codes link together

---

2. Shimazaki Tōson, *Tōson zenshū* [hereafter abbreviated *TZ*], 17 vols. (Tokyo: Chikuma Shobō, 1966–71), 16:331.

the distinct realms of man and beast in symbolic nodes, as in, for example the image of "purple eyes." I call these kinds of metaphors "hidden metaphors."[3] I believe that Tōson self-consciously extrapolated this method from the aesthetic analysis of the Grotesque he found in Ruskin's *Modern Painters*. However, proving that hypothesis is not my goal here, either. What I would like to examine here is not so much the problem of Tōson's awareness of his own methodology, but the problem of the visual sensibility that produced these half-human, half-beastly images, a visuality that is prior to any conscious choice of methodology.

From a different perspective, I might say that what interests me here is the way that transparent objectivity and opaque hallucination are fused in Tōson's passages of natural description. We already know how Tōson, inspired by passages in which Ruskin discussed the beauty of clouds, set about observing nature. Certainly, passages of natural description that can be regarded as the result of that work are visible throughout *Broken Commandment*. One thing that should draw our attention, however, is that in situations where a panoramic natural vista is portrayed in the mode of visual transparency, the prospect is usually shared with another observer. Even in situations when the two are not gazing out at the scenery together, as in cases when Inoko Rentarō is physically absent, Ushimatsu takes in the scene before him with an interior visual intentionality that aims to link the two men in mutual sympathy. In this sense, natural description in the mode of visual transparency is precisely the actualization of a visual intentionality that creates a space that is open to others.

Tōson apparently began to sketch out the first notes for *Chikuma River Sketches* (*Chikumagawa no suketchi,* 1912) sometime around 1900, but the sort of writing style he was using at that time remains uncertain.[4] As far as we can judge from the *Sketches* we have today, however, it seems clear that at the time he decided to publish the work, Tōson consciously chose a method of description based on the idea of sharing nature with some other person. In fact, he may have initially decided to practice the description of natural scenes precisely as a

3. "Hidden metaphor" (*an 'yu*), a word used frequently in the 1960s and 70s by critics such as Yoshimoto Takaaki, describes a kind of literary trope that appears most commonly in tanka and haiku. Used in contrast to the more common terms *hiyu* (simile) and *in 'yu* (metaphor), *an 'yu* denotes a nonlogical, nonconventional connection in the mind of the writer between one event and another, or one sensation and another.

4. The verbal sketches of natural scenery that Tōson produced under Ruskin's influence in the years leading up to *Broken Commandment* were not published for a decade. When they did appear in print, first as a series of magazine articles and later as the book *Chikuma River Sketches*, they were newly revised by Tōson, and because the original sketches are lost, the extent of this later rewriting is unknown. All quotations from this work below are adapted from the translations that appear in Shimazaki Tōson, *Chikuma River Sketches*, trans. William E. Naff (Honolulu: University of Hawaii Press, 1991).

way of cultivating a sensibility that was more open to others. For example, "I am presently teaching students about your age in a school near the ruins of Komoro castle. Try to imagine how we await the spring in these mountains and just how short it always proves to be. [. . .] Have you ever visited a farm? The front yard here is broad and spacious so that you can go directly around to the back door by passing alongside the kitchen" (*Sketches*, 5–7).

The "you" in this case is the "My dear Yoshimura (or better, Shigeru)" (*Sketches*, 3) mentioned in the preface. As we can see from this and other examples, what enhances the objectivity and transparency of natural description for Tōson is nothing other than the sense of sharing or symbiosis with some other. The idea that the description of natural scenes could restore and elevate one's humanity was a prominent theme in this era, and what I have just described was Tōson's way of putting this motif into practice. When Kunikida Doppo first began to record the results of his attempts at actual observations, he was forced to cast it in the form of conversations with his younger brother back at home in *Letters to my Beloved Brother (Aiteitsūshin*, 1894–95). There, too, circumstances that resemble those of *Chikuma River Sketches* appear to be at work.

However, in *Broken Commandment*, alongside such descriptions of scenes meant to be shared with others, we also find descriptions of nature that cannot be shared with anyone else—descriptions such as occur in the scene where Ushimatsu hears the disembodied voice of his father:

> Again he heard his father's voice. . . . Ushimatsu stopped, peering through the faint starlight: no sign of any human shape, no sound. What was it that was deluding him on this bitter night, when even the prowling dogs were silent?
> *"Ushimatsu! Ushimatsu!"* Again . . . he shuddered, distraught and feverish. It *was* his father's voice, hoarse but still resonant, calling to him from the distant valley of Nishinoiri, beneath the peaks of Eboshi. . . . He looked up. Like the earth, the sky was at rest: voiceless, soundless. The daytime breeze had died, the birds vanished; nothing remained but the cold gleam of the scattered stars and the awe-inspiring spectacle of the Milky Way, trailing like a wisp of smoke across the majestic heavens. As his gaze lingered on the sea of indigo above him, it seemed to dissolve into a vision of the world beyond; he heard it again, a voice like that of a father seeking out the soul of his child, echoing through the cold, starry spaces in search of his son. But what did it mean? Ushimatsu walked about the yard, bewildered.
> (*Commandment*, 63–64)

It is not that no effort is made here toward achieving a transparency of vision. However, the appearance of this supernatural omen of ill-fortune is not simply due to the fact that his surroundings are shrouded in the darkness of night: it is the result of the closing off of any visual intentionality toward others. In fact, just before this event, Ushimatsu has been overwhelmed by bitter self-reproach and suspicious looks because of the tennis match after the Emperor's Birthday festivities in which he was paired with the "eta child" Senta. His obvious emotional instability looks odd even to his friend Ginnosuke, and when Ushimatsu tries to speak of his mysterious experience, Ginnosuke simply dismisses it, laughing it off: "See? Neither of us heard anything—only you. Proof again it's your nerves" (*Commandment*, 65). Hence, it is when Ushimatsu lacks any reciprocal relationship with other people that he first encounters what is, in this sense, "solitary nature"; it reveals its naked face to him, a face that threatens humans with auguries of ill-fortune. We are acquainted with this sort of frightening experience from Doppo's "The Banks of the Sorachigawa" ("Sorachigawa no kishibe," 1902); here, because Ushimatsu too is in a state of mental self-torture, he is forced to undergo the same sort of experience of nature. Ushimatsu's gaze— because it is in the process of losing all grounds for thrusting nature back toward objectivity, toward the status of being simply the object of the gaze—is exposed to a crisis: he is in danger of being bewitched by a transcendental nature.

Ushimatsu's feelings are also, of course, closed off from all others at the scene of the bull's slaughter. When he stares at the "peculiar skin color" and "red faces" of the slaughterhouse men as something like evil omens, it is as if he fears that his own "brand" might somehow appear as well. More than anything, Ushimatsu fears that the men will see through the secret of his "identity." It is precisely because these persons are present that he becomes increasingly uneasy about sharing this scene with others. His efforts elsewhere to achieve a transparency of vision indicate a kind of visual intentionality that attempts to overcome conventional norms of visuality, to go beyond perceptual stereotypes. But when he isolates himself emotionally in the slaughterhouse scene, this aspect of his visual intentionality diminishes, and his sensibility is even more strongly permeated by conventional consciousness, with all its discriminatory stereotypes.

* * * * *

Until now, however, scholars and critics have largely ignored *Broken Commandment*'s structure of expression. Of course, all of them probably understand that, theoretically, description does not simply reflect the outside world. For example, when the depicted surroundings are only roughly outlined, and the embodied visual intentionality that tries to live out this situation finds itself obstructed—on the evening when Ushimatsu hears the voice of his father, for example, or at the slaughterhouse—it is overwhelmed by a passive emotionality. In contrast to this, in visually transparent natural description we can discern a visual intentionality that is actively trying to take in its surroundings in an affinitive way, to engage its situation. The fatal flaw of *Broken Commandment* criticism has been its failure to take into account the question of visual intentionality. This is not only a problem with *Broken Commandment*; there has been an even more egregious misunderstanding of Masaoka Shiki's assertions about, and his practice of, *shasei* (sketching).[5]

In "The Haiku World of 1896" ("Meiji no 29-nen no haikukai," 1897), Shiki takes up recent poetry by Takahama Kyoshi and calls it "time haiku."[6] He cites in particular two poems:

> On a straw hat/stolen from a scarecrow/the rain beats harder

and

> "Oh, if only I lived here," I think/looking at the moon from the ruined temple

and argues that

> These lines of Kyoshi's express a subjective time different from the foregoing [Buson's *The long days pile up/and become the distant past*, and *The heat of the sun/crossing Hageyama/coming home after an outing*]. They do not speak of a past or a future that is the same as the present, nor of things that must necessarily follow from the present as a result of cause and effect, or of things that are likely to happen in everyday life. Rather, they take up entirely disassociated things, things that the reader could hardly imagine given the present situation (I speak of things which are naturally disassociated), and draw (coincidental) distinctive connections between them. Who would see a person with a straw hat in the rain and think that it had belonged to a scarecrow? Yet Kyoshi has here taken up just this kind of peculiar situation. Who would think that a person looking at the moonlight from an old temple might one day become its resident? Yet Kyoshi has taken up this kind of peculiar situation. This is where Kyoshi's poems break away from the old masters.[7]

---

5. Masaoka Shiki (1867–1902) was an influential poet and literary theorist, especially with regards to the genres of tanka and haiku. His advocacy of *shasei* (lit., "to copy from life") involved a rejection of the traditional rhetorical devices, vocabulary, and thematic conventions that marked those genres; they were to be replaced with vivid, pictorial images taken from the imagination's encounters with everyday life.
6. Takahama Kyoshi (1874–1959) and Kawahigashi Hekigotō (1873–1937), who is discussed below, were haiku poets and disciples of Shiki's.
7. Masaoka Shiki, *Shiki zenshū* [hereafter abbreviated *SZ*], 25 vols. (Tokyo: Kōdansha, 1975–78), 4:521.

If we think about the particular objective scene that Kyoshi's haiku portrayed, what he saw before him was merely a person hurrying along the road as a heavy rain beat down on his straw hat, or a person gazing up at the moon from the precincts of a dilapidated temple. The idea that the straw hat had been borrowed from a scarecrow, or that the person was visiting a temple because he wanted to live there, derive from the writer's imagination. But Shiki does not call the poems "imaginative haiku"; he calls them "time haiku."

Why is this? As we can see from expressions like "stolen" and "If only I could live here," the writer stands to some extent in the position of a character who exists within the depicted setting, which is to say that he tries to live out the visual intentionality of such an immanent position. From this, an inevitable (and yet unexpected, even to the author) past in which something was "stolen," or a future in which one might "live here," takes shape. Hence, the phrase "time haiku": it seems that Shiki read out of these poems the creation of a visually intentional time. He places great value on expressions of imaginative "subjective time" and in turn criticizes such haiku as Hekigotō's picturesque

> camellias fall/a red camellia/then a white one

or

> a lantern/on a starry, moonlit night/shines on the well-edge

because he says they "tend toward realistic, life-like description, with almost no poetic technique at all. [. . .] What sort of value these pictures and haiku possess as fine art or as literature remains to be seen" (*SZ* 4:505–6).

In "Trends in the New School of Haiku" ("Haiku shinpa no keikō," 1899), published two years later, Shiki compares Kyoshi's haiku

> Silk-making village/no room in any house/passed through it and went on

with two haiku by Buson,

> I passed a temple where there were peonies—ah, the regret

and

> Firelight in the houses/which refuse me lodging—/snow-covered village:

> Kyoshi is not speaking here of regret for what is past, nor does he depict the scene from the time he was refused lodging. He has already passed through this village, whose houses have been given entirely over to silkworm-raising; he has not yet come to the next village, where he might be able to find a room. *Neither looking back at the past nor forward into the future, it describes the exquisite emotion that arises in the present moment as he is in the process of walk-*

ing. Buson and Taigi, to say nothing of Bashō and Kikaku, were never able to perceive this. (*SZ* 5:171; italics in the original).

Shiki praises here the freshness of the idea of a self that lives out in visual intentionality the process of moving between past and future, that is to say, *the present moment.*

But can we really interpret the expression "Oh, if only I lived here" as meaning "[I] might one day become its resident"? Does "pass*ed* through it and *went* on" really permit Shiki's present-tense reading that "he is in the process of walking"? Doubts of this sort linger, but at least these examples illuminate the way Shiki understood the haiku method he called *shasei.* It becomes even clearer when we read Shiki's proclamation of *shasei* in the essay "Descriptive Prose" ("Jojibun," 1900) that *shasei* consists of living out a specific scene through visual intentionality, or of generating a specific image while living out a visual intentionality.

* * * * *

We have already touched upon the reasons why *shasei* has come to be seen as simply the contemplation of landscape. Karatani Kōjin and Hasumi Shigehiko, transforming that simplification into an *a priori*, have subsequently set forth the grounds for a "system" of landscape. The confusion that arises from this simplification is especially spectacular in Karatani's case, because the "literary history" he relies on is remarkably slipshod. Let us begin by looking at an example or two from his *Origins of Japanese Literature.* After he takes up Doppo's "Those Unforgettable People" ("Wasureenu hitobito," 1898), citing Paul Valéry's *Degas, Danse, Dessin* (1938), and Etō Jun's "The Sources of Realism" ("Riarizumu no genryū," 1971), Karatani opines "that Kunikida Doppo was influenced by [*shasei*] is indisputable."[8] In order to say this sort of thing, one has to have pretty loose definitions of the terms "*shasei*" and "influence." If in fact "literary history" amounted to this, one would certainly want to join Karatani in saying "yet if we stand back from conventional literary historical concepts like 'influence,' it becomes clear without any doubt that what all of the writers of the 1890s encountered was 'landscape'" (*Origins*, 31).

If only Karatani would also have cast a doubtful eye toward the knowledge he derives from "literary history"! He mistakenly uses the word "suffix" to describe the verb *tsukamatsuru* and the auxiliary verb *gozaru.* Moreover, ac-

---

8. Karatani Kōjin, *The Origins of Modern Japanese Literature,* trans. ed. Brett de Bary (Durham: Duke University Press, 1993), 31.

cording to Karatani, Futabatei's *Ukigumo* "despite its use of the [suffix] *da*, [. . .] cannot be considered a *genbun itchi* work" (*Origins*, 51), because it is written using the prose style of *ninjōbon* and Bakin—he says this even as he quotes the opening passage of *Ukigumo*![9] Naturally, as we read on and encounter these sorts of problems, what becomes most apparent is the sloppiness of Karatani's own "epistemological constellation" (*Origins*, 22) and the dubious "origins" of his own literary historical knowledge. What he ought first of all to have done was to objectify and rigorously examine the "origins" of his own *idée fixe* (itself a kind of "system"): that Japanese literary historians have not been able to read modern literature as anything other than the history of the construction of "the modern self." But instead he tries to gloss over his own lack of rigor with the deliberate ambiguity that characterizes his reading of specific expressions.

For example:

> Up until that point, as soon as a shrine came into view, I had interrupted my conversations to pray silently, but now I was able to walk to school chatting happily all the way. I was not distressed that I had been forced to sign the "covenant of believers in Jesus." Through monotheism I had become a new person. I began to eat beans and eggs again. The thought that there was just a single God was so exhilarating that I felt I had understood the whole of Christian doctrine. My body and soul were brought back to health by the spiritual freedom conveyed on me by this new creed, and I intensified my efforts in my studies. Ecstatic over the vitality with which my body had been newly endowed, I wandered through fields and hillsides, as the spirit moved me, marveling at the birds soaring through the skies, and at lilies blooming in the valleys: through nature I attempted to converse with the God of nature.[10]

9. The opening passage of *Ukigumo* is much closer to the *kokkeibon* writing style of such Edo period comic authors as Shikitei Sanba than it is to the prose style of the *yomihon* genre in which Bakin specialized. In the English translation of *Origins*, the original Japanese text's references to Bakin are replaced by references to Sanba.

10. Quoted in *Origins*, 87. This is a translation back from the Japanese translation of Uchimura's original English-language text. The original English passage reads: "While I used to stop my conversation as soon as a temple came in view, for I had to say my prayer to it in my heart, they [Uchimura's friends] observed me to continue in cheer and laughter all through my way to the school. I was not sorry that I was forced to sign the covenant of the 'Believers in Jesus.' Monotheism made me a new man. *I resumed my beans and eggs.* I thought I comprehended the whole of Christianity, so inspiring was the idea of one God. The new spiritual freedom given by the new faith had a healthy influence upon my mind and body. My studies were pursued with more concentration. Rejoicing in the newly-imparted activity of my body, I roamed over fields and mountains, observed the lilies of the valley and birds of the air, and sought to commune through nature with nature's God." Published under the name "A Heathen Convert," in *How I Became A Christian: Out of My Diary* (Tokyo: Keiseisha, 1895), 15.

According to Karatani, this is a passage from *How I Became a Christian,* translated into Japanese by Yamamoto Taijirō and Uchimura *Kanzō*.[11] Karatani seems to have read these reminiscences as if they were a relatively accurate reproduction of Uchimura's experiences during the time he attended Sapporo Agricultural College. Karatani writes,

> I know of no other document which describes the conversion from polytheism to monotheism so dramatically. Through monotheism, for Uchimura, nature became for the very first time "simply nature." Uchimura felt he had attained a freedom of spirit—in fact, spirit itself—through his conversion. Taken out of context, the passage above seems more evocative of Old Testament spirituality than of Christianity. One has the sense, moreover, of a discovery of landscape here. Nature, formerly veiled by diverse prohibitions and significations, becomes "simply nature" when it is seen as the creation of a single God. Yet this kind of nature (or "landscape") exists only by virtue of the existence of the spirit or of an inner world. (*Origins*, 88)

Yet, as we can infer even from the translation, with its passages such as "marveling at the lilies blooming in the valleys, at the birds soaring through the skies," the experiences from the earlier time that Uchimura recalls and records here have been transformed into an imaginary projection directed at readers from Christian nations: they are refracted through expressions characteristic of the Bible. This becomes still clearer when we refer to the original English-language text, with its "lilies of the valley and birds of the air."

Karatani's methodological consistency might perhaps have been preserved if he had grasped this point in particular. Uchimura's autobiography was directed mainly toward American Christians and so of course was written in English. What Karatani calls Uchimura's "discovery of landscape" could only occur under the "system" formed by these two preconditions. What is more, Uchimura says nothing in the passage just quoted, nor in any other place, that could be construed as demonstrating how, as Karatani maintains, nature had been "formerly veiled by diverse prohibitions and significations." Uchimura says nothing more than that the days of his youth were dominated by "heathen superstitions." Although this is not mentioned in the autobiography, Hokkaido in the 1880s was still in an undeveloped, rustic state, and Uchimura received at the Agricultural College a relatively high-level education in the techniques of natural science: observation, testing, and analysis. Furthermore, practical agri-

---

11. Kamei is pointing out a mistake here: the second translator was not Kanzō himself, but rather Uchimura Miyoko. Kamei also points out orthographic errors in Karatani's transcription of the work's Japanese title.

cultural training exposed him to nature as the object of physical labor. In this sense, he had certainly encountered "simple nature." But this experience occurred independently of his conversion to Christianity; in fact, Uchimura agonized over his inability to see in this nature any of the signs of God mentioned in the Bible. When we view the expressions of sympathy with nature found in his autobiography against this sort of experience, the partiality of those expressions, their projected or imaginary quality, becomes apparent.

Even if we could see anywhere in Uchimura's autobiography the articulation of a "landscape," we would have to regard its "origin" as being the "origin" of a certain kind of linguistic expression. It would have to be set within the context of the following sort of remark:

> The philosopher Leibnitz has said: "With the exception of the soul, all we are able to apprehend directly is God. We can know only *indirectly* any exteriority that can be discovered using the tactile senses."
>
> But if that is the case, how are we to distinguish Superstition from Faith? How do we know that a belief that does not depend on reason does not amount to the worship of herrings' heads? What then is the proof that the concept of "God" is not simply a delusion in the minds of superstitious people?
>
> *That belief of which the truth becomes clearer and clearer, I call 'faith,' while that which grows more and more obscure I call 'superstition.'* Truth is that which is in harmony with our own natures, so that when I believe it, there is joy and agreement with all of my being; falsehood is that which destroys the harmony of my self, which cannot but oppress all or part of my happiness. *An ample feeling of contentment is the sign that I have been able to understand the Truth,* and when I am able to grasp the Truth, both my logical faculties and my emotions repeat "Amen," the mountains and the hills let loose their voices and sing before me, and the trees in the fields all clap their hands. *(Record of Redemption,* 1893)[12]

This "Truth" is not the truth of natural science. The Uchimura who wrote this had already cast aside his position as a natural scientist, gone to America, grappled with theology, and returned to Japan. For Uchimura, neither the nature that is objectified in the natural sciences nor the nature that is apprehended by sensibility—in short, nothing belonging to what Leibnitz called "any exteriority that can be discovered using the tactile senses"—could any longer be considered the source of Truth or emotional inspiration. *"The power of nature to move men's*

---

12. Japanese title: *Kyūanroku.* Reprinted in Uchimura Kanzō, *Uchimura Kanzō zenshū* [hereafter abbreviated *UKZ*], 40 vols. (Tokyo: Iwanami Shoten, 1980–84), 2:230–31.

souls is passive, not active. It appears joyful to those who are happy and sad to those who are unhappy. The cherry blossoms on the eastern slope give joy to thousands, yet they can reflect limitless enmity as well. Things are the servants of the spirit; they can never be its master" *(Record of Redemption, UKZ* 2:156).

For Uchimura, the objectification of nature, which in turn led to an objectification of the self—that is, the separation of subject and object—was the original sin. He did not, therefore, employ the mode of expression that characterized most natural description; the literature of the period, which conferred the greatest literary value on aesthetic depictions of the external world, could not for him be considered literature at all. The objectification of nature could only mean the alienation of the self from God, from the state where subject and object were undifferentiated. Any truth or power to inspire deriving from a nature that had lost its Godliness could be no more than indirect and ambiguous. Uchimura worked earnestly to refine his own spirituality. In *How I Became a Christian*, it sounds as if he was from time to time—especially during his stay at Amherst College—vouchsafed moments of great joy, in which his spirituality was transported to a higher place and he felt at one with nature. These were the moments that produced a cognition like that seen in the foregoing passage. Yet Uchimura did not try to express those experiences in his own *words*; he deliberately chose to refract them through the expressions of the Bible, because that was the mode of writing best suited to describing this kind of privileged experience. His "reproduction" of the earlier period he spent at Agricultural College was produced after the fact, made possible by this writing style that he had subsequently acquired. Although he undoubtedly achieved subjecthood by virtue of his being subjected to a monotheistic God, that subject was in no respect one who "discovered landscape."

If we were to call this steady gaze of spirituality "turning one's back on the outside world," or "[the attainment of] interiority," and if we regarded even prose as remote from Rousseau[13] as Uchimura's biblically refracted expressions as being "the discovery of landscape," then it might be possible to agree with Karatani that "when nature is seen as the creation of a single God, it becomes 'simply nature.' Yet this kind of nature (or 'landscape') exists only by virtue of the existence of the spirit or of an inner world." If we define the concept in this way, however, it no longer even remotely fits Doppo, let alone Shiki.

Of course, not every Christian of the time was like Uchimura. Here is a passage from Kozaki Hiromichi's *Why I Believe* (*Shinkō no riyū*, 1889):

---

13. Karatani cites Rousseau's writing as the first historical instance of the discovery of a landscape in prose.

> By their nature, there is a quality of elegance in people that worships the beauty of nature in the regularity and orderliness of all the myriad things in heaven and earth. When an animal sees some rare coloring, it experiences a certain sensation. But the concept of elegance lies elsewhere, invisible to it. The beauty of nature, like the wonder of pictures, music, and poetry are all for animals no more than a gold coin to a cat; they cannot perceive any such sensation at all. Only humans look at the beauty of nature and rejoice, paint pictures of it, compose poetry about it, or set it to music, and in this way they are able to consort with the Deity. That which is regarded as art differs widely depending on the time and place. Yet the existence of such a concept, like the concept of virtue, emerges among human beings in all places and all eras alike. (*MBZ* 88:53)

There is no sign here of a belief that the objectification of nature amounts to alienation from some primordial state blessed by God. Nature is the source of beauty, or it is transcendent beauty itself, and when it is contemplated, the "thought cannot but reach the invisible Eternal Creator" (*MBZ* 88:48). The concept of "art" or "the arts" as a universal—that which the genres of painting, poetry, and music all had in common—came into being through the mediation of this concept equating nature with beauty. Kozaki refers to the perception of color in animals, and mentions the regional and historical differences in concepts of art; he seems to have been aware of Darwin's theories. He uses this scientific knowledge to explain why the concept of art itself was universal to all humanity. In doing so, Kozaki manifests a position often taken by Christian intellectuals of the period, the attempt to portray Christianity as consistent with evolution and theories of progressive historical development.

We can only say that Christianity hastened "the discovery of landscape" if we speak about the thought of Kozaki and others of his ilk. Of course, Uchimura too had studied Darwin. William Smith Clark, who transplanted Christianity to the Sapporo Agricultural College, was a botanist who did not countenance evolutionary theories. Uchimura entered the college shortly after Clark's return to America and was compelled to convert to Christianity in the wake of the deep influence Clark had left behind. But at the same time, he learned about the theory of evolution from the college's foreign teachers of hygiene and microscopy. This was enough to make him agonize deeply over the problem of how the Truth of the Bible and scientific knowledge were to be reconciled; they stood in direct contradiction to one another with regard to the existence of God, two antinomian outlooks. Unlike Kozaki, Uchimura could not pick and choose among scientific teachings in search of a jury-rigged solution. After a violent struggle, Uchimura arrived at what was for his era an epoch-making understanding, one that used the concept of *alienation* to understand nature that had been objectified through acts of contemplation.

Nevertheless, contemporary literature progressed in the direction suggested by Kozaki Hiromichi. During this same period, the Christian educator Iwamoto Yoshiharu asserted in "Literature and Nature" ("Bungaku to shizen," 1889) that "The greatest literature is that which is able to reflect nature just as it is [. . . .] Man's knowledge arises entirely from nature, just as man's virtue is nourished entirely by nature. How could man's beauty alone not also derive from it?" (MBZ 32:25). Although criticized by Mori Ōgai, the idea that truth and beauty were founded in nature was generally accepted by non-Christian intellectuals as well. On top of this, Kikuchi Tairoku's *Rhetoric and Chinese-Style Prose* (*Shūji oyobi kanbun*, 1879), a translation of the entry on "Rhetoric and Belles Lettres" in the Chambers' Encyclopedia, had set off an explosion in interest in rhetoric: if literature was one of the Arts, how was its particular beauty expressed in composition? In addition, the study of geology became popular in the 1870s and 1880s. Writings reminiscent of the old travel narrative genre (*kikōbun*) began to appear, as in Sakuma Shun'ichirō's *The True System of Japanese Geography* (*Nihon chiri shōshū*, 1889): "I recently traveled into the heartland, heading north on the Suido road. . . ." In the midst of this trend, Shiga Shigetaka's *On Japanese Landscape* (*Nihon fūkeiron*, 1894) called for the cultivation of a national spirit (nationality) that drew its inspiration from the beauty of nature. All of these elements were synthesized to form the Meiji genre of travel literature (*kikō bungaku*).[14]

Karatani cites Yanagita Kunio's preface to *Anthology of Travel Writing* (*Kikōbunshū*, 1930):

> In this passage we find Yanagita narrating the "discovery of landscape" in terms of a change in the way *kikōbun* were actually written. Let me suggest that this transformation consisted of the liberation of travel literature from the literary, from the convention of what Yanagita describes as "a string of poems and elegant writing [*bibun*]." Why, in fact, was it that for so many centuries Japanese recognized as landscapes only the famous places celebrated in literature and could be satisfied with "stringing together poems and elegant writing"? It was because this was the "landscape" given to them by their encounter with Chinese literature—the Imperial poetry anthology, the *Kokinshū* (905), provided the basic model. Even Motoori Norinaga did not deviate from tradition on this point. The iconoclast was Masaoka Shiki,

---

14. See chapter twelve for an extended exploration of this genre.

who exclaimed that "Ki no Tsurayuki was a terrible poet and his anthology, the *Kokinshū*, is rubbish!" (Adapted from *Origins*, 52)

Here again, Karatani's reading of the text lacks methodological consistency. If
Yanagita referred to Tsurayuki's *Tosa nikki* as "a string of poems and elegant
writing," then the question to ask first of all would have been about the "origins" of the concept "elegant writing." Yanagita's remarks—"This is the reason
why books describing scenery which have begun to appear in recent years have
so often been dismissed, and scorned as vulgar, by connoisseurs of literature,
and why the efforts of those who wish to bequeath such documents to posterity
have been viewed as the products of futile toil" (quoted in *Origins*, 52)—applied to the travel literature that flourished during the 1880s and 1890s. Surely,
this travel literature was marked by a visual intentionality that sought to break
with the formalistic mannerism that "recognized as landscape only the famous
places celebrated in literature." But it was also a movement that aimed for the
creation of new "poems and elegant writing"; it was a movement deeply interested in the problems of rhetoric and of aesthetic expression. Shiki's many works
of *kikōbun,* starting with "Record of the Hanging Bridge" ("Kakehashi no ki,"
1892), were no exception.

Here, we return to Shiki, who in "Haiku Wastebasket" ("Haikai
hogukago," 1897) writes:

> While the writer appropriates rather than creates raw material, he re-
> fines that material and makes it over according to his own ideal; in
> this respect, we may call the writer a second-order creator. Through
> adorning and refining, the raw material takes on a perfected beauty –
> or again, the material may be destroyed, and even its unique inherent
> beauty may be lost. It all depends on the technical skill of the refiner
> (the writer). [. . .] Creation produced the universe with no conscious
> plan, and there is little of the vulgar in nature. Accordingly, that which
> is vulgar in a work can usually be attributed to human agency or arti-
> ficiality. It is for this reason that works that reflect nature directly
> have little vulgarity. Yet it is easy for the vulgar to attach itself to
> places where adornment is added to writing. This is why, although
> people with great ability are unequaled in their power to adorn a work
> of literature, to add to it everything necessary to bring it to perfec-
> tion, those who are just beginning in this line of study would do bet-
> ter to reflect nature directly. At least they will be able to avoid vul-
> garity. (*MBZ* 53: 211–12)

Yanagita's phrases about "connoisseurs of literature" who "dismissed and scorned
as vulgar" those "books describing scenery which have begun to appear in recent years" probably referred to those who held literary conceptions like Shiki's;

and of course we should remember that Shiki's comments above probably include a self-critical reflection on his own earlier *kikōbun* works.

Shiki's probably took the concept "material" from Herbert Spencer's economics. It was Sōseki who had drawn Shiki's attention to Spencer, it seems. In an 1890 letter to Shiki, Sōseki writes, "This is the way I define my own prose":

> Because prose *is an idea which is expressed by means of words on paper,* I see *idea* as the *Essence* of prose. The way of *arranging the words* is without doubt an *element;* but it is not as important as the *idea,* which is the *essence.* In order to create what in economics is called *wealth,* you need *raw material* and *labor. Labor* does no more than *modify* the *raw material.* If there is no *raw material* to begin with, no matter how skilled the *labor,* there is no use from the start; in the same way, if in the first place you don't have an *idea,* the *words' arrangement* is completely useless.[15] (*SZ* supplemental vol. 1:471)

If my assumption is correct, that which Shiki called "sketching" was a practice aimed at obtaining what Sōseki called "raw material." Refining this raw material, Shiki's "making it over according to one's own ideal," was, perhaps, its elevation to *idea.* According to Shiki, "The scene as it actually exists is like a naturally beautiful woman; she cannot escape having a certain number of flaws, and for this reason, the eyebrows, for example, must be improved and more desirable ones penciled in, and powder and rouge are applied, while figured silk and brocade are draped over her—all in order to perfect her beauty" ("Haiku Wastebasket," *MBZ* 53:211). Sōseki's *idea* corresponds to the term "technique" (*ishō*) as it is used in Shiki's article, "The Haiku World of 1896," which appeared in the same month as "Haiku Wastebasket." Shiki sought the basis of beauty in nature, and thought that nature contained little that was vulgar. It was on this basis that he argued that those "who are just beginning in this line of study would do better to reflect nature directly. At least they will be able to avoid vulgarity." This is an extension of the view of nature held by Kozaki Hiromichi and Iwamoto Yoshiharu (although, in Shiki's case, without the attendant Christian belief); but his assigning of nature to the dimension of "raw material" can be regarded as Shiki's own distinctive contribution. In opposition to nature, he posits "technique," human subjectivity. Shiki never rejects rhetoric; rather, he criticizes as "vulgar" any rhetoric that is not solidly grounded in "technique." We have already described how he designated an embodied visual in-

---

15. In this passage, italicized words appear in English in the original.

tentionality as the basis for poetic "technique." Hekigotō may have created distinct and vivid impressions in such "sketch-like miniatures" ("Haiku World of 1896," *SZ* 4:503) as:

> camellias drop/a red camellia/ then a white one

and

> a lantern/on a starry, moonlit night/shines on the well-edge.

Yet in the end, according to Shiki, his works were flawed haiku, haiku that lacked technique.

* * * * *

However, Shiki's advocacy of *shasei* was not confined to criticism of hackneyed haiku composed with lifeless "technique"; it confronted something much more terrifying. Hasumi Shigehiko may not have had Shiki in mind when he wrote the following, but he seems to have intuited a threat much like the one Shiki encountered.

> But landscape slips right through the net of aesthetic sensibility; it functions instead as a mechanism that carefully organizes the openings in that net's mesh, usurping the gaze's authority to assay aesthetic judgments. What I am saying is that landscape inserts that which had been thought of as sensibility into the system of circulation of "knowledge," alongside imagination and thought, so that it [landscape] continuously functions as an educational apparatus, administering its [the system's] networks of exchange and distribution. This education is none other than the ceaseless activity of articulating being and of domesticating thought, sensibility, and imagination into a system that suits this landscape-as-apparatus. Accordingly, a sensibility that reacts to the landscape with wonder or even boredom is already interpolated into the narrative of beauty incessantly told by this landscape-as-apparatus. Being does not "read" landscape. It is landscape that "reads" being.[16]

This is a passage from Hasumi's "Beyond Landscape." What is unconvincing about Karatani Kōjin's discussion of landscape is not only his lack of basic knowledge of literary history—at the time of writing he had not, apparently, read several of the works to which he refers—but that while he debates "land-

---

16. Hasumi Shigehiko, "Fūkei o koete," in *Hyōsō hihyō sengen* (Tokyo: Chikuma Shobō, 1979), 167–217. This passage appears on 169.

scape," he fails completely to problematize the relationship between gaze, body, and sensibility. In comparison, Hasumi makes no reference to literary history and does not mention works by any other writers—in other words, the "landscape" to which he refers claims no relevance outside his own text—but insofar as he has introduced into the discussion the problematic nature of the gaze, he has arrived at an intellectual conclusion that far surpasses Karatani's.

Let us admit that the gaze possesses, as Hasumi says, a kind of authority. This is because the gaze privileges the seeing person in relation to the seen object. It denigrates the object into something passive, into an object that is subjected to articulation and interpretation. In other words, the gaze creates a structure of discrimination.

However, the *thing* that is objectified in this manner is all the more able, for that very reason, to draw the gaze onto itself, to usurp the gaze and to dominate the consciousness of the gazing person by virtue of its passivity. In short, we can also talk about the authority possessed by the object of the gaze. Precisely by being seen, it becomes able to dominate and control the way it is seen, and it is able to hide those aspects of itself which are not objectified. It was Uchimura Kanzō, as discussed above, who regarded this conflict between the gaze and its object as a tragedy akin to man's original sin.

While Uchimura was mainly concerned with the problem of the intersubjective relationship between persons, he takes up the following passage from the Book of Genesis:

> And when the woman saw that the tree was good for food, and that it was pleasant to the eyes, and a tree to be desired to make one wise, she took of the fruit thereof, and did eat, and gave also unto her husband with her; and he did eat. And the eyes of both were opened, and they knew that they were naked, and they sewed fig leaves together, and made themselves aprons. (Genesis 3:6–7, King James Version)

Uchimura argues that, "the 'tree of knowledge is really the tree of discernment [*bunbetsu*]: when humans eat its fruit they believe they are able of their own accord to discern what is good from what is evil, and that they can now make their way through the world without God" (*Record of Redemption, UKZ* 2:190).

According to this understanding, the authority of the gaze was a privilege that rightly belonged only to God. It was with the awakening to consciousness of humans and their subsequent objectifying of self and other that the conflict between gaze and concealment broke out. Relations between people now took the form of a relationship of alienation. "Thus the history of the human species took an entirely new direction; man had to learn for himself, fight for himself, take responsibility for himself; and the strong were victorious, the weak defeated" (*Record of Redemption*, *UKZ* 2:191). It was this kind of autonomy, which had exacted a particularly cruel toll on modern man, that Uchimura considered the worst of all possible outcomes. His originality lay in his keen awareness of the tragic situation that had led people to become antagonistic with one another, in which human beings became literally their own worst enemies, and in the way he contrived somehow to maintain an autonomous existence in the midst of that catastrophe even as he searched for a way of overcoming it.

Ever since humans had appropriated the gaze that had once been God's special privilege, they formed relationships in which they became *things* (objects) to one another, while any nonhuman object was even further denigrated to the dimension of pure objectness. However, this state was also constantly haunted by a fear that the gaze might be commandeered by its object, the terror that *things* might be looking back. Of course, Uchimura Kanzō was not the only one to have sensed this fear. When Ushimatsu in *Broken Commandment* hears the voice of his father, the object of his gaze seems like something otherworldly, and he is overcome by fear at the prospect of being bewitched by it. Likewise, the terror he feels in the slaughterhouse arises from the possibility that the objects of his discriminatory gaze—the burakumin slaughterhouse men—might at any moment look back at him, destroying the privilege of his gaze and exposing his identity as a burakumin, as the object of social discrimination.

In Masaoka Shiki's writings, this fear is not always so evident. What I mean by this is that vision for him meant living out the world of objects through visual intentionality, venturing into the depths of that object world, touching for himself the thickness of *things*. In the midst of this object world, the privilege of the gaze was relativized. Shiki even took this process of breaking down the privilege of the gaze and made it the plot composition of one of his fictional pieces.

Tamae, the main character of Shiki's unpublished story "*Higan* Lilies" ("Manjushage," ca. 1897), is the eldest son of the Nomura family, "the grandest family in the first ward" (*SZ* 13:297). "He was in the flower of his sixteenth or seventeenth year, was by nature clever and kind, and was in addition a fine scholar" (*SZ* 13:298), yet he is apt to fall into melancholic silence. To escape from his nurse's officious advice, he ventures outside and arrives "behind the small shops outside town; finally he caught his breath; it was as if he had become aware of himself for the first time" (*SZ* 13:300). Amidst nature in the outskirts of the city, he tastes a measure of freedom, but:

> All of a sudden a sound reached his ear, and he stopped and looked around; he had come to Mitsunofuchi. As if he had just thought of something, he began to look for a place to walk where there was no road, between the trees off in that direction, here on this tuft of grass;

finally he veered away from the wood on the embankment and went out into the green of the meadows. When he turned around and looked, he saw a mound rising up in the middle of the fields about fifty feet distant from the embankment and one giant tree, he could not tell how high, that soared into the clouds; underneath them, at the peak of their blossoming, *higan* lilies grew so thickly that there was no space between them. They reflected the light of the sun now setting in the west, as if a red carpet were spread out over the ground. He saw that in the middle of them there sat a young girl; I'll ask her, he said to himself, and taking the raised path between the fields, he made his way around to the little mound and gazed at the back of the young girl. She might have been a beggar; the obi on her dirty, patched kimono had a strip of Chinese crepe attached to it, but was tied around her like a rope, and her hair was bound up crudely in back. Beside her legs, which were straight out in front of her, there was a basket with a few flowers and grasses in it; she was picking lilies, and without any particular care, tying them up with string. (*SZ* 13:301)

This may look like a perfectly ordinary passage of description inserted into the story, but note how the nature depicted by the narrator who is immanent to the depicted setting is then transformed into *a nature that is lived out* by the work's characters: the point of view of the narrator becomes virtually identical with that of the hero. This mode of writing was almost without precedent in 1897; it had only just been invented.

In other words, the nature depicted in fiction up until this had consisted of nothing more than inert landscape descriptions, the lifeless backdrop scenery to the stage on which the characters appeared. Even in Tokutomi Roka's sketches in *Nature and Man* (*Shizen to jinsei,* 1900)—although he produced that period's most original passages of aestheticized landscape description, and although the sketches represented a new variation on the genre of travel writing—the landscape objectified therein was never drawn according to the visually intentional gaze of someone who actually lived it. Even at its best, it was never more than nature depicted just as it was seen, drawn with a colorist's eye for the momentary, instant-by-instant changes in its tints and pigments. This was why Roka was able to use some of those sketches without any alteration in his novel *Nami-ko* (*Hototogisu,* 1898), and why some of the descriptions from *Nami-ko* were written such that they would not look out of place in *Nature and Man*. The characters in the novel who gaze at the landscape are portrayed by the writer as if they themselves were part of it:

It was evening at Ikao, the famous town of hot springs in Jōshū. A lady stood gazing at the beautiful scene revealed through an open screen in the third story of the Chigira Hotel. Her age was eighteen or thereabouts. Her hair was dressed in a tasteful *mage*, and she wore a gray crape gown, relieved by green bows at her breast.

She was of a fair and clear complexion, and though her eyebrows were a little too close together and her cheeks were somewhat thin, she seemed to be as gentle in nature as she was slender and graceful in figure. She was not like the plum-blossom, daring to bloom in the bleak north wind, nor like the cherry-flower, whose petals are blown hither and thither like butterflies in the spring morn. She was, indeed, like the shy daisy dimly discovering itself in the dusk of a summer eve.

In the evening of that spring day the far-away hills of Nikko and Shio, and those on the borders of Echigo, as well as the nearer peaks of Onoko, Komochi, and Akagi, were glorious in the rays of the sinking sun. Even the cawing of crows, flying from a tree just beneath, seemed to be toned with gold, as two fragments of cloud floated out from behind Akagi. The lady at the screen in the third story was watching their movement.[17]

Namiko, the heroine, is portrayed through the same consciousness that characterizes the aestheticized descriptions of scenery in Roka's sketches and other works of elegant prose. While she is supposed to be regarding the same landscape as the immanent narrator, the author completely ignores her own unique way of viewing the landscape. Even in the scene that depicts her walking through the mountains of Ikaho, nature is not depicted as her own lived space. The narrator's gaze and sensibility dominate everything, paying no heed to the individual qualities that distinguish the work's various characters.

In contrast to this, the immanent narrator in Shiki's "*Higan* Lilies" hews closely to the distinct perspective of the hero. As for the standard process that characterizes the rise of such a mode of expression, we can posit the following: the narrator who is immanent to the depicted scene possesses a self-exhibiting tone (the foregrounding of rhetoric, what Jakobson calls the prosodic feature), a tone that—as it repeatedly makes contact with the distinctive sensibility of a particular character—gradually yields to a transcendental synthesis of the two, achieving thereby what Hiromatsu Wataru calls the dimension of the *indefinite person* (man, one; in Japanese: *hito*).[18] This process can also be seen at work in

---

17. Tokutomi Kenjiro [Roka], *Nami-Ko: A Realistic Novel*, trans. Sakae Shioya and E.F. Edgett (Boston: Herbert B. Turner & Co., 1904), 1–2.
18. Hiromatsu Wataru (b. 1933) is a leading philosopher of the postwar era who has published many works dealing with such topics as materialism and phenomenology. Kamei here cites *The Structure of Communal Subjective Existence in the World* (*Sekai no kyōdō-shūkanteki sonzai kōzō*) (Tokyo: Keiso Shobo, 1972). Kamei gives the words in the parenthetical expression in roman letters: the English "man" and the French indefinite pronoun *on*.

Ukigumo, to a certain extent; but at the end of that novel—because the two entities are finally collapsed into a single dimension—the mode of expression contracts to contain only the protagonist Bunzō's subjective world. But in *"Higan* Lilies," the immanent narrator preserves to the end a relationship with the protagonist that is characterized by neither fusion nor separation; this mode of expression, which Noguchi Takeuchi[19] might criticize as ambiguous and duplicitous, makes possible the work's dramatic unfolding.

We can describe this as follows: the gaze of the immanent narrator overlaps with Tamae's sphere of interest. This gives birth to what is literally a privileged gaze and also simultaneously actualizes a way of looking at the objective world that corresponds to Tamae's sensibility. The circumstances that arise here can be easily guessed from the passage quoted above. The young girl whom Tamae discovers is the daughter of a flower-seller. Yet, the narrator is not reduced to a single dimension that is coterminous with Tamae. In the next scene, the girl is portrayed as the daughter of a snake-handler, who is shunned as an outcaste and discriminated against by the people of the village. In this scene, however, the gaze of the narrator never takes up the girl's perspective. The girl remains throughout the object of the gaze, never its subject. In this sense, it is as if the gaze of the narrator here stands in for that of the absent Tamae. Then, when Tamae reappears, certain facts about the girl that were revealed only to the immanent narrator have already become a part of Tamae's consciousness. This can only mean that Tamae's consciousness has already been captured by the object of its gaze, the flower girl.

The two have become lovers. While Tamae waits for the girl on Taishōzuka, he falls asleep and has a strange, bewitching dream, reminiscent of a scene from "The Harlot with the Heart of a Snake" ("Jasei no in") in Ueda Akinari's *Tales of Moonlight and Rain* (*Ugetsu monogatari*, 1768).

> It was rather strange, he thought, but he fell asleep straightaway; perhaps it was the saké. He had been sleeping deeply for a while, he thought, when he became unbearably uncomfortable; two or three golden snakes had appeared and wrapped themselves around his throat, as if to suffocate him, and he woke up yelling. His back was bathed in cold sweat. As he could no longer endure the fright that hung on him, he leapt up; he had fallen asleep on the grass in front of Taishōzuka, and he had had a dream. He thought someone was there,

19. Noguchi Takehiko (b. 1937) is an important contemporary literary critic. Kamei here cites his book, *The Japanese Language in Fiction* (*Shōsetsu no Nihongo*), vol. 13 of *Nihongo no sekai*, 16 vols. (Tokyo: Chūō Kōronsha, 1980–86), which is discussed at greater length in chapter twelve.

and he looked around, but there was no one there, no one coming
toward him out of the gathering dusk of the evening. (*SZ* 13:319)

The structure of this passage is rather complex. The dream of being overtaken
by the golden snakes is a dream within a dream: he dreams he has drunk saké
and fallen asleep, whereupon he dreams of the snakes; the fright of this is so
great that it breaks through both dreams, and he returns to reality on Taishōzuka.
Of course, the golden snakes are a hidden metaphor for the girl (or the relationship between Tamae and the girl), just as the bull, the *ushi,* is a hidden metaphor
for the hero of *Broken Commandment,* Ushimatsu. When he awakes, Tamae has
the strange feeling that someone is looking at him. Along with the fear that
lingers from the dream, he is made to sense omens of ill-fortune in the object of
his privileged gaze: the object seems to be looking back at him. Amidst this
fear, the privileged status of his consciousness, his consciousness of being privileged, collapses.

> Ah, what a strange dream. But I probably dreamt what I was thinking
> about. [. . .] It's a bother, no matter which way you look at it. A hu-
> man being born perfect in every way, without so much as a hair miss-
> ing from her head, ought to be able to mix with anyone she wants to.
> Does that sort of logic exist in this world? Now that the four classes
> are all equal, so long as she is not diseased or a criminal, she is a
> pure, chaste girl, like an angel, and we are wrong to look down on
> her, thinking in our hearts that she is shameful. (*SZ* 13:319)

Here, the positions of the subject who looks and the *thing* that is looked
at are reversed. Tamae is forced by his parents to marry the daughter of a powerful family. On that day, the flower-girl secretly enters his house. When night
falls, the weather suddenly breaks, and in the midst of the storm Tamae hears
the voice of a goblin and sees the girl and the golden snakes. He can no longer
tell whether this is a dream or reality. He loses his mind, and the girl disappears
from the village forever.

The fact that Shiki was trying his hand at this sort of fantastic novel at
precisely the same time he was making the case for *shasei* realism, for sketching from real life, is a key problem for anyone who hopes to understand Shiki's
oeuvre. From my point of view, this novel is of interest precisely because it
harbors within it the methodology of Shiki's *shasei;* it is an excellent example
of how the logic of *shasei* was transformed into a logic of the novel. To put it
another way, an obsessive privileging of visual description leads one, unexpectedly, to a direct encounter with the monstrosity of the *thing* that is alienated and
discriminated (against) through visual objectification. This finally leads not only
to terror but also fascination: the gazing subject falls under the spell of the hu-

man being who is figured within the *thing* via such hidden metaphors as a bull or snake. Tayama Katai, it appears, experienced this bewitching horror too; the details can be had in "The Last of Jūemon" ("Jūemon no saigo," 1902). And the reason Hasumi Shigehiko's "Beyond Landscape" seems somehow incomplete and unfulfilling is that it never takes up this drama that unfolds between the gaze and the *thing*.

Shiki, Tōson, and Katai, while venturing into the territory of that drama, strengthened the visual transparency of natural description as a way of subjugating that horror, that fear. I have already touched on how Tōson practiced visual transparency in the form of a natural description that was opened out to some other viewer. In this sense, the introduction of "*Higan* Lilies," which expresses Tamae's experience in arriving on the outskirts of town as his "for the first time being aware of himself," is quite symbolic. It is true that there is a sort of artlessness about the expression "after a while he came back to himself," but this "self," this "I," is one that stands alone, having escaped the strain of being with others, and it is in this isolated state that it becomes possessed by an evil spirit. Shiki had worked through this crisis in his experimental practice novel ("*Higan* Lilies"), and so for him the effaced "self" objectified in the *shasei* mode of expression had to be as much as possible a "self" or "I" distilled into an indefinite person, into a *one*. This was not a self-exhibiting mode of expression that foregrounded individual preferences and quirks, but one that mobilized the eye of *one* so purified as to lack all apparent individuality, a *one* who projected itself into the object world, thereby illuminating with visual transparency the order of *things*. It is perhaps for this reason that in Shiki's mode of expression, the *words* seem highly transparent.

Yet for Shiki to proceed in this direction, he had to abandon novel writing. When we consider this, another enormous question rears its head. Did the drama between the gaze and its object that we see in "*Higan* Lilies" force Shiki to adopt the novelistic genre, or did the characteristic devices of the novel genre instead lead him to this drama? When we begin to think along these lines, we understand how closely, in an unexpected way, Kōda Rohan's "Encounter With a Skull" and Izumi Kyōka's "The Holy Man of Mt. Kōya" ("Kōya hijiri," 1900) stand to Shiki and Katai.[20] One reason Karatani Kōjin's argument lacks persuasive power lies in his failure to read the subtle differences in the significance of "landscape" between different genres—sketches, memoirs, novels and so on. He writes,

---

20. While Shiki and Katai are closely identified with sketching and realism, Rohan and Kyōka are noted for their fantastic tales, written in non-*genbun itchi* styles.

This passage [in Kunikida Doppo's "Those Unforgettable People"] clearly reveals the link between landscape and an introverted, solitary situation. [. . .] It is only within the "inner man," who appears to be indifferent to his external surroundings, that landscape is discovered. It is perceived by those who do not look "outside." (*Origins*, 25)

Karatani cites only passages that reconstitute nature through the mediation of acts of memory and recollection. Not surprisingly, the result of this arbitrary selection is that he detects the appearance of interiority in descriptions of landscape. He seems not to realize or care that multiple perspectival dimensions can exist within a single expression.

Chapter Twelve
Until the Disciplining of Nature:
Travel Writing at Home and Abroad[1]

TRANSLATED BY MICHAEL BOURDAGHS

In this chapter, Kamei traces through the transformation in the construction of nature that occurred in Meiji literature, especially works of travel writing. He begins by examining works that depict foreign, colonial space in a contemptuous manner: here the gazing subject distances himself from the world he sees and refuses to acknowledge any complicity with it. But this logic breaks down in fiction: in Mori Ōgai's works, we find a new tendency to use scenic descriptions as a means for achieving a new self-awareness. This requires the gazing subject actively to commit himself to the world he sees. Likewise, in the stories of Kunikida Doppo, we see a sense of alienation from the earlier genre of travel writing, one that provides the logic for a new kind of fiction. There, the presence of an auditor breaks through the sense of isolation from the landscape that marked earlier travel writing. This also gives birth to an anxiety over the very possibility of communication, so that Doppo's sensibility harbors a fear of speechlessness and attempts to locate some language that will allow contact, dialogue between the thing that is nature and the self. The privilege of the gazing subject collapses, and nature emerges as something with an independent voice, as something that exceeds the capacity of (and thereby relativizes) the ability of human minds to objectify it as "landscape." Subsequently, fictional works arose that posit contact between traveler and "native" as a kind of violation, one that produces an evil and vengeful nature. In all of these forms,

---

1. The Japanese title of the chapter is "Shizen ga kanri sareru made," lit., "Until nature is managed." The word *kanri* ("management," also translated as "disciplined" below) was widely used in the 1970s and 1980s, especially in the phrase "managed society" (*kanri shakai*), akin to the Frankfort School's notion of "administered society," to critique the imposition of bureaucratic administration on all levels of social life in modern Japan.

> *an autonomous nature emerged, and yet with the rise of the natural-*
> *ism of Tayama Katai and others, nature lost its autonomous status: it*
> *became managed, something with no existence beyond its objectifi-*
> *cation by the human subject. It is here that Kamei locates the crisis*
> *of modern Japanese literature, one that persists to the present day.*

The traveler does not merely pass through as an observer, but in one form or another *commits* himself in relation to some problem involving the "natives." At this moment, he commits a violation of some essential taboo. Here we find one basic pattern of the modern novel. We might call it the crisis of landscape, the birth of nature.

The modern concept of travel unfolded through a logic that equated transportation and communication technologies with civilization and enlightenment. The awareness that transportation played an important role in economic and cultural development achieved theoretical explication in such works as Taguchi Ukichi's *A Short History of Japanese Development* (*Nihon kaika shōshi*, 1877–82),[2] but even prior to this, we can cite such incidents as the lifting of the regulations on domestic travel and, even earlier, the beginning of travel to the West.[3] The first literary work to clearly reflect this ideology is Kanagaki Robun and Fusō Kan's *By Shank's Mare Through the West* (*Seiyō dōchū hizakurige*, 1870–76), where we find the following passage:[4]

> For Yajirō and Kitahachi, too, I will speak about the transformation
> of all the nations of the world brought about by the progress of civi-
> lization. [. . .] In the beginning, there were those peoples who knew
> not how to cook food, nor how to weave clothing, nor how to erect

2. Taguchi Ukichi (1855–1905) was an important economist in Meiji Japan and one of the first advocates in Japan of liberal economic theory.

3. During the Edo period, despite the existence of a well-developed network of highways such as the Tōkaidō road linking Edo and Kyoto, travel was highly regulated: a series of barriers were manned by armed guards, and only travelers carrying proper documents were allowed to pass through. In most cases, travel by women was completely banned. The system began to break down in the last decades of the period, and these regulations were officially lifted in 1871. Sporadic travel to the West began in the last decades of the Edo period, including the 1860 Embassy to the United States.

4. *Shank's Mare Through the West* was written as a sequel to one of the most popular *gesaku* fiction works of the late Edo period, *Shank's Mare* (*Tōkai dōchū hizakurige*, 1802–22) by Jippensha Ikku (1765–1831). Ikku's comic narrative, which traces the travels of its protagonists along the Tōkaidō and other highways, continued to be widely read in Meiji, and even today the names of its two protagonists, usually abbreviated to Yaji and Kita, remain household words in Japan. An English translation by Thomas Satchell is available (*Shank's Mare* [Rutland, VT: Charles E. Tuttle Co., 1960]). The Yaji and Kita of *Through the West* are supposed to be grandsons of the original duo.

shelters and mark boundaries, who wandered hither and thither hunting animals for food, who had no such thing as money, who lived in
the wilds together with fowl and beast, who did not know how to
conduct agriculture. The people of that time are called uncivilized,
or, in the Western term, "semibarbarian." (*MBZ* 1:108)

The logic employed here is borrowed from *A Brief Geography* (*Yochishi
ryaku*, 1870–75), edited by Uchida Masao.[5] In this work, Uchida classifies the
"degree of civilization" of various peoples into four categories ("savage,"
"semibarbarian," "half-civilized," and "enlightened") and from this perspective
provides detailed introductions to the natural environment, folk customs, and
governmental structures found on each continent. At the time, it was one of the
more reliable texts available in the field of human geography. The authors of
Shank's Mare Through the West combine the categories "savage" and
"semibarbarian" in the above-quoted explanation, which is spoken by one of
the work's characters. Here, the discriminatory *sense* that was latent in the com-
parisons between urban Edo and the rural countryside in Jippensha Ikku's *Shank's
Mare* is legitimized through the logic of civilization and enlightenment and then
expanded and rendered manifest as a discriminatory *view* of other Asian nations. In *Shank's Mare Through the West* a commitment to equate the West with
Enlightenment is legitimated along the lines suggested by Uchida, and for this
reason the characters Yajirō and Kitahachi embrace no awareness of having committed any wrongs as they scornfully trample over "native" customs. Moreover,
this scornful gaze is also turned toward the interior of Japan, as in the following
passage:

Even today, these sorts of customs remain in such places as Arabia,
Siberia, and the Tartar. Yet within our own imperial land, too, there
are not many places like the three great cities [Kyoto, Osaka, and
Tokyo], and if you go to remote areas you find places where it is hard
to believe that you are in the world of humans. (*MBZ* 1:109)

These passages are of course exaggerated in order to provide a comic,
gesaku-like effect, but the way in which the discovery of landscape harbored
social prejudice is also clear from other expressions, such as the following passage from Narushima Ryūhoku's *Diary of a Journey to the West* (*Kōsei nichijō*,

---

5. Uchida Masao (1838–76) was an intellectual involved in the early Meiji Civilization and Enlightenment movement, alongside such figures as Fukuzawa Yukichi (1835–1901) and Katō
   Hiroyuki (1836–1916). His *Brief Geography*, a summary of Western geography textbooks, is
   considered one of the classic texts of the movement.

1881–84). Because I want to compare this to Mori Ōgai's *kikōbun* travel narratives, I will quote it at length:

> 29th: Rain. At 11:00, spotted in the distance off to the right a single line of blue: the cape of Malacca. It alternated rapidly between rain and clear skies today, and around 2:00 spotted to the left a lighthouse atop a small island; sticking out in a straight line behind it is Sumatra. In the straits where it faces Malacca lies the Port of Singapore.
>
>> Malacca to the south, Sumatra to the north,
>> The serpentine lay of the land, two snakes slither,
>> Slither through the ocean, but never meet,
>> Where the two heads face off, myriad sails flutter.[6]
>
> At 6:00, we reached the port. This port, located 1.17° above the equator, is called New Port. There are not many houses, but many coal depots—it was built to serve as a port of call for mailboats. The landscape around us as we entered the port was exceedingly beautiful. Mailboats are able to lay anchor right next to the shore, which makes landing very easy. The children from the port, all of them naked, ride out in small melon-shaped boats, selling stationery supplies, and when passengers throw coins into the water, they dive under the water to grab them; floating in the water, they look like tadpoles. The natives all have black faces and go barefoot; they wrap themselves in a saffron cloth, leaving half of their body exposed, like the pictures of Arhat saints. Those among them who appear to own a little property all seem to be followers of Islam and wear bucket-like caps on their heads, while women and children go about barefoot and with their shoulders exposed, and some of them drill holes and wear gold rings in their noses, a sight that is exceedingly strange. [. . .]
>
> October 1 (Fri.): Woke early and together with everyone again headed for the market in the old port city. The road we traveled went past beautiful plants and flowers, and as for geological features, the whole area consisted of a red soil. In the houses along the road, natives and Chinese people live mixed together; in particular there are many immigrants from around the Minguang River. At an inn named the New Renkō, we ate noodles with chicken and drank rice wine. In the front of the shop there are many Cōchin trays lined with bonsai plants. A sign reads, "Look with your eyes, but do not touch with your hands: those who know principle will understand." [. . .] Natives came to the mouth of the port. Not a few species of rare and unusual animals, parrots and long-tailed monkeys and the like, were on sale, and the prices did not seem to be very high.
>
>> A number of savages gather in the port,
>> Chattering away as they lay out local products,

6. These lines (and those that appear below at the end of this quotation) are written in 4–3 meter as *kanshi*, poems written in *kanbun*, a Japanified form of Chinese.

Woolly hair, black faces, their legs all red,
I laugh: the monkey-seller looks like a monkey (*MBZ* 4:119)

As one would expect, the manner of grasping the scenery here displays a certain literary talent. The observation here is more detailed and marked by a stronger sense of aesthetic contemplation than that found, for example, in the description of the same place in Nakai Ōshū's *Travels in the West: New Narrative of a Sea Voyage* (*Seiyō kikō: kōkai shinsetsu*, 1870). The difference is probably due to a weakening in the sense of political urgency by the time of Narushima's visit. (Nakai was a samurai from the feudal domain of Kagoshima; after leaving the service of his domain, he traveled secretly to England in 1866 with the backing of Gotō Shōjirō of the Tosa domain. He returned to Japan the following year, and *Travels in the West* is a record of his experiences abroad). Nonetheless, the flip side of Narushima's literary flair is the same sort of arrogant contempt that we found in the depiction of Aden in *Shank's Mare Through the West*—for example, "I laugh: the monkey-seller looks like a monkey."

In many ways, a work that we introduced in the last chapter, Sakuma Shunichirō's human geography textbook, *The True System of Japanese Geography* (*Nihon chiri shōshū*, 1889), could be called a Japanese version of *A Brief Geography*. Along with accounts describing the discovery of landscape typical of *kikōbun* travel narratives (e.g., "I recently traveled through the whole of our nation. [. . .] As I left the Musashino region and entered the Kai region, I was struck by the unparalleled excellence of the mountain scenery"), it also introduces the local customs of each region in Japan. Although the perspective here does not display overt prejudice, in fact this apparently unbiased mode of description harbors a latent discrimination in the way it repeatedly emphasizes certain supposedly unenlightened customs. As I will touch on again later, it was Kunikida Doppo who felt alienated from this *kikōbun* standpoint, prompting him to leave that genre and to move instead in the direction of the novel.

Let us return to Uchida's *Brief Geography* to examine what it describes as the driving force behind the movement from barbarity to enlightenment. It is clear even from the reflection of the work found in *Shank's Mare Through the West* that it located this in the system of land ownership, particularly the system of ownership for agricultural land, under which people "erect shelters and mark boundaries."

> Semibarbarians, when compared with the previously discussed group [savages], are somewhat advanced in their knowledge, and in them we see the existence of private property. [. . .] The first type among them are called nomads. [. . .] The second type are partially nomadic and partially agricultural, and among its numbers are some that es-

tablish villages and live in a fixed place for a year, sometimes even
two or three years. [. . .] The third type engages in agriculture and
herds livestock, or, in some cases, in fishing and hunting. [. . .] As
village size grows larger, some emerge that could be called states,
and among these are some in which *laws* exist and people submit to
the guarantees of their chief.

That this way of thinking was an extremely widespread ideology at the
time is also confirmed by Yano Ryūkei's *Tale of the Floating Castle* (*Ukishiro
monogatari*, 1890). This work is marked by a grand plot on a scale rarely seen
in Japanese literature: it narrates the tale of an adventurer who not only re-
nounces his Japanese citizenship and attempts to establish an ideal republic in a
new land, but also attempts to liberate the nations of Southeast Asia from colonization at the hands of the Western powers. Even this work, however, includes
passages that tend to legitimate colonization. The hero plans first to seize a
deserted island in the South Seas, which he will name Kaiō Island—Ruler-of-
the-Ocean Island—and then:

> After Kaiō Island, we will proceed to take Madagascar. [. . .] Let us
> discuss the barbaric, unenlightened nature of this nation. . . . [. . .]
> From that position [Madagascar] we will extend our reach to capture
> the neighboring region of the African interior. [. . .] But in the area
> from its midpoint of 20° to the equator, there lie more than three
> million square miles of territory (several dozen times the size of the
> territory of Japan) that have yet to be organized. (*MBZ* 15:90)

The justifications offered for this interventionism is that these lands are barbaric and unenlightened and that they accordingly lack any stable organization
(a governmental system established on the basis of land ownership). We find an
example of the same thinking applied to the situation within Japan in an English-language report that William Clark, the first head of the Sapporo Agricultural College, submitted to the head of the Hokkaido Colonization Office:

> Agriculture is the surest foundation of national prosperity. It feeds
> the people, converts the elements into property, and furnishes most
> of the material for manufactures, transportation and trade. The busi-
> ness of country can be most profitably and earnestly done by resident
> citizens who are intelligently and earnestly devoted to its welfare,
> and they alone can be relied on for its defense in time of foreign
> invasion. As soon as practicable, therefore, the migratory fishermen
> of Hokkaido should be converted into permanent settlers. (*First An-
> nual Report of Sapporo Agricultural College*, 1877)

In this, we clearly see a negative evaluation of nomadic hunters and fishermen
made from the perspective of the State, which acknowledged only agriculture

as a legitimate land ownership system. Clark understood the purpose of the Sapporo Agricultural College to be the cultivation of officials who, as the leadership core of such a land ownership system, would devote their intelligence and energy to fostering national prosperity. The Christianity that he brought with him aimed to convert students into this sort of person, starting from their interiority.

Uchimura Kanzō's autobiographical reminiscences, which I referred to in the preceding chapter and which Karatani Kōjin discusses in his *Origins of Modern Japanese Literature*, are written under a consciousness that views the folk beliefs he held prior to his forced conversion to Christianity as barbaric superstitions, both in spirit and flesh. To put it another way, Uchimura writes a sort of *kikōbun* travel narrative in the sense that it treats the problems of man and nature in Hokkaido in an abstract and distanced manner, utterly ignoring the incursion of the new agricultural land ownership system and his own complicity with it.

> Rejoicing in the newly-imparted activity of my body I roamed over
> fields and mountains, observed the lilies of the valley and birds of
> the air, and sought to commune through nature with nature's God.[7]

We might even go so far as to say that to "observe" in this condition of spiritual and physical exaltation, nay, that this exaltation in and of itself can only be realized on the basis of a fundamental abstraction, a repressing of the connection between the observing self and the object of its gaze.

Uchimura, already having committed himself to Western Enlightenment, has no consciousness of having committed any transgression against the "natives." We do, however, detect from time to time in his writing a nostalgic longing for the stoic calm of *heretical* nations, a longing that arises perhaps out of his latent sense of guilt.

Virtually the sole exception to this pattern in this period comes in Shiga Shigetaka's *Incidents in the South Seas* (*Nanyō jiji*, 1887),[8] which displays a dawning awareness of the dark side of civilization and enlightenment, gained through contact with the "natives" of Micronesia who were being subjected to violent colonial subjugation at the hands of the Western powers. It evoked what

---

7. Uchimura Kanzō, published under the name "A Heathen Convert," *How I Became A Christian: Out of My Diary* (Tokyo: Keiseisha, 1895), 15.
8. Shiga Shigetaka (1863–1927), a graduate of Sapporo Agricultural College and a member of the nationalist Seikyōsha school that dominated Japanese intellectual life in the 1890s, was a geographer. His best-known work is *Japanese Landscapes* (*Nihon fūkei ron*, 1894), discussed below.

we might call the problem of the Third World of that era, a counterforce to the eurocentric worldview. Likewise, in contrast to the majority of travel narratives, where interest was focused on the "exterior" that lay outside the author's sphere of daily life, Shiga's *Japanese Landscapes* (*Nihon fūkei ron*, 1894) was written in a form that switched the direction of the gaze toward the "interior"— Japan. But because Shiga's critique of the dark side of civilization and enlightenment was not sufficiently rigorous, even his theory of "landscape" largely abstracts away the concrete problems facing "natives" and shows a tendency to lapse into purely aesthetic travel narrative.

* * * * *

I have spent a number of pages here reconfirming what is in fact a matter of common knowledge. My purpose in adopting this sort of macroscopic approach was to enable an explication of the special characteristics of "nature" as it appears in modern literature. Nonetheless, having said that, I have no desire to produce yet another barren discussion of authorial views of nature, described through such ambiguous concepts as "external nature" and "internal nature." I want to reject that sort of argument and instead explore how the landscape discovered by the gaze of travelers, as described above, altered the very structure of the novel, and also, from the opposite perspective, how nature was transformed within the structure of the novel and how this in turn has influenced our own sensibility.

For example, Ōta Toyotarō, the protagonist of Mori Ōgai's "Maihime" ("The Dancing Girl," 1890) was once a writer of travel narratives.

> It is now five years since the hopes I cherished for so long were fulfilled and I received orders to go to Europe. When I arrived here in the port of Saigon, I was struck by the strangeness of everything I saw and heard. I wonder how many thousands of words I wrote every day as I jotted down random thoughts in my travel diary. It was published in a newspaper at the time and was highly praised. . . .[9]

This passage and others like it have hitherto received little attention, but when read through the approach I am pursuing here, they take on new meaning. We find here a sense of self-awareness, one that exceeds the possibilities of the travel narrative genre and leads to the choice of the novelistic genre of a private

---

9. Mori Ōgai, "Maihime," trans. Richard Bowring, *Monumenta Nipponica* 30:2 (Summer 1975): 167–82. This passage appears on 167.

memorandum, an I-I sort of communication that ultimately produces an internal objectification of the self.[10]

Of course, Toyotarō's travel writings are not actually quoted in the work, but we are not entirely without the means to infer their nature.

> 11th [of September, 1884]. Early morning. The boat passes through the straits between Malacca and Sumatra. Mountain ranges intermittently wind in serpentine fashion from north to south. The waves are calm, like floor mats. A poem:
>
> > Last night, winds brought fierce strife
> > This morning, the winds stop, bringing smiles to faces anew
> > Human emotions, how is this sea different from them?
> > One day with furrowed brows, one day with smooth.
>
> 8:00 a.m. We reach Singapore, the so-called New Port. The boat docks in the harbor. The harbor resembles Saigon. Along the coast, there are many sooty warehouses. Young children paddle up in boats and beg us to throw coins in the water. They dive in and pick them up, missing not one in a hundred. Their boats are narrow and small and resemble hollowed-out melons. It is recorded in the *Miscellany of Reinan*[11] that 'the boat-dwelling Tan people can go into the water without drowning. They always swim to retrieve things left in the water for the benefit of visitors.' These too belong to this type.
>
> 11:00 a.m. We hire a carriage and see a number of temples and gardens. On the road, the soil color is red, similar to that in Saigon. There are many Chinese people who open stores and sell food or pull rickshaws to make a living. The natives have a dusky yellow color to their bodies. Around their shoulders and waist they wrap a red and white cloth. The women wear gold rings in their noses, and all go barefoot. Those who are Muslims wear bucket-shaped caps. There are ox-carts. The oxen's shoulder-peaks stick out like camel humps. There are abundant coconut trees and sugarcane planted in the gardens. At the Chinese temple, the door plaque reads Kanshu Kaikan. There are some unremarkable British and French chapels. We visited some gardens. People bind the bonsai to create dolls, like our chrysanthemum dolls. We lodge at the Hotel Europe. It is of much lower quality than the Hotel Hong Kong. We returned to our ship at 3:00 in the afternoon. [. . .] After dinner, we leisurely approached the harbor. There are numerous islands scattered throughout the harbor, and also many ships and boats as well. The ships and boats are coming and

10. See the discussion of "I-I communication" or "autocommunication" in Yuri M. Lotman, *Universe of the Mind*, trans. Ann Shukman (London: I.B. Tauris, 1990), esp. 20–35. Kamei discusses this concept at greater length in chapters nine and ten.

11. *Reinan zakki* (*Lingnan zaji*) is a miscellany record of foreign customs written by the Chinese scholar-official Wu Zhenfang (active in the late 1600s) and first published in 1796.

going among the islands. This is the island of Malacca. The British
opened the harbor in order to obtain a stranglehold on two oceans,
the Sea of China and the Indian Ocean. Of course, the magnificent
setting is beyond description. A poem:

> It is said that the savages' smoke hides the water-village
> But in the harbor now I see a thousand boats
> The British have the Midas touch
> The hard iron now suddenly glitters.

Another poem:

> In the dusk, I leave the boat, stand in the shadows of trees
> Through the forest I hear a temple bell,
> Children with skin as black as lacquer
> Chatter in their savage tongue and sell colorful eggs.

Today I sent a letter to home. The temperature is 85° Fahrenheit.
(*MBZ* 27:347)

This is the passage describing Singapore from Ōgai's "Diary of a Journey to the West" ("Kōsai nikki," written 1884, published 1889), written in
kanbun. Of course, for the purpose of comparison, I have selected the description of the same place that we saw depicted in Ryūhoku's *Diary of a Journey to
the West*, yet we are still given pause by the striking resemblance between these
two passages: it is as if they had been written in mutual consultation. We receive the same impression from the corresponding passage in Nakai Ōshū's *Travels in the West: New Narrative of a Sea Voyage*. Of course, this is partially due
to the fact that these travelers were all taken to similar places, but this extraor-
dinary resemblance also enables us to make more general inferences about the
kind of travel narratives that were being produced in this period.

When we examine these passages closely, however, we also find in Ōgai's
travel narrative a distinguishing characteristic: it uses the spectacle before the
eye as a means for objectifying that which constrains the self, the limits of the
self. By means of this spectacle ("But in the harbor now I see a thousand boats")
a preconceived notion ("It is said that the savages' smoke hides the water-vil-
lage") is objectified for him. When Ryūhoku calls the children who dove into
the water to pick up coins "tadpoles" and points out the "natives" to explain that
they were like "Arhat saints," he is mainly concerned with transmitting information to the reader. We do not see a tendency there to select *words* that adhere
to his own feelings. While this sort of visual intentionality is not entirely lacking in Ōgai, it is clear, at least insofar as the *kanshi* poems by the two writers are
concerned, that whereas Ryūhoku molds his poems with an aim toward producing a clear impression of the external world, Ōgai seems determined to weave
his own mode of being into his expressions. Even when he describes the "natives" selling things, he first objectifies his own position (situation): "In the
dusk, I leave the boat, stand in the shadows of trees." Then, together with the

reverberations of a "temple bell" heard "through the forest," he hears them "chatter in their savage tongue." In this manner, Ōgai's description conveys the gazing traveler's loneliness. When we look at their respective biographies, we might conclude that Ryūhoku's feeling of ennui was greater, and it may be for precisely that reason that he abandoned any attempt to depict interiority and instead clung to impressions of the external world. It is when adherence to the external world reaches an extreme that a distanced, sardonic observation—"I laugh: the money-seller looks like a monkey"—is born, and accordingly the "chattering" that he hears can only reverberate harshly, as a kind of "loud howling." In this sense, we can say that while Ryūhoku viewed things with a dry eye, the echoes of a melancholic tone seem to color the "chatter in their savage tongue" that Ōgai heard.[12] This tendency is not limited to this single passage; in nearly all of Ōgai's travel narratives, the spectacle before his eyes is depicted in a manner that includes a growing awareness of that which constrains the self. For example,

> 26th. We reach the port of Aden. [. . .]
> A poem:
>> Ten thousand leagues, the boat crosses wild waves,
>> These tears stain my traveler's robes,
>> Bare mountains, red plains, no green grass,
>> Ah, to have scenery like my hometown!
> Another:
>> Who could look around at others and smile?
>> I am surprised: yellow dirt floats even on the waves.
>> We are not river willows, but how can we bear this?
>> The red sun bakes the mountain, boils the sea. (*MBZ* 27: 349)

In fact, however, we do not find the discovery of a particularly new kind of landscape in Ōgai's travel diaries. But if we speak of the Ōgai who wrote "Maihime," he seems at that time to have felt that he could not yet again present his travels to the public. We can even speculate that this decision to abandon the travel narrative genre was projected onto "Maihime" in the form of Toyotarō's awareness of the impossibility of writing in that genre. Of course, it is not my intention to collapse Ōgai and Toyotarō together. What I want to stress, based on the sort of connections I have been drawing here, is that this Toyotarō, having rejected the travel narrative, goes on to choose the form of a confes-

---

12. The characters translated here as "chatter" used by both Ryūhyoku and Ōgai (*shūshū*) can refer both to the chatter of birds, insects, or monkey and to the sound of someone crying out of sadness; hence, it is similar to the English noun "cry."

sional record. A logic of the novel arises out of this rejection of the travel narrative genre.

> At first this pain was a mere wisp of cloud that brushed against my heart, hiding the mountain scenery of Switzerland, dulling my interest in Italy's ruins [. . . .] If my remorse were of a different nature, I could perhaps soothe my feelings by expressing them in poetry. But it is so deeply engraved upon my heart [. . . .] I think I will try to record the outline of my story. ("Maihime," 151–52)

Here, we find "remorse," the "heart," detected as being that which obstructs his interest in the landscape, and an awareness that a confessional record is the necessary and inevitable genre for transcribing what is in this "heart." Note that this mode of writing represents an expansion of the aspect that already existed in Ōgai's earlier travel narratives, a further development of his method of using the object before his eyes as a means for objectifying the limitations of the self. Rather than describe in detail the objects that appear before his eyes, Toyotarō uses them as a means for turning a doubting eye on the internal constraints—his mode of life as a "mere passive, mechanical being," forced to be "a walking dictionary" and "an incarnation of the law" ("Maihime," 153)—that were rendered manifest via those external objects. He then describes the process by which those constraints (i.e., the self) collapse, thereby bestowing a properly novelistic structure onto this confessional record. In this sense, "Maihime" is a novel structured around the critical gesture of rejecting the contemporary travel narrative genre.

In it, the great boulevards of Berlin function as symbols of the West, of civilization and enlightenment. Toyotarō escapes from them into a dark alleyway.

> One evening I sauntered through the Tiergarten and then walked down Unter den Linden. On the way back to my lodgings in Monbijoustrasse, I came in front of the old church in Klosterstrasse. How many times, I wonder, had I passed through that sea of lights, entered this gloomy passage, and stood enraptured, gazing at the three-hundred-year-old church that lay set back from the road. Opposite it stood some houses with the wash hanging out to dry on poles on the roof, and a bar where an old Hebrew with long whiskers was standing idly by the door; there was also a tenement house with one flight of steps running directly to the upper rooms and another leading down to the home of a blacksmith who lived in the cellar. ("Maihime," 170)

If the above expression was intended to reproduce the landscape in order to realize all the more the sense of being "enraptured," he would have depicted the appearance of the old church in much greater detail. But instead, he chooses to focus on reproducing his own position (situation). His sense of being "enraptured" comes from entering into, *committing* himself to the domain of the "natives" who have been left behind in Berlin's rise as a glittering international city. It is through this sort of impulsive obsession, of which he is still barely aware, that the "three-hundred-year-old church" attracts his eye. He then *commits* himself to the life of the girl he encounters in front of the church and finally ends up *committing* a grave violation of taboo, a violation that creates new constraints on his position.

In this way, the *écriture* of a confessional record, an I-I system of communication that occurs within Toyotarō, makes possible a new mode of expression. This mode depicts the external world through a visual intentionality that aims mainly to express the self's own obsession. To put it more precisely, the scene above does not depict the landscape as seen by Toyotarō when he was in Berlin; rather, it depicts a landscape that includes as part of itself the "enraptured" Toyotarō that existed at that time, a landscape that becomes available to observation only at a later time, as an object of recollection (onboard the ship in Saigon harbor).

* * * * *

Kunikida Doppo was another writer who created a structure for the novel out of this motif of becoming alienated from the *kikōbun* travel narrative genre and its characteristic form of landscape. .

> A little beyond the Tama river at Futago there is the post town of Mizonokuchi, in the middle of which stands the Kameya inn. It was right at the beginning of March. The sky was overcast and a strong North wind was blowing, making the place seem even colder and more forlorn than usual – it was a gloomy enough place at the best of times. The snow which had fallen the previous day still lay on the ground and drops of rain, dancing in the wind, fell from the eaves on the southern side of the inn's uneven thatched roof. There were even cold ripples in the muddy water trapped in the footprints made by straw sandals on the road. It was dusk, and most of the shops had not long put up their shutters, but for all that it was very quiet in the darkened town. Being an inn, there was still a light shining brightly through the door of Kameya's, but there seemed to be no guests that night and it was quiet inside. In fact the only sound was the occasional tapping of a pipe on the edge of the brazier.[13]

---

13. Adapted from "Those Unforgettable People," 36–46 in Kunikida Doppo, *River Mist and Other Stories*, trans. David Chibbet (Tokyo: Kodansha International, 1982). This passage appears on 36–37.

This is the opening passage from "Those Unforgettable People" ("Wasureenu hitobito," 1898). The image of a deserted village may have been triggered by eighteenth-century British literature, but in such details as the attention paid to "footprints made by straw sandals" we find a mode of expression deriving from real lived experience, one that could not have been born in the absence of some individual's unique obsession. At the time, this mode of writing was exceptional: it places at the beginning of the work the "native" world, the spectacle of its desolate early spring that pre-exists the arrival of the traveler.

Latent in this passage is an unidentifiable, unnamable speaking subject, what I have called the non-person narrator. But now let us rewrite this scene, replacing this speaking subject with Ōtsu, the protagonist, who makes his appearance shortly after this passage. With only a few minor changes—the addition of "One day I went . . ." at the outset and a few other alterations in wording and aspect—this passage could be woven into the embedded "Unforgettable People" story that Ōtsu subsequently narrates to Akiyama. That is to say, the work employs a particular device: it opens with an expression that foreshadows its conclusion, where the Kameya innkeeper becomes one of Ōtsu's "unforgettable people." The author acknowledges this device in the work's concluding passage:

> Two years passed. Ōtsu was living in a part of Tōhoku. [. . .] One rainy evening in the same season of the year as when he had stayed in Mizonokuchi, Ōtsu was sitting alone at a table, deep in thought. He had in front of him the manuscript "Those Unforgettable People" which he had shown to Akiyama those two years ago. The latest entry was under the heading "The Kameya innkeeper."
> Of Akiyama there was no mention. (46)

But what makes these people "unforgettable"? And why couldn't Akiyama become one of them?

Without the positing of Akiyama as an auditor,[14] the work would resemble a *kikōbun* travel narrative in its purest form. The manuscript that Ōtsu carries with him is apparently an abbreviated, I-I form of *kikōbun*, simply a "sketchy outline of something which really happened" (40). Of course we cannot know if it is written in *kanbun* like Ōgai's "Diary of a Journey to the West," but we can hypothesize that it consists of a private language, *words* chosen chiefly for their close adherence to his own feelings rather than out of a desire to communicate with some other. If we think of it in this way, it is only through the

---

14. See Kamei's explication of the term *kikite* ("auditor" or "listener") in chapter ten.

urging of the auditor Akiyama that its mode of expression is transformed into the writing style we find in the story "Those Unforgettable People."

As a result of this transformation, something new becomes visible to Ōtsu himself:

> All my life I have tortured myself with the problems of humanity and because of that I have become disillusioned with any hopes I may once have had for a great future for myself. Suffering has made me an unhappy man and on nights like this when I sit up late under the lamp light, I find it difficult to bear the isolation, and so I seek sympathy. My ego is crushed and I long for human company. It is then that I recall things that happened a long time ago, and I remember my friends. At such times it is often these people I have described who come to mind, usually without any conscious thought on my part. Well, perhaps not so much the people themselves, but the people as they stand in the scenes in which I first saw them, if you see what I mean. Perhaps I am different from other men. Others walk along the quiet road balanced between heaven and earth and in the end they return hand-in-hand to a truly eternal heaven. At least perhaps they do. This is what I feel at such times and always cry. I cannot help myself. And when I feel this way, I have no existence of my own, so neither does anyone else. I just have a secret longing for this or that person. (45–46)

At this point, it is no longer possible for him to be a traveler with a fixed sense of direction and purpose, like Nakai Ōshū and his ilk. While it is not the case that he completely lacks any sense of direction, his future goals bring him only a sense of oppression. Ōtsu becomes a restless wanderer, and it is from this perspective that he recalls the "natives" he happened to gaze at in passing and feels a desire to situate them within the scene of that moment. As is clear from the introductions to the scenes of the various "unforgettable people," he also places his own figure within the depicted scene from that moment. But unlike Toyotarō in "Maihime," he never directly commits himself to that world, that life. Instead, his visual intentionality lingers as a simple nostalgia for them, and it is with an intuition of a mutual isolation in life borne by all that the scene is called up to mind. With the calling up of these memories, the temporal phase of his life is made to undergo a revolution, and it is only then that nature comes into view.

Ōtsu only becomes aware of this motif behind the "unforgettable people" through the act of explaining it to Akiyama. It is in this sense that the work contains within itself a critique of the *kikōbun* genre (and its authorial position), which treats the other as a part of the landscape to be gazed at in passing, with no attempt made to query its relationship to the gazing self. It is the positing of an auditor, Akiyama, that enables this critique.

This is not limited to "Those Unforgettable People." In many of Doppo's stories, we find a character who suddenly becomes talkative when he locates a suitable auditor. It was through this unleashing of talkativeness that Doppo became, along with Sōseki, one of the few authors to master what I have called the conversational writing style. But Sōseki developed a conversational writing style that was able to open up a deeper level of meaning beyond the depicted exchange of opinions, even as it depicted a conversation that consisted of flashes of wit and clever epigrams used to *evade* the main issue at stake. Doppo's talkative characters, on the other hand, are forced onto an increasingly abstract, conceptual level by their doubts over their ability to communicate their own unique experiences to an interlocutor. In his attempt to explain why certain characters in scenes are burned into his visual memory like an obsession, Ōtsu at first cites "a sense of the calmness of heaven and earth, an awareness of the mystery of man's existence" (43). But this fails to dispel his unease, and finally he reaches the objectification of his own dilemma that we see in the passage cited above.

At the same time, however, Doppo's works also frequently manifest an anxiety directed toward people who do not speak, a dread of the silent. The first of Ōtsu's "unforgettable people" is a solitary man gathering things on a deserted shoreline. Next comes a pack-horse man who passes by singing a popular song at the foot of Mount Aso, and then the lute-playing monk to whom no one pays any attention. While these figures are not entirely lacking in *words*, they do seem to be closed off into a kind of silence in their lack of concern for attracting the ears of others. Following them, the next of the "unforgettable people" to appear is the innkeeper, with his curt, "unfriendly" manner (37). "Old Gen" ("Gen oji," 1897) relates the tale of an incommunicative ferryman who has his *words* restored when he adopts the beggar child Kishū, only to commit suicide in despair over the persistent silence of Kishū, in whom all human feeling is dead.[15]

In fact, this anxiety over speechless beings can be said to form Doppo's unique sensibility.

> With his back to the north wind, a child is sitting on the withered white grass of a sand dune, watching the evening sun as it sets beyond the Isu mountains. He waits for his father's ship, which is long overdue, and his heart is lonely and sad. Dead reeds on the bank of the Saigo river rustle in the salt-laden breath of the wind as it blows and ice formed at their roots in the full of the midnight tide, unseen by the eyes of men, though shattered by the morning ebb-tide, re-

---

15. A translation is available in Kunikida Doppo, *River Mist and Other Stories*, 10–22.

mains unmelted throughout the day, etching white lines at the water's edge in the dusk. If a weary traveler were to stop by this stream, is it possible that he could look around him unaware and pass on unfeeling? For this is the grove of Holy Rokudai which even after the passing of seven hundred years, still compels pity as the icy winds howl through its branches.

A boat makes it way against the gentle river current amidst the drifting fallen leaves. In other days one might have heard a jovial boatman's song come echoing from the boat to proclaim the frosty night to come, but this man—whether he is farmer or fisherman it is impossible to tell—just looks about him, saying nothing. He neither speaks nor laughs nor sings, but just rows silently on in his loneliness.[16]

This is the opening passage from "The Bonfire" ("Takibi," 1896), thought to be Doppo's earliest fictional work. It is described through the eyes of a person who seems to live in this place, and yet at the same time we also find the eye of a traveler being presupposed. This structure is not found in the poem of the same name ("Takibi," included in the collection *Sankō suichō*, 1898) that celebrates the same scene; it seems that this doubling of the self through the positing of a traveler's gaze is the characteristic conception that marks Doppo's prose writing. It is only when viewed through this doubled eye that the "native" becomes one who "neither speaks nor laughs nor sings."

To remain speechless, however, does not mean that one has nothing within one's heart worthy of being spoken. Among Ōtsu's "unforgettable people," the sense of their reality, of their being actually existing persons, gradually increases as we move from the image of the man gathering things on the shore to the Kameya innkeeper. Along the trajectory of Doppo's career, too, we see a similar progression: from the story "Bonfire," with its figure of "this man—whether he is farmer or fisherman it is impossible to tell," through "Old Gen," we see an increasing tendency to touch on the unspoken pathos hidden in the heart of the "native." When Ryūhoku or Ōgai look at "natives," it never occurs to them that each of the "natives" must harbor his or her own unique thoughts and feelings. In subsequent travel literature depicting the customs and landscape of Japan itself, too, when we encounter such things as the voices of peddlers or the words used in giving directions along the road, they register only as markers of "native" strangeness and rusticity. But in Doppo's works, the common people who make up Ōtsu's "unforgettable people" each bears his or her

---

16. Translation modified from "The Bonfire" in Kunikida Doppo, *River Mist and Other Stories*, 23–27. This passage appears on 23. Rokudai was a Buddhist monk murdered in the twelfth century; his grave is located near the setting being described.

own unique life. They are treated as beings who do in fact harbor *words*, but who lack the ability to speak those hidden *words* aloud.

Moreover, Doppo's characteristic protagonist, with his tendency to double himself by positing the eye of a traveler, is positioned midway between that speechless being and the auditor who unexpectedly causes the protagonist to become talkative. When the consciousness of this go-between selects a particular scene, it usually chooses the liminal space between nature and human settlement, that is, the edge or outskirts of a town. The Kameya Inn where Ōtsu stays is positioned on such a boundary, a trait it shares with the site of Toyotarō's encounter with Elis in "Maihime." Ōtsu himself enjoys the presence of a suitable interlocutor in Akiyama, and yet his consciousness seems to be trained mainly on the persons who suffer the burden of speechlessness. In fact, it is probably because Akiyama is an artist that Ōtsu feels compelled to speak of scenes that rise to mind only when he feels the privilege of his gazing position collapse: "my ego is crushed . . ." (45). The *words* in the passage cited above conclude with Ōtsu's expression of a feeling of gentle intimacy with all beings: "Never at other times do I feel such freedom from the struggle for wealth and fame. Never do I feel such a profound sympathy for all things" (46).

In the end, it seems that Doppo's protagonists desire to hear even the *words* that lie hidden within nature.

As is well known, the "I" of "Musashino" ("Musashino," 1898)[17] learns how to understand "the beauty of deciduous woods" from "Futabatei Shimei's translation of the short story *The Rendezvous* by Ivan Turgenev" (101–2). Of course, we can call this the acquisition of a new mode of *looking* at nature, but when we pay close attention to the passage he quotes from *Rendezvous*, it becomes apparent that what moved him so deeply was in fact something else.

> One moment fleecy white clouds were trailing across the sky, covering it, and the next, without any warning, there would be a rift in the clouds revealing patches of blue sky which shone forth like the eyes of a man shining with wisdom. [. . .] It was not the cheerful, laughing sound of early spring; it was not the gentle wafting sound of summer; nor was it the long conversational sound or the nervous chatter of late autumn. No, it was a melancholy whispering which sometimes you could catch and sometimes not. (101)

Judging from his decision to single out and quote this sort of passage, it seems that what strongly attracted him was the notion of an animate nature. He wanted to touch on the secret "whispering" of nature.

---

17. Quotes below adapted from the translation as it appears in Kunikida Doppo, *River Mist and Other Stories*, 97–112.

This is not simply a matter of using numerous expressions that involve personification. Here, nature itself possesses embodiedness and animation. It is unclear precisely when Doppo first became acquainted with *Rendezvous*, but we can at least aver that this quotation of *Rendezvous* proclaims the necessity of his writing "Musashino" at around the same time as he wrote "Old Gen" and "Those Unforgettable People." These works all signal a rediscovery of *Rendezvous*.

In other words, what we see here is nothing but the process by which nature is distinguished from landscape and rendered into something independent in its own right. In *Rendezvous*, the relationship between the gaze and its object (nature) was relativized. Doppo's protagonists are marked by a deep sympathy for *things*; they are able to spy out the unique sense of actual existence that adheres to each *thing*. The "I" in "Musashino" too clearly hears the secret whispering of nature: for example, the sound of rain when it passes through a woods, or again:

> Under the bridge there was the gentle murmur of the water—not the sound made by water as it dashes against the river banks, nor yet that of shallow water. There was a rich fullness of water, and it flowed through a deep clay channel with dampened walls so that water tangled with water, jostled against water, all the while itself giving off this sound. (109)

Even in an ordinary, commonplace phenomenon like hearing the sound of a river, he spies out the sound, the immanent and unique language that is produced by this *thing* water itself.

In this manner, Doppo's protagonists recognize an I-I form of private language, a secret whispering that arises from within the *thing* itself, just as they likewise spy out the fullness of the "inner speech" that the ostensibly speechless people carry on within themselves. Moreover, they then try to convey this "inner speech" to their auditors. Even "Musashino" is structured around the fundamental concept of its being narrated to an auditor: "you," the reader. It seems that it was Doppo who was able to actualize in practice—albeit minus the concept of God—what Uchimura Kanzō called seeking "to commune through nature with nature's God."

Most likely this is because Doppo himself was able to exchange with *things* the *words* of a kind of *thing*-to-I language. When it is assumed that an object has no autonomous existence, that it exists only as the object of a gaze, and when expression from the start takes as its motive a self-to-other (i.e., self-to-reader) form of communication, the writing style is characterized by attempts at self-exhibition through the use of witty observations or unusual rhetorical devices. In fact, the majority of literary *kikōbun* travel narratives and fiction from this time was written in this sort of ornately stylized prose. It is these authors who should be called "inward persons."[18] They were forced to use witty observations and displays of rhetoric in the attempt to prove their existence to the other. This was because their self-consciousness was closed off, both from *things* and from other people. Among Doppo's works, "Bonfire" consists more or less of ornately stylized prose, but this is not simply because it is written in the pseudo-classical style. It was, after all, quite possible to write ornately stylized prose even in the modern *genbun itchi* style. Rather, it is because the expressions in "Bonfire" are composed in a form that foregrounds the rhetorical pains and labors that went into them. After "Bonfire," Doppo moved quickly to pioneer the mode of expression we find in "Musashino" and "Those Unforgettable People," one that unlocks the singularity and weight of being of the *thing* itself for the reader. From the manner in which Ōtsu is situated in "Those Unforgettable People" and the "I" in "Musashino," we can posit that the initial motive behind this was not the desire to open a line of communication to the reader, but rather the gradual accumulation of a *thing*-to-I "inner speech." It is by reconstructing this "inner speech" into "external speech" directed at an auditor (Akiyama, "you") that the scene produced through the *thing*-to-I circuit is then opened up to view.

It is possible to construct a novel around nothing more than this sort of disclosure. A narrative event is not always a precondition of the novel. Herein lies Doppo's originality as a writer.

Of course, this was only possible because his writing style had already acquired sufficient quality. Let us return again to the opening passage of "Those Unforgettable People."

> The snow which had fallen the previous day still lay on the ground and drops of rain, dancing in the wind, fell from the eaves of the southern side of the inn's uneven thatched roof. There were even cold ripples in the muddy water trapped in the footprints made by straw sandals on the road.

This passage presents nature as revealed within a "landscape," but it presents it via an "external speech" constructed by refiguring the speaking subject's "inner speech." The mode of expression here is born out of a sensibility that has directly communed with, touched upon nature in this scene. In this sense, Doppo's

---

18. "Inward persons" (*naiteki ningen*) is a phrase often used to describe the inwardly focused characters (and authors) typical of much late Meiji fiction published after the turn inward that followed the suppression of the public, political activities of the People's Rights movement.

writing style does not provide unmediated contact with the interior, but rather is formed through both a striving toward an indicative structure that holds the other (the auditor) ceaselessly present to consciousness and a visual intentionality toward the actual specificity of *things*. Earlier, I argued that the speaking-subject position that Ōtsu subsequently assumes was already latent within this opening passage. To put this the other way around, it is by including a latent Ōtsu-like speaking subject position within this other-oriented indicative structure and this *thing*-oriented attention toward specificity that objectivity in description is achieved. This is how the *realism* of the sort seen in this passage was established.

This transformation of nature into something autonomous, however, also necessarily leads to a confrontation with nature's lack of concern for humanity. We can call Kishū from "Old Gen," in so far as he has lost all human sensibility, a person who has returned to nature, and Old Gen's despair at his absolute silence foreshadows the daunting indifference of existence, of *things*. "The Banks of the Soragachi River" ("Soragachi no kishibe," 1902) is a story built around a particular encounter with nature, wherein the "elegant whispering" (*MBZ* 66:174) of nature heard in Hokkaido turns out to be a sneering laugh directed toward all living beings, including people.

* * * * *

In this period, we also find works that take the following structure: a traveler exchanges meaningless gossip with, for example, an old woman at a tea shop, an encounter that serves as a premonition of the violation of some taboo that will subsequently carry him into some terrifying experience.

Among the best-known works along these lines are Sōseki's *The Miner* (*Kōfu*, 1908) and *The Three-Cornered World* (*Kusamakura*, 1906). A number of Izumi Kyōka's works also belong, including "The Holy Man of Mt. Kōya" ("Kōya hijiri," 1900), "One Day in Spring" (published originally in two parts as "Shunchū" and "Shunchū gokoku," 1906), and *The Grass Labyrinth* (*Kusa meikyū*, 1908).[19] Among earlier works, Rohan's "Encounter with a Skull" comes to mind. Of course, the interlocutor with whom the protagonist exchanges gossip is not always an old woman at a tea shop: in "Encounter with a Skull," it is the innkeeper, and in "Holy Man of Mount Kōya" it is not so much the young

---

19. The first two works are available in translation in Izumi Kyōka, *Japanese Gothic Tales*, trans. Charles Shirō Inouye (Honolulu: University of Hawaii Press, 1996).

girl at the tea shop as the peasants met along the road. There are also cases where the traveler is a long-term sojourner. But what all these protagonists share in common is their lack of an actual, practical goal (a travel destination). Moreover, the warning they receive, be it from a tea-shop woman or a peasant, does not in particular hint at some terrifying experience. For example, there is this very practical warning from "Holy Man of Mount Kōya": "That's the old road people used to take fifty years ago. It'll get you to Shinshū all right, and it cuts off a good seventeen miles overall. But you can't get through anymore" ("Kōya," 30). In fact, the local people themselves frequently seem unaware of the terrifying situation that awaits the traveler.

Considered in this light, the local people fill the role of a *sae no kami*, a deity placed on the edge of a village to ward off evil deities: if you can pass them by without any contact, then nothing untoward will happen. The very act of exchanging *words* with them implies the premonition of something terrible: this is the narrative structure shared by all of these works. To *commit* oneself to them by establishing a relationship through conversation is already in itself to *commit* some sort of violation. Having abstracted this pattern out from these works, we find that it also fits such works as "Maihime" and Tayama Katai's "The End of Jūemon" ("Jūemon no saigo," 1902).

The lineage of this pattern can be traced back to Edo literature, but this does not explain why it became such a prominent presence in the major works of the Meiji 30s. It is clear, however, that memories of the Edo period, when the right to travel were severely restricted, were being revived at that time. Sōseki's *Miner* is based on an actual incident, but runaways like its protagonist were not necessarily unusual—this is clear from such works as Wada Kyutarō's *From a Prison Window* (*Gokusō kara*, 1925–26).[20] Rohan depicts runaways in "The Wandering Balladeer" and in "The Whaler," and according to his "Record of a Desperate Journey" ("Tokkan kiko," 1893), Rohan himself was at one time a runaway.[21] To cite a few other actual historical figures of this type, there are Katsu Kokichi from *Musui's Story* (*Musui dokugen*, written 1843) and Miyazaki Tōten as depicted in his autobiography, *My Thirty-Three Years' Dream* (*Sanjūnen*

---

20. Wada Kyūtarō (1893–1928) was an anarchist activist. In 1924, he was sentenced to an indefinite prison term after he plotted the assassination of an army general in revenge for the murder of his mentors, Ōsugi Sakae and Itō Noe, the previous year. *From A Prison Window* is a collection of poetry and prose that he wrote while in prison.
21. "Record of a Desperate Journey," included in *Chintō sansui* (1893), a collection of Rohan's travel writings, is an autobiographical account of Rohan's 1887 journey from Hokkaido to Tokyo.

no yume, 1902).[22] The picaro type that Saeki Shōichi describes in *Modern Japanese Autobiographies* finds its truest form in these persons.[23]

But such characters as the protagonist of "Holy Man of Mount Kōya" or the artist in *Three-Cornered World* in fact are not driven by the feeling of despair that is shared by the actual and fictional runaways discussed above. Being a runaway is not necessarily the key to this problem. What is essential here is this: on a whim, a superfluous person lacking any purposeful destination exchanges *words* with some "native"—in other words, a prohibition is constructed against acts of *committing*, and the superfluous person is then punished for violating it. In this sense, we can position these works as belonging to the next stage of development beyond that of "Unforgettable People." It is "Holy Man of Mount Kōya" that begins to animate the surrounding landscape, filling it with specters reminiscent of the monsters of local folklore the instant the protagonist brushes aside the warning from the peasant and enters the old road. The following is the opening from Kyōka's "One Day in Spring":

> "Excuse me, sir."
> "Who, me?"
> The still of the spring day, the absence of other people, no doubt, had made it possible for the reply to come so quickly. How else could it be? The old man, wearing a loosely fitting headband on his wrinkled forehead, had a sleepy, almost drunken expression as he calmly worked the soft ground warmed by the sun. The damp and sweaty plum blossoms nearby, a flame ready to flutter away into the crimson sunset, swayed brilliantly with the chatter of small birds. Their voices sounded like conversation to the old man, but even in his rapturous trance, he must have known that the sound of a human voice could only be calling for him.
> Had he known the farmer would answer so promptly, the passerby might have thought twice about saying anything. ("One Day in Spring," 73)

---

22. Katsu Kokichi (1802–50) was a low-ranking samurai late in the Edo period. His autobiography, which includes passages describing his experiences as a runaway, was written in 1843 but first published in 1899–1900. An English translation is available: Katsu Kokichi, *Musui's Story: The Autobiography of a Tokugawa Samurai*, trans. Teruko Craig (Tucson: University of Arizona Press, 1988). Miyazaki Tōten (1871–1922) is best known as a Japanese who was active in various nationalist revolutionary movements in China during the first decades of the twentieth century. A translation of his autobiography is available: Mizakai Tōten, *My Thirty-Three Years' Dream: the Autobiography of Miyazaki Tōten*, trans. Eto Shinkichi and Marius B. Jansen (Princeton: Princeton University Press, 1982).

23. Saeki Shōichi, *Kindai Nihon no jiden* (Tokyo: Kodansha, 1981). In his survey of modern Japanese autobiographies, Saeki describes the picaro-type (a roguish vagabond) of protagonist found in the autobiographies of such figures as Ozaki Saburō (1842–1918).

The wanderer here seems to be a drifter, ignorant of local circumstances. On a stroll he happened by chance to see a snake enter the two-story house on the corner. Wondering if he should alert the women in the house about this, he calls out to the old man, whom he presumes must know the women. Moreover, as if he sensed a premonition of what is to come, he even hesitates here to engage in *words*. Subsequently he walks on a bit further and sees another snake in a field of rape blossom flowers. Then, at the stone steps leading up to the Kunoya Kannon, he unexpectedly encounters a herd of horses.

> He found himself enclosed in a triangle formed by a line that con-
> nected the snake at the corner house, the snake in the rape field, and
> this herd of horses. ("One Day in Spring," 78)

This seems an unremarkable spatial relationship, but Kyōka possessed a unique receptivity that allowed him to feel something in it, as if under some sort of magic spell: "How very strange!" (78). We see something similar in other Kyōka works, such as "Stars, Woman" ("Hoshi jorō," 1908). The protagonist's consciousness of something "very strange" becomes an autosuggestion, creating a mental situation in which he is apt to fall under the spell of mysterious visions.

Even with this gloss, the opening's mode of expression is hard to follow.

> The old man, wearing a loosely fitting headband on his wrinkled fore-
> head, had a sleepy, almost drunken expression as he calmly worked
> his hoe—if they scattered into the soft dirt beneath it, damp and
> sweaty, a flame ready to flutter away into the crimson sunset, the
> plum blossoms swayed brilliantly with the chatter of small birds. Their
> voices sounded like conversation to the old man. . . .

An intrusive expression like this seems excessively ornate for the purpose of describing the appearance of the old man. After all, the basic indicative structure of this scene is to express the appearance of the old man and his surroundings as viewed from the standpoint of the passerby. As seen by the passerby, the old man is fused with nature to such an extent that he seems to hear *words* not so much from a human voice but in the chirping of birds. In turn, the *words* of the passerby *commit* a disruption of this harmony. To put it another way, the passerby's human *words* here have the effect of crushing the *words* (inner speech) of a thing-to-person communication that exists within nature. This gives birth to an expansion and intensification of the indicative function of the language here. The external world that exists for the old man (indicated by the passage that extends from the "damp and sweaty plum blossoms" to "their voices sounded like conversation . . .") and the objectification that exists from the perspective of the passerby are knitted together, bringing an excessively ornate form to the basic indicative structure.

To approach this from a different angle, what existed here at first was a self-sufficient world in which nature and people were in harmony. The passerby who enters into this on a whim forces onto this nature a gaze that captures it as a landscape. The expansion or distortion of the indicative structure that subsequently occurs is like a spasm produced by the tension between this gaze and nature. The nature to which the old man is linked displays a calm self-sufficiency:

> The three rows of earth the farmer had so industriously spaded gave forth a pleasing, joyful smell. And yet there was something lonely about the field, the clumps of milk vetch showing here and there, and the green, dust-covered fava-bean sprouts, severed from their roots and returned to the soil. ("One Day in Spring," 74)

But things are different for the passerby. He pushes on with his walk, passes the two women working their looms, and then comes upon the field of rape blossoms.

> To his dazzled eyes, it was as if the two weavers at their looms had been vaguely copied onto a piece of white paper, and that the remaining space around them had been painted yellow. The contrast between the rape blossoms and the colors of the two women—their kimonos, their scarves, even the pieces of fabric they were weaving—made them stand out in his mind. Of course, he couldn't say if this method of highlighting was effective or not. But the image did hold him spellbound as he imagined a line of gold on red, the top of a weaver's shuttle leaping in a circle, searing his eyes, flying into the grass by the stream's edge, disappearing like an extinguished flame. ("One Day in Spring," 77)

In short, the second snake has slithered past him. His gaze was attempting to realize an aesthetic totalization by folding the image of the women he had just seen into the landscape that appears before his eyes. It is precisely at this instant, as if out of nature's malice, that the snake slithers past: the Japanese phrase idiomatically translated above as "he saw" literally translates as "shot his eye." This is because the pictorial totalization of the landscape that he visually intended sought not an unforced harmony between nature and people, but rather bore an arrogance that forcibly attempted to extract beauty by arranging people within nature. Here, he realizes something intuitively. While the earth beneath the old man's feet was filled with the warm affection of nature, what he finds at his own feet is a snake slithering past. "How very strange!"

My reason for choosing to explore this work here is of course that its opening provided suitable material to follow my discussion of Doppo's "Those Unforgettable People." But there is one other reason: it is because Noguchi Takehiko also takes up this passage in his book, *The Japanese Language in Fiction*.[24] Noguchi's perceptive decision to select such works as "One Day in Spring" and "Grass Labyrinth" from among Kyōka's many works and the power of his analysis, which identifies a "principle of interchangeability" underlying Kyōka's mode of expression, represent Noguchi at the height of his powers. He defines this "principle of interchangeability" in the following manner:

> To put it simply, in the language of Kyōka's fiction, tenor [the actually existing thing that is being compared to something else] and vehicle [the absent thing which is being used as a figure for the tenor] are not only capable of switching places at will, in fact they are interchangeable to the extent of fusing into a single unit in which they are of equal semantic value. (Noguchi, 218)

This is a quality acquired through the skillful manipulation of the connotations of *words*. For example, take the following expressions from "Grass Labyrinth":

> Those four o'clock flowers [*oshiroi no hana*] are spectacular. [. . .] One tall white mountain lily [*yamayuri*] towered above the others, in bloom with its head hanging down. It was enough to startle me. (Quoted in Noguchi, 216)

Noguchi interprets this passage in the following manner:

> The phrase *oshiroi no hana* indicates first of all an object, the flower known as a "four o'clock." To that extent, it is denotative. But the phrase also literally means a flower [*hana*] of [*no*] white facial powder [*oshiroi*]. Accordingly, here *oshiroi no hana* becomes a single metaphor, in which the flower serves as vehicle for the tenor, white facial powder. In short, it is a synthesis of the connotations possessed by each of the two words *oshiroi* and *hana*. [. . .] "*Yamayuri*" likewise certainly indicates the mountain lily that is the object of vision here. Still [. . .], if a mountain lily were simply blooming, "in bloom with its head hanging down," there would be no reason for it to "startle" anyone. Here, "with its head hanging down" serves as a kind of vehicle for the unwritten "facing downward." (Noguchi, 216–17)

---

24. Noguchi Takehiko, *Shōsetsu no Nihongo*, vol. 13 of *Nihongo no sekai*, 16 vols. (Tokyo: Chūō Kōronsha, 1980–86).

In short, a certain *word* refers to a certain thing and at the same time objectifies a second image, so that in seeing expressions such as *oshiroi no hana* or *yamayuri*, the reader is supposed to somehow perceive "the seemingly feminine phantom that the wandering priest saw earlier" (Noguchi, 218).

But, as is already clear from this explanation, this "principle of inter-changeability" only functions insofar as it is born out of earlier narrative developments. If readers did not know the storyline up to that point, it is highly un-likely that they would perceive anything that would "startle" somebody in such commonplace expressions as *oshiroi no hana* or white mountain lily "in bloom with its head hanging down." The same difficulty undermines Noguchi's analy-sis of "One Day in Spring." About the mode of expression in the opening pas-sage of that story, Noguchi writes:

> In the world of Kyōka's fiction, already from the first lines, the lan-guage contains the entirety of the work. [. . .] As with the Buddhist concept of the "seed"—the latent potentiality of all phenomena—all of the events that will presently occur in the work originate in the language itself; everything unfolds out of it. (Noguchi, 226–27)

But Noguchi fails to explain concretely how it is those events "originate" and "unfold" from the language. We cannot but see this as a major weakness in Noguchi's argument, which after all took as its overall project the explanation of how fiction is created through the expressive powers that "originate" within language itself.

Let me restate this as a theoretical problem. Noguchi puts forward as primary the thesis that "the chain of connotations of the novelistic word gives birth to the referential fictional image" (Noguchi, 169), the result of his attempt to apply Sōseki's F+f formula from *On Literature* (*Bungakuron*, 1907). The prob-lem arises from his overemphasis on the "*emotive* value of words" (Noguchi, 100) as constituting the function of connotation. As a result, he not only distorts Sōseki's *On Literature*, but also fails to understand the ways in which the mode of the indicative structure (the unfolding of cognition) leads specifically to the novelistic genre. For example, in describing the expression contained in the famous passage describing the dawn on Daisen Mountain at the conclusion of Shiga Naoya's *A Dark Night's Passing* (*An'ya kōro*, 1919), Noguchi proclaims its "matchless accuracy," yet fails to explain what structure of expression the "mobilization of the referential function" (Noguchi, 265) produces in order to give the impression of "matchless accuracy." What are the similarities and dif-ferences between the indicative structures of expression in the novelistic genre that give the impression of "accurate" description and those that provide a similar impression in other genres? Because Noguchi's problematic fails to consider this question, his reading of *A Dark Night's Passing* ends up reproducing the most commonplace sort of interpretations.

In general, the methodologies of structuralism and semiotics were established as approaches that shunted the author off to the side. This was a productive development in so far as it led to the discovery of connotations at the level of the historically distinct forms of expression shared by a particular era, so that it thereby transcended approaches that focused on the author's biography or attempted to explain matters through recourse to the author's "interior." Nonetheless, the majority of scholars who up until now have employed these methods have produced nothing better than solipsistic, self-contained readings that remain within the boundaries of a single work. I believe that in order to overcome this ahistorical solipsism, in order to reintroduce the question of the author, we must explore how the author's expressive subjectivity is rendered into an object for consciousness within that author's expressions, just as we must rigorously trace through the unfolding of the narrator's modes of cognition (i.e., the indicative structure) and expression (self-consciousness). In fact, Noguchi Takehiko tries to combine his semiotic methodology with a more author-oriented approach, attempting to read the author's subjectivity in the act of enunciation (or again in the degree of the author's self-referentiality) within the acts of enunciation performed by the characters that appear in a work. But lacking sufficient concern for the mediating stratum of the narrator, he ends up arbitrarily choosing examples (quotations) that serve only to reinforce the conventional images of the authors he discusses. Moreover, he depicts these authorial images only in terms of the "connotations of words" (their emotive value).

Above all, the structure of expression should be seen as a process, the unfolding of cognition. It was based on this mode of reading that I attempted to grasp the mode of expression in the opening passage of "One Day in Spring":

> The old man, wearing a loosely fitting headband on his wrinkled forehead, had a sleepy, almost drunken expression as he calmly worked his hoe—if they scattered into the soft dirt beneath it, damp and sweaty, a flame ready to flutter away into the crimson sunset, the plum blossoms swayed brilliantly with the chatter of small birds. . . .

I was caught up by the two figurative expressions, "into the soft dirt beneath it, damp and sweaty" and "a flame ready to flutter away into the crimson sunset." Both expressions modify "plum blossoms," but when examined from the standpoint of cognition, the plum blossoms modified by "if they scattered" are mediated by a certain supposition about them. As is clear from the fact that this expression includes the image of the old man—"if they scattered into the soft dirt beneath [the hoe], damp and sweaty"—this represents an attempt to imagine the world of the old man himself. On the other hand, we also find here an attempt to imagine the scene of an incredibly magnificent sunset, a desire that seems to belong to the wanderer. Looked at in this way, what we find here is a doubling of the world within a single expression. This was the starting point for my analysis.

As the story progresses, we encounter someone attracted by the latter sort of magnificence, one who ends up being led by it into an experience so terrifying that he commits suicide: the "gentleman" whose tale is narrated by the priest at the Kunoya Temple.

> Having lived here for a while, he [the gentleman] was more than used to the steps. He quickly climbed to the main hall, where the moonlight shone on the pillars and wooden planks, and looked out at the burning clouds on the ocean's horizon, shimmering crimson, the chaos of twilight, water and mountains all absorbed into one huge lake, the light of the setting sun leaking through the eaves, wisps of clouds gradually disappearing like a scattering of red and white lotus blossoms. Had he stayed there on the veranda, aboard the Vessel of the Law, he wouldn't have had to drown in that sea of passion.
> But then a most unusual thing happened—
> He heard the sound of flutes and drums coming from behind the temple— ("One Day in Spring" 107)

In its mentality and aesthetic feeling, the sensibility of this "gentleman" (as reflected in the priest's manner of speaking) is closest, among all the characters in the work, to that of the wanderer. When we examine the expressive structure here, we see that this similarity is what causes this sensibility to be woven into the passages of narrative description (*ji no bun*), which subsequently adhere to the perspective of the wanderer. In short, the wanderer is possessed by this sensibility.

During his stay at the temple, as narrated by the priest, this "gentleman" falls in love with the beautiful young wife of a wealthy local resident. Then, with his mind overwhelmed by the beauty of the evening sunset, he is lured by the sound of drums to climb up the hill behind the temple. When he leaves the unfamiliar mountain path, he encounters a stage constructed in a village in the valley. On the stage there stands the woman he loves. "The gentleman stood transfixed. Then someone quickly stepped forward, brushing his back as he passed. It was a black shadow" ("One Day in Spring," 113). The shadow walks onto the stage and sits back-to-back with the woman, facing toward the "gentleman." It has the gentleman's face. The gentleman suddenly realizes that there are other spectators around him.

The woman on the stage, her bosom bared, leans back against the figure of the man on the stage (the doubled self of the "gentleman"). "Under her weight, the man fell back, and the stage slipped down and down into the earth," and he heard "a voice that sounded all the way from the tops of the mountains to the valley" ("One Day in Spring," 114). Surely this is an apparition, caused by the spell of the same "very strange" space that the wanderer encountered earlier in the story. In the instant that the gentleman's alter ego attempts to realize the gentleman's desire, a desire that touches on a local prohibition, in that moment on the hallucinatory stage there occurs a sudden reversal, the equivalent of having a snake slither past one's feet.

* * * * *

In concluding, there is one other thing I must note, relevant not just to "One Day in Spring" but to all of the works I have discussed here, beginning with Rohan's *Encounter With a Skull*. In them, the other party with whom the protagonist or narrator undergoes a terrifying experience is almost always a being burdened with some sort of prohibition. Moreover, what shapes his or her destiny is the dark side of Japan's modernity, the negative mirror-image cast by those who were left behind in the rise of the new order. Among the "natives," the premodern communal hallucination that took the form of taboos has already disappeared, but its place is taken by the dark side of modernity, transformed into a kind of prohibition, one that takes on the afterimage of a folk mentality.

By chance, the travelers in these works exchange *words* with some person playing the role of a *sae no kami*, a village boundary deity. As a result, the travelers are drawn into contact with this being, who has been transformed into a prohibition. In the process, each traveler undergoes a unique encounter with nature.

When we look at it in this way, the position occupied by such works as Sōseki's *Three-Cornered World* or Katai's "The End of Jūemon" is self-evident. Particularly in the latter work, we encounter *nature as prohibition*—specifically, in the personified form of Jūemon and his young companion. Note that in these works the evil will of nature that assails the travelers on their journey before they brush against the prohibition is mitigated, so that *prohibited nature* exists only on the conceptual level as an abstract problem for the narrator. In short, here the evil will of nature is directed mainly toward the "natives."

When we investigate Katai's stories and novels, from "Forgotten Waters" ("Wasuremizu," 1896) through "Jūemon," it becomes clear that Katai sought to motivate the necessity for depicting nature in the motif of the protagonist's return to his hometown (or to some previously visited place). The issue that this raises is the theme of *nature as hometown,* present in works beginning with Miyazaki Koshoshi's "Homecoming" ("Kisei," 1890),[25] but I do not have the space to take that up in detail here. But the changes in the character of expression in Katai's works after "Forgotten Waters" developed roughly in parallel with the history I have touched on here of the production of an independent, autonomous nature in the modern novel. Regardless of the problematic composition of "The End of Jūemon," the contradictions in Katai's view of nature, and the shortcomings of his theories of representation, it seems that there was a certain logic behind the important role that his works and theories of composition played in establishing the school of *natural*-ism in Japan.

To put this another way, while the plot composition of "Jūemon" does include elements reminiscent of Izumi Kyōka or of Natsume Sōseki's *Three-Cornered World,* it is a work that internally achieved a sloughing off of that style, and with it the Japanese novel became able, at least on a conceptual level, to objectify nature. Mediated by this new conceptual or ideational status, nature began to appear everywhere in the novel—including in the *interior* of human beings. Even as the novel was premised on the autonomy of the nature that surrounded the human world, in fact this nature was already dismembered, partitioned according to human convenience. This nature arrived already appropriated and exploited. What do I mean by dismembered and appropriated? For example, a conversation between characters in a work is suddenly cut off, just as the ethicality of the hero comes under serious scrutiny, and in that moment of silence nature appears—in other words, natural description is inserted into the scene as an emotional pretext or as a topos for evading the question of ethics. This sort of natural description, which today seems a bit old-fashioned, first became widely used from the beginning of the Meiji 40s—from around 1907. Novels dismember nature and structure it as the space of human affairs, thereby projecting onto it the fictional norm of an interior naturalism. Without this framework, the "accurate" description of the dawn on Daisen Mountain in *A Dark Night's Passing* could never have appeared; neither could the metaphysical conversion of nature into a place of refuge for those who have committed a transgression in human affairs.

The majority of the fiction written today still consists of variations on this framework. To bring matters somewhat closer to home, in so-called Hokkaido Literature, the extent to which Hokkaido's nature is foregrounded demonstrates

---

25. Miyazaki Koshoshi (1864–1922) was a poet, novelist and critic active in the Minyūsha literary circle of the 1890s. "Homecoming," his most famous work, is a story based on the author's own visit to his rural hometown.

the degree to which this framework has been granted the status of an *a priori*.[26] No matter how much the severity of Hokkaido's nature and the importance of historical conditions are stressed, so long as this framework remains the premise by which one "perceives" literature, the nature depicted will never be anything but a nature that is administered and disciplined by this framework, a managed nature. The sudden boom since the 1960s of novels that depict the customs, folklore and scenery of Hokkaido finds its fundamental reason for existence in this phenomenon. Moreover, what has in turn disciplined this *literature* is the so-called theory (or history) of Hokkaido Literature, which is closely linked to the institutionalized system of "literary studies." This is because at the time the historical compilation of literature dealing with Hokkaido was first undertaken, it was conducted under the assumption that the rise of naturalism, which was most responsible for establishing this framework, provided the benchmark for the establishment of a modern Japanese literature.

It is also important to note that this situation is in fact nearly universal in today's Japan. In the previous chapter, I criticized Karatani Kōjin's *Origins of Modern Japanese Literature*, but I am in fact in sympathy with Karatani's motive of resisting literary history, the mode of being through which literature has been disciplined. But without clearly objectifying the framework that underlies this, we can never overcome it. From my perspective, his method of dealing with passages quoted from various works demonstrates a failure to understand the fundamental framework and hence seems utterly arbitrary. My dissatisfaction with Noguchi Takehiko's work arises from the same point. Both in quantity and quality, the forms of linguistic expression that the Japanese people acquired from the late Edo through the Meiji periods are so rich and diverse as to boggle the imagination. Why were some of them "perceived" to be literature, while others were not acknowledged as such? The aim of my work here has been to solve that problem, and in order to do so I have tried to examine expressive structures along the axis of *words*, looking at how nature, sensibility, embodiedness, and consciousness were positioned within them. In pursuing this problem, we should use whatever methodologies are useful—be it formalism, structuralism, or semiotics. But we have to be aware that the energy of the Meiji period gave birth to an incredible variety of expressions, a plurality that relativizes those methodologies and that is capable of hitting back at them. But Noguchi's methodology, while undeniably skillful at times, is on the whole too

26. Kamei has spent much of his career teaching at Hokkaido University in Sapporo. "Hokkaido Literature" became a prominent category of literary studies in Japan in the 1960s and 1970s as scholars such as Wada Kingo studied shared characteristics in literary works set in Hokkaido and/or written by authors with Hokkaido ties.

frail. My emphasis on and historical rehabilitation of the immanent functioning of what I have called the non-person narrator was of course for the purpose of defining the essential character of certain expressions. But I also used this notion because I thought it was an effective mechanism for elucidating how nature and sensibility were situated within those expressions. I must also admit that, as I came to see connections between this and Bakhtinian methodologies, I was spurred on by an interest in matching my own skills against those of the Bakhtin school.

At any rate, what I have accomplished here is nothing more than the honing of a particular tool that is useful for elucidating the frameworks through which we compose our sensibility, as well as our consciousness of self and other through our interaction with nature. Our present situation, in which nature is dismembered and disciplined and in which we have lost any image of its autonomous totality, was first produced in the structure of the novel.

Afterword to the Japanese Edition (1983)

TRANSLATED BY MICHAEL BOURDAGHS

The present book collects a series of articles I published in the journal *Gunzō* under the titles "Transformations of Sensibility" (*Kansei no henkaku*) and "Transformations of Sensibility Revisited" (*Kansei no henkaku sairon*). Because the original articles were published over the course of five years, I have taken this opportunity to correct certain inconsistencies in language, as well as to add new material.

In an earlier work, *The Theory of Contemporary Expressions* (*Gendai no hyōgen shisō*)—a revised edition is now available under the title *The Body: The Beginning of Expression* (*Shintai: hyōgen no hajimari*)—I used the perspective of theories of the body to examine the recent wave of new literary theory and to explore the principles of linguistic expression. The criticism I received then can be broadly categorized into two types. First, there were those who said that, in terms of linguistic theory, my ideas were confused because I seemed ignorant of the trends that had arisen in European linguistics since Saussure. From my perspective, though, these critics have only revealed their own ignorance of the linguistic theories developed by Tokieda Motoki and Miura Tsutomu, based on the expressive structures of Japanese.

Second, there were those who were concerned with my work primarily as literary theory and who expressed doubts as to whether the many special characteristics of expression that mark contemporary literature could be fully explicated using my methods, or again who were dissatisfied with my apparent lack of concern for the contemporary crisis of literature. In a sense, these criticisms were justified.

Of course, I too felt strongly motivated by the sense that humanity faces a crisis in the present day, and it was for this very reason that I sought in theories of the body a direction for breaking through that crisis. As a result, I came to have contacts with a group working on these problems in very practical ways: they have for example established a space where children can encounter a variety of literatures and peoples, and they have promoted bilingualism and a range of physical activities. The reason my work took this direction is, I think, because I deliberately rejected the idea of blunting the contemporary sense of alienation by painting it over with sentiments such as "self"-love. To put it bluntly, I was disgusted by the stench of dishonesty that emanated from this sort of thinking. It seemed to me that I had to investigate the possibilities and limitations of the view of literature that was born out of this sort of thinking, from the perspective of its theoretical soundness and the basic principles of its grasp of literature and humanity. Because I approached the question with this at the front of my mind, I lacked a perspective wide enough to see that this view of literature too had its foundation in the history of modes of expression.

The theories of the body and Miura Tsutomu's linguistic theory are of course not omnipotent in their ability to elucidate the numerous modes of expression used in literature: that much is self-evident. But they are also not completely bereft of potential. In my efforts to open up new possibilities and to expand existing ones, it was necessary to grasp sensibility through a theory of the body. At the same time, it was also necessary to create a method of analysis that used theories of expression to explicate the self-consciousness of sensibility (i.e., the rendering of sensibility into language). What I have aimed at in this book in particular is to trace through and explicate historically the process by which a self-awareness of sensibility was achieved in the modern period. In this, the concept of the non-person narrator, which I developed from some of Miura Tsutomu's ideas, was very useful.

To put this more precisely, as I explored the various modes of expression current from the Meiji 10s to the Meiji 30s (i.e., roughly from the late 1870s to the late 1900s), a unique characteristic, what I have called the non-person narrator, came into focus, and I found Miura Tsutomu's linguistic theories useful in developing this discovery and in creating a methodology appropriate to it. In tracing through the rise and transformations of this narrator, the history of expressions of sensibility and the process by which a certain mentality was constructed became visible. Contemporary literature in fact has inherited only a very small part of the multiple modes of expression I have explicated in this book. I have attempted to locate the roots of the contemporary view of literature in the history of expressions, as well as to expose its partiality.

During roughly the same period as I was pursuing this task, new methodologies such as structuralism and semiotics began to flourish and undertook the task of puncturing the fundamental concepts that underlie the contemporary view of literature. It goes without saying that I was in sympathy with this, and because I began to negotiate actively with them during the course of this project, I too came to be considered one of the advocates of these methodologies. But in fact, the promoters of those methodologies have done nothing but to impose one-sidedly their concepts onto Japanese literary works. I could not shut my eyes to their lack of sensitivity to the subtle fluctuations that characterize actual expressions. There is a clear difference, both conceptually and functionally, between the non-person narrator that I explore here and the narrator that is theorized in those methodologies. This is because the motives behind our use of these concepts are completely opposite. Even if the advocates of the new methodologies criticize from the perspective of situationist theory the popular appropriation of their methods, in the end they only lapse into an authoritarianism that aims only to defend their institutionalized system. What is really needed is a critical reconstruction of those methodologies.

For these and other reasons, my work has made little headway. Both Hashinaka Yūji, the previous editor of *Gunzō*, and Tsuji Akira, its present editor, have kindly indulged my idiosyncratic manner of working, and Kagoshima Masao has been a constant source of encouragement. Thanks to them, my work has reached its present state. With the kind consideration of Komago Yasushi, it has now been collected and published in book form. I am very grateful to them and wish to express my heartfelt thanks to them here.

Index

ABOUT THE AUTHOR

Kamei Hideo is Professor Emeritus at Hokkaido University and Director of the Otaru Municipal Museum of Literature. He is the author of numerous books and articles and one of the most respected scholars of modern Japanese literature today.

ABOUT THE TRANSLATION EDITOR

Michael Bourdaghs holds a Ph.D. in East Asian Literature from Cornell University and is currently Assistant Professor in East Asian Languages and Cultures at UCLA. His research focuses on modern Japanese literature, popular culture, and critical theory.

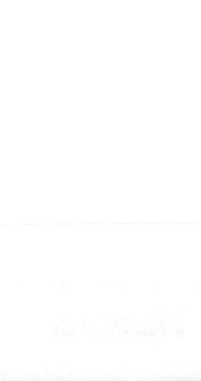

Printed and bound by CPI Group (UK) Ltd, Croydon, CR0 4YY

13/04/2025

14656505-0004